Equity Valuation

For other titles in the Wiley Finance series
please see www.wiley.com/finance

Equity Valuation

Models from Leading Investment Banks

Edited by

Jan Viebig
Thorsten Poddig
and
Armin Varmaz

John Wiley & Sons, Ltd

Other Wiley Editorial Offices

John Wiley & Sons Inc., 111 River Street, Hoboken, NJ 07030, USA

Jossey-Bass, 989 Market Street, San Francisco, CA 94103-1741, USA

Wiley-VCH Verlag GmbH, Boschstr. 12, D-69469 Weinheim, Germany

John Wiley & Sons Australia Ltd, 42 McDougall Street, Milton, Queensland 4064, Australia

John Wiley & Sons (Asia) Pte Ltd, 2 Clementi Loop #02-01, Jin Xing Distripark, Singapore 129809

John Wiley & Sons Canada Ltd, 6045 Freemont Blvd, Mississauga, ONT, L5R 4J3, Canada

Wiley also publishes its books in a variety of electronic formats. Some content that appears in print may not be
available in electronic books.

Library of Congress Cataloging in Publication Data

Viebig, Jan, 1969–
    Equity valuation : models from leading investment banks / Jan Viebig, Thorsten Poddig, and
    Armin Varmaz.
       p. cm. — (The Wiley finance series)
    Includes bibliographical references and index.
    ISBN 978-0-470-03149-0 (cloth : alk. paper)
    1. Stocks—Mathematical models. 2. Portfolio management—Mathematical models.
    3. Valuation—Mathematical models. 4. Investment analysis—Mathematical models.
    I. Poddig, Thorsten. II. Varmaz, Armin. III. Title.
    HG4661.V54 2008
    332.63′221—dc22

                                  2008002738

British Library Cataloguing in Publication Data

A catalogue record for this book is available from the British Library

ISBN 978-0-470-03149-0 (H/B)

Typeset in 10/12pt Times by Integra Software Services Pvt. Ltd, Pondicherry, India
Printed and bound in Great Britain by Antony Rowe Ltd, Chippenham, Wiltshire

Contents

Foreword

Every student of finance or applied economics learns the lessons of Franco Modigliani and Merton Miller. Their landmark paper, published in 1958, laid out the basic underpinnings of modern finance and these two distinguished academics were both subsequently awarded the Nobel Prize in Economics. Simply stated, companies create value when they generate returns that exceed their costs. More specifically, the returns of successful companies will exceed the risk-adjusted cost of the capital used to run the business. Further, these returns and the securities of the underlying companies must be judged against an uncertain backdrop, such that the risk-adjusted expected returns are attractive.

Investors seek to identify these successful companies. They strive to calculate the appropriate pricing of securities. How can this best be done? Every practitioner knows that the two simple declarative sentences at the beginning of this paragraph belie the complexity of the search for successful companies and financial instruments that offer favorable prospects for investors. The world is messier than models. Accounting data can be unreliable, economic conditions can change, investor risk tolerance can shift, and low-probability scenarios can occur.

This book is written from the perspective of practitioners, and the editors have chosen leaders in the field who can describe the theory and implementation behind their various approaches. The contributors to *Equity Valuation: Models from Leading Investment Banks* also describe the potential weakness of different models. This perspective is essential to understanding why there is no single magical solution. Investors are urged to use models as tools, often very powerful tools, but not as replacements for sound analysis and common sense.

Most successful investors believe that the fundamentals of economic and company performance will ultimately determine the performance of financial assets. Indeed, models are typically constructed in the hope of identifying deviations from fundamentally determined prices for entire classes of financial assets as well as specific securities. In Part I, Jan Viebig and Thorsten Poddig, the lead authors of this book, describe the basics of many valuation models, which are linked to key metrics such as cash flow, earnings and book value.

To paraphrase the authors, valuing a company would be simple if balance sheets and income statements were always accurate. In the real world, balance sheets may not fully reflect the fair value of assets, debt and equity, and earnings per share may not capture the sustainable earnings power of the company. Even when there is no intention to deceive, there is an underlying tension between corporate accounting, which seeks to take a snapshot at a specific point in time and to do so in a timely way, and the economic reality.

Even well-constructed models can lead to errors if the inputs to the model are wrong. This happens most often when there are notable changes, for example, in the macroeconomic backdrop or a structural shift in technology. In such cases, model inputs tend to be simple extrapolations of the past rather than a guide to the future. Part II describes a situation in which another technique, often referred to as Monte Carlo simulation, can be used to best advantage. When there is a wide range of possible scenarios, and fundamental outcomes, Monte Carlo techniques often provide answers that are approximately correct. Under similar circumstances, one-scenario models provide answers that are precisely wrong.

In Part III, Tom Larsen and David Holland describe two approaches that are used to adjust accounting measures and emphasize long-term returns. Both the Economic Value Added (EVA) approach developed by Stern Stewart and the Cash Flow Return on Investment (CFROI) system developed by Holt Value Associates attempt to emphasize those metrics that are most related to long-term company performance. By examining the returns that companies can generate on their cash flows and invested capital, these approaches seek to determine which managements are adding true value to their companies and, hence, shareholders. The implications can be critical. For example, in the early 1990s, analysts at Goldman Sachs concluded, using an EVA-type approach, that most large corporations in Japan were generating disappointing returns on their capital employed. This led to a (correct) multiyear bearish view on Japanese equities.

Trevor Harris and his colleagues at Morgan Stanley have developed ModelWare which attempts to assess the intrinsic value of enterprises. Their approach, described in Part IV, begins with adjustments to reported accounting data, attempting to move accounting metrics closer to economic reality for each company. They then apply the basic concepts of the discounted cash flow approach described in Part I, such as the tradeoff between risk and reward, and consider the components of return on equity, including operating margins, asset turnover, and financial leverage. Their discussion provides an extremely useful review of the state of model building among professional investors.

Part V, written by David Bianco, describes the model developed at UBS which considers the value-added growth potential of each company, referred to as the Economic Growth Quotient (EGQ). This approach incorporates the principles of discounted cash flow and economic profit analysis. Further, Bianco applies regression analysis to help explain why certain companies are more highly valued in the marketplace than others, looking at factors such as return on capital.

In Part VI, Jan Viebig, Daniel Stillit and Thorsten Poddig provide readers with a glimpse into yet another type of model, one that is best applied to leveraged buyout (LBO) analysis. Unlike many other approaches which attempt to assess the public value of a security, the LBO model takes the view of a private equity investor. In such cases, returns are linked not only to current and extrapolated performance of the company, but also to the benefits of control, and the possibility of restructuring the company's operating and financial structures. Goldman Sachs has made such a model available to our clients; it is fully interactive, and allows the user to change critical inputs and to assess alternative scenarios.

Aswath Damodaran has written Part VII, a superb summary of valuation approaches and alternatives. Professor Damodaran is the author of one of the most widely used and acclaimed text books on the topic of valuation. His contribution to this volume provides an overview of the basic principles that support theoretically sound valuation methodologies and also lays out several of the underlying issues now confronting users of valuation methods. These include the accounting challenges affecting both income statements and balance sheets. Damodaran also describes the logical extension of these computational techniques to new securities and applications. Examples include real options valuation and the assessment of relative valuation.

This detailed yet readable book concludes in Part VIII with an up-to-date discussion by Varmaz, Poddig and Viebig on the current issues under discussion by practitioners and academics alike. These include the manner in which models may be improved, extended to other asset categories, and broadened to portfolio management as well as security selection. This book will give you the context in which to judge different approaches and to understand the basis on which these models may fail or succeed. A complete bibliography will be useful to students and practitioners alike.

The approach at my own firm is one of discipline, and we are proud of our emphasis on economic and investment theory and model building. But this must be viewed against a backdrop of common sense, recognizing that the underlying structures and assumptions may change. John Maynard Keynes, best noted for his contributions to economic theory in the twentieth century, was also an accomplished investor. Indeed, his work in the 1930s on the marginal efficiency of capital lays the groundwork for much modern finance. I will therefore give Lord Keynes the last word on being overly dependent on models and theory, and failing to recognize that models may be precisely wrong. Even when the model's result is ultimately correct, timing can be variable. In a quote often attributed to him, he noted that "Markets can remain irrational longer than you can remain solvent."

Abby Joseph Cohen, CFA
Goldman, Sachs & Co.
New York, NY

September 2007

Preface

The goal of this book is to open the doors of leading investment banks to our readers and to explain in a clear and user-friendly way how portfolio managers and financial analysts at leading investment banks analyze firms. This book reveals how experts at leading investment banks such as Deutsche Bank, Goldman Sachs, Morgan Stanley, Credit Suisse and UBS really value companies. Unlike most other publications, *Equity Valuation: Models from Leading Investment Banks* does not focus on just one valuation model but discusses different valuation frameworks used in the investment industry today. The book is organized as follows:

Part	Title	Authors	Organization
	Foreword	Abby Joseph Cohen	Goldman Sachs
I	Discounted Cash Flow (DCF) Models	Jan Viebig, Thorsten Poddig	DWS Investment GmbH University of Bremen
II	Monte Carlo Free Cash Flow to the Firm (MC-FCFF) Models	Jan Viebig, Thorsten Poddig	DWS Investment GmbH University of Bremen
III	HOLT CFROI® Framework	Tom Larsen, David Holland	Harding Loevner Management Credit Suisse
IV	Morgan Stanley ModelWare's Approach to Intrinsic Value	Trevor S. Harris, Juliet Estridge, Doron Nissim	Morgan Stanley Morgan Stanley Columbia Business School
V	UBS VCAM and EGQ Regression-based Valuation	David Bianco	UBS
VI	Leverage Buyout (LBO) Models	Jan Viebig, Daniel Stillit, Thorsten Poddig	DWS Investment GmbH UBS University of Bremen
VII	Valuation 101: Approaches and Alternatives	Aswath Damodaran	Stern School of Business, New York University
VIII	Final Thoughts on Valuation	Armin Varmaz, Thorsten Poddig, Jan Viebig	University of Bremen University of Bremen DWS Investment GmbH

This preface provides a summary of the content and the key concepts of each part, and introduces the authors.

Part I

Content	Today almost every sophisticated valuation model used by leading investment banks is based on discounted cash flows. Jan Viebig and Thorsten Poddig give a systematic overview about the most important discounted cash flow models used in practice and illustrate the models by hands-on examples. Readers already familiar with basic valuation models are encouraged to skip Part I.
Authors/ Organization	Jan Viebig is a managing director at DWS Investment GmbH. He manages hedge funds for DWS from Frankfurt. DWS Investment GmbH is part of Deutsche Asset Management (DeAM), the global asset division of Deutsche Bank. Thorsten Poddig is Professor of Finance at the University of Bremen.
Key concepts	Discounted Cash Flow (DCF) Model, Dividend Discount Model (DDM), Cash Flow Statement, Free Cash Flow to the Firm (FCFF) Model, Cost of Capital, Capital Asset Pricing Model (CAPM), Competitive Advantage Period (CAP), Terminal Value.

Part II

Content	According to an old adage, forecasting is especially difficult if it involves the future. Financial analysts do not know the future with certainty when building valuation models. Using Baidu.com as a real-life example, Jan Viebig and Thorsten Poddig introduce step-by-step Monte Carlo Free Cash Flow to the Firm (MC-FCFF) models to the reader. Combining modern valuation theory and statistical analysis allows investment professionals to build more realistic valuation models in a world full of uncertainty. Readers can download the complete models discussed in Part II from our website: www.wiley.com/go/equityvaluation.
Authors/ Organization	Jan Viebig is a managing director at DWS Investment GmbH in Frankfurt. Thorsten Poddig is Professor of Finance at the University of Bremen.
Key concepts	Monte Carlo Free Cash Flow to the Firm (MC-FCFF) Model, Financial Value Driver Approach.

Part III

Content	Tom Larsen and David Holland compare two of the most widely used valuation metrics in Part III of this book: the Economic Value Added (EVA) approach developed by Stern Stewart and the Cash Flow Return on Investment (CFROI) framework originated by HOLT Value Associates. Both models are rooted in the valuation framework pioneered by Miller/Modigliani and are widely used by consultants, portfolio managers, investment bankers and corporate managers all over the world. Post Enron, most people do not dispute the fact that accounting

	data can be misleading to investors. Studying Part III helps investors, educators and the general public to understand how investment professionals adjust accounting data to understand the true performance of a company.
Authors/ Organization	Tom Larsen is Head of Research at Harding Loevner Management in Somerville, New Jersey. Before joining Harding Loevner Management, Tom Larsen worked as a senior policy analyst at the renowned CFA Institute. David Holland is a managing director at Credit Suisse and co-head of the HOLT Valuation & Analytics Group. HOLT Value Associates was the premier developer and provider of the CFROI valuation model to portfolio managers worldwide. The firm was recently acquired by Credit Suisse.
Key concepts	Cash Flow Return on Investment (CFROI), Economic Value Added (EVA).

Part IV

Content	ModelWare's organizing principle is as simple as convincing: Separating operating from funding activities helps to better understand how companies create (or destroy) value. One of the strengths of the model is that the logic of accounting relationships is retained consistently. At the heart of ModelWare is a new analytical concept called "Profitability Tree" which illustrates that return on equity is driven by the effect of financial leverage and return on net operating assets. The "Profitability Tree" links rearranged financial statement information and performance metrics. Investors can use ModelWare to analyze operating margins, asset turnover ratios and other performance metrics implied in current share prices. Another helpful concept introduced by Morgan Stanley is the "Profitability Map" which shows how operating margins and operating asset turnover ratios evolve over time in a two-dimensional space. The "Profitability Map" is an essential valuation tool as margin and efficiency improvements usually justify higher valuations.
Authors/ Organization	Trevor Harris is a managing director and vice chairman of client services at Morgan Stanley, and formerly headed the Global Valuation and Accounting team in Equity Research. Prior to joining Morgan Stanley, Trevor Harris was the Jerome A. Chazen Professor of International Business and Chair of the Accounting Department at Columbia Business School. Juliet Estridge is a vice president at Morgan Stanley. Doron Nissim is Associate Professor and Chair of the Accounting Department at Columbia Business School.
Key concepts	ModelWare, Profitability Tree, Profitability Map.

Part V

Content	David Bianco introduces the reader to UBS Value Creation Analysis Model (VCAM) and its Economic Growth Quotient (EGQ). VCAM is a standardized discounted cash flow model which allows investors to analyze the value accretive growth potential of companies. Regression-based valuation is a new, innovative analytical concept which tries to explain why some companies trade at higher valuation multiples than others. The economic logic behind UBS's regression-based valuation framework is compelling: The higher the expected present value of a company's growth potential relative to its economic book value, the higher should be its observed valuation multiple. David Bianco uses a linear regression model to visualize the relationship between valuation multiples (EV/NOPAT) and a specifically developed explanatory variable named EGQ.
Authors/ Organization	David Bianco is UBS's Chief US Equity Strategist. According to Barron's, David Bianco is one of the "top strategists" in the United States. UBS is a premier investment banking firm and a key global asset manager.
Key concepts	Value Creation Analysis Model (VCAM), Economic Growth Quotient (EGQ).

Part VI

Content	Part VI describes the methodology and the mechanics of LBO models developed by leading investment banks such as UBS, Deutsche Bank, Goldman Sachs, Credit Suisse and Morgan Stanley. Unlike DCF models, LBO models value companies from the perspective of a private equity investor who recapitalizes the financial structure of a company and restructures operations to enhance profitability and capital efficiency. LBO models reveal that the value of controlling a company can be substantial from the perspective of a financial investor.
Authors/ Organization	Jan Viebig is a managing director at DWS Investment GmbH. Daniel Stillit is a managing director conducting restructuring and M&A situations research at UBS, one of the world's flagship financial firms. Thorsten Poddig is Professor of Finance at the University of Bremen.
Key concepts	Leverage Buyout (LBO) Model, Internal Rate of Return (IRR), Multiple Approach.

We believe that the authors of Parts III, IV and V do a good job in describing HOLT CFROI, ModelWare and UBS VCAM, arguably the three most sophisticated proprietary models used by financial analysts and portfolio managers to value equities today. They are all experts in the field of equity valuation who helped to develop or improve these models. The aim of the two remaining parts is to discuss valuation from a theoretical perspective without supporting one approach over the other. Readers interested in valuation theory might want to read Part VII first in which Aswath Damodaran, the author of several best-selling text books on investment valuation, gives an excellent overview about alternative valuation concepts.

Part VII

Content	In Part VII, Aswath Damodaran discusses four basic approaches to valuation and how value enhancement is framed in each approach. First, he looks at discounted cash flow models and their variants – certainty equivalents, excess return models and adjusted present value models. Second, he examines accounting valuation models – book value and liquidation value. Third, he evaluates relative valuation models, where assets are priced based upon how the market is pricing similar assets. Finally, he considers real options models, where value can be derived from increasing flexibility and potential opportunities in the future, and the interaction between corporate strategy and finance in value enhancement.
Authors/ Organization	Aswath Damodaran is Professor of Finance and David Margolis Teaching Fellow at the Stern School of Business at New York University. He is the author of several highly praised books including *Damodaran on Valuation, Investment Valuation, The Dark Side of Valuation, Corporate Finance: theory and practice*, and *Applied Corporate Finance: a user's manual*. His papers have been published in the *Journal of Financial and Quantitative Analysis*, the *Journal of Finance*, the *Journal of Financial Economics* and the *Review of Financial Studies*.
Key concepts	Discounted Cash Flow Models, Certainty Equivalents, Excess Return Models, Accounting Valuation Models, Relative Valuation Models, Real Options Models.

Part VIII

Content	The aim of Part VIII is to focus on the underlying theory behind the models discussed in the previous parts of this book. Reviewing the literature, the authors discuss alternatives to incorporate risk into the DCF framework and show how asset allocation and DCF valuation can be linked in practice.

(Continued)

Authors/Organization	Armin Varmaz recently finished his Ph.D at the University of Bremen where he works for Thorsten Poddig. Thorsten Poddig is Professor of Finance at the University of Bremen. Jan Viebig is a managing director at DWS Investment GmbH in Frankfurt.
Key concepts	Risk Premium, Utility-based Valuation, Certainty Equivalents, Risk Neutral Probabilities, Asset Pricing Models.

The book is richly endowed with real world, hands-on examples. Combining valuation theory with practical insights, we hope that *Equity Valuation: Models from Leading Investment Banks* can be read with profit by students, investment professionals, corporate managers, and anyone else seeking to learn about equity valuation.

Acknowledgments

We would like to express our appreciation to several people who helped us writing and editing this book. First, our gratitude goes to Klaus Kaldemorgen, the speaker of the board of DWS Investment GmbH. We are extremely grateful for the continuing support that we received from DWS Investment GmbH and Klaus Kaldemorgen's openness to new ideas and valuation concepts. Most likely, he would add that he is always open to new thoughts as long as they help us to make money for clients. But this is another story. We wish to thank all portfolio managers at DWS Investment GmbH including Martin Tschunko, Marc-Alexander Kniess, Hansjörg Pack and Thomas Gerhardt for their suggestions, analysis and common sense.

Peter Hollmann, a partner at Goldman Sachs in Frankfurt, introduced us to Abby Joseph Cohen, one of Wall Street's most respected strategists. We are extremely grateful that Abby Joseph Cohen wrote the Foreword to our book in August/September 2007, an extremely volatile time in financial markets. Dagmar Kollmann (CEO Morgan Stanley Bank AG), Stefan Hüttermann and Philipp Salzer (both Credit Suisse), Klaus Fink and Jens Schaller (both UBS) opened the doors for us to leading investment banks. Working for an investment bank is a time-consuming job. Tom Larsen, David Holland, Trevor Harris, Juliet Estridge, Doron Nissim, David Bianco and Daniel Stillit spent many evenings and weekends writing articles for this book. Working with them was a privilege and a great learning experience for us. We could not have written this book without the support from Deutsche Bank, Goldman Sachs, Morgan Stanley, Credit Suisse, and UBS.

We are very thankful that Aswath Damodaran, one of the leading experts in the field of equity valuation, contributed to this book. We also thank Magnus von Schlieffen, Merrill Lynch, and Nicola Riley, University of Bremen, for their support. We are very grateful for the kind support from Stephan Beeusaert and Giz Armitage at Palisade, the developer and provider of @Risk. For their efforts, judgment, and motivation we wish to thank Pete Baker, Viv Wickham and Chris Swain at John Wiley & Sons, Ltd.

Jan Viebig
Thorsten Poddig
Armin Varmaz

September 2007

Abbreviations

APT	Arbitrage Pricing Theory
APV	Adjusted present value
ARPU	Average revenue per user
BOY	Beginning of year
BV	Book value
CAGR	Compounded annual growth rate
CAP	Competitive advantage period
CAPEX	Capital expenditures
CAPM	Capital Asset Pricing Model
CDP	Competitive disadvantage period
CEO	Chief executive officer
CEQ	Certainty equivalent
CF	Cash flow
CFBH	Cash flow to bond holders
CFFF	Cash flow from financing activities
CFFI	Cash flow from investing activities
CFFO	Cash flow from operating activities
CFNF	Cash flow from net financing
CFO	Chief financial officer
CFROI	Cash flow return on investment
COGS	Cost of goods sold
DA	Depreciating assets
D&A	Depreciation and amortization
DCF	Discounted cash flow
ΔD	Net debt issuance
DDM	Discounted dividend model
DGM	Dividend growth model
DPS	Dividend per share
EBIT	Earnings before interest and taxes
EBITDA	Earnings before interest, taxes, depreciation and amortization
EBV	Economic book value
EGQ	Economic growth quotient
EP	Economic profit
EPA	Economic profit analysis
EPIC	Economic profitability of invested capital

EPS	Earnings per share
ERP	Equity risk premium
ESO	Employee stock options
EV	Economic value
EVA	Economic value added
FCFE	Free cash flow to equity
FCFF	Free cash flow to the firm
FCFO	Free cash flow from operating activities
FV	Future value
FYE	Fiscal year end
GAAP	Generally accepted accounting principles
GCF	Gross cash flow
GDP	Gross domestic product
GI	Gross investment
IC	Invested capital
INT	Interest payments
IPO	Initial public offering
IPR&D	In-process research and development
IRR	Internal rate of return
IV	Intrinsic value
IVC	Incremental value creation
LBO	Leveraged buyout
LIBOR	London Interbank Offered Rate
LIFO	Last in, first out
MC-FCFF	Monte Carlo Free Cash Flow to the Firm
MVL	Market value line
NDA	Non depreciating assets
NFE	Net financial expense
NFO	Net financial obligations
NIBCL	Non-interest-bearing current liabilities
NOA	Non-operating assets (Part I)
NOA	Net operating assets (Part IV)
NOPAT	Net operating profit after taxes
NOPBT	Net operating profit before taxes
NOPBTA	Net operating profit before taxes and amortization
NOPLAT	Net operating profit less adjusted taxes
NPV	Net present value
OI	Operating income
OPATO	Operating asset turnover
OPEBS	Other post-employment benefits
OM	Operating margin
OPEX	Operating expenses
PE	Price/earnings ratio
PEG	PE to growth ratio
PP&E	Property, plant and equipment
PV	Present value
PVGO	Present value of growth opportunities

R&D	Research and development
REV	Revenues
RIV	Residual income valuation
RNP	Risk neutral probability
ROA	Return on assets
ROE	Return on equity
ROGI	Return on gross investment
ROIC	Return on invested capital
ROIIC	Return on incremental invested capital
RONA	Returns on net assets
RP	Debt repayments
SG&A	Selling, general and administrating expenses
SPE	Special purpose entity
SM	Service mark
TAX_{adj}	Taxes, adjusted
TV	Terminal value
US GAAP	US general accepted accounting principles
VCAM	Value creation analysis model
VCH	Value creation horizon
WACC	Weighted average cost of capital

Part I
Discounted Cash Flow (DCF) Models[1]
Jan Viebig[2] and Thorsten Poddig[3]

[1] DWS Investment GmbH, © 2008 Jan Viebig.
[2] Managing Director, DWS Investment GmbH.
[3] Professor of Finance, University of Bremen.

1
Introduction

The fundamental value[1] of each investment is the present value of its expected, future cash flows discounted at an appropriate risk-adjusted rate. Virtually every sophisticated equity valuation model used by leading investment banks today is based on discounted cash flows (DCF). The structure and the names of the models might differ, but the underlying idea is always the same. They are all rooted in the present value framework for equity valuation pioneered by Merton Miller and Franco Modigliani in the early 1960s.[2]

Economists use models to simplify the complexity of the real world. A good valuation model is simple and helps investors to make informed decisions. Many financial analysts today forget that a good model is simple, not complex. Financial economists subjectively make simplifying assumptions to focus on specific valuation aspects while neglecting other aspects. As a result, a plethora of "different" discounted cash flow approaches exists today, each with its own acronym: dividend discount models (DDM), free cash flow to the firm (FCFF) and Economic Value Added (EVA), to name just the most popular models discussed in academic literature.

Financial analysts at leading investment banks have added proprietary discounted cash flow models and new acronyms. The most sophisticated DCF models used by financial analysts today are, in our opinion, Credit Suisse's Cash Flow Return on Investment (CFROI) model, Morgan Stanley's ModelWare and UBS's Value Creation Analysis Model (VCAM). In Part VI we discuss leveraged buyout (LBO) models used by Goldman Sachs, UBS and other leading investment banks. These models will be presented later in this book by leading experts who helped to develop and enhance the models. This part gives an overview of the discounted cash flow approach to prepare the reader for the problems that can arise in practice.

Part I of this book is organized as follows: Chapter 2 discusses present value calculation and the interpretation of fundamental value, Chapter 3 gives an overview of the most popular DCF models and explains how investors can estimate the main input factors of these models.

Using Baidu.com, Inc. as a practical example, Part II of this book demonstrates how investors can formulate Monte Carlo Free Cash Flow to the Firm (MC-FCFF) models. Monte Carlo simulations enable financial analysts to take the uncertainty of future cash flows and expected discount rates into account when valuing stocks.

---

[1] In literature, the *fundamental* value of an investment is often also called *intrinsic* or *fair* value.
[2] Miller and Modigliani (1961).

2
The Fundamental Value of Stocks
and Bonds

The fundamental value of an investment is the present value PV_0 of its expected, future cash flows. Given a risk-free rate of 4%, an investment A that pays a cash flow (CF_A) of USD 100 000 at the end of one period with certainty is worth USD 96 154 today as an investor receives USD 100 000 at the end of one period if he/she invests USD 96 154 today at a risk-free rate of 4%:

$$PV_0 = CF_A \times \frac{1}{(1+i_A)^t} = \frac{100\,000}{1.04^1} = 96\,154 \Leftrightarrow$$

$$CF_A = PV_0 \times (1+i_A)^t = 96\,154 \times 1.04^1 = 100\,000$$

If investment A currently traded below its fundamental value of USD 96 154 – for example, at USD 90 000 – an arbitrageur could borrow USD 90 000 at 4%, invest it in investment A and realize a risk-less profit of USD 6400 before transaction costs at maturity [USD 100 000 − 90 000 × 1.04]. If investment A traded above its fundamental value – for example, at USD 105 000 – an arbitrageur could borrow investment A at a small borrowing fee from the owner of the asset, sell it for USD 105 000 in the market and invest the proceeds of the short sale at the risk-free rate. At maturity the investor would realize a risk-free profit of USD 9200 before borrowing fees and transaction costs [USD 105 000 × 1.04 − USD 100 000]. As a result of these arbitrage transactions, the price of the asset which trades below its fundamental value would increase and the price of the asset which trades above its fundamental value would fall until all arbitrage opportunities are eliminated and the market price equals its fundamental value (*arbitrage-free pricing*).

The expected returns which are foregone by investing in an asset rather than in a comparable investment are called *opportunity cost of capital*. The opportunity cost i of a risky asset B is simply the sum of the risk-free rate r_f plus a risk premium π which adequately reflects the uncertainty of future cash flows generated by asset B:

$$i_B = r_f + \pi_B$$

A US dollar, euro or yen received today is worth more than the same amount of money received tomorrow in the eyes of most investors. Investors are usually only willing to forgo current consumption and invest in a risk-free asset if they receive interest on the investment. If the interest rate increases, people are typically more willing to delay consumption into the future. Classical economists postulate that the interest rate is the price that brings consumption and investment into equilibrium. However, investors not only have to decide how much to consume and how much to save but also if they want to hold wealth in the form of cash or to purchase long-term assets. According to Keynes, the risk-free rate r_f can be viewed as reward for parting with liquidity.[1]

Common sense suggests that risk-free investments yield lower returns than risky assets. Risk-averse investors are willing to invest in risky assets only if they can expect to receive a risk premium π in addition to the risk-free rate which adequately reflects the uncertainty of future cash flows of that asset. By definition, the risk premium of a risky asset B is the difference between the expected return i on asset B less the risk-free rate.[2]

$$\pi_B = i_B - r_f$$

The fundamental value of a risky investment depends on the expected returns (opportunity costs) that investors can achieve elsewhere on a comparable investment with the same characteristics. The fundamental value decreases (increases) if the opportunity costs increase (decrease). The price of identical assets with the same expected return and risk should be equal in competitive financial markets. If prices of identical assets were different, arbitrageurs would simply buy the cheap and short sell[3] the more expensive but otherwise identical asset to capture a risk-free arbitrage profit. Arbitrage ensures that assets trade very close to fundamental values *in equilibrium*, i.e. after all arbitrage opportunities are eliminated.

Cash flows and discount rates must be consistent: Nominal cash flows must be discounted at nominal discount rates, cash flows in real terms at real discount rates. Let us assume that the real risk-free rate is 1.5%, the expected inflation rate 2.5%, the risk premium 4% and that the expected cash flow of asset B at the end of period 1 is USD 100 000. The nominal opportunity cost of capital of asset B is simply the sum[4] of the real risk-free rate $r_{f,real}$, the expected inflation rate r_{inf} and the risk premium π_B. The fundamental value of asset B is 92 593:

$$PV_{0,B} = CF_{1,B} \times \frac{1}{1 + \left(r_{f,real} + r_{inf} + \pi_B\right)} = \frac{100\,000}{1 + (0.015 + 0.025 + 0.04)} = \frac{100\,000}{1.08} = 92\,593$$

Implicitly, we have assumed that investors compare characteristics of assets and have a preference for high returns, low risk and liquidity. In other words, we have assumed that greed, fear and impatience generally dominate investment decisions. A brief look at how bonds are priced in financial markets shows that the present value approach describes realistically how assets are priced in competitive financial markets. If the present value rule holds, the price of a bond P_B equals the present value of its future cash flows c_t:[5]

$$P_B = \frac{c_{1,B}}{(1 + y_B)^1} + \frac{c_{2,B}}{(1 + y_B)^2} + \ldots + \frac{c_{T,B}}{(1 + y_B)^T}$$

---

[1] Keynes (1997), p. 167.
[2] The annualized, historical geometric average of equity risk premia relative to bills over the 105-year period from 1900 to 2004 was 5.5% for the United States, 6.4% for Japan, 3.6% for Germany, and 4.3% for the United Kingdom. Dimson *et al.* (2005), p. 39.
[3] Short selling (building a short position) a stock is simply the opposite of buying it (building a long position): A short seller of a stock borrows it from the owner of the asset and sells it in the market hoping that the price declines so that she can buy it back at a lower price. The short seller of a stock not only realizes the price difference, but also has to pay borrowing fees and dividends, if any, to the owner of the stock and receives interest on the proceeds of the short sale.
[4] Discounting the expected cash flow in the amount of USD 100 000 by the product of one plus the real rate of interest multiplied by one plus the inflation rate and one plus the risk premium leads almost to the same result:

$$USD\ 100\,000/(1.015^*1.025^*1.04) = USD\ 92\,422.$$

[5] Fabozzi (1997), pp. 25–105.

The yield y is the interest rate that makes the present value equal to the price of the bond. The yield-to-maturity is the yield that an investor would realize if she holds the bond until maturity. By convention, the yield-to-maturity of a semi-annual bond with $k = 2$ payments per year is expressed by doubling the semi-annual discount rate i. Table 2.1 shows that a bond that pays semi-annually USD 2.5 over five years (10 periods) and USD 100 at maturity T should trade at USD 100 (par value) if the yield of identical bonds (opportunity cost) is 5% and at USD 99.56 if the required yield is 5.1%.

Table 2.1 Present value calculation to value bonds

	Scenario 1: $y = 5\%$			Scenario 2: $y = 5.1\%$		
t	Cash flows c	$PV = c/(1+i)^t$	$PV \times t$	Cash flows c	$PV = c/(1+i)^t$	$PV \times t$
1	2.5	2.4390	2.4390	2.5	2.4378	2.4378
2	2.5	2.3795	4.7591	2.5	2.3772	4.7544
3	2.5	2.3215	6.9645	2.5	2.3181	6.9543
4	2.5	2.2649	9.0595	2.5	2.2605	9.0419
5	2.5	2.2096	11.0482	2.5	2.2043	11.0213
6	2.5	2.1557	12.9345	2.5	2.1494	12.8967
7	2.5	2.1032	14.7221	2.5	2.0960	14.6720
8	2.5	2.0519	16.4149	2.5	2.0439	16.3510
9	2.5	2.0018	18.0164	2.5	1.9931	17.9375
10	102.5	80.0728	800.7284	102.5	79.6833	796.8328
Σ		100.0000	897.0866		99.5635	892.8997

In reality, differences between bond prices and the present values of future cash flows to bond holders are usually very small. Otherwise, arbitrageurs would try to capture a risk-free profit by buying undervalued bonds and short selling overvalued bonds. Yield changes are the main value driver of bonds. The modified duration quantifies the sensitivity of a bond to small yield changes. The Macaulay duration and the modified duration in scenario 1 are 4.485 and 4.37:

$$D_{Macaulay} = \frac{\sum\limits_{t=1}^{n} t \, \frac{c_t}{(1+i)^t}}{k \sum\limits_{t=1}^{n} \frac{c_t}{(1+i)^t}} = \frac{897.0866}{2 \times 100} = 4.485433 \Rightarrow D_{MOD} = \frac{D_{Macaulay}}{(1+i)} = \frac{4.485433}{1.025} = 4.37$$

If the yield-to-maturity y increases by 10 basis points (0.1% or 0.001) from 5% to 5.10% the price of the bond should approximately fall by -0.437% (from USD 100 to USD 99.56):[6]

$$\frac{\Delta P}{P} = -D_{MOD} \times \Delta y = -4.37 \times 0.001 = -0.00437 = -0.437\%$$

The present value rule also applies to equities. The fundamental value of a stock is simply the sum of future cash flows to equity holders discounted at the opportunity costs of equity. However, there are at least four important differences between stocks and bonds:

---

[6] Modified duration gives only an initial approximation of the percentage price change of a bond due to small yield changes. As the price/yield relationship of a bond is not linear, investors also have to consider the second derivative (convexity) if large yield changes are considered. Fabozzi (1997), pp. 90–94.

(1) *The future cash flows of stocks are more uncertain than those of bonds*: Coupon payments are usually constant and can be predicted with a high degree of confidence. Cash flows to equity holders cannot be predicted with the same high degree of confidence. Scenario analysis and Monte Carlo simulations are therefore essential tools for equity analysts who want to take the uncertainty of future cash flows into consideration.

(2) *Equity holders do not receive a redemption value at maturity*: They are the owners of a company and therefore, theoretically, entitled to receive cash flows until infinity. As it is not practically possible to discount cash flows until infinity, equity analysts usually discount cash flows over a finite period of time $t = 1, \ldots, T$, the so-called competitive advantage period, and calculate a terminal value which captures the value of expected cash flows after the competitive advantage period. The fundamental value of a stock is the sum of the discounted cash flows to equity holders during the competitive advantage period and the discounted value of the terminal value. The terminal value is – in contrast to the redemption value of a bond – a purely theoretical construct.

(3) *In contrast to the opportunity costs of debt, the opportunity costs of equity cannot be readily observed in financial markets*: Financial economists have constructed various models to estimate the costs of equity. The most widely used model to quantify the costs of equity is the Capital Asset Pricing Model. The CAPM describes how assets are priced under equilibrium conditions.

(4) *The number of value drivers is more plentiful for stocks than for bonds*: Yield changes are clearly the most important value driver for bonds. The duration quantifies the price sensitivity of a bond to small yield changes. Opportunity costs are also an important value driver for equities. However, there are several other value drivers which have a strong impact on the value of equities, including sales growth, operating margins, capital expenditures and change in net working capital, to name just the most prominent value drivers of stocks. Building a model to price equities is more complicated than valuing bonds.

The fundamental value quantifies the present value of future cash flows. It expresses how much an investment is worth in equilibrium assuming that no arbitrage opportunities exist. Some investors argue that equity valuation models are not helpful in making investment decisions as market prices often deviate from their fundamental values for an extended period of time. Of course, market prices can deviate from their fundamental values for a long time. It is not sufficient to simply select overvalued and undervalued stocks. Investors are well advised only to buy undervalued and short sell overvalued stocks if they have valid reasons to believe that a stock price will move to its fundamental value over time.[7] Some investors claim that fundamental values are extremely sensitive to highly subjective inputs. They are right as fundamental values are never objective, but depend on subjective expectations of an uncertain future. Investors should also be aware that financial analysts and their employers have their own interests.

Valuation models are most useful if investors (a) are able to identify stock prices which deviate significantly from their fundamental values and (b) have valid reasons to believe that the prices of these stocks will move to their fundamental values over time. Believers in efficient market theory often claim that stock prices always fully reflect all available

---

[7] These reasons are often called "catalysts". In chemistry a catalyst is a substance that accelerates a reaction. In the parlance of finance the word catalyst is often used for information that triggers or accelerates stock price adjustments.

information.[8] However, valuation models are useful not only for active fund managers, but also for believers in efficient markets. If market prices equal fundamental values, believers in efficient markets can apply DCF models to analyze what expectations are implied in current market prices.[9]

Fundamental values are based on the premise that a company will employ its assets to generate cash flows, will continue its operations and will not liquidate its assets. In reality, the going-concern assumption does not always hold. The going-concern assumption does not hold for companies involved in mergers, acquisitions or restructurings. A hedge fund manager who short sells a stock believing that it is trading well above its fundamental value suffers a large loss if a financial or strategic investor buys this company and pays a large control premium. The fundamental value reflects only the value of the cash-generating, operating assets of a firm. Often companies hold an excess amount of cash on their balance sheets not needed to continue the firm's operation. Fundamental values do not reflect the value of excess cash and other non-operating assets which are not utilized to generate operating cash flows. DCF valuation is a useful exercise to understand what an investment is worth in equilibrium. Like every model, DCF models are based on simplifying assumptions. Trading on the basis of fundamental values can be painful if the no-arbitrage argument or the going-concern assumption does not hold. In summary:

(1) Virtually every sophisticated equity valuation model used by leading investment banks today is a discounted cash flow (DCF) model. The fundamental value of an investment derived by DCF models is the present value of its expected, future cash flows.

(2) Investors compare assets and have preferences for high returns, low risk and liquidity. The expected return which is foregone by investing in a specific asset rather than in a comparable investment is called opportunity cost of capital. The fundamental value of an asset depends on its opportunity cost of capital.

(3) While the present value rule applies both to bonds and equities, several important differences exist: Cash flows to equity holders are more uncertain; equity holders do not receive a redemption value at maturity; the opportunity costs of equity cannot readily be observed in the markets and therefore must be modeled; interest rate sensitivity measured by duration is the key value driver of bonds, the value drivers of equities are more plentiful.

(4) When applying DCF models, investors have to estimate the expected cash flows during the competitive advantage period, the terminal value and the opportunity cost of capital. The opportunity cost of capital consists of the risk-free rate plus a risk premium, which adequately reflects the uncertainty of future cash flows. Cash flows and opportunity costs should be consistent.

(5) Fundamental values are calculated assuming that a company will employ its operating assets to generate cash flows, will continue its operation and will not liquidate its assets. The going concern assumption does not hold if companies are involved in mergers, acquisitions or restructurings. The fundamental value does not reflect the value of non-operating assets which are not utilized to generate operating cash flows.

---

[8] The so-called efficient market hypothesis is not a theoretical system of sentences which are logically related but a definition formulated by Eugene F. Fama: "A market in which prices always 'fully reflect' available information is called 'efficient'." Fama (1970), p. 383. Financial economists do not agree how quickly stock prices react on new information and whether investors always interpret information rationally. The work on efficient capital markets is summarized in Fama (1991) and Malkiel (2003).

[9] Rappaport and Mauboussin (2001), pp. 7–14.

3

Discounted Cash Flow Models: The Main Input Factors

3.1 ANALYTICAL BALANCE SHEETS AND FREE CASH FLOW DISCOUNT MODELS

Theoretically, the value of a firm is determined by the value of its assets A financed by debt D and equity E: $A = D + E$. The value of equity equals the value of assets minus the value of debt: $E = A - D$. Assuming that only one class of common shares is outstanding, the value of one share s can be calculated by the value of common equity E divided by the number of shares n outstanding: $s = E/n$.

Valuing a company would be very simple if the balance sheet always reflected the fair market value of assets, debt and equity. Unfortunately, accountants preparing financial statements have to follow generally accepted accounting principles (GAAP). US GAAP requires that fixed assets are valued at historical costs less depreciation. The reported book value of property, plant and equipment, often bought years ago, is generally not equal to its current market value. The reported value of current assets is also heavily influenced by accounting conventions. Companies are, for example, allowed to use different methods for inventory accounting. The recognition of intangible assets, including goodwill, trademarks, and patents, is especially problematic. US GAAP, for example, generally requires that research and development (R&D) costs are charged to expenses when incurred while some financial economists argue that R&D costs should be capitalized as intangible assets and be amortized. Companies often tend to understate indebtedness and hide debt from the balance sheet. Leasing and special purpose vehicles are classic examples of off-balance sheet debt. If a lease is treated as an operating rather than a capital lease, no obligation is shown on the balance sheet of the lessee. The amount of reported pension liabilities depends on various highly subjective assumptions.[1] Investors have numerous reasons to mistrust book values reported on corporate balance sheets.

The analytical view of a financial analyst differs from the view of an accountant on a balance sheet for three principal reasons:

(1) Corporate balance sheets report only the value of existing assets. They do not reflect the expected value of future investments.
(2) They also do not separate operating assets which a company utilizes to generate operating cash flows from non-operating assets.
(3) They do not isolate long-term providers of capital. Current liabilities are shown on the right hand side of traditional balance sheets.

---

[1] Kieso *et al.* (2004).

Financial analysts typically rearrange balance sheets created by accountants. Figure 3.1 shows a rearranged, analytical balance sheet.

Assets	Liabilities
A.1 Fundamental value of existing operating assets A1.1 Fundamental value of existing fixed assets A.1.2 Fundamental value of existing working capital $WC = CA - CL$	D. Market value of long-term debt
A.2 Fundamental value of future investments A.2.1 Fundamental value of future investments in fixed assets A.2.2 Fundamental value of future investments in working capital A.3 Value of non-operating assets	E. Residual value of equity $(E = A - D)$

Figure 3.1   Analytical balance sheet

The rearranged, analytical balance sheet isolates long-term providers of capital reflecting the value of long-term debt and equity. Current liabilities are moved from the right to the left side of the balance sheet and included in working capital (WC) as the difference between current assets (CA) and current liabilities (CL).[2] As book values of assets usually do not reflect the fair value of assets, financial analysts estimate the value of the operating assets by discounting the expected future cash flows which a company will generate by utilizing its operating assets. To stay in business and to generate future cash flows companies have to invest in fixed assets and in working capital. Usually not only property, plant and equipment but also inventories, accounts receivables and other current assets increase when companies grow. Financial analysts discount future cash flows to estimate the value of both operating assets in place (A.1) and the value of future investments (A.2). To calculate the value of an enterprise the value of non-operating assets (A.3) must be added. The present value of future cash flows does not include the value of non-operating assets.

The value of equity is the residual claim on the value of operating and non-operating assets owned by the company less the market value of debt ($E = A - D$). *Free* cash flows (FCF) are defined as cash flows from operations which a company can distribute to its providers of capital after investing in working capital and fixed assets. The operating cash flows after capital expenditure are an important performance measure because they quantify the cash that a company generated by its operations after maintaining and expanding its asset

---

[2] When calculating invested capital, cash flows and weighted average cost of capital, we included current liabilities consistently in net working capital. The expression *debt, or D,* is used for long-term debt not including current liabilities in Part I of this book.

base. A company can use its FCF to pay dividends, to reduce debt, to buy back shares or to make acquisitions. If companies do not invest in future growth opportunities or distribute cash to debt and equity holders, but rather leave it unutilized on their balance sheets, the cash represents a non-operating asset.

Basically two types of free cash flow models exist: free cash flow to the firm (FCFF) and free cash flow to equity (FCFE) discount models.[3] FCFF are free cash flows after investing in working capital and fixed assets but before interest payments which can be distributed to all providers of long-term capital (debt and equity). As it is not practically possible to discount FCFF until infinity, financial analysts usually discount FCFF by the weighted cost of capital, or WACC,[4] over a finite period of years, $t = 1, \ldots, T$, the so-called competitive advantage period. The terminal value, or TV, quantifies the value of cash flows after the competitive advantage period, $t = T + 1, \ldots, \infty$:[5]

$$EV = \sum_{t=1}^{\infty} \frac{FCFF_t}{(1 + WACC)^t} = \sum_{t=1}^{T} \frac{FCFF_t}{(1 + WACC)^t} + \frac{TV_{EV}}{(1 + WACC)^T}$$

The FCFF model is an enterprise valuation model. To calculate the fundamental value of equity $V_{E,0}$, financial analysts have to subtract the market value of debt D_M from the enterprise value EV: $V_{E,0} = EV - D_M$. Alternatively, financial analysts can directly estimate the fundamental value of equity $V_{E,0}$ by discounting FCFE by the cost of equity i_E:

$$V_{E,0} = \sum_{t=1}^{\infty} \frac{FCFE_t}{(1 + i_E)^t} = \sum_{t=1}^{T} \frac{FCFE_t}{(1 + i_E)^t} + \frac{TV_E}{(1 + i_E)^T}$$

FCFE are the free cash flows after funding investments and after interest payments. FCFE are the source for dividend payments. If analysts discount expected, future dividends (the cash flows that the company really distributes to equity holders) instead of FCFE (the cash flows which the company could potentially distribute to equity holders), DCF models are referred to as dividend discount models (DDM). All DCF models lead to the same result if consistent inputs are used. Cash flows and discount rates must be consistent:

(1) Risk premia and discount rates should adequately reflect the uncertainty of expected, future cash flows. Discounting highly uncertain cash flows by low discount rates is arguably one of the most prominent mistakes made by financial analysts.
(2) Free cash flows to the firm must be discounted by a firm's weighted average cost of capital provided by debt and equity holders. Free cash flows to equity which quantify the free cash flows after interest payments to debt holders must be discounted by a firm's costs of equity.
(3) Cash flows and discount rates must be expressed in terms of equal purchasing power: Nominal cash flows should be discounted by nominal discount rates, real cash flows by real discount rates.

---

[3] Damodaran (2002), pp. 351–422.
[4] The calculation of the weighted average cost of capital is explained in section 3.3.3.
[5] The calculation of terminal values is discussed in section 3.3.4.

A word of caution before we discuss the most popular DCF models: Some financial economists argue that traditional DCF models fail to consider the managerial flexibility to expand, to delay or to abandon projects in response to unexpected market developments. The option to adapt and revise future decisions has an option value which can be estimated by applying real option models.[6] Real option models applied in corporate finance and corporate strategy are often complex and currently not widely used by financial analysts. In Part II Monte Carlo simulations are introduced which become increasingly popular among financial economists to deal with uncertainty investors face when making investment decisions.[7]

3.2   THE DIVIDEND DISCOUNT MODEL

The dividend discount model (DDM) is the most simplified form of a discounted cash flow model. Dividends are cash flows equity holders actually receive from a company. According to the rule of consistency, dividends must be discounted by costs of equity. Dividend discount models are equity not enterprise valuation models. Several versions of the dividend discount models exist, each based on different simplifying assumptions.

The most basic form is the *perpetuity version* which is based on two extremely simplifying assumptions:

(1) Investors receive constant dividends in perpetuity.
(2) Costs of equity are constant forever.

According to the present value rule, the fundamental value of equity $V_{0,E}$ is the present value of constant, future dividends D_1 distributed to all equity holders in one year from now discounted by the constant costs of equity i_E. If the two assumptions hold and dividends and costs of equity are in fact constant, the present value formula can be simplified as shown below:[8]

Equation I: $$V_{0,E} = \frac{\overline{D_1}}{\left(1+\overline{i_E}\right)^1} + \frac{\overline{D_1}}{\left(1+\overline{i_E}\right)^2} + \ldots + \frac{\overline{D_1}}{\left(1+\overline{i_E}\right)^\infty}$$ $\left|\text{multiply by}\left(1+\overline{i_E}\right)\right.$

Equation II: $$V_{0,E}\left(1+\overline{i_E}\right) = \overline{D_1} + \frac{\overline{D_1}}{\left(1+\overline{i_E}\right)^1} + \frac{\overline{D_1}}{\left(1+\overline{i_E}\right)^2} + \ldots + \frac{\overline{D_1}}{\left(1+\overline{i_E}\right)^{\infty-1}}$$ $\left|\begin{array}{l}\text{subtract I from II} \\ \text{for } t \to \infty \text{ the final} \\ \text{term is 0}\end{array}\right.$

Equation III: $$V_{0,E}\left(1+\overline{i_E}\right) - V_{0,E} = \overline{D_1}$$

Perpetuity DDM: $$V_{0,E} = \frac{\overline{D_1}}{\overline{i_E}} \Leftrightarrow V_{0,share} = \frac{\overline{DPS_1}}{\overline{i_E}}$$

After rearranging the present value equation, the perpetuity DDM states that the fundamental value of equity is equal to the constant dividends paid to all shareholders in one year from now, D_1, divided by the constant cost of equity i_E. If both sides of the formula are divided by the number of shares outstanding, the fundamental value of one share equals the constant dividend per share DPS_1 distributed to shareholders in one year from now divided by the constant cost of equity i_E.

---

[6] Copeland and Antikarov (2001), pp. 3–27.
[7] In practice, financial analysts discount expected cash flows by one plus the risk-adjusted interest rate. Grinold and Kahn argue that risk-adjusted expected cash flows should be discounted by one plus the risk-free rate of interest instead. The idea to introduce risk-adjusted probability distributions is complex, not widely used in practice and therefore not discussed here. Grinold and Kahn (2000), pp. 199–224.
[8] Barker (2001), p. 35.

In the most popular form of the dividend discount model, the *dividend growth model (DGM)*,[9] assumption (1) is replaced by the more realistic premise that dividends are not constant but grow at a constant rate g over time. Again, it is assumed that costs of equity are constant over time. Starting with the present value formula and the premise that dividends grow at a constant rate g, the DGM equation can be derived as follows:[10]

Equation I:
$$V_{0,E} = \frac{D_0 (1+\overline{g})^1}{(1+\overline{i_E})^1} + \frac{D_0 (1+\overline{g})^2}{(1+\overline{i_E})^2} + \ldots + \frac{D_0 (1+\overline{g})^\infty}{(1+\overline{i_E})^\infty}$$
$\left|\begin{array}{l}\text{multiply by } (1+\overline{g}) \\ \text{divide by } (1+\overline{i_E})\end{array}\right.$

Equation II:
$$\frac{V_{0,E} (1+\overline{g})}{(1+\overline{i_E})} = \frac{D_0 (1+\overline{g})^2}{(1+\overline{i_E})^2} + \frac{D_0 (1+\overline{g})^3}{(1+\overline{i_E})^3} + \ldots + \frac{D_0 (1+\overline{g})^{\infty+1}}{(1+\overline{i_E})^{\infty+1}}$$
$\left|\begin{array}{l}\text{subtract II from I} \\ \text{for } t \to \infty \text{ the final} \\ \text{term is } 0\end{array}\right.$

Equation III:
$$V_{0,E} - \frac{V_{0,E} (1+\overline{g})}{(1+\overline{i_E})} = \frac{D_0 (1+\overline{g})^1}{(1+\overline{i_E})^1}$$

DGM:
$$V_{0,E} = \frac{D_0 (1+\overline{g})}{\overline{i_E} - \overline{g}} \Leftrightarrow V_{0,share} = \frac{\overline{DPS_0} (1+\overline{g})}{\overline{i_E} - \overline{g}}$$

The DGM simply states that the fundamental value of equity is the amount of dividends distributed in one year from now $D_0(1+g)$ divided by the difference between constant costs of equity i_E and the constant growth rate g. According to the DGM, the value of one share equals the dividend per share expected in one year from now divided by the difference of the cost of equity and the expected growth rate.

The shareholder assembly of Deutsche Telekom, the German telecoms operator, decided on April 26, 2005 to pay a dividend of EUR 0.62 per share for 2004. On April 26, 2005, Deutsche Telekom shares closed at EUR 15.33 and traded at 10:30 a.m. the next morning at EUR 14.70 ex dividend. Bloomberg showed on that day that trailing earnings per share (EPS) over the last 12 months were EUR 1.10. Nelson, another provider of financial information, reported that the 31 analysts who covered Deutsche Telekom expected EPS of EUR 1.30 for the full year 2005 on average.

According to the Capital Asset Pricing Model, which will be discussed in greater detail in section 3.3.3, the estimated cost of equity of Deutsche Telekom was 8.3% (Table 3.1).[11]

Table 3.1   Inputs DGM Deutsche Telekom

Dividend per share DPS 2004	EUR 0.62
Earnings per share EPS 2004	EUR 1.10
Estimated earnings per share 2005	EUR 1.30
Estimated cost of equity (CAPM)	8.3%
Estimated growth rate forever	4%

According to the DGM, a share of Deutsche Telekom was worth EUR 14.99 assuming a constant growth rate of 4% p.a.:[12]

---

[9] The Dividend Growth Model is often called the Gordon Growth Model after its originator.

[10] D_0 represents the last annual dividend currently received, $D_0(1+g)$ the dividend expected one year from now. The formula shown above therefore differs slightly from Barker (2001), p. 35.

[11] The CAPM was applied using a risk-free rate of 3.5%, a beta of 0.72 and a risk premium of 6.7%: $3.5\% + 0.72 * 6.7\% = 8.3\%$.

[12] Please note that we used 2004 as base period $t = 0$.

$$V_{0,E} = \frac{D_0\,(1+\bar{g})}{\bar{i}_E - g} = \frac{0.62\,(1+0.04)}{0.083 - 0.04} = 14.99$$

Using the more optimistic analysts' EPS estimates of EUR 1.30 for 2005 and an assumed payout ratio of 56% (EUR 0.62/EUR 1.10), the expected dividend for fiscal year 2005 equals EUR 0.73 (EUR 1.30 * 0.56). Assuming a constant dividend growth rate of 4% for the period beyond 2005, the fundamental value of one share of Deutsche Telecom equals EUR 16.98:

$$V_{0,E} = \frac{D_1}{\bar{i}_E - g} = \frac{0.73}{0.083 - 0.04} = 16.98$$

The example explains how investors can incorporate EPS estimates of financial analysts into DGM models. It also illustrates how sensitive the fundamental value is to changes in expected dividends. Small changes in growth expectations and/or estimated costs of equity have a substantial impact on the fundamental value derived by the DGM. If the growth rate, for example, fell from 4% to 3% in the second example, the fundamental value per share would fall from EUR 16.98 to EUR 13.77, or almost 19%.

Financial economists often suggest valuing shares by applying more realistic *multi-stage dividend growth models*.[13] Using Multi-Stage DGM, financial analysts can incorporate different growth assumptions over different time periods in their models. The *two-stage dividend discount model* is the most widely used Multi-Stage DGM. Two-Stage DGM are most appropriate if (1) explicit forecasts of future dividends over a finite forecast period exist (usually formulated by financial analysts), or if (2) dividends grow at an abnormal rate during an initial period and more moderately thereafter.

In case (1), *Two-Stage DGM with explicit dividend forecasts for a finite period of time*, the fundamental value per share equals the present value of dividends per share (DPS) during the explicit forecast period plus the present value of the terminal value TV. The terminal value can be determined by applying the standard DGM. It reflects the value of the expected dividends after the explicit forecast period $t = T + 1, \ldots, \infty$ which shareholders expect to receive forever. The terminal value must be discounted to determine its present value:

$$V_{0,share} = \frac{DPS_1}{\left(1+\bar{i}_E\right)^1} + \frac{DPS_2}{\left(1+\bar{i}_E\right)^2} + \cdots + \frac{DPS_T}{\left(1+\bar{i}_E\right)^T} + \frac{TV}{\left(1+\bar{i}_E\right)^T}$$

$$TV = \frac{DPS_T\,(1+\bar{g}_{TV})}{\bar{i}_{E,TV} - \bar{g}_{TV}}$$

In case (2), *Two-Stage DGM with an initial high growth rate*, financial analysts assume that dividends grow at a high growth rate g_{HG} in an initial high growth period and at a slower rate g_{TV} during the terminal value or stable growth period. The fundamental value of a share is

---

[13] Damodaran (2005), pp. 536–547.

the sum of the present value of the dividends during the high growth period and the present value of the dividends after the high growth period reflected by the terminal value.[14]

$$V_{0,share} = \frac{DPS_0 \left(1 + g_{HG}\right)\left(1 - \dfrac{\left(1 + g_{HG}\right)^T}{\left(1 + \overline{i_{E,HG}}\right)^T}\right)}{\overline{i_{E,HG}} - \overline{g_{HG}}} + \frac{\dfrac{DPS_T \left(1 + \overline{g_{TV}}\right)}{\overline{i_{E,TV}} - \overline{g_{TV}}}}{\left(1 + \overline{i_{E,HG}}\right)^T}$$

(present value of DPS during	(present value of DPS during
the initial abnormal-growth period	the terminal value period
$t = 1, \ldots, T$)	$t = T + 1, \ldots, \infty$)

The high growth period is often called the competitive advantage period. By definition, the competitive advantage period is the period in which the return on capital exceeds the cost of capital. Using equity valuation models, the competitive advantage period is the period in which the return on equity (ROE) is higher than the cost of equity i_E: ROE $> i_E$. A company that earns high returns on capital attracts competition. Instead of using historical growth rates or analyst estimates, investors can forecast future growth rates by applying the *fundamental growth equation*. The retention ratio b is the percentage of net income that a company retains in its business to enable future growth. By definition the retention ratio, or plow-back ratio, is one minus the payout ratio. According to the fundamental growth equation, the expected growth rate g equals the retention ratio b multiplied by ROE:[15]

$$g = b \times \text{ROE} \qquad b = 1 - \text{Payout ratio}$$

The art of valuation is not to build more sophisticated models, but to understand how other people value investments. In his famous example of a beauty contest, John Maynard Keynes linked investing in the stock market to judging a beauty contest:

> ... It is not a case of choosing those which, to the best of one's judgment, are really the prettiest, nor even those which average opinion genuinely thinks the prettiest. We have reached the third degree where we devote our intelligences to anticipating what average opinion expects the average opinion to be. And there are some, I believe, who practice the fourth, fifth and higher degrees. ... [16]

Discounted cash flow models are excellent tools to analyze other investors' opinions. Damodaran (2005) applied a Two-Stage DGM to value shares of Deutsche Bank using the in Table 3.2.[17]

Applying the Two-Stage DGM formula, Damodaran (2005) calculated a present value of dividends during the high growth period of EUR 7.22, a discounted terminal value of EUR 47.59 and a fundamental value per share of EUR 54.81:

---

[14] Dividends in period $t = 1$, or $DPS_0(1 + g_{HG})$ are multiplied by factor $1 - [(1 + g_{HG})T/(1 + i_{E,HG})T]$ to calculate the value of a geometric series of dividend payments which grow at a constant rate g_{HG} over a finite period of time. Damodaran (2002), p. 337.
[15] Damodaran (2005), p. 541.
[16] Keynes (1997), p. 156.
[17] The following example is taken from Damodaran (2005), pp. 546f.

Table 3.2   Inputs Two-Stage DGM Deutsche Bank

Dividend per share DPS 2003	EUR 1.50
Earnings per share EPS 2003	EUR 4.33
Retention ratio b during the CAP[18]	65.36%
ROE	11.26%
Cost of equity during the CAP[19]	8.76%
Assumed length of CAP	5 years
Cost of equity during the TVP[20]	8.87%
Growth rate during the TVP	4%

$$V_{0,share} = \frac{1.50\,(1+0.0736)\left(1 - \dfrac{(1+0.0736)^5}{(1+0.0876)^5}\right)}{0.0876 - 0.0736} + \frac{\dfrac{3.53}{0.0887 - 0.04}}{(1+0.0876)^5} = 7.22 + 47.59 = 54.81$$

Some of Damodaran's inputs need further explanation. The growth rate during the high growth period was calculated by applying the fundamental growth equation:

$$g_{HG} = b_{HG} \times ROE_{HG} = 0.6536 \times 0.1126 = 0.0736$$

Using a growth rate of 7.36% translates into an estimated EPS of EUR 4.65 for 2004, EUR 4.99 for 2005, EUR 5.36 for 2006, EUR 5.75 for 2007 and EUR 6.18 for 2008. In most cases analysts use 3, 5 or 10 years as length of the competitive advantage period, usually without even trying to explain their reasons for choosing a specific time span. Damodaran's high growth period lasts 5 years. Financial analysts often use the "DuPont formula"[21] to decompose ROE:

$$\frac{\text{Net income}}{\text{Average equity}} = \frac{\text{Net income}}{\text{Net sales}} \times \frac{\text{Net sales}}{\text{Average assets}} \times \frac{\text{Average assets}}{\text{Average equity}}$$

$$\text{ROE} = \text{Profit margin} \times \text{Asset turnover} \times \text{Financial leverage}$$

ROE equals net income less preferred dividends, if any, divided by average equity. Management can enhance a firm's ROE not only by increasing profit margins and asset turnover, but also by employing more debt (less equity) to finance its asset base at the expense of higher risk due to financial leverage.[22] The profit margin reflects how well a company manages its costs. Asset turnover quantifies how efficiently a company uses its average assets in place to generate sales during a reporting period. Financial leverage measures the relationship between average assets, which can be financed by debt and equity, and average

---

[18] The retention ratio during the competitive advantage period (CAP) equals to $1 - 1.50/4.33 = 0.6536$.

[19] To calculate the cost of equity during the competitive advantage period (CAP), Damodaran (2005) applied the Capital Asset Pricing Model with a risk-free rate of 4.05%, a beta of 0.98 and a risk premium of 4.82%: $4.05\% + 0.98*4.82\% = 8.76\%$.

[20] To calculate the cost of equity during the terminal value period (TVP), Damodaran (2005) applied the Capital Asset Pricing Model with a risk-free rate of 4.05%, a beta of 1 and a risk premium of 4.82%: $4.05\% + 1*4.82\% = 8.87\%$.

[21] In the 1910s, Donaldson Brown, an engineer working in DuPont's financial department, developed a return on investment formula to decompose DuPont's return on investment into profitability and asset efficiency company-wide. Different versions of his formula were later used to decompose return on investment and return on equity. The ROE decomposition formula is perhaps the most widely used version of the "DuPont formula".

[22] Ferris *et al.* (1992), pp. 233–235.

equity employed during a period. The DuPont formula helps investors to better understand the sources of ROE.

The discounted terminal value represents over 86% of the fundamental value of Deutsche Bank's shares. This illustrates how important input factors are which go into the terminal value calculation. By definition, ROE equals costs of equity in the terminal value period: $ROE_{TV} = i_{E,TV}$. The retention ratio b_{TG} during the terminal value period can be calculated by applying the fundamental growth equation. Using a terminal value growth rate of 4% leads to a terminal value payout ratio of 54.9% and a dividend of EUR 3.53 in $T + 1 = 6$:

$$g_{TV} = b_{TV} \times ROE_{TV} \Rightarrow 0.04 = b_{TV} \times 0.0887 \Rightarrow b_{TV} = 0.451 \text{ and } (1 - b_{TV}) = 0.549$$

$$DPS_6 = EPS_5 (1 + g)(1 - b) = 6.18 \times 1.04 \times 0.549 = 3.53$$

Damodaran concluded that shares of Deutsche Bank trading at EUR 66, at the time he did his valuation, were overvalued compared to a fundamental value of EUR 54.81 based on his assumptions discussed above.[23] At the beginning of 2006, shares of Deutsche Bank traded at EUR 82. Are valuation exercises therefore useless? Table 3.3 reflects the earnings and dividends expectations for Deutsche Bank by leading investment banks at the beginning of 2006[24].

Table 3.3 Earnings and dividend expectations for Deutsche Bank

	Damodaran[25]			UBS (March 20, 2006)[26]			Merrill Lynch (April 3, 2006)[27]			Lehman Brothers (February 3, 2006)[28]		
	EPS	DPS	ROE	EPS	DPS	ROE	EPS	DPS	ROE	EPS	DPS	ROE
2004	4.65	1.61	11.26	4.68	1.70		4.35	1.70	9.5	4.65	1.70	
2005	4.99	1.73		6.64	2.50	12.5	7.42	2.50	14.1	7.44	2.50	
2006	5.36	1.86		8.89	3.20	14.3	7.67	2.69	13.5	7.11	2.75	11.9
2007	5.75	1.99		9.67	3.50	14.3	8.54	3.15	14.1	7.69	3.00	11.8
2008	6.18	2.14		10.43	3.80	14.6	9.38	3.56	14.4	8.24	3.25	11.8

Damodaran (2005) correctly anticipated that Deutsche Bank entered into a high growth period but did not foresee the increase in earnings to its full extent. In 2005, Deutsche Bank's income before income taxes increased to EUR 6.1 billion compared to EUR 4 billion in 2004 mainly because of its highly profitable investment banking business.[29] Deutsche Bank's dividend per share of EUR 1.70 for fiscal year 2004 (paid on May 19, 2005) increased by 47% to EUR 2.50 for fiscal year 2005 (paid on June 2, 2006). Analysts at UBS Investment Research who applied a dividend growth model to value shares of Deutsche argued in March 2006:

---

[23] Damodaran (2005), p. 547.
[24] Financial analysts make different adjustments to earnings. Earnings and ROE data from different analysts must therefore be interpreted and compared with great caution.
[25] Damodaran (2005), p. 546f.
[26] UBS Investment Research (2006).
[27] Merrill Lynch (2006).
[28] Lehman Brothers (2006). Table 3.3 reflects stated – not adjusted – EPS, as stated earnings are used in the report to calculate ROE.
[29] Deutsche Bank (2005), p. 50.

... Our price target of €110 is based on a Gordon growth model, in which we assume a sustainable ROE of 14.6%, a perpetual growth rate of 4.0%, and cost of equity of 10%. ....[30]

At the beginning of 2006, the earnings per share and dividend estimates of most analysts were significantly higher than Damodaran's earlier forecasts. It is therefore no surprise that shares of Deutsche Bank traded well above Damodaran's fundamental value of EUR 54.81.[31] Dividend discount models are helpful tools to translate earnings expectations into fundamental values. The result, however, depends on subjective assumptions made under uncertainty.[32] The model is extremely sensitive to input changes. Expected dividends are the product of expected earnings multiplied by an expected payout ratio. If companies are not expected to distribute earnings to shareholders over an extended period of time in the future, it is often practically impossible to apply dividend discount models.

Dividends are the amount of cash which a company actually distributes to its shareholders. Free cash flows to equity (FCFE), on the other hand, are cash flows after investment and after interest payments to debt holders which a company could distribute to its shareholders. Theoretically, FCFE models and dividend discount models are equivalent. The main advantage of a dividend discount model is its simplicity. Formulating FCFE models, on the other hand, forces financial analysts to analyze the earnings potential of a company in more detail. Analyzing revenues, operating expenses, investment needs and other factors which drive free cash flows to equity helps investors to understand how a company generates economic earnings (free cash flows) which could be distributed to shareholders. Free cash flows are the ultimate source to pay dividends in the future. We applied a dividend discount model to value shares of Deutsche Telekom above. However, Deutsche Telekom might not be able to pay dividends in the future if, for example, price pressures in the telecom industry increase further, or if Deutsche Telecom has to invest more in its infrastructure to stay competitive. When applying dividend discount models, analysts typically assume that companies pay a certain amount of dividends in the future without carefully analyzing the true earnings potential of a firm. Formulating free cash flow models, on the other hand, forces analysts to carefully analyze the revenue potential, the cost structure and the investment needs of a firm.

Most financial analysts apply free cash flow to the firm (FCFF) models instead of free cash flow to equity (FCFE) models. Free cash flows to the firm are cash flows after investment but before interest payments which could be distributed to both debt and equity holders, i.e. all providers of capital. FCFF models are more popular among practitioners than FCFE models, because it is more intuitive to value the complete firm and then subtract the value of debt instead of analyzing only the value of a firm which is financed by equity. If consistent inputs are used, FCFF and FCFE models lead to the same results. In the next chapter we leave dividend discount models behind us and focus on free cash flow models which make the earnings generation process of a firm – from revenues over operating earnings to free cash flows – more transparent.

---

[30] UBS Investment Research (2006), p. 2.
[31] Deutsch Bank shares traded at EUR 94.50 on March 20, 2006, when UBS Investment Research raised its price target from EUR 105 to EUR 110. UBS Investment Research (2006), p. 1.
[32] For general remarks on uncertainity see Part VIII of this book.

3.3   THE FREE CASH FLOW TO THE FIRM (FCFF) MODEL

Instead of applying dividend discount (DDM) or free cash flow to equity (FCFE) models to directly value the equity of a company, financial analysts can alternatively value the entire enterprise by using free cash flow to the firm (FCFF) models and then subtract the value of debt to derive the equity value. As most financial analysts prefer FCFF to FCFE models, we concentrate on FCFF models. FCFF models can be built in four steps:

(1) Estimate FCFF during the competitive advantage period (CAP).
(2) Discount FCFF by the weighted average cost of capital (WACC).
(3) Calculate the terminal value.
(4) Determine the enterprise value and the value of equity.

The value of one single share is simply the value of (common) equity divided by the number of (common) shares outstanding. These four steps will be explained in greater detail in the following chapters. Above we have argued that free cash flow models make the earnings generation process – from revenues over operating earnings to free cash flows – more transparent. Valuing companies on the basis of reported earnings might lead to the wrong conclusion if management uses creative accounting tricks ("window dressing") to overstate reported earnings. Before we discuss in detail how to estimate FCFF, we explain why investors should care about cash flows and mistrust reported earnings.

3.3.1   Stirling Homex: why cash is king!

Searching for "cheap" stocks, investors often calculate and compare valuation ratios. The price/earnings (PE) ratio, the quotient of the current stock price to current or expected future earnings per share (EPS), is arguably the most popular valuation ratio. Unfortunately, reported net income and EPS are often distorted by different interpretations of accounting conventions and therefore misleading. Revenue and expense items which are shown on the income statement do not necessarily lead to cash receipts and payments. The following case study illustrates why financial economists often mistrust reported earnings and recommend reconciling net income to operating cash flows.[33]

In February 1970 Stirling Homex, founded by two brothers David and William Stirling, went public.[34] The shares were sold to the public at USD 16.50 and traded above USD 51 in the middle of March.[35] On July 10, 1972, Stirling Homex filed for bankruptcy.[36] John Brooks, writing for *The New Yorker* at the time, called the 1960s the "go-go years" of the stock market. According to him, the success of an initial public offering depended on three things: a persuasive tongue, a resourceful accountant and a story.[37] Stirling Homex manufactured and installed modular homes. ". . . Their 'story' was instant housing. The current national obsession . . . was A Decent Home for Every American. . . . "[38] Jerry Dienstag, who worked at the time as a corporate lawyer for Stirling Homex, told his wife Eleanor in fall 1971, a few months before Stirling Homex filed for bankruptcy: ". . . You have no idea what it's

---

[33] To study this case study in more detail, see: Ferris and Barrett (1985). The Stirling Homex case is also discussed in two Harvard Business School Case Studies: Barrett (1983) and Wilson (1977).
[34] Stirling Homex Corporation (1970).
[35] Ferris and Barrett (1985), p. 1.
[36] Wilson (1977), p. 1.
[37] Dienstag (1976), p. 28.
[38] Dienstag (1976), p. 29.

like. One day the treasurer tells me he's worried about meeting the payroll and the next day I find out David [Stirling] bought himself another jet! . . . For starters, we still owe the bank $35 million. Then we've got an incredibly high overhead, and David keeps turning out these modules and assigning them to so-called projects that never get built. . . . "[39]

The problem was front-end loading or fraudulent reporting of revenues. Stirling Homex produced thousands of modular housing units, sealed them in plastic and recognized revenues without having proper customers who were willing and able to pay for the produced units. ". . . When the company collapsed, some 10 000 modular units valued somewhere around $35 million were discovered sealed in plastic and stored in fields around the country. Full purchase and payments existed for only 900 of these units. . . . "[40] Until the company collapsed, the Stirling brothers enjoyed corporate high life including limousine services and corporate airplanes.[41] Equity holders lost a fortune when the company finally filed for bankruptcy. Their mistake: They believed in a story, relied on reported earnings and did not carefully analyze cash flows. In summer 1970 Stirling Homex looked like a healthy growth company to investors focusing on net income. Reported net income had increased from USD 2.0 million in fiscal year 1970 to almost 3.3 million in fiscal year 1971, an increase of roughly 60% (Table 3.4).

Table 3.4 Stirling Homex Corporation: consolidated statement of income[42]

In USD	FY 1971	FY 1970
Revenues		
Manufacturing division	29 482 271	16 492 770
Installation division		
Trade	7 230 878	5 601 357
Affiliate	–	459 941
Equity in undistributed net income of subsidiary	134 579	–
Total revenues	**36 847 728**	**22 554 068**
Cost and expenses		
Cost of sales		
Manufacturing division	17 729 078	9 919 327
Installation division	6 601 413	5 240 388
Administrative and selling expenses	4 048 113	2 390 604
Interest expense	1 838 461	648 181
Total costs and expenses	**30 217 065**	**18 198 500**
Income before federal and state income taxes	**6 630 663**	**4 355 568**
Federal and state income taxes		
Current	368 000	1 965 982
Deferred	3 010 000	2 320 379
	3 378 000	2 320 379
Net income	**3 252 663**	**2 035 189**
Average common shares outstanding	8 881 938	8 649 483
Earnings per common share	**0.37**	**0.24**

---

[39] Dienstag (1976), p. 138.
[40] Wilson (1977), p. 1.
[41] Wilson (1977).
[42] Stirling Homex Corporation (1971).

The Committee of Sponsoring Organizations of the Treadway Commission (COSO) more recently analyzed a large number of alleged accounting frauds of public companies in the United States of America over an 11-year period and concluded that in over half of the frauds premature or fictitious reporting of sales revenues played a decisive role.[43] Investors are well advised to mistrust reported earnings and study corporate reports in detail. One of the most rewarding exercises for investors is studying footnotes. Footnote 3 to the consolidated financial statements for fiscal year 1971 explained the revenue recognition policy of Stirling Homex: ". . . Sales of modules (Manufacturing Division) are recognized when units are manufactured and assigned to specific contracts. . . . " Stirling Homex made investors believe that these contracts were guaranteed by the US Department of Housing and Urban Development (HUD). In fact, only non-legally binding letters of designation by local housing authorities existed which were not guaranteed by HUD.[44] Stirling Homex recognized earnings on its income statement for modules which were not delivered to customers and reported receivables on its balance sheet although collectibility was highly unlikely.

Ratio analysis can help investors to better understand the quality of reported earnings. Front-end loading of sales revenues can best be identified by calculating receivable turnover ratios and receivable collection periods. The receivable collection period measures how many days receivables are outstanding before cash is collected:

$$(\text{Average}) \text{ receivable turnover} = \frac{\text{net sales}}{(\text{Average}) \text{ accounts receivable}}$$

$$(\text{Average}) \text{ receivable collection period} = 365 \text{ days}/(\text{Average}) \text{ receivable turnover}$$

$$= 365 \text{ days} \times \frac{(\text{Average}) \text{ accounts receivable}}{\text{net sales}}$$

Footnote 3 to Stirling Homex's consolidated financial statements for fiscal year 1971 showed that receivables had increased dramatically (Table 3.5).

Table 3.5 Stirling Homex Corporation: receivables[45]

In USD	July 31, 1971	July 31, 1970
Contract receivables:		
Billed	10 382 626	10 559 145
Unbilled	24 633 799	4 626 370
Total	35 016 425	15 185 515
Income tax refund receivable	2 498 672	–
Current portion of long-term receivables	12 500	17 500
Other receivables	317 975	283 104
	37 845 572	**15 486 119**

Investors who carefully studied the footnotes learnt that receivables had increased considerably in fiscal year 1971 and, even worse, that 65% of all receivables – USD 24.6

---

[43] The Committee of Sponsoring Organizations of the Treadway Commission (1999), p. 6.
[44] Barrett (1983), p. 2.
[45] Stirling Homex (1970, 1971).

million out of USD 37.8 million – were classified as "unbilled receivables". Stirling Homex recognized sales and reported receivables on its balance sheet, but did not even send bills to most of its clients. The receivable turnover dropped in fiscal year 1971 from 1.46 to 0.97.[46] As a consequence, the receivable collection period increased from 251 days (365 days/1.46) in fiscal year 1970 to 375 days (365 days/0.97) in fiscal year 1971. The increase in the collection period reflected a deteriorating quality of receivables and reported revenues. At the end, Stirling Homex did not collect cash at all, but filed for bankruptcy in 1972.

Analyzing cash flow statements can help investors to detect front-end loading or fraudulent reporting of revenues. Today, Statement of Financial Accounting Standards No. 95 (FAS 95) requires that companies reporting under US GAAP classify cash flows as cash flows from operations (CFFO), cash flows from investing (CFFI), and cash flows from financing (CFFF). Companies can either use the direct or the indirect method for cash flow reporting. Companies using the direct method have to classify (directly) whether cash receipts and payments are generated by operating, financing or investing activities. To avoid the laborious classification of multitudinous cash in- and outflows, the vast majority of companies apply the indirect method by reconciling net income (indirectly) to cash flows from operations. The indirect method forces companies to reveal the difference between net income and cash flow from operating activities by removing the effects of deferrals and accruals.[47] Cash flow statements can indirectly be prepared from balance sheets and income statements. The first step is for financial analysts to simply calculate the changes in balance sheet positions and classify whether the changes are due to operating, investing or financing activities (Table 3.6).

Table 3.6 Stirling Homex Corporation: consolidated balance sheet[48]

In USD	FY 1971	FY 1970	Change **	Activity
Assets				
Cash	3 196 457	2 778 077	418 380	Check: change in cash = CFFO + CFFI + CFFF
Preferred stock proceeds receivable	19 000 000		19 000 000	Financing
Receivables	37 845 572	15 486 119	22 359 453	Operating
Inventories	4 492 543	3 751 224	741 319	Operating
Prepaid expenses and other current assets	226 530	124 765	101 765	Operating
Investment in unconsolidated subsidiary	1 134 579		1 134 579	Investing
Long-term receivables	4 225 349	541 124	3 684 225	Operating
Property, plant and equipment at cost, less accumulated depreciation and amortization	9 426 941	5 245 745	4 710 312	Investing (**USD 529 116 added: depreciation expense)

---

[46] Dividing net sales of USD 36.9 million (USD 22.6 million) by receivables of USD 37.8 million (USD 15.5 million) leads to a receivable turnover of 0.97 (1.46) in FY 1971 (FY 1970). Financial economists often divide net sales by average receivables as net sales are realized over a period of time (a reporting period) and receivables are measured at a specific point in time (at the end of a reporting period). The average receivable turnover in FY 1971 was 1.38 (USD 36.8 million/USD 26.7 million).
[47] Financial Accounting Standards Board (1987), p. 4.
[48] Stirling Homex Corporation (1971).

Deferred charges, less accumulated amortization	2 558 792	944 109	2 046 800	Investing (**USD 432 117 added: amortization of deferred charges)
Total assets	**82 106 763**	**28 871 163**		
Liabilities and stockholder's equity				
Current portion of long-term debt	295 630	333 036	−37 406	Financing
Notes payable to banks – unsecured	37 700 000	11 700 000	26 000 000	Financing
Accounts payable	4 025 254	2 480 834	1 544 420	Operating
Due to unconsolidated subsidiary	76 894		76 894	Financing
Accrued expenses and other liabilities	577 377	232 819	344 558	Operating
Current and deferred income taxes	3 528 125	1 387 338	2 140 787	Operating
Long-term debt	236 588	496 489	−259 901	Financing
Deferred income taxes	2 098 767	587 265	1 511 502	Operating
Option deposit on land contract	235 000		235 000	Operating
Cumulative convertible preferred stock	500 000		500 000	Financing
Common stock	89 092	88 974	118	Financing
Additional paid-in capital	26 554 452	8 446 738	18 107 714	Financing
Retained earnings	6 370 333	3 117 670	3 252 663	Check income statement: net income
Less treasury stock at cost	−180 750		−180 750	Financing
Total shareholder's equity	33 333 127	11 653 382		
Total liabilities and shareholder's equity	**82 106 762**	**28 871 163**		

After calculating the changes in all balance sheet positions, net income can be reconciled into cash flows by adding back depreciation and amortization and removing the effects of deferrals and accruals (Table 3.7).

Table 3.7 Stirling Homex Corporation: cash flow statement[49]

In USD	
Net income	**3 252 663**
Depreciation expense	+529 116
Amortization of deferred charges	+432 117
Change in receivables	−22 359 453
Change in long-term receivables	−3 684 225
Change in inventories	−741 319
Change in option deposit on land contract	+235 000
Change in prepaid expenses and other current assets	−101 765
Change in accounts payable	+1 544 420

[49] Stirling Homex Corporation (1971).

Table 3.7   (Continued)

In USD	
Change in accrued expenses and other liabilities	+344 558
Change in current and deferred income taxes	+2 140 787
Change in deferred income taxes	+1 511 502
Cash flow from operating activities (CFFO)	**−16 896 599**
Change in property, plant, and equipment at cost	−4 710 312
Change in deferred charges	−2 046 800
Change in investment in unconsolidated subsidiary	−1 134 579
Cash flow from investing activities (CFFI)	**−7 891 691**
Change in current portion of long-term debt	−37 406
Change in notes payable to banks – unsecured	+26 000 000
Change in due to unconsolidated subsidiary	+76 894
Change in long-term debt	−259 901
Change in cumulative convertible preferred stock	+500 000
Change in common stock	+118
Change in additional paid-in capital	+18 107 714
Change in preferred stock proceeds receivable	−19 000 000
Change in treasury stock at cost	−180 750
Cash flow from financing activities (CFFO)	**25 206 669**
CFFO + CFFI + CFFF	**418 380**

Stirling Homex reported positive net income of USD 3.3 million in fiscal year 1971. Investors that were not preoccupied with net income, but analyzed operating cash flows carefully at the end of fiscal year 1971, detected that Stirling Homex did not generate but rather utilized huge amounts of cash: The cash flow from operating activities (CFFO) in fiscal year 1971 was *minus* USD 16.9 million! The company "burnt" huge amounts of cash for operating (*minus* USD 16.9 million) and investing activities (*minus* USD 7.9 million). The cash flow from financing activities (CFFF) reflects that the company had raised USD 19 million from equity investors and only survived because banks pumped huge amounts of money (USD 26 million) into a company that produced homes for non-existent customers. The example of Stirling Homex shows how misleading net income – and therefore price/earnings ratios – can be, if the quality of reported sales and earnings is low. Analyzing cash flow statements, studying footnotes and calculating financial ratios can help investors to identify accounting problems and avoid expensive mistakes when making investment decisions.

The Stirling Homex case study illustrates why investors should mistrust reported earnings. Table 3.7 explains how investors can reconcile reported net income to cash flows from operations (CFFO). Reconciling net income to cash flows from operations helps investors to understand why cash flows from operations differed from reported net income. Financial analysts should be able to formulate and analyze cash flow statements. Cash flows from operations are the difference between cash receipts and payments generated by operating activities. However, companies have to invest in net working capital and in fixed assets to grow revenues and ultimately cash flows from operations. *Free* cash flows are defined as cash flows from operations after investing. In the next section we will discuss how investors can estimate free cash flows.

3.3.2   FCFF during the competitive advantage period

The FCFF formula

Free cash flows to the firm (FCFF) are the cash flows that a company generated during a reporting period from operations after investing. Investments can be classified as investments in property, plant and equipment (PP&E) and investments in net working capital (NWC). Companies invest in long-term and current assets to maintain and expand their asset base and, ultimately, to grow future revenues and cash flows. The word *free* in free cash flows means after investments. Free cash flows to the firm can be distributed to the providers of capital without jeopardizing the future operations of a firm. Companies can use free cash flows to the firm at their discretion to pay dividends, to buy back shares, to retire debt or to fund mergers and acquisitions. Theoretically it is possible to distinguish between several levels of discretionary cash flows (Table 3.8).

Table 3.8   Definition of FCFF and discretionary cash flows

CFFO
Less capex and ΔNWC
$\qquad$ = FCFF (or discretionary cash flow level I)
$\qquad$ Less dividends and share buybacks
$\qquad\qquad$ = Discretionary cash flow level II
$\qquad\qquad$ Less debt retirement
$\qquad\qquad\qquad$ = Discretionary cash flow level III
$\qquad\qquad\qquad$ less M&A
$\qquad\qquad\qquad\qquad$ = Discretionary cash flow level IV

Free cash flows to the firm (FCFF) are defined as cash flows from operating (CFFO) minus capital expenditures (CAPEX) and change in net working capital (ΔNWC). Financial analysts typically use earnings before interest and taxes (EBIT) as a basis to calculate FCFF:[50]

$$FCFF_t = EBIT \times (1 - \tau_t) + D\&A_t - CAPEX_t - \Delta NWC_t \pm ADJ_t$$

Taxes are a major cost of doing business for most companies. Earnings before interest and taxes are therefore multiplied by $(1 - \tau)$, where τ denotes the cash tax rate of a company as a percentage of operating profits. From a cash flow perspective, the amount of cash taxes which a company actually paid must be deducted from operating earnings. The income tax expenses under accrual accounting usually differ from the amount of taxes which a company actually paid. Temporary differences between book taxes and cash taxes typically arise if companies use accelerated depreciation to compute taxable income and straight-line depreciation to compute reported earnings[51].

---

[50] Damodaran (1996), p. 237.
[51] Temporary differences between income tax expenses (financial reporting) and income tax payable (tax reporting) lead to deferred tax liabilities or deferred tax assets. Deferred tax liabilities (assets) represent an increase in taxes payable (refundable) in future years. Kieso *et al.* (2004), pp. 959–1015.

Depreciation and amortization (D&A) must be added back to operating earnings as it represents a non-cash charge. Capital expenditures and changes in net working capital lead to cash outflows and are therefore subtracted from operating earnings to calculate FCFF. Financial analysts often make additional adjustments (ADJ) to reported earnings to eliminate accounting distortions.

Earnings before interest and taxes (EBIT) are a widely used definition of "operating profits". EBIT are revenues less operating expenses (OPEX). Operating expenses include costs of goods sold (COGS), expenses for selling, general and administration (SG&A), research and development (R&D) and other expenses stemming from operating activities:

$$EBIT = REV - OPEX$$

$$= REV - (COGS + SG\&A + R\&D + OPEX_{Others})$$

Table 3.9 shows a condensed income statement. Operating profits (losses) are profits which a company derives from its operating activities *before* interest income (expense) and before other income (expenses). Please note that not only regular, but also irregular, items are reported in net income. Restructuring charges which often include write-offs and other one-time items are a typical example for irregular items. Irregular items fall into five categories: discontinued operations, extraordinary items, unusual gains and losses, changes in accounting principles and changes in estimates.[52] While financial analysts are interested in operating income from continuing operations, they have to carefully analyze irregular

Table 3.9 Condensed income statement

	Abbreviation
Sales revenues	
Less sales discounts, sales returns and allowances	
Less business tax and surcharges	
Total net revenues	REV
Less operating costs and expenses:	OPEX
costs of revenues (or: costs of goods sold)	COGS
selling, general and administrative	SG&A
research and development	R&D
share-based compensation	
Operating (loss) profit (or: earnings before interest and taxes)	EBIT
Plus interest income (expense)	INT
Plus other revenues and gains (or: irregular income)	
Minus other expenses and losses (or: irregular expenses)	
Net (loss) income before tax	
Less taxation	
Net (loss) income	NI

---

[52] Kieso *et al.* (2004), pp. 132–141.

items as companies often try to overstate operating profits by classifying normal operating expenses as irregular items.

During management meetings, institutional investors usually spend a significant amount of time learning from senior management how revenues and operating margins will develop over time and how much capital will be spent to fund future investments. Expected revenues in period t are usually modeled as revenues in period $t-1$ multiplied by one plus the expected revenue growth rate g^e. Expected operating profits can be expressed as revenues multiplied by expected operating margins (EBIT^e/REV^e). The rearranged FCFF formula incorporates revenue growth rates and operating margins and can be used to forecast future, expected FCFF^e:

$$\text{FCFF}_t^e = \left[(\text{REV}_{t-1} \times (1 + g_t^e)) \times \left(\frac{\text{EBIT}^e}{\text{REV}^e} \right)_t \right] \times (1 - \tau_t^e)$$
$$+ \text{D\&A}_t^e - \text{CAPEX}_t^e - \Delta\text{NWC}_t^e \pm \text{ADJ}_t^e$$

Free cash flow to the firm (FCFF), free cash flow to equity (FCFE) and net operating profit after taxes (NOPAT) are widely used measures to quantify the operating performance of companies. The following formulae demonstrate how the three measures are related. Free cash flows to the firm (FCFF) can be expressed as the sum of free cash flows to equity holders (FCFE) and cash flows to bond holders (CFBH):

$$\text{FCFF} = \text{FCFE} + \text{CFBH}$$

Cash flows to bond holders are the difference between interest payments (INT) and net debt issuance (ΔD). Net debt issuance equals new borrowings (B) less debt repayments (RP).

$$\text{CFBH}_t = INT_t - \Delta D_t$$
$$\Delta D_t = B_t - RP_t$$

Free cash flows to equity (FCFE) are the free cash flows after operating expenses (OPEX), interest payments (INT), taxes (TAX), capital expenditures (CAPEX), change in net working capital (ΔNWC) plus depreciation and amortization (D&A) and net debt issuance (ΔD):

$$\text{FCFE}_t = (\text{REV}_t - \text{OPEX}_t - \text{INT}_t - \text{TAX}_t) + \text{D\&A}_t - \text{CAPEX}_t - \Delta\text{NWC}_t + \Delta D_t$$

Net debt issuance, or ΔD, increases free cash flow to equity holders. Dividends are cash flows which equity holders actually receive. Free cash flows to equity, on the other hand, can be viewed as free cash flows after investments which a company could distribute to its shareholders. Free cash flows to the firm are free cash flows after investments which could be distributed to both debt and equity holders.

The FCFF formula can be simplified by canceling interest payments (INT) and net debt issuance (ΔD). However, interest payments are tax deductible. The following formula takes the tax-shield benefit of interest payments into account. Stern Stewart & Co., the consulting firm that invented the EVA framework,[53] calculates adjusted taxes (TAX$_{adj}$) as the difference

---

[53] EVA is a trademark of Stern Stewart & Co.

between the accounting tax provision reported on the income statement less the increase in deferred taxes, i.e. the taxes which the company did not in fact pay, plus tax savings from interest expenses.[54] Adjusted net profits after taxes are usually referred to as net operating profits after taxes, or NOPAT.[55] The following formula expresses that FCFF are equivalent to NOPAT plus depreciation and amortization less investments:

$$FCFF = \left[REV_t - OPEX_t - TAX_{adj,t} \right] + D\&A_t - CAPEX_t - \Delta NWC_t$$
$$= NOPAT_t + D\&A_t - CAPEX_t - \Delta NWC_t$$

Net in net operating profits after taxes means *net of depreciation*.[56] Both NOPAT and FCFF measure economic profits derived from operations after taxes. The key difference between NOPAT and FCFF is that depreciation and amortization rather than capital expenditures and change in net working capital are subtracted from operating profits to derive NOPAT.[57] From a financing perspective, NOPAT can be derived by adding preferred dividends, minority interest provisions and interest expenses after taxes back to income available to common equity. Table 3.10 illustrates that adjustments to income and capital must be made consistently. Preferred stock, minority interest and interest bearing debt must be added back to invested capital if investors want to calculate consistent returns on capital (NOPAT / Invested capital).

Table 3.10 Calculation of net operating profits after taxes (NOPAT) and invested capital[58]

Net operating profits after taxes (NOPAT)	Invested capital (IC)
= Income available to common equity	= Common equity
+ Preferred dividends	+ Preferred stock
+ Minority interest provision	+ Minority interest
+ Interest expense after tax	+ Interest bearing debt
+ Increase in equity equivalents	+ Equity equivalents

To eliminate accounting distortions, increases in equity equivalents such as increases in deferred taxes, increases in LIFO reserves and goodwill amortization are added to operating income. The consulting firm Stern Stewart & Co. has identified over 160 potential reclassifications and other adjustments to reported earnings.[59] Stern Stewart & Co., for example, classify research and development costs (R&D) and other "value-building capital outlays" as investments rather than expenses.[60] Please note that the reclassification of operating expenses such as R&D costs as investments requires additional tax adjustments.

---

[54] Stewart (1999), p. 105.
[55] Stewart (1999), pp. 85–95.
[56] Stewart (1999), p. 86.
[57] Please note that depreciation and amortization (D&A) is included in costs of goods sold (COGS), selling, general and administrative expenses (SG&A), and research and development expenses (R&D).
[58] Stewart (1999), pp. 87–92.
[59] Ehrbar (1998), pp. 161–181.
[60] Stewart (1999), pp. 28f, 60–62.

Modeling FCFF requires a good understanding of a firm's business model and the industry in which the company operates. Four central economic insights should be considered when modeling FCFF:

(1) *Economies of scale*: When revenues increase, companies usually obtain a reduction in average unit costs. This reduction is known as economies of scale. Economies of scale result, for example, from lower overhead costs per unit of production, learning effects and more efficient use of technology, capital and labor. When revenues grow expected operating margins often increase as a result of declining average unit costs. Assumptions on operating margins must be consistent with expected revenue growth rates.

(2) *Business cycles*: Financial economists have identified business cycles of different periodicity. Nikolai Kondradieff identified long waves in production and prices which last in excess of 40 years. Clément Juglar suggested that business cycles recur every 8 to 10 years. Joseph Schumpeter distinguished Kitchin cycles (named after Joseph Kitchin) of 40 months. Boom periods are regularly followed by recessions. Monetary supply, consumption, investment, sentiment and several other economic variables influence economic activity. Credit expansion and contraction regularly distort economic activity. Overinvestment leads to oversupply, and subsequent inventory liquidation to economic slumps. Underconsumption periodically triggers economic crises.[61] Financial analysts who extrapolate price and output trends in a linear fashion disregard economic activity fluctuating in cycles. Forecasting FCFF requires a good understanding of the business cycle, especially if the companies operate in highly cyclical industries.

(3) *Competitive life cycles*: Like human beings companies are born, they grow up and finally pass away. Three stylized competitive life cycle stages can be distinguished.[62] Stage 1: Young companies typically require high investments. Capital expenditures typically exceed depreciation at the beginning of the life cycle. Some companies achieve high return on invested capital as a reward for innovation in their early life cycle. Stage 2: Companies that generate high returns on invested capital attract competitors. When competitors enter highly profitable industries and imitate successful innovators, high rates of return fade to average cost of capital over time.[63] As long as returns on invested capital are higher than cost of capital, companies generate positive economic returns. Mature companies with little investment requirements which produce high cash flows are often called cash cows. Finally in stage 3, competition has eroded economic returns in excess of cost of capital. In this stage, companies often leave unprofitable industries, close capacities, sell unprofitable assets or try to reinvent themselves by introducing new services or products. Companies that are unwilling or unable to restructure usually fail. Mature companies typically have different growth prospects and capital needs than companies which are in earlier life cycles. Growth rates, margins and capital needs typically change when companies enter into a new stage of their life cycle.

(4) *Consistency between revenues and investment*: Companies that want to grow revenues and free cash flows usually have to invest in fixed assets and working capital. Inconsistency between expected revenue growth rates and expected investments in fixed and current assets is arguably one of the most important mistakes when modeling FCFF.

---

[61] Faber (2002), pp. 47–144.
[62] Madden distinguishes four stages: high innovation stage, fading cash flow return on investment (CFROI) stage, mature stage and failing business model stage. Madden (2005), pp. 7f.
[63] Madden (2002), pp. 13–63.

Investment needs of companies are industry specific: Building a new semiconductor plant currently requires investments of over USD 2 billion. The business model of an internet company, on the other hand, is typically more scaleable and requires less capital to grow sales. Financial analysts look at a wide range of ratios to measure how effectively companies utilize their assets and compare how much investment is (typically) required to enable growth (in an industry). Analyzing historical capex-to-sales and change in net working capital-to-sales ratios helps to better understand the relationship between revenues and investment needs.

In reality, the inputs of a FCFF model cannot be estimated with certainty. Monte Carlo simulations – discussed in Part II – can help financial analysts to incorporate the uncertainty of future growth rates, EBIT margins, cash tax rates, and investment needs when modeling expected FCFF during the competitive advantage period. One of the most critical input factors is the length of the competitive advantage period which will be discussed in the next section.

The competitive advantage period and the logic of EVA models

A company creates economic value as long as its return on invested capital exceeds its cost of capital. One of the most important questions for investors is to determine how long the period lasts in which cost of capital is lower than return on capital. This period is usually called the competitive advantage period. Joel Stern and Bennett Stewart, founding partners of Stern Stewart & Co., formulated a performance measure that quantifies how much value a company added for its shareholders during a period. Economic Value Added, or EVA, is positive if the return on invested capital r is higher than the opportunity cost i on invested capital IC:[64]

$$EVA = (r - i) \times IC \qquad r = \frac{NOPAT}{IC}$$

Invested capital is the amount of cash invested in the business.[65] The return on invested capital r equals net operating profits after taxes, or NOPAT, divided by invested capital. In other words, EVA is the residual income after subtracting a capital charge, $i \times IC$, from NOPAT:[66]

$$EVA = NOPAT - i \times IC$$

The competitive advantage period (CAP) is the time period in which a company generates positive economic value, or EVA. A company can generate economic value for its shareholders only if returns on investment r are higher than opportunity costs of invested capital:[67]

$$CAP: \qquad r > i \Rightarrow EVA \text{ is positive}$$

---

[64] Stewart (1999), pp. 136–150.
[65] Dierks and Patel (1997), p. 52.
[66] Stewart (1999), p. 224.
[67] Theoretically, the statement is wrong if invested capital is negative. However, in reality invested capital is almost never negative.

A company destroys economic value, on the other hand, if cost of capital exceeds return on invested capital. If we refer to the period in which returns on capital are lower than cost of capital as the capital *dis*advantage period (CDP), we can state:

$$\text{CDP:} \quad r < i \Rightarrow \text{EVA is negative}$$

If return on invested capital is lower than cost of capital, managers are forced to restructure, to divest or to close unprofitable businesses. Innovative companies often generate high returns on invested capital in the early stages of their life cycle. However, high return on invested capital attracts competitors. High return on invested capital typically falls if new competitors enter a highly profitable industry or if existing competitors try to gain market share. If low cost producers, for example, enter an industry, price pressures increase and returns on capital fall as a result. If there are no barriers to entry and exit, return on invested capital fades to cost of capital over time:[68]

$$\textit{Under competition:} \quad r \xrightarrow{t} i \Rightarrow \text{EVA} \xrightarrow{t} 0$$

A company can no longer generate economic value, or EVA, for its shareholders if competition has eroded excess return on capital above cost of capital. The terminal value period, TVP, is by definition the period in which return on invested capital equals cost of capital:

$$\text{TVP}: r = i \Rightarrow \text{EVA} = 0$$

EVA is a useful performance measure focusing on the economic spread between return on invested capital and cost of capital. But it is not an entirely new concept. It is simply a rearrangement of the standard DCF formula. Assume that a company can invest EUR 200 000 in a project today with an opportunity cost of capital of 12% which generates a single cash flow of EUR 240 000 in one year from now. If consistent inputs are used, the standard DCF and the EVA approach both lead to the same present value:

$$\text{PV}(C_t) = C_0 + \frac{C_1}{(1+i)} = -200\,000 + \frac{240\,000}{1.12} = 14\,286$$

$$\text{PV(EVA)} = \frac{(r-i) \times \text{IC}}{(1+i)} = \frac{\left(\left[\dfrac{240\,000}{200\,000} - 1\right] - 0.12\right) \times 200\,000}{1.12} = 14\,286$$

The EVA approach can help investors to gain new insights because it brings to light whether a firm is earning its cost of capital. However, the EVA model is just a rearranged DCF model expressing the same economic rationale: The value of each investment is the discounted value of its future cash flows. When formulating FCFF models, financial analysts are well advised to make their assumptions on return on invested capital, cost of capital and invested capital transparent and check if the model's implied EVAs are realistic.

---

[68] Madden (2002), pp. 13–63.

Over time, companies can earn returns on capital in excess of cost of capital and generate economic value only if they have sustainable competitive advantages. Warren Buffett, one of the world's most successful investors, searches for companies with lasting competitive advantages. He asks how well high returns on capital are protected by "economic moats": ". . . In business, I look for economic castles protected by unbreachable 'moats' . . . ."[69]

Porter (1998) argues that five forces determine a firm's ability to earn returns on capital in excess of cost of capital:

(1) Rivalry among existing firms.
(2) Threat of potential entrants.
(3) Threat of substitutes.
(4) Bargaining power of suppliers.
(5) Bargaining power of buyers.

These five competitive forces influence prices, costs, required capital expenditures and therefore industry profitability. Companies usually have shorter competitive advantage periods if they face rapid innovation and are threatened by substitutes, existing rivals and new entrants. If the bargaining power of buyers is low, companies can demand high prices for their products and services. Costs for raw materials and other input factors on the other hand are a heavy strain on profitability, if suppliers can take advantage of their superior bargaining power. The sustainability of a firm's competitive advantages depends on the strength of these five competitive forces.[70]

According to Porter, three generic types of competitive advantages exist: cost advantage, differentiation and focus.[71] Companies possess a competitive advantage if they are the lowest cost producer in their industry. Warren Buffett argues: ". . . But the ultimate key to the company's success is its rock-bottom operating costs, which virtually no competitor can match. . . . "[72] A good example of a low cost producer is Ryanair, Europe's largest low fares airline, which offered standard, no-frills services to 27.6 million passengers in fiscal year 2005 while strictly controlling costs.[73] Alternatively, companies can gain a competitive advantage over their rivals by following a differentiation strategy. Real or perceived differentiation can be achieved by exceptional product features, superior technology or appealing branding. Apple Inc., for example, can command premium prices because the company successfully differentiated itself from competitors by introducing innovative products like the Macintosh desktop and notebook computers, the iPod digital music player and the iTunes music store and by establishing a unique brand.[74] Last but not least, companies can seek to achieve a competitive advantage by focusing on a narrow segment. Instead of offering a wide range of products, focusers exploit differentiation or cost advantages in well-defined target segments which are often neglected by large corporations.[75] A typical example of a successful one product company is Tomtom, today Europe's largest provider of navigation systems. The company focused early on a niche market neglected by large consumer electronic

---

[69] Buffett (1995).
[70] Porter (1998), pp. 4–11, Mauboussin et al. (2001).
[71] Porter (1998), pp. 11–26.
[72] Buffett (1995).
[73] Ryanair Holdings, plc (2005).
[74] Apple Computer, Inc. (2005).
[75] Porter (1998), pp. 11–26.

companies and benefits today from fast growing consumer demand for car navigation devices.[76]

Competitive advantage periods are the intellectual link between competitive strategy and valuation.[77] Applying Porter's concept of the five competitive forces, investors can analyze the sustainability of a firm's competitive advantage. However, the length of the competitive advantage period cannot be estimated precisely. Investors can only analyze how fast excess returns on capital faded historically to cost of capital in particular industries.[78] Using the EVA formula discussed above, financial analysts can measure how much value comparable companies added for shareholders over time in the past to get a better understanding of industry dynamics. Companies are comparable if they possess similar competitive advantages. As the length of the competitive advantage period is uncertain and instable, investors are well advised to simulate *conceivable* competitive advantage periods of different lengths. One of the biggest pitfalls when valuing companies is to assume that companies can achieve high excess returns on capital forever. Companies that gained a competitive advantage and earn high returns – like Ryanair, Apple Computer and Tomtom – attract competitors. Successful investors – like Warren Buffett – ask how long competitive advantages are protected by "economic moats" and try to anticipate changes in a firm's competitive position not reflected in its current share price.

3.3.3 Weighted average cost of capital (WACC)

The WACC formula

Companies can employ both debt and equity to finance assets. Companies utilize assets to generate revenues and ultimately cash flows. The appropriate rate to discount FCFF is the weighted average cost of total capital (debt and equity). FCFE are free cash flows after funding investments and after paying interest to debt holders which belong to a firm's equity holders. FCFE and dividends must be discounted by the cost of equity (Table 3.11).

Table 3.11 Rule of consistency between cash flows and discount rates

Model	Cash flow definition	Cash flow can be distributed to	Appropriate discount rate
Enterprise model (FCFF model)	FCFF	Providers of both debt and equity (before interest payments to debt holders)	Weighted average cost of capital (debt and equity), or WACC
Equity model (dividend discount or FCFE model)	Dividends or FCFE	Equity holders (after interest payments to debt holders)	Cost of equity

To calculate the weighted average cost of capital, or WACC, the costs of debt and equity must be weighted by the proportion of long-term debt and equity to total long-term capital

---

[76] Tomtom (2006).
[77] Mauboussin *et al.* (2001).
[78] Madden (2002), pp. 13–63.

employed by the firm. The weighted average cost of capital is the average of the cost of long-term debt i_D and equity i_E weighted by the proportions of long-term debt w_D and equity w_E employed to finance the firm's assets. In contrast to the cost of equity, interest payments are tax deductible. To adjust the WACC for the tax-shield benefit of interest expense, the cost of debt before taxes i_D must be multiplied by one minus the tax rate τ.

The weights w_D and w_E can be calculated by dividing the market values of long-term debt D_M and equity E_M, respectively, by the total market value of long-term debt and equity employed by the firm:[79]

$$w_D = \frac{D_M}{D_M + E_M} \qquad w_E = \frac{E_M}{D_M + E_M}$$

Financial analysts often use the book value of long-term debt instead of the market value of debt D_M, when calculating the weights of debt and equity to total capital. The book or carrying value of a bond issued above or below par value usually equals its face value plus/minus any unamortized premiums or discounts. Discounts and premiums to par value are usually amortized and charged to interest expense over the life of the debt.[80] Financial analysts can use the book value instead of the market value of bonds when calculating the weights w_E and w_D, as the difference between the carrying value and the market value of a bond is usually negligible.

While analysts can generally use the book value of long-term debt instead of its market value, they face several challenges when measuring a firm's true debt burden: Companies frequently keep debt off the balance sheets by using various forms of off-balance sheet financing. The debt burden of unconsolidated subsidiaries in which the parent has no controlling interest is typically not shown on the parent's balance sheet. Since Enron collapsed, most investors are familiar with the special purpose entities (SPE) which Enron used to hide liabilities from investors. Similarly, under US GAAP, no obligations are reported on the balance sheet for leases which meet certain criteria and are classified as operating leases.[81] In addition, investors should carefully analyze if reported pension obligations reflect the net present value of future pension obligations. Accounting for defined benefit obligations is particularly problematic.[82] Obligations which are not fully reflected on the balance sheet must be added to reported debt.

The market value of equity E_M usually differs substantially from the book value of equity shown on the balance sheet. The market value of common equity equals the number of common shares outstanding times the current share price of common equity. If preferred shares are outstanding, the market value of preferred equity must be calculated separately by multiplying the number of preferred shares outstanding with its current share price of preferred equity.

---

[79] The market value of equity is the product of the current stock price and the number of shares outstanding. In cases where several (common, preferred) share classes exist, the current share prices must be multiplied separately by the number of each share class outstanding.
[80] Kieso et al. (2004), pp. 669–723.
[81] Kieso et al. (2004), pp. 1085–1147.
[82] Kieso et al. (2004), pp. 1017–1084.

Cost of debt and cost of equity

The opportunity cost of debt i_D is simply the risk-free country rate plus a risk premium which adequately reflects the risk of the firm's outstanding bonds. If a company has a credit rating from Standard & Poor's,[83] for example, financial analysts only have to add the country specific risk-free rate r_f and the rating premium r_p to calculate the cost of debt.[84] Let us assume that the yield on 10-year US government bonds is 4.78% and the risk premium for BBB corporate bonds is 3%. Given these assumptions, the after-tax cost of debt $i_{D,ex}$ for a company with a BBB rating and an assumed tax rate of 28% is 5.60%:

$$i_{D,ex} = (1 - \tau)\left(r_f + r_{p,BBB}\right) = (1.00 - 0.28)\,(4.78\% + 3.00\%) = 5.60\%$$

Risk-free rates and corporate bond spreads can be observed in the markets. The cost of equity i_E, on the other hand, is not readily available on Reuters, Bloomberg nor can it be found in daily newspapers. Financial analysts have to apply risk factor models to estimate the cost of equity. The standard model to estimate the opportunity cost of equity is still the Capital Asset Pricing Model (CAPM).[85] According to the CAPM, the opportunity cost of equity $i_{E,j}$ of asset j equals the expected, risk-free rate r_f on default-free securities plus asset j's beta β_j multiplied by the market risk premium. The market risk premium, or equity risk premium, is the expected return on the market portfolio $E(r_m)$ minus the risk-free rate r_f.

$$i_{E,j} = r_f + \beta_j\left(E(r_m) - r_f\right)$$

Investors invest in risky equity securities only if they can expect to receive an equity risk premium in excess of the risk-free rate which compensates them for bearing equity-specific risk. The CAPM postulates that investors are rewarded only for the systematic market risk which cannot be eliminated by diversification. One reason for the popularity of the CAPM among financial analysts is that only few input factors are required:

(1) The *risk-free rate* r_f is the expected return on a security that has no default risk. By definition, the expected returns of risk-free securities do not correlate to the returns of risky assets. Financial analysts usually use the 10-year rate on Treasury bonds or bills to quantify the risk-free rate.

(2) The *beta of a security* β_j is the slope of a linear regression between the (excess) returns of security r_j and the (excess) returns on the market portfolio r_m. It measures the sensitivity of the returns on asset j to movements of the returns on the market portfolio. Financial analysts typically use broad market indices, like the S&P 500 index, as proxies for the unknown market portfolio. The beta coefficient equals the covariance between the

---

[83] Long-term credit ratings in the four highest Standard & Poor's categories, AAA, AA, A, and BBB, are referred to as "investment grade", debt rated BB, B, CCC, CC and C as "speculative grade" or "junk bonds". Debt rated D is in default. Standard & Poor's (2003), pp. 7–10.

[84] If a company is not rated by a rating agency, financial analysts usually apply the rating premium of rated companies with comparable interest coverage ratios. Financial analysts often add back depreciation and amortization expenses to reported operating earnings and leasing payments to interest expenses before they compare interest coverage ratios (adjusted operating earnings/adjusted interest expense). McKinsey & Company, Inc. (2000), p. 174.

[85] Sharpe (1964), Lintner (1965), and Mossin (1966).

returns of asset r_j and the returns on the market portfolio r_m divided by the variance of the returns on the market portfolio:

$$\beta_j = \frac{\text{cov}\left(r_j, r_m\right)}{\text{var}\left(r_m\right)} = \frac{E\left[\left(r_j - E\left(r_j\right)\right)\left(r_m - E\left(r_m\right)\right)\right]}{E\left[\left(r_m - E\left(r_m\right)\right)^2\right]}$$

Sharpe used 60 monthly returns in his early studies to calculate regression betas.[86] The following chart shows the regression line between 60 monthly returns of Intel and the S&P 500. The beta of 2.2 expresses that investors can expect shares of Intel to increase (decrease) by 2.2% when the S&P 500 increases (decreases) by 1%. The beta of a stock measures how "aggressively" or "defensively" a stock reacts to movements of the overall market. Intel Corporation's beta of 2.2 reflects that Intel's shares are more sensitive to movements of the broad equity market than the market portfolio which has, by definition, a beta of 1. The systematic risk of Intel Corporation is above market average as semiconductor companies like Intel Corporation operate in a capital intensive, highly cyclical industry.

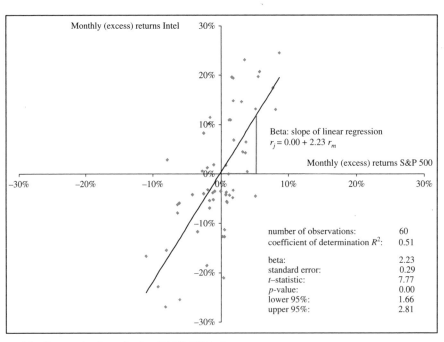

Figure 3.2   Regression beta for Intel/S&P 500 index

With a t-statistic of 7.77[87] we can reject the hypothesis H_0 that Intel Corporation's beta is zero. As a rule of thumb, the beta coefficient is statistically significant at a

---

[86] Sharpe (1971), p. 10 and Sharpe and Cooper (1971), p. 11. Today, financial analysts most often use 60 or 36 monthly returns or 52 weekly returns to calculate regression betas. Of course, the regression beta depends on the chosen time period.
[87] The t-statistic equals the beta coefficient divided by its standard error.

0.05 significance level if the absolute t-statistic is larger than 2. The coefficient of determination R^2 expresses that the movements of the overall market explain 51% of the variation in Intel Corporation's returns. Historical betas are biased estimates of future betas: High historical betas often overestimate and low historical betas often underestimate future betas. Blume (1971) found that historical beta coefficients β_1 tend to regress to the mean over time and recommended using adjusted betas β_2 corrected for the historical rate of regression:[88]

$$\beta_2 = 0.34 + 0.66 \, \beta_1$$

Beta coefficients, like other input variables of FCFF models, are not constant over time. Future, expected betas can be estimated under uncertainty only with statistical errors. The difference between the upper 95% and the lower 95% beta coefficients is usually large – in Intel Corporation's regression the difference is 1.15 (2.81 – 1.66)! Cautious investors are therefore well advised to do stress tests and to apply the upper and lower 95% beta in addition to the expected beta when calculating costs of equity.

(3) The *market risk premium*, or equity risk premium, is the difference between the expected return on a well-diversified equity portfolio minus the expected risk-free rate. Stocks are generally riskier than government bonds. It is therefore no surprise that equity investors demand a risk premium in excess of the risk-free rate. While the equity premium is a forward looking number, financial economists are usually analyzing historical returns on stocks and bonds to better understand the future excess returns on stocks relative to bonds. Financial economists have found that the average return on stocks was superior to the average return on short-term government bonds over different periods in the past. According to Siegel (2005), the equity premium increased from 1.90% to 3.46% and finally to 6.09% over the periods 1802–1870, 1871–1925 and 1926–2004.[89] The high average excess return on equities relative to bonds creates an equity premium puzzle: Investors must be extremely risk averse to accept puzzlingly low returns on fixed income securities relative to equities.[90] Dimson *et al.* (2006) calculated historical equity risk premia for the United States and several international equity markets over the period 1900–2005: The risk premium relative to short-term government bonds was on (geometric) average 5.5% for the United States, 6.7% for Japan, 4.4% for the United Kingdom, and 3.8% for Germany. Equity risk premia were historically extremely instable over time. The standard deviations are 19.6% for the United States and even higher for other large markets for the 1900–2005 period.[91] Using the Monte Carlo method discussed in Part II, financial analysts can incorporate the high volatility into FCFF models.

In summary, while the cost of debt is readily observable in financial markets, investors can estimate the cost of capital only by using financial models. Most financial analysts apply

---

[88] Blume (1971), pp. 8f. Using Marshall's method of correction, historical betas of 2.0 and 0.5 would translate into adjusted betas of 1.66 ($0.34 + 0.66 * 2.0$) and 0.67 ($0.34 + 0.66 * 0.5$). Marshall's method of correction is, for example, used by Bloomberg to calculate adjusted betas.

[89] The main reason for the increase of the equity risk premium over the three periods was the decline in returns on short-term government bonds. The real return on US stocks was on (geometric) average 7.02%, 6.62% and 6.78% and the real returns on short-term government bonds was 5.12%, 3.16% and 0.69%. Siegel argues that the equity premium has been unusually high since 1926 and may be closer to historical norms of 3% in the future. Siegel (2005) and Siegel (1992).

[90] Mehra and Prescott (1985).

[91] Dimson *et al.* (2006), pp. 40–43. For Germany, the years 1922–1923 were excluded. Financial economists generally use geometric instead of arithmetic averages to calculate equity premia because of the compounding effect.

Table 3.12 Equity risk premia relative to short-term bills, 1900–2005 (Source: Dimson *et al.* (2006))

Country	Geometric mean in %	Arithmetic mean in %	Standard deviation in %
France	6.8	9.3	24.2
Germany	3.8	9.1	33.5
Italy	6.6	10.5	32.1
Japan	6.7	9.8	27.8
United Kingdom	4.4	6.1	19.8
United States	5.5	7.4	19.6

the CAPM to estimate cost of equity because it requires few inputs: The risk-free rate, the security's beta coefficient and the equity risk premium. Given its wide use among financial analysts, the CAPM is discussed in more detail on pp. 42–45.

Leverage and cost of equity

Often reliable beta coefficients for individual firms cannot be estimated. Return series for newly issued stocks are too short to calculate regression betas. If a company materially changed its business model or its financial structure, past return series are often not meaningful. Financial analysts often apply the average cost of equity of a peer group or industry as a proxy for the cost of equity of individual firms. When calculating average costs of equity for a peer group, financial analysts have to consider that financial leverage impacts on cost of equity.

If a firm increases its debt to equity ratio, its equity beta and therefore its cost of equity increase (effect 1). On the other hand, increasing its financial leverage means that a firm uses a higher proportion of debt which is usually cheaper than the cost of equity (effect 2). If capital markets are perfect, the two effects offset each other exactly. According to Miller and Modigliani, a firm cannot increase its value by changing its capital structure.[92] The following example illustrates the Miller and Modigliani proposition: Assume that the debt to equity ratio of firm j is 1:1 and its equity beta 1.4, the risk-free rate (r_f) 5% and the market risk premium (π) 5.5%. The asset beta (β_A) is simply the average of the equity beta β_E and the debt beta β_D weighted by the proportion of equity E_M and debt D_M to total capital.[93] As the beta of debt is by definition zero if perfect capital markets are assumed in which investors can borrow at the risk-free rate, the equation can be simplified:

$$\beta_A = \frac{E_M}{(E_M + D_M)}\beta_E + \frac{D_M}{(E_M + D_M)}\beta_D \xrightarrow{\beta_D = 0} \beta_A = \frac{\beta_E}{\left(1 + \dfrac{D_M}{E_M}\right)} = \frac{1.4}{\left(1 + \dfrac{1}{1}\right)} = 0.7$$

Using the CAPM, the cost of equity $i_{E,j}$ of firm j equals:

$$i_{E,j} = r_f + \beta_{E,j}(\pi) = 5\% + 1.4 \times 5.5\% = 12.7\%$$

---

[92] Modigliani and Miller (1958), pp. 268–271.
[93] As discussed above, E_M and D_M represent the market value not the book value of equity and debt.

As we assumed that the debt to equity ratio is 1:1, the weighted average cost of capital, or WACC, of firm j is:

$$\text{WACC}_j = \left(\frac{E_M}{(E_M + D_M)}\right) i_{E,j} + \left(\frac{D_M}{(E_M + D_M)}\right) i_{D,j} = \frac{1}{2} \times 12.7\% + \frac{1}{2} \times 5\% = 8.85\%$$

Financial analysts might argue that cost of debt is cheaper than cost of equity and the firm should therefore increase its debt to equity ratio, for example, to 2:1. However, if the firm increases its financial leverage, the equity beta $\beta_{E,j}$ and the cost of equity $i_{E,j}$ increase but the WACC remains constant at 8.85%:[94]

$$\beta_{E,j} = \beta_A \times \left(1 + \frac{D_{M,j}}{E_{M,j}}\right) = 0.7 \times \left(1 + \frac{2}{1}\right) = 2.1$$

$$i_{E,j} = r_f + \beta_{E,j}(\pi) = 5\% + 2.1 \times 5.5\% = 16.55\%$$

$$\text{WACC}_j = \left(\frac{E_{M,j}}{(E_{M,j} + D_{M,j})}\right) i_{E,j} + \left(\frac{D_{M,j}}{(E_{M,j} + D_{M,j})}\right) i_{D,j} = \frac{1}{3} \times 16.55\% + \frac{2}{3} \times 5\% = 8.85\%$$

In both scenarios the WACC is 8.85%. Assuming perfect capital markets, financial leverage does not impact on a firm's WACC. To illustrate the impact of financial leverage, we assumed perfect capital markets in which taxes do not matter. In reality, interest expense is tax deductible, but cost of equity is not and, hence, taxes do have an impact on WACC as equity holders benefit from the tax shield. To simplify matters we also assumed that the cost of borrowing remains constant when leverage increases. In reality, financial leverage impacts on the rating and hence the cost of debt of a firm especially if the firm is in distress. However, we can draw two important conclusions from the example:

(1) Financial leverage influences both the equity beta and the cost of equity of a firm.
(2) A firm's WACC is independent of its capital structure if capital markets are perfect.

Financial analysts can apply the average cost of equity of a peer group as a proxy for the cost of equity of an individual firm. First, a peer group of comparable companies bearing similar market risk to the individual firm must be identified. Second, the regression betas for the firms within the peer group must be estimated and weighted. Assume that the arithmetic averages of the betas, the debt to equity ratios[95] and the tax rates of the firms that constitute the peer group are $\beta_{pg,av}$, $(D_M/E_M)_{pg,av}$ and $t_{pg,av}$, respectively. The unleveraged beta of the peer group $\beta_{pg,av,unlev}$ is simply:[96]

$$\beta_{pg,av,unlev} = \frac{\beta_{pg,av}}{\left[1 + (1 - t_{pg,av})\left(\frac{D_M}{E_M}\right)_{pg,av}\right]}$$

---

[94] Modigliani and Miller (1958), Miller and Modigliani (1961).
[95] Again, market values not book values of debt and equity must be used to calculate debt to equity ratios.
[96] Damodaran (2002), pp. 57–59, Copeland et al. (2000), p. 309.

If the current debt to equity ratio and the current tax rate of the individual firm j are $(D_M/E_M)_j$ and τ_j, respectively, firm j's leveraged beta $\beta_{j,lev}$ and – applying the CAPM – cost of equity $i_{E,j}$ equal:

$$\beta_{j,lev} = \beta_{pg,av,unlev} \times \left[1 + (1 - \tau_j) \left(\frac{D_M}{E_M} \right)_j \right]$$

$$i_{E,j} = r_f + \beta_{j,lev} \times \pi$$

Using adjusted peer group betas to estimate cost of equity has three key advantages:

(1) Cost of equity can be estimated for firms with short return series.
(2) The standard error of the regression coefficients averages out if a large group of comparable companies is chosen.
(3) Estimated beta coefficients reflect the current financial leverage not the firm's financial leverage during the regression period.[97]

However, the estimated cost of equity $i_{E,j}$ is an appropriate estimate of the true cost of capital only if the chosen peer group bears the same systematic market risk as the individual firm – and if the CAPM holds. It is time to have a more thorough look at the CAPM.

The Capital Asset Pricing Model

The Capital Asset Pricing Model (CAPM) was developed by Sharpe, Lintner and Mossin in the mid-1960s.[98] It is still the most widely used model for estimating the opportunity cost of equity $i_{E,j}$.

$$i_{E,j} = r_f + \beta_j \left(E(r_M) - r_f \right)$$

As discussed above, the beta coefficient β_j can be interpreted as the slope of a linear regression between the excess returns of a stock j (dependent variable) and the excess returns of the market portfolio (independent or explanatory variable) and measures the sensitivity of an individual stock j to movements of the overall market. The CAPM postulates that investors are only rewarded for systematic market risk which cannot be eliminated by diversification.[99] The CAPM is one of the most important models in capital market theory based on a few simplifying assumptions:

(1) *All investors follow Markowitz's approach:*[100] They prefer low variances σ^2 (risk) and high expected returns $E(R)$ (reward). Investors are able to estimate the mean and standard deviation for all available investments. Markets are perfect, taxes and transaction costs are irrelevant. Risk-averse investors should choose between efficient portfolios offering minimum levels of risk for given levels of expected return (or maximum levels of expected return for given levels of risk). Investors can determine efficient portfolios by

---

[97] Damodaran (2002), pp. 196–200.
[98] Sharpe (1964), Lintner (1965), and Mossin (1966).
[99] The CAPM is discussed in detail in Sharpe and Alexander (1990), pp. 134–240.
[100] Markowitz (1952).

minimizing the portfolio variance σ_P^2 under the constraint that the expected portfolio return $E(R_P)$ should equal a specific target return E:

$$\text{Min } \sigma_P^2 = \sum_{i=1}^{n} \sum_{j=1}^{n} w_i w_j \, \text{cov}_{i,j} \qquad s.t. \quad E(R_P) = \sum_{i=1}^{n} w_i E(r_i) = E$$

$$\sum_{i=1}^{n} w_i = 1$$

The terms w_i and w_j represent the weights and $\text{cov}_{i,j}$ the covariance between the returns of assets i and j. The so-called efficient frontier connects all efficient portfolios in the two-dimensional risk/return space.

(2) *A risk-free asset is available*: If investors can invest not only in portfolios of risky securities but also in a risk-free asset, the curved efficient frontier becomes a linear efficient market line as the covariance between the returns of a risk-free asset and a risky asset is by definition zero. Optimal portfolio selection only involves building portfolios which consist of an efficient tangency portfolio of risky securities and the risk-free asset. The weighting of the two assets depends on the risk/return expectations and the preferences of the individual investor.

(3) *All investors have homogeneous expectations, they can invest and borrow at the same risk-free rate and have the same one-period horizon*. In equilibrium, a unique efficient tangency portfolio, called the market portfolio M, exists on the efficient frontier in which all available securities have a proportion which is non-zero.[101] The efficient frontier, now called capital market line, is the same for all investors. The slope of the capital market line is the so-called reward-to-variability[102] or Sharpe ratio:[103]

$$\frac{E(R_M) - r_f}{\sigma_M}$$

Now, we can derive the CAPM mathematically. Let us assume that a portfolio consists of only two assets: a risky asset i and the market portfolio M with weights of w_i and $(1 - w_i)$, respectively. The expected return and standard deviation of the two-asset portfolio are:

$$E(R_P) = w_i E(R_i) + (1 - w_i) \, E(R_M)$$

$$\sigma_P = \left[w_i^2 \sigma_i^2 + (1 - w_i)^2 \, \sigma_M^2 + 2 w_i (1 - w_i) \text{cov}_{i,M} \right]^{0.5}$$

A marginal change in the weight w_i of risky asset i has the following impact on the expected return and standard deviation of the two-asset portfolio:

---

[101] Presuming that all investors have homogeneous beliefs, there would be no demand for an asset if its proportion in the market portfolio were zero. As a result, its price would fall and its expected return would rise. At some point, all investors would buy it. Hence, its proportion in the market portfolio must be non-zero in equilibrium.

[102] Sharpe (1966), pp. 122f.

[103] Sharpe (1994).

$$\frac{\partial E\left(R_P\right)}{\partial w_i} = E\left(R_i\right) - E\left(R_M\right)$$

$$\frac{\partial \sigma_P}{\partial w_i} = 0,5 \left(w_i^2 \sigma_i^2 + \left(1 - w_i\right)^2 \sigma_M^2 + 2w_i \left(1 - w_i\right) \mathrm{cov}_{i,M}\right)^{-0,5}$$

$$\left(2w_i \sigma_i^2 - 2\sigma_M^2 + 2\mathrm{cov}_{i,M} - 4w_i \mathrm{cov}_{i,M}\right)$$

If two equilibrium conditions hold, we can logically derive the CAPM:

(1) In equilibrium, there is no excess demand for asset i: $w_i = 0$.
(2) According to Jevons' law of one price, there is only one price for risk in equilibrium.

The marginal reward-to-variability ratio of our two-asset portfolio and the slope of the capital market line, the Sharpe ratio, must be equal:

$$\frac{\frac{\partial E\left(R_P\right)}{\partial w_i}}{\frac{\partial \sigma_P}{\partial w_i}} = \frac{E\left(R_i\right) - E\left(R_M\right)}{\frac{\left(\mathrm{cov}_{i,M} - \sigma_M^2\right)}{\sigma_M}} = \frac{E\left(R_M\right) - r_f}{\sigma_M} \Rightarrow E\left(R_i\right) = r_f + \beta_{i,M}\left(E\left(R_M\right) - r_f\right)$$

We have shown that the expected return of a risky asset i is linearly related to the systematic market risk under equilibrium conditions. The CAPM is widely criticized for several reasons. The claim that the assumptions are not realistic is true, but least important. All economic models are based on simplifying assumptions which are not completely fulfilled in reality. More important is Roll's critique that the CAPM cannot be tested without complete knowledge of the true composition of the market portfolio M.[104] In reality we do not know the composition of the true market portfolio which includes by definition all available assets. Market indices, which are usually used to test the CAPM, are not necessarily efficient portfolios. The most severe critique, however, is the claim that the linear relation between beta and expected returns does not hold empirically. One of the most controversial questions among financial economists is whether the CAPM yields accurate predictions.[105]

Fama and French (1992) analyzed the cross-sectional variation in average stock returns over the 1941–1990 period and concluded that the relation between average return and beta is weak.[106] Fama and French (1996) argued that a three-factor model yields more accurate predictions than the CAPM:[107]

$$E\left(R_j\right) = r_f + \beta_j \left(E\left(R_M\right) - r_f\right) + s_j \left(F_{size}\right) + h_j \left(F_{B/M}\right)$$

The first half of Fama and French's equation is identical to the CAPM. The beta β_j coefficient measures the sensitivity of portfolio j to the excess return on a market portfolio. The coefficient s_j measures the sensitivity of portfolio j to the difference between the returns of a portfolio of stocks with small market capitalizations and the returns of a portfolio of stocks with large market capitalizations. The return spread is usually referred to as size factor

[104] Roll (1977).
[105] Fama and French (1992), Black (1993).
[106] Fama and French (1992).
[107] Fama and French (1996).

(F_{size}). The term h_j represents portfolio j's sensitivity to the return spread between portfolios of stocks with high and low book equity to market equity (B/M) ratios. The three-factor model presumes that portfolios formed on size and book to market ratios can be used to explain expected returns. The main disadvantage of the model is that it cannot be logically derived. Like other multi-factor models, the three-factor model is based only on empirical studies of historical returns and therefore prone to data snooping biases.[108] It is questionable if multi-factor models really yield superior return estimates for single stocks.[109]

To summarize, the CAPM is a model which explains how risky assets are priced *in equilibrium*. In contrast to multi-factor models which are based on empirical studies, the CAPM can logically be derived from a few simplifying assumptions. The CAPM is still the preferred model to estimate the opportunity costs of single stocks. It only requires a few inputs. Applying the CAPM is therefore less time consuming than using multi-factor models. However, systematic market risk might not be the only factor explaining the variation in stock prices. While financial economists do not agree which factor model is most appropriate to estimate the opportunity cost of equity, most economists would agree that cost of capital can only be estimated under uncertainty. We therefore recommend combining a factor model – like the CAPM – and the Monte Carlo method to simulate possible realizations of equity premia and opportunity cost of capital.[110]

3.3.4   Terminal value calculation

The fundamental value of a firm is theoretically the present value of its future cash flows from now until infinity discounted at an appropriate risk-adjusted rate. As it is impossible to estimate cash flows until infinity, analysts usually estimate the present value of future cash flows during a limited forecasting period, $t = 1, \ldots, T$, the so-called competitive advantage period. The value of a firm, or enterprise value EV, equals the present value of future FCFF during the competitive advantage period and the present value of cash flows after the explicit forecasting period.

$$EV = \sum_{t=1}^{\infty} \frac{FCFF_t}{(1+WACC)^t} = \sum_{t=1}^{T} \frac{FCFF_t}{(1+WACC)^t} + \frac{TV_T}{(1+WACC)^T}$$

The value of future cash flows after the explicit forecasting period, $t = T + 1, \ldots, \infty$, is often referred to as terminal value[111] TV, residual value,[112] or continuing value.[113] The terminal value which can be viewed as equivalent to the redemption value of a bond is a purely theoretical concept. Bond investors receive a series of coupon payments and a redemption value at maturity. By contrast, there is no redemption value that equity investors receive at a certain point in time. Firms usually do not stop operations, liquidate all assets and distribute the cash receipts to equity holders at an ex ante determined point in time.

---

[108] Lo and MacKinlay (1990).
[109] While theoretically interesting, the Arbitrage Pricing Theory (APT) which was proposed as an alternative to the CAPM is rarely applied by practitioners. Analysts usually prefer the mean variance capital asset pricing model because of its simplicity. Ross (1976); Roll and Ross (1980).
[110] The CAPM is also discussed in Part VIII of this book.
[111] Damodaran (2002), pp. 303–321.
[112] Rappaport (1998), pp. 40–47.
[113] Copeland et al. (2000), pp. 267–288.

If we assume that free cash flows grow at a constant rate g_{TV} forever during the terminal value or stable-growth period, we can apply the perpetuity formula which we derived earlier:[114]

$$TV_T = \frac{FCFF_T \left(1 + \overline{g_{TV}}\right)^1}{\left(1 + WACC_{TV}\right)^1} + \frac{FCFF_T \left(1 + \overline{g_{TV}}\right)^2}{\left(1 + WACC_{TV}\right)^2} + \ldots + \frac{FCFF_T \left(1 + \overline{g_{TV}}\right)^\infty}{\left(1 + WACC_{TV}\right)^\infty}$$

$$TV_T = \frac{FCFF_T \left(1 + \overline{g_{TV}}\right)}{WACC_{TV} - \overline{g_{TV}}} \Rightarrow TV_0 = \frac{TV_T}{\left(1 + WACC_T\right)^T}$$

The terminal value captures the value of the cash flows after the explicit forecast period at point T. It must be discounted by the weighted average cost of capital of the competitive advantage period, $WACC_T$, to derive its present value at $t = 0$. It is not unusual that the terminal value captures the large majority of the total enterprise value of a firm. Valuation models are extremely sensitive to changes in the input factors which go into the terminal value calculation: the constant growth rate, g_{TV}, the free cash flow to the firm at $t = T$, $FCFF_T$, and the weighted average cost of capital, $WACC_{TV}$. Financial analysts often get it wrong and use unrealistic inputs when calculating terminal values:

(1) *The constant growth rate g_{TV} during the terminal value period*: Using the perpetuity with growth formula presumes that free cash flows grow at a constant rate g_{TV} during the terminal value period. The growth rate during the terminal value period cannot exceed the growth rate of the overall economy. If Microsoft, for example, grew at a higher rate than US GDP forever, the value of Microsoft would at some point be larger than the whole US economy. While Microsoft could grow not only in its domestic market, but also internationally, even Bill Gates would not argue seriously that Microsoft will dominate the US economy at some point in the future. Convergence between real interest rates and real economic growth rates is one of the standard assumptions of neoclassical economists.[115] Assuming that the risk-free interest rate and the economic growth rate will converge in the long run, financial analysts often use the risk-free interest rate as a proxy for the growth rate in the steady state, terminal value period. Applying the risk-free interest rate as a proxy for the growth rate also ensures that the difference between the $WACC_{TV}$ and the growth rate g_{TV} is positive as companies usually have to pay risk premia above the risk-free rate for debt and equity.[116] Earlier we defined return on invested capital as net operating profit after taxes, or NOPAT, divided by invested capital IC:

$$r = \frac{NOPAT}{IC}$$

As return on invested capital and opportunity cost of capital are by definition equal in steady state, a firm cannot add economic value (EVA) by increasing invested capital during the terminal value period:

$$EVA = (r - i) \times IC \xrightarrow{r_{TV} = i_{TV}} EVA_{TV} = 0$$

---

[114] See section 3.2.
[115] Economic growth theories are discussed in: Samuelson and Nordhaus (1998), pp. 517–537.
[116] Damodaran (2002), pp. 305–307.

Free cash flow to the firm equals NOPAT times $(1 - b)$, where the plowback ratio b represents the percentage of NOPAT reinvested in net working capital and net long-lived assets. Applying the fundamental growth equation which states that the growth rate equals the return on invested capital r times the plowback ratio b, we can rearrange the terminal value formula by substituting FCFF by NOPAT:[117]

$$FCFF = NOPAT \times (1 - b) \xrightarrow{g = r \times b \Rightarrow b = \frac{g}{r}} FCFF = NOPAT \times \left(1 - \frac{g}{r}\right)$$

$$TV_T = \frac{NOPAT_T \times \left(1 - \frac{\overline{g_{TV}}}{r_{TV}}\right) \times (1 + \overline{g_{TV}})}{WACC_{TV} - \overline{g_{TV}}}$$

The rearranged terminal value formula expresses that the terminal value does not only depend on the assumed growth rate but also on the assumed return on invested capital during the terminal value period. The assumed growth rate g_{TV}, the assumed return on invested capital r_{TV} and the implied plowback ratio b_{TV} must be consistent. While companies usually invest less in the business during the terminal value period than in the high growth period, a constant growth rate in steady state still requires some investment in property, plant and equipment and net working capital. Financial analysts often use high growth rates which imply returns on invested capital and plowback ratios which are unrealistically high for mature companies in steady state.

(2) *Free cash flows to the firm $FCFF_T$ during the terminal value period*: Depending on the nature of the industry and the business model of a firm, FCFF and NOPAT are often cyclical. Financial analysts tend to overestimate (underestimate) the value of a firm if they use peak (trough) cash flows or earnings at $t = T$ instead of normalized economic earnings. Using the perpetuity formula with growth requires that financial analysts use normalized FCFF or NOPAT which a company is expected to generate over the complete business cycle in steady state. The growth rate g_{TV} represents the expected long-run growth trend in FCFF. The cash flow or earnings estimates should reflect the cash generating power of a mature firm which entered steady state.

(3) *Weighted average cost of capital $WACC_{TV}$ during the terminal value period*: Weighted average costs of capital are opportunity costs of capital. According to the rule of consistency between cash flows and opportunity cost of capital, $WACC_{TV}$ must adequately reflect the risk of the firm during the terminal value period. The risk profile of a company is usually different during the high growth period and the terminal value period. The weighted average cost of capital during the terminal value period, $WACC_{TV}$, should reflect that the firm entered steady state:

$$WACC_{TV} = (1 - \tau_{TV})i_{D,TV}w_{D,TV} + i_{E,TV}w_{E,TV}$$

The terms τ_{TV}, $i_{D,TV}$, $i_{E,TV}$, $w_{D,TV}$ and $w_{E,TV}$ represent the expected tax rate, the expected opportunity cost of debt and equity and the proportion of debt and equity used to finance assets during the terminal value period. While it is difficult to anticipate whether the capital structure of a firm will be significantly different in the terminal value period

---

[117] Copeland *et al.* (1990), pp. 269–271.

compared to the high growth period, mature companies are usually less sensitive to the business cycle than growth companies. Financial analysts applying the CAPM to estimate cost of equity can incorporate the different risk profile of a firm in steady state by using lower betas.

The terminal value usually captures a large proportion of the complete value of a firm. Professional portfolio managers often suspect that buy-side analysts manipulate terminal values to justify desired target prices. Manipulating terminal values is arguably the easiest way to influence intrinsic enterprise values. Analysts who report terminal values but do not make transparent their assumptions on implied growth rates, return on invested capital, plowback rates and normalized free cash flows are most likely of limited help. Investors are well advised to carefully analyze terminal values.

Using Baidu.com, Inc. as a practical example, Part II of this book demonstrates how investors can formulate Monte Carlo Free Cash Flow to the Firm (MC-FCFF) models. Monte Carlo simulations enable financial analysts to take the uncertainty of future cash flows and expected discount rates into account when valuing stocks.

References

Apple Computer, Inc. (2005), Annual Report Pursuant to Section 13 or 15(d) of the Securities Exchange Act of 1934, for the Fiscal Year Ended September 24, 2005.

Barker, R. (2001), *Determining Value*, Financial Times Prentice Hall.

Barrett, M.E. (1983), Stirling Homex (A), Harvard Business School Case Study 9-173-193, Rev. October 25.

Black, F. (1993), Beta and return, *The Journal of Portfolio Management*, Fall, 8–18.

Blume, M.E. (1971), On the assessment of risk, *The Journal of Finance*, March, 1–10.

Buffett, W. (1995), Berkshire Hathaway, Inc., Shareholder Letter, http://www.berkshirehathaway.com/letters/1995.html.

Copeland, T., and Antikarov, V. (2001), *Real Options*, Texere.

Copeland, T., Koller, T., and Murrin, J. (2000), *Valuation: Measuring and Managing the Value of Companies*, Third Edition, John Wiley & Sons.

Damodaran, A. (2002), *Investment Valuation*, Second Edition, John Wiley & Sons.

Damodaran, A. (2005), *Applied Corporate Finance*, Second Edition, John Wiley & Sons.

Deutsche Bank, Annual Review 2005.

Dierks, P.A., and Patel, A. (1997), What is EVA, and how can it help your company, *Management Accounting*, November, 52–58.

Dienstag, E. (1976), *Whither Thou Goest: The Story of an Uprooted Wife*, E.P. Dutton & Co., Inc.

Dimson, E., Marsh, P., and Staunton, M. (2006), *Global Investment Returns Yearbook 2005*, Published by ABN AMRO, February.

Ehrbar, A. (1998), *EVA: The Real Key to Creating Wealth*, John Wiley & Sons.

Faber, M. (2002), *Tomorrow's Gold: Asia's Age of Discovery*, CLSA Books.

Fabozzi, F.J. (1997), *Handbook of Fixed Income Securities*, Fifth Edition, McGraw-Hill.

Fama, E. (1970), Efficient capital markets: a review of theory and empirical work, *The Journal of Finance*, May, 383–417.

Fama, E. (1991), Efficient markets II, *The Journal of Finance*, December, 1575–1617.

Fama, E.F., and French, K.R. (1992), The cross-section of expected stock returns, *The Journal of Finance*, June, 427–465.

Fama, E.F., and French, K.R. (1996), Multifactor explanations of asset pricing anomalies, *The Journal of Finance*, March, 55–84.

Financial Accounting Standards Board (1987), Statement of Financial Accounting Standards No. 95, Statement of Cash Flows, November.

Ferris, K.R., and Barrett, M.E. (1985), *Stirling Homex Corporation*, Thunderbird, The American Graduate School of Management.

Ferris, K.R., Tennant, K.L., and Jerris, S.I. (1992), *How to Understand Financial Statements: A Nontechnical Guide for Financial Analysts, Managers, and Executives*, Prentice Hall.

Grinold, R.C., and Kahn, R.N. (2000), *Active Portfolio Management: A Quantitative Approach for Providing Superior Returns and Controlling Risk*, Second Edition, McGraw-Hill.

Keynes, J.M. (1997), *The General Theory of Employment Interest and Money*, Originally published 1936, Prometheus Books.

Kieso, D.E., Weygandt, J.J., and Warfield, T.D. (2004), *Intermediate Accounting*, Eleventh Edition, John Wiley & Sons.

Lang, M. (2004), *Employee Stock Options and Equity Valuation*, The Research Foundation of CFA Institute 2004.

Lehman Brothers (2006), Deutsche Bank, Research Note by Joanna Nader, February 3.

Lintner, J. (1965), Security prices, risk, and maximal gains from diversification, *The Journal of Finance*, 587–616.

Lo, A., and MacKinlay, C. (1990), Data snooping biases in tests of financial asset pricing models, *Review of Financial Studies*, 3, 431–468.

Madden, B.J. (2002), *CFROI Valuation: A Total System Approach to Valuing the Firm*, Third Edition, Butterworth-Heinemann.

Madden, B.J. (2005), *Maximizing Shareholder Value and the Greater Good*, Learning What Works.

Malkiel, B.G. (2003), The efficient market hypothesis and its critics, *Journal of Economic Perspectives*, Winter, 59–82.

Markowitz, H.M. (1952), Portfolio selection, *The Journal of Finance*, March, 77–91.

Mauboussin, M.J., Schay, A., and McCarthy, P. (2001), Competitive advantage period (CAP), At the intersection of finance and competitive strategies, Credit Suisse First Boston Equity Research, October 4.

Mehra, R., and Prescott, E.C. (1985), The equity premium: a puzzle, *Journal of Monetary Economics*, 15, 145–161.

Merrill Lynch (2006), Deutsche Bank: Positive management changes, Research Note by Stuart Graham and Neil McDermid, April 3.

Miller, M.H., and Modigliani, F. (1961), Dividend policy, growth, and the valuation of shares, *The Journal of Business*, October, 411–433.

Modigliani, F., and Miller, M.H. (1958), The cost of capital, corporation finance and the theory of investment, *The American Economic Review*, June, 261–297.

Mossin, J. (1966), Equilibrium in a capital market, *Econometrica*, October, 768–783.

Mulford, C.W., and Comiskey, E.E. (2002), *The Financial Numbers Game, Detecting Creative Accounting Practices*, John Wiley & Sons.

Porter, M.E. (1998), *Competitive Advantage: Creating and Sustaining Superior Performance, With a New Introduction*, Free Press.

Rappaport, A. (1998), *Creating Shareholder Value: A Guide for Managers and Investors*, Second Edition, The Free Press.

Rappaport, A., and Mauboussin, M.J. (2001), *Expectations Investing: Reading Stock Prices for Better Returns*, Harvard Business School Press 2001.

Roll, R. (1977), A critique of the asset pricing theory's tests, *Journal of Financial Economists*, 4, 129–176.

Roll, R., and Ross, S.A. (1980), An empirical investigation of the arbitrage pricing theory, *The Journal of Finance*, December, 1073–1103.

Ross, S.A. (1976), The arbitrage theory of capital asset pricing, *Journal of Economic Theory*, 13, 341–360.

Ryanair Holdings, plc (2005), Annual Report & Financial Statements.

Samuelson, P.A., and Nordhaus, W.D. (1998), *Economics*, Sixteenth Edition, Irwin/McGraw-Hill.

Sharpe, W.F. (1964), Capital asset prices: a theory of market equilibrium under conditions of risk, *The Journal of Finance*, September, 452–442.

Sharpe, W.F. (1966), Mutual fund performance, *The Journal of Business*, January, 119–128.

Sharpe, W.F. (1971), Risk, market sensitivity and diversification, Graduate School of Business, Stanford University, Research Paper No. 50, November.

Sharpe, W.F. (1994), The Sharpe ratio, *The Journal of Portfolio Management*, Fall, 49–58.

Sharpe, W.F., and Cooper, G.M. (1971), Risk-return classes of New York stock exchange common stocks, 1931–1967, Technical Report No. 3.

Sharpe, W.F., and Alexander, G.J. (1990), *Investments*, Fourth Edition, Prentice Hall.

Siegel, J.J. (1992), The equity premium: stock and bond returns since 1802, *Financial Analysts Journal*, January–February, 28–38.

Siegel, J.J. (2005), Perspectives on the equity risk premium, *Financial Analysts Journal*, November/December, 61–72.

Standard & Poor's (2003), Corporate rating criteria, Internet Version, http://www2.standardandpoors.com/spf/pdf/fixedincome/CorpCrit2003r-jun.pdf

Stewart, G.B. (1999), *The Quest for Value*, Second Edition, HarperCollins Publishers.

Stirling Homex Corporation (1970), Prospectus, February 19.

Stirling Homex Corporation (1971), 1971 Annual Report.

Swartz, M. (2004), *Power Failure, The Inside Story of the Collapse of Enron*, Mimi Swartz with Sherron Watkins, First Currency Paperback Edition, April.

Tomtom (2006), Fourth Quarter Results Release 2005, February 14.

The Committee of Sponsoring Organizations of the Treadway Commission (1999), Fraudulent financial reporting: 1987–1997, An analysis of U.S. public companies, Research Report Prepared by Mark S. Beasley, Joseph V. Carcello, Dana R. Hermanson, March.

UBS Investment Research (2006), Deutsche Bank, Research Note by Philipp Zieschalg, Alastair Ryan, Daniele Brupbacher, 20 March 2006.

Ulam, S.M. (1991), *Adventures of a Mathematician*, Third Edition, University of California Press.

Wilson, D.A. (1977), Stirling Homex, Harvard Business School Case Study 9-177-197, April 1.

Part II
Monte Carlo Free Cash Flow to the Firm (MC-FCFF) Models (Deutsche Bank/DWS)[1]
Jan Viebig[2] and Thorsten Poddig[3]

[1] DWS Investment GmbH, © 2008 Jan Viebig.
[2] Managing Director, DWS Investment GmbH.
[3] Professor of Finance, University of Bremen.

4

Introduction

In Part I we discussed the main input factors of FCFF models. In Part II we will explain how investors can apply the model in practice. Figure 4.1 maps the FCFF approach. We will apply the model to Baidu.com, Inc., a Chinese internet company listed on NASDAQ. Part II is structured as follows. In Chapter 5, we demonstrate how analysts of leading investment banks formulate standard FCFF models. Financial analysts usually incorporate expected values of various input factors into FCFF models. However, the inputs into FCFF models are highly uncertain. In Chapter 6 we introduce the Monte Carlo method and incorporate distributions of possible realizations of our main value drivers into our FCFF model.

	Year 0	Year 1	Year 2	...	Year T
Revenue growth driver 1					
Revenue growth driver n					
Revenue growth g					
Net revenues (Rev)	Rev_0	$Rev_1 = Rev_0(1+g_1)$	$Rev_2 = Rev_1(1+g_2)$	...	$Rev_{T-1}(1+g_T)$
minus COGS					
minus SG&A					
minus R&D					
minus other OpEx					
EBIT (reported)					
plus/minus adjustments					
EBIT (adjusted)					
Taxable Income					
Tax rate t					
Future EBIT (1–t)		$Rev_1 \times (EBIT/Rev)_1 \times (1-t_1)$	$Rev_2 \times (EBIT/Rev)_2 \times (1-t_2)$	...	$Rev_T \times (EBIT/Rev)_T \times (1-t_T)$
plus D&A					
minus Capex					
minus ΔNWC					
FCFF	$FCFF_0$	$FCFF_1$	$FCFF_2$	...	$FCFF_T$
Present value of FCFF during CAP		$PV_1 = FCFF_1/(1+WACC)$	$PV_2 = FCFF_2/(1+WACC)^2$	...	$PV_T = FCFF_T/(1+WACC)^T$
ROIC = profit margin × IC turnover					
WACC					
EVA = (ROIC−WACC) * IC	$(ROIC_0-WACC_0)>0?_0$	$(ROIC_1-WACC_1)>0?$	$(ROIC_2-WACC_2)>0?$	...	$(ROIC_T-WACC_T)>0?$

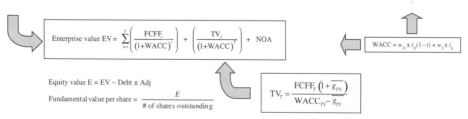

$$\text{Enterprise value EV} = \sum_{t=1}^{T}\left(\frac{FCFF_t}{(1+WACC)^t}\right) + \left(\frac{TV_T}{(1+WACC)^T}\right) + NOA$$

$$WACC = w_D \times i_D(1-t) + w_E \times i_E$$

Equity value E = EV − Debt ± Adj

$$\text{Fundamental value per share} = \frac{E}{\text{\# of shares outstanding}}$$

$$TV_T = \frac{FCFF_T\left(1+\overline{g_{TV}}\right)}{WACC_{TV} - g_{TV}}$$

Figure 4.1 FCFF model

5
Standard FCFF Model

... One summer morning, the sun dawned wicked hot over Wall Street, where the watchword was Baidu.com. If Baidu meant nothing to you, oh how out of it you were. Billed as the Google of China, Baidu went public at 27, opened that day at 66 and swiftly hit 151.... Baidu, it seems, must be Mandarin for Inefficient Market Hypothesis, ... [1]

On August 4, 2005, the Chinese language Internet search provider Baidu.com, Inc. went public. The Chinese company founded in January 2000 helps internet search users to find information online and enables online marketing customers to bid for priority placements in search results using Baidu's auction-based pay-for-performance service. The initial public offering (IPO) was priced at USD 27. The American Depository Shares (ADS) opened at USD 66 and closed at USD 122.54 on its first trading day. USD 122.54 per ADS translated into a market capitalization of roughly USD 4.2 billion, an astonishingly high market capitalization for a company that generated only USD 13.4 million in net revenues and USD 1.3 million in operating profits in 2004.

The media dubbed Baidu as the "Google of China". In its prospectus, Baidu reported that the research firm iResearch expected the Chinese internet user base to grow from 115 million in 2005 to 187 million in 2007.[2] The media hype surrounding Google and the projected growth potential of the online market in China were presumably the dominant reasons why Baidu's shares jumped almost fivefold on its first trading day. On September 13, 2005, Baidu's shares closed at USD 112.25 in New York. Some market participants were surprised that both Goldman Sachs and Piper Jaffray initiated coverage on Baidu with an "Underperform" rating on September 14, 2005, only a few weeks after the IPO in which both companies had acted as underwriters. Goldman Sachs' internet analysts argued in September 2005:[3]

... Although we recognize the strategic value of owning the stock of the leading search company in China and how one could use aggressive "blue sky" valuation parameters to justify the current stock price, we advise clients not to use this approach aggressively. Our P/E-to-normalized-growth valuation analysis suggests an implied fair value of ~$27 while our DCF analysis suggests a value of $24. ... [4]

On September 22, 2005, when Credit Suisse First Boston initiated coverage Baidu's shares traded at USD 80.50:

---

[1] *BusinessWeek*, European Edition, October 3, 2005.
[2] Baidu.com, Inc. (2005a), pp. 1–9.
[3] Goldman Sachs (2005), PiperJaffray (2005).
[4] Goldman Sachs (2005), p. 1.

Table 5.1 Baidu.com, Inc.: consolidated statement of operations data[5]

(in thousands except for per ADS data)	For the year ended December 31,				For the three months ended March 31,		
	2002	2003	2004		2004	2005	
	RMB	RMB	RMB	USD	RMB	RMB	USD
Net revenues	10 542	36 638	110 909	13 401	17 150	42 628	5151
Operating costs and expenses	(29 567)	(47 933)	(99 905)	(12 071)	(16 208)	(39 889)	(4819)
Operating (loss)/profit	(19 043)	(9295)	11 004	1330	942	2739	332
Net (loss)/profit	(18 577)	(8885)	12 005	1450	1038	2501	303
Net (loss)/income per ADS – Diluted	(2.44)	(0.87)	0.43	0.05	0.04	0.08	0.01
Weighted average number of shares used in per share calculation – diluted	7622	10 189	28 124	28 124	26 930	29 808	29 808

> ... We are a believer in Baidu's strong fundamentals in the Internet paid-search market. However, due to its premium valuation we are initiating coverage of Baidu with an UNDERPERFORM rating and a 12-month price target of US$52.0. . . . [6]

A few weeks later on October 27, 2005, Morgan Stanley issued a research report with an "Underweight" rating, again arguing that Baidu's shares, which traded at the time at USD 81.05, were significantly overvalued compared to its intrinsic DCF value:

> ... Baidu's current share price is higher than our DCF value per share, using a 13% discount rate plus a free cash flow exit multiple of 11 (at a terminal growth rate of 4%). The current DCF value assumes a revenue CAGR of mid-30% and a margin expansion from high 10% to mid 30% over next ten years. DCF is our preferred valuation methodology because it incorporates our long-term view about the company's operation. . . . [7]

In fall 2005, financial analysts at Goldman Sachs, PiperJaffray, Morgan Stanley and Credit Suisse First Boston all agreed that Baidu's shares trading on the NASDAQ under the ticker symbol BIDU were overvalued compared to its fundamental or intrinsic value. In the following chapters we demonstrate how leading investment banks employed DCF models to value Baidu.com, Inc. in fall 2005. In section 5.6 we will compare the results of their models with the stock price performance in the 2005 to 2007 period. The "financial value driver approach" discussed in section 5.4 can help investors to formulate more realistic DCF models and to analyze DCF models formulated by financial analysts. Usually, financial analysts at leading investment banks start with analyzing historical and forecasting future revenues and operating margins when formulating DCF models. That is where our discussion of Baidu's fundamental value begins, too.

---

[5] Baidu.com, Inc. (2005a), pp. 8–9. The data is prepared in accordance with US GAAP. RMB is the official abbreviation for Renminbi, the Chinese currency (8.2 RMB ≈ 1 USD).
[6] Credit Suisse First Boston (2005), p. 4.
[7] Morgan Stanley (2005).

5.1 NET REVENUES

Top line growth is arguably one of the most important value drivers of a firm. Modeling future revenues starts with carefully analyzing historical revenues reported on a company's income statements. US GAAP requires that public companies disclose information about operating segments. Baidu.com, Inc. is almost a single product or service company. In 2004, over 90% of its revenues came from online marketing services, the remaining part from enterprise search software and related services (7%) and portal search services (2%). Coming from a very low base, Baidu's net revenues increased in 2003 by 267% and in 2004 by 187%.[8]

Typically, financial analysts assume that competitive advantage periods of high growth companies last five to 10 years.[9] However, the assumed length of the competitive advantage period can vary dramatically. To forecast future net revenues, financial analysts usually apply what we call the "revenue growth driver approach": Telecom analysts, for example, often forecast revenues by predicting the number of future users and average revenues per user. Semiconductor analysts predict future product mixes and prices per product. Retail analysts formulate expectations on expected same store sales, etc. The art of modeling revenues is to identify and forecast the most relevant drivers which determine a firm's future revenues. The factors driving the top line of a company are industry specific. Financial analysts typically apply one of the following approaches to forecast future revenues:

(1) *ARPU approach*: Financial analysts can try to forecast future revenues, or REV, of a company j by multiplying the expected number of customers or users n and the expected average revenue per user (ARPU):

$$REV_j = n_j \times ARPU_j$$

This approach is widely used by telecom and internet analysts. Average revenues per user or customer (ARPU) are an important ratio reflecting the purchasing power and willingness of a firm's clients. Portfolio managers who invested in telecom operators in emerging markets in the past have experienced that wealthier customers often sign up early and are therefore more profitable than new users. In September 2005, Goldman Sachs forecasted that Baidu.com, Inc. would generate 37% compounded annual growth rates (CAGR) from 2006 to 2009 and significantly higher revenue growth rates in 2005 and 2006. Goldman Sachs's mid-term revenue growth predictions were mainly driven by expected growth in advertisers of over 30% and growth in revenue per advertiser of 4%.[10] Revenues from online marketing services accounted for 91% of Baidu's total gross revenues in 2004. Table 5.3 reflects how Goldman Sachs forecasted Baidu's online marketing revenues for the 2005 to 2007 period using the ARPU approach in fall 2005.[11]

With hindsight, we know today that Baidu's online marketing revenues grew much stronger than analysts predicted in fall 2005. In 2005 Baidu had over 76 000 active online customers and generated online marketing revenues in the amount of USD 38.1 million, representing a 187.6% increase from 2004.[12] Online marketing revenues in 2006 grew

---

[8] Baidu.com, Inc. (2005a), pp. 68–74 and p. F-4.
[9] Please note that Credit Suisse First Boston assumes that the competitive advantage period lasts for 10 years but only provides revenue and margin forecasts for the period 2005 to 2010. Credit Suisse First Boston (2005), pp. 49 and 55.
[10] Goldman Sachs (2005), p. 3 and pp. 15–19.
[11] Goldman Sachs (2005), pp. 33–36.
[12] Baidu.com, Inc. (2006c), pp. 29 and 55, Baidu.com, Inc. (2006a).

Table 5.2 Baidu.com, Inc.: net revenues[13]

STEP 1: Model net revenues

in thousands of RMB (if not otherwise stated)	Year t − 1	Year 0	Year 1	Year 2	Year 3	Year 4	Year 5	Year 6	Year 7	Year 8	Year 9	Year 10
For the year ended December 31,	2003	2004	2005E	2006E	2007E	2008E	2009E	2010E	2011E	2012E	2013E	2014E
Revenues:												
Online marketing services	31 775	106 854										
Enterprise search software and related services	2803	7958										
Portal search services	5993	2639										
Total revenues	40 571	117 451										
Less: Business tax and surcharges	−1933	−6452										
Growth in net revenues	267%	187%	149%	70%	58%	47%	36%	28%	21%	18%	12%	10%
Goldman Sachs September 14, 2005			137%	71%	51%	35%	26%	21%	17%			
Morgan Stanley October 27, 2005			160%	68%	64%	58%	46%	34%	25%	18%	12%	10%
Credit Suisse September 22, 2005			144%	89%	49%	37%	37%	22%				
Net revenues in thousands of RMB	38 638	110 909	275 609	467 157	735 772	1 077 906	1 465 953	1 869 090	2 261 599	2 668 686	2 988 929	3 287 822
Net revenues in thousands of USD		13 401	33 984	57 603	90 724	132 911	180 759	230 467	278 865	329 061	368 549	405 403

[13] Baidu.com, Inc. (2005a), pp. F-1 to F-49, Morgan Stanley (2005), p. 15, Goldman Sachs (2005), p. 22, Credit Suisse First Boston (2005), p. 55. PiperJaffray (2005) did not provide sufficient long-term estimates which could have been used in a FCFF model. If necessary, growth rates were calculated from absolute figures provided in the research reports. RMB amounts were translated in USD at a constant rate of 8.11 RMB per USD.

Table 5.3 Baidu.com, Inc.: ARPU approach

	2003	2004	2005E	2006E	2007E
Average active online marketing customers	24 795	34 663	70 100	110 100	158 100
New online marketing customers	14 828	9868	35 437	40 000	48 000
Revenue per online marketing customer [USD] ("ARPU")	157	380	474	518	544
Online marketing revenues [USD million]	3.9	13.2	33.2	57.0	86.0
Implied growth rate		236%	152%	72%	51%

by 169.5% to USD 106.2 million from 2005.[14] Table 5.3 reflects one scenario which seemed possible in fall 2005. In Chapter 6 we will explain how analysts can simulate thousands of possible scenarios instead of concentrating on just one possible realization of an uncertain future.

(2) *Market share approach*: Alternatively, financial analysts can estimate future revenues by multiplying the expected market share s_j of a company j by the expected total revenues, or $REV_{i,j}$, of industry i in which company j operates:

$$REV_j = s_j \times REV_{i,j}$$

Using forecasts from iResearch and ZenithOptimedia, Goldman Sachs predicted that the online advertising market in China will grow from USD 397 million in 2004 to USD 3057 million in 2009. According to Goldman Sachs, pay-for-performance search revenues will grow from USD 67 million in 2004 to USD 1157 million in 2009.[15] Baidu's share of the Chinese search traffic was 37%, Yahoo's 32% and Google's 19% in 2005 according to Morgan Stanley, but Baidu competes not only with search engines but also with portals like Sina, Sohu and Netease – all listed on NASDAQ[16] – for the limited advertising budgets of mainly small and medium enterprises in China.[17]

(3) *Price/volume approach*: Financial analysts covering industrials and consumer goods companies often estimate future prices p^* and volumes v^* per product to forecast future revenues. Let us assume that a company produces $l = 1, \ldots, n$ products, then its expected revenues equal:

$$REV^*_j = \sum_{l=1}^{n} p^*_{j,l} \times v^*_{j,l}$$

Applying the price/volume approach requires a good understanding of a firm's business model and of price and volume trends in the respective industry.

(4) *Trend extrapolation approach*: A common practice among analysts is to extrapolate historical growth trends – linearly or exponentially – into the future. As discussed above

---

[14] Baidu.com, Inc. (2007a).
[15] Goldman Sachs (2005), p. 7.
[16] The ticker symbols are SINA, SOHU and NTES.
[17] Morgan Stanley (2005), p. 5.

growth rates are influenced by life and business cycles. Initial high revenue growth rates usually slow down when the revenue base increases ("base effect")[18] and when companies enter into a more mature stage of their life cycle. Revenue growth rates of cyclical companies are often heavily influenced by business cycles. Extrapolating historical growth rates into the future usually leads to unrealistic results. Only a few companies, for example utilities, are typically able to grow their revenues at a more or less constant rate over longer periods of time.

(5) *Near term guidance approach*: Some analysts simply incorporate company forecasts into their models for the near future. However, companies typically only formulate revenue and profit forecasts for the next quarter or fiscal year. After its IPO, Baidu started to provide revenue forecasts for the following quarter (Table 5.4).

Table 5.4 Baidu.com, Inc.: revenue drivers and revenue guidance[19]

	2002	2003	2004	Q1 2005	Q2 2005
Reporting date	August 4, 2005 (prospectus)	August 4, 2005 (prospectus)	August 4, 2005 (prospectus)	August 4, 2005 (prospectus)	August 23, 2005 (Q2 2005 results)
RMB/USD	8.2270	8.2772	8.2768		
Total net revenues [USD million]	1.3	4.7	13.4	5.2	8.4
Online marketing revenues [USD million]	0.5	3.8	12.9	5.2	8.1
Active online marketing customers	9960	24 700	34 600	31 768	41 248
Online marketing revenues per online marketing customers	52.4	154.9	372.8	163.6	196.4
Revenue guidance for next quarter [USD million]					9.6–10.0

Later we will see that Baidu's stock price climbed significantly in May 2006 when Baidu reported revenues higher than its own revenue forecasts for the first quarter 2006 and fell dramatically when Baidu reported second quarter results in July 2006 which were only "in line" with its own revenue guidance. Financial analysts and the media pay great attention if a company "disappoints investors" or "beats analysts' forecasts". If a company successfully guides "its" analysts, analysts' forecasts and company guidances are almost identical. In its quarterly report on August 23, 2005, Baidu gave its first post-IPO revenue guidance.

---

[18] Usually it is easier to grow a very low revenue base than a multi-billion revenue base at high growth rates. This observable phenomenon is often referred to as base effect. Abnormally high growth rates of young companies which often have a revenue base close to zero are usually not sustainable.

[19] Baidu.com, Inc. (2005a), pp. 68–76, Baidu.com, Inc. (2005b), p. 2.

Baidu is in a very early stage of its life cycle and operates in an emerging economy and in a very nascent industry.[20] While advertising revenues are usually cyclical in nature in mature markets, financial analysts believed in fall 2005 that Baidu will enjoy high non-cyclical growth rates in the future which will decline from 149% in 2005 to 10% in 2014. On average, the three investment banks expected that Baidu's net revenue will grow from only USD 13 million in 2004 to USD 405 million in 2014. We hope that the reader by now not only understands how Wall Street models revenues but also that these estimates are highly uncertain. Baidu.com, Inc. is a good example illustrating why we recommend incorporating uncertainty into FCFF models by applying the Monte Carlo method discussed below.

5.2   COST STRUCTURE AND OPERATING INCOME

By definition, operating income – or more precisely earnings before income and taxes (EBIT) – equals net revenues, or REV_{net}, minus operating expenses. Operating expenses reported on the income statement include cost of revenues or cost of goods sold (COGS), selling, general and administrative expenses (SG&A), research and development expenses (R&D), as well as other operating expenses.

$$EBIT_{adj}(1-\tau) = [REV_{net} - (COGS + SG\&A + R\&D + Others) \pm ADJ](1-\tau)$$

Taxes can be considered as operating expenses as a company has to pay taxes if it intends to continue its operations. Companies have to pay taxes on taxable income. Modeling future taxable income and effective tax rates is almost impossible. To simplify matters, financial analysts usually forecast tax rates, or τ, as a percentage of operating earnings. The tax rate as a percentage of operating earnings usually differs from the tax rate as a percentage of taxable income. As discussed in section 3.3.2, interest payments are tax deductible. Baidu does not benefit from tax shields as the company's assets are completely financed by equity. If tax-deductible expenses exceed taxable revenues, companies report net operating losses for tax purposes. Tax rules permit companies to carry net operating losses back or forward over specific periods of time. Companies receive refunds for income taxes paid in the past if they carry net operating losses back. Tax loss carryforwards, on the other hand, result in future tax savings if taxable revenues exceed tax-deductible expenses in the future.[21] For simplicity we assumed that the product of expected operating profits and the chosen tax rate adequately reflect the true cash tax burden of the company. The dynamics of possible tax loss carryforwards are not incorporated into our models.

Some managers use creative accounting tricks to misstate financial performance. Basically, there are three main ways to fool investors:

(1) *Overstating revenues*: Front-end loading or fraudulent reporting of revenues is one of the most common ways to manipulate profits. Manufacturers often use channel stuffing to meet analysts' expectations by forcing distributors to order products which cannot be sold to end-customers and recognizing revenues prematurely at the date of shipping.[22]

---

[20] Online advertising sales accounted for 3 to 4% of total advertising expenditures in the United States, Japan and South Korea, but only for 1.6% in China in 2004. Morgan Stanley (2005), p. 4.
[21] Kieso *et al.* (2004), pp. 974–980.
[22] Mulford and Comiskey (2002), p. 171.

The Stirling Homex case discussed in Part I, section 3.3.1 is another typical example of front-end loading of revenues.

(2) *Understating debt*: Managers often try to fool investors by hiding debt. Enron used a complex structure of special purpose entities (SPE) to hide its growing debt from investors until it finally collapsed.[23] Under US GAAP a lessee does not have to report liabilities if a lease does not meet four capitalization criteria and therefore qualifies as operating lease. Off-balance sheet financing is widely used in capital intensive industries, for example in the airline industry. Companies can lower debt to equity ratios by not reporting assets and liabilities on their balance sheets.[24]

(3) *Understating operating costs*: Companies use numerous ways to understate operating costs. Companies often capitalize costs instead of expensing them immediately to meet analysts' expectations by deferring operating costs in the future.[25] Not only can companies delay write-offs to meet analysts' expectations, but they can also write down inventory aggressively to lower future operating costs.[26] Managers often classify normal costs from operations as restructuring charges or other extraordinary costs to hide operating costs from investors. New chief executive officers tend to take big baths and write down assets in order to blame problems on predecessors and make future earnings look good.[27]

Investors should be aware of these accounting tricks and adjust reported operating income to eliminate accounting distortions before estimating future operating income if necessary. Carefully analyzing cash flows is in our opinion the best way to detect creative accounting.[28] In section 5.3 we will explain how investors can reconcile operating profits into operating cash flows. Analysts often adjust reported earnings to get a better understanding of a firm's "true" economic costs and profitability. Some financial economists argue that operating leases and research and development expenses should not be expensed but rather capitalized and amortized over time to better match costs and future revenues. If analysts capitalize operating leases, for example, they have to consider that not only do rent expenses decrease and interest expenses and amortization increase, but also that lease liabilities increase. Adjustments (ADJ) to earnings and capital must be made consistently!

Analyzing historical COGS, SG&A, R&D and other operating expenses helps investors to better understand the cost structure and the business model of a firm. In practice, it is almost impossible to accurately forecast the different operating costs separately over a multi-year competitive advantage period. Instead of subtracting expected operating expenses from expected net revenues, financial analysts typically estimate future operating profits by multiplying expected net revenues with expected operating profit margins. Below we used average operating margins and tax rates estimated by leading financial analysts covering Baidu.com, Inc. to illustrate how Wall Street models future operating profits. High growth companies often benefit from economies of scale if revenues grow much stronger than overhead costs and operating margins increase. In fall 2005, financial analysts forecasted that, on average, Baidu's adjusted EBIT margins would increase from 22% in 2005 to 42% in 2014.

---

[23] Swartz (2004), pp. 380f.
[24] Kieso *et al.* (2004), pp. 1085–1147.
[25] In the mid-1990s, for example, AOL capitalized marketing costs as "deferred subscriber acquisition costs" and later extended the amortization period. Schilit (2002), pp. 33–36 and 115–117.
[26] Mulford and Comiskey (2002), pp. 247–249.
[27] Mulford and Comiskey (2002), p. 81.
[28] Of course, not only reported earnings but also cash flows can be manipulated. However, manipulating earnings is typically easier than manipulating cash flows.

Table 5.5 Baidu.com, Inc.: operating income and operating profit margins[29]

STEP 2: Model operating income

in thousands of RMB (if not otherwise stated)	Year $t-1$	Year 0	Year 1	Year 2	Year 3	Year 4	Year 5	Year 6	Year 7	Year 8	Year 9	Year 10
For the year ended December 31,	2003	2004	2005E	2006E	2007E	2008E	2009E	2010E	2011E	2012E	2013E	2014E
Total net revenues	38 638	110 909	275 609	467 157	735 772	1 077 906	1 465 953	1 869 090	2 261 599	2 668 686	2 988 929	3 287 822
Minus COGS	−20 703	−32 985										
Minus SG&A	−16 930	−39 004										
Minus R&D	−5 191	−11 406										
Minus share-based compensation	−5 109	−16 510										
Total operating costs and expenses	−47 933	−99 905										
EBIT (reported)	−9 295	11 004										
EBIT (reported) margin	−24%	10%										
Adjustment: plus share-based compensation	5 109	16 510										
EBIT (adjusted)	−4 186	27 514	60 648	137 451	244 564	369 666	550 279	736 613	889 957	1 082 337	1 237 254	1 392 015
EBIT (adjusted) margin	−11%	25%	22%	29%	33%	34%	38%	39%	39%	41%	41%	42%
Goldman Sachs September 14, 2005			20%	27%	32%	32%	33%	35%	39%	41%	41%	42%
Morgan Stanley October 27, 2005			24%	27%	31%	35%	37%	39%	40%	41%	41%	42%
Credit Suisse September 22, 2005			22%	34%	36%	36%	43%	45%				
Taxable income												
Taxes	0	(481)										
Tax rate [% of taxable income]												
Tax rate [% of EBIT (adjusted)]	0%	2%	9%	9%	9%	12%	12%	12%	10%	15%	13%	13%
Goldman Sachs September 14, 2005			8%	9%	7%	7%	7%	7%	7%	16%	13%	13%
Morgan Stanley October 27, 2005			10%	9%	9%	12%	12%	13%	13%	13%	13%	13%
Credit Suisse September 22, 2005			8%	9%	11%	16%	16%	16%				
EBIT $(1-\tau)$ (adjusted) in thousands of RMB	−4 186	27 033	55 387	125 144	222 648	326 390	485 712	649 413	802 975	924 943	1 075 075	1 208 220
EBIT $(1-\tau)$ (adjusted) in thousands of USD	−516	3 333	6 829	15 431	27 453	40 245	59 890	80 076	99 010	114 050	132 562	148 979

[29] Baidu.com, Inc. (2005a), pp. F-1 to F-49, Morgan Stanley (2005), p. 15, Goldman Sachs (2005). p. 22, Credit Suisse First Boston (2005). p. 55. PiperJaffray (2005) did not provide sufficient long-term estimates which could have been used in an FCFF model. If necessary, adjusted operating margins and tax rates were calculated from absolute figures provided in the research reports to make data comparable. USD amounts were translated in RMB at a constant rate of 8.11 RMB per USD.

One word of caution has to be made: Baidu granted a substantial amount of options in the past.[30] In 2004, share-based compensation accounted for roughly 150% of reported EBIT and 15% of net sales. Most analysts add back share-based compensation as issuing options does not result in a cash outflow at the grant date. However, existing and future options represent a claim against equity and should therefore be taken into consideration when valuing the equity of a firm. While issuing options does not result in a cash outflow at the grant date, employee stock options do have several cash effects when employees exercise their options: First, companies receive cash inflows from financing to the amount of the strike price when employees exercise their options. Second, if companies repurchase shares which can be issued to option holders, cash flow from financing leaves the firm. Third, tax savings from so-called non-qualified stock options can be substantial.[31] Most financial analysts add back share-based compensation and only adjust shares outstanding for the dilution effect of options.[32] We followed current market practice and added share-based compensation back to operating earnings and used the number of diluted shares outstanding when calculating the fundamental equity value per share. Theoretically, not only debt but also the estimated value of existing and future options must be subtracted from the estimated enterprise value as share-based compensation represents a claim against equity.[33]

Before making investment decisions, investors should carefully analyze both Wall Street's revenue and profit margin expectations and question if these expectations are realistic. In section 5.4 we explain how investors can use what we call the "financial value driver approach" to more realistically forecast and analyze profit margins. But before discussing the financial value driver approach, we demonstrate how to reconcile operating income to free cash flows to the firm.

5.3   RECONCILING OPERATING INCOME TO FCFF

Discussing the Stirling Homex case,[34] we argued that a thorough analysis of cash flow statements can help investors to avoid expensive mistakes when making investment decisions. Revenues and expenses reported on the income statement do not necessarily result in cash in- and outflows. To reconcile operating income to operating cash flows, depreciation, amortization and other non-cash charges must be added to operating earnings. In addition,

---

[30] Baidu.com, Inc. (2005a), pp. F-1 to F-49, Morgan Stanley (2005), p. 15, Goldman Sachs (2005), p. 22, Credit Suisse First Boston (2005), p. 55. PiperJaffray (2005) did not provide sufficient long-term estimates which could have been used in an FCFF model. If necessary, adjusted operating margins and tax rates were calculated from absolute figures provided in the research reports to make data comparable. USD amounts were translated in RMB at a constant rate of 8.11 RMB per USD.

[30] Baidu.com, Inc. (2005a), pp. 62–66 and F-14.

[31] Lang (2004), p. 5. An example: In 2002, employees of Dell exercised 63 million shares at a strike price of USD 3.11 when Dell's shares traded at USD 23.24. As a result, Dell received cash inflows from financing in the amount of USD 196 million [USD 3.11 × 63 million shares]. Assuming that Dell repurchased the shares to avoid dilution, it paid USD 1464 million [USD 23.24 × 63 million shares]. The estimated tax savings in the amount of USD 355 million were also substantial [(USD 23.24 − USD 3.11) × 63 million shares × 0.28 tax rate]. The net cash effect from options in the amount of USD 913 million (USD 196 − 1464 + 355 million) was substantial compared to Dell's reported operating income of USD 1789 million in 2002. Lang (2004), pp. 26, 18–20 and 62–64.

[32] Under US GAAP companies must report basic and diluted earnings per share (EPS). To calculate diluted EPS, options that are in the money must be added to basic shares outstanding. Adjustments are made for the cash flows from financing received from employees but not for the tax implications of options. Assume that 50 options are outstanding with a strike price of USD 20 and that the shares currently trade at USD 80. The company receives USD 1000 when options are exercised [USD 20 × 50 options]. With these proceeds, the company can buy back 12.5 shares [USD 1000/USD 80 per share]. As a result, diluted EPS would be calculated not on the basis of 50 but 37.5 new shares [50 new shares − 12.5 repurchased shares]. Lang (2004), pp. 50f.

[33] Lang (2004), p. 6.

[34] See Viebig and Poddig, Part I, section 3.3.1 in this book.

all effects of accruals and deferrals of future cash receipts and payments must be removed. Changes in receivables and accrued expenses are typical examples of accruals which lead to cash receipts and payments not in the current, but in future periods. Changes in inventory, deferred tax assets and deferred revenues are typical deferrals of past cash receipts and payments. An increase in net working capital reduces cash flows, a decrease in net working capital releases cash. To generate future cash flows, a company does not only have to invest in net working capital but also in property, plant and equipment and other non-current assets. When revenues increase, net working capital usually *increases* as a company typically has to invest in inventories, receivables and other current assets to support its growth. Baidu's net working capital less cash *decreased* in the past – mainly because of the strong increase in customer deposits. It is questionable whether Baidu's clients will help the company to finance its growth in the future.

Table 5.7 reflects how Baidu's adjusted EBIT can be reconciled to free cash flows to the firm from a pure cash flow perspective. We deliberately decided not to capitalize research and development (R&D) expenses and operating leases. Capitalizing R&D expenses makes sense from an economic perspective if it helps to better match R&D expenses and future revenues generated by research and development efforts. Amortizing capitalized expenses requires subjective assumptions on the asset life of capitalized assets. Assuming that R&D assets have a life of 3 years, capitalizing R&D expenses would lead to an increase in EBIT of 7.091 million in 2004 (plus RMB 11.406 million in R&D expenses, minus RMB 4.315 million in amortization expenses). In addition, capital expenditures would increase by RMB 7.091 million in 2004. While the net effect on FCFF is zero as not only EBIT but also capital expenditures increase, capitalizing R&D expenses leads to an increase in assets of RMB 16.162 million.

Table 5.6 Baidu.com, Inc.: Capitalizing R&D expenses[35]

in thousands of RMB		R&D expense	Amortization expense	Unamortized R&D assets	
				Portion	Total amount
Current year t_0	2004	11 406		1.00	11 406
year t_{-1}	2003	5191	1730	0.67	3461
year t_{-2}	2002	3885	1295	0.33	1295
year t_{-3}	2001	3868	1289	0.00	0
Sum	Total		4315		16 162

Adjustments to operating earnings should not be made mechanically. Before capitalizing R&D expenses, financial analysts should question if capitalizing R&D expenses really allows them to better match R&D costs and revenues generated by R&D efforts. This requires that the life of R&D assets can be estimated reliably. While we showed how to capitalize R&D expenses, we applied a more conservative and less time-consuming approach and expensed Baidu's R&D costs immediately when calculating FCFF.

Some companies lease assets instead of borrowing money and buying them. If leases qualify as so-called operating leases, no assets and liabilities must be reported on the balance

[35] Baidu.com, Inc. (2005a), p. 68, Baidu.com, Inc. (2006c).
[36] Kieso *et al.* (2004), pp. 1085–1147.

Table 5.7 Baidu.com, Inc.: free cash flows to the firm (FCFF)[37]

STEP 3: Reconcile operating income to FCFF

in thousands of RMB (if not otherwise stated)	Year t − 1	Year 0	Year 1	Year 2	Year 3	Year 4	Year 5	Year 6	Year 7	Year 8	Year 9	Year 10
	2003	2004	2005E	2006E	2007E	2008E	2009E	2010E	2011E	2012E	2013E	2014E
For the year ended December 31,												
EBIT (1 − τ) **(adjusted)**	(4186)	27 033	55 387	125 144	222 648	326 390	485 712	649 413	802 975	924 943	1 075 075	1 208 220
depreciation and amortization (D&A)												
depreciation of fixed assets	4888	8893										
amortization of intangible assets	0	1050										
plus total D&A	4888	9943	30 667	42 000	52 333	56 000	60 333	65 667	64 500	60 000	62 000	64 000
Goldman Sachs September 14, 2005			28 000	37 000	52 000	55 000	60 000	66 000	73 000	60 000	62 000	64 000
Morgan Stanley October 27, 2005			29 000	34 000	40 000	46 000	50 000	52 000	56 000			
Credit Suisse September 22, 2005			35 000	55 000	65 000	67 000	71 000	79 000				
ΔNWC less cash												
Δ in accounts receivable (incl. allowance for doubtful accounts)	(1518)	(8381)										
Δ in inventories	0	0										
Δ in prepaid expenses and other current assets	250	(1483)										
Δ in current deferred tax assets	0	0										
Δ in non-current assets	(1268)	(9864)										
[increases in current assets: negative figures]												
Δ in customers' deposits	6265	17 590										
Δ in accrued expenses and other liabilities (from CF-statement)	1580	10 713										
Δ in deferred revenue	5013	(1158)										
Δ in deferred income	0	0										
Δ in total current liabilities	12 858	27 145										
[increases in current liabilities: positive figures]												

---

[37] Baidu.com, Inc. (2005a), pp. F-1 to F-49, Morgan Stanley (2005), p. 15, Goldman Sachs (2005), p. F-1 to F-49, Morgan Stanley (2005), p. 15, Goldman Sachs (2005), p. 22, Credit Suisse First Boston (2005), p. 56. PiperJaffray (2005) did not provide sufficient long-term estimates which could have been used in an FCFF model. If necessary, depreciation and amortization and changes in net working capital were calculated from absolute figures provided in the research reports to make data comparable. RMB amounts were translated in USD at a constant rate of 8.11 RMB per USD.

minus total ΔNWC less cash [positive numbers reflect decreases in NWC less cash!]	11 590	17 281	41 667	46 333	65 000	75 667	78 667	82 667	107 000	113 000	79 000	63 000
Goldman Sachs September 14, 2005			48 000	56 000	76 000	74 000	72 000	70 000	73 000			
Morgan Stanley October 27, 2005			51 000	54 000	84 000	121 000	144 000	149 000	141 000	113 000	79 000	63 000
Credit Suisse September 22, 2005			26 000	29 000	35 000	32 000	20 000	29 000				
Cash flow from operations before capex	12 292	54 257	127 720	213 478	339 981	458 057	624 712	797 746	974 475	1 097 943	1 216 075	1 335 220
capex												
acquisitions of fixed assets	(6402)	(25 415)										
acquisitions of intangible assets	0	(11 905)										
capitalization of internal use software costs	(1556)	(2155)										
capitalization of R&D	0	0										
capitalization of operating leases	0	0										
minus total Capex	(7958)	(39 475)	(81 000)	(65 667)	(92 333)	(113 333)	(140 333)	(158 667)	(180 000)	(251 000)	(204 000)	(224 000)
Goldman Sachs September 14, 2005			(81 000)	(35 000)	(51 000)	(59 000)	(69 000)	(76 000)	(85 000)			
Morgan Stanley October 27, 2005			(81 000)	(101 000)	(142 000)	(187 000)	(237 000)	(269 000)	(275 000)	(251 000)	(204 000)	(224 000)
Credit Suisse September 22, 2005			(81 000)	(61 000)	(84 000)	(94 000)	(115 000)	(131 000)				
FCFF	4334	14 782	46 720	147 811	247 648	344 723	484 379	639 080	794 475	846 943	1 012 075	1 111 220
Discount factor			1.13[38]	1.28	1.44	1.63	1.84	2.08	2.35	2.66	3.00	3.39
Present value of expected FCFF or PV(FCFF)			41 345	115 758	171 632	211 425	262 901	306 962	337 700	318 586	336 904	327 352
Sum of PV(FCFF) in thousands of RMB	2 430 567											
Sum of PV(FCFF) in thousands of USD	299 700											

38 Most (but not all) analysts discount free cash flow which a company generates during the current reporting year by one plus the opportunity cost of capital even if the valuation is made in the middle or at the end of the year. One could argue that it would be more appropriate to discount Baidu's expected FCFF generated in 2005 by one plus the discount rate over 0.25 instead of 1 year as the valuation was made in fall 2005. Fiscal year 2005 was used as "first" year as Baidu had not reported financial results for 2005 at the date of valuation.

sheet of the lessee under US GAAP.[36] We recommend capitalizing operating leases only if a company leases a material amount of operating assets. Please note that capitalizing operating lease expenses affects both operating income and debt.[39] Adjustments must be made consistently when calculating FCFF and invested capital. Table 5.7 reflects how Baidu's adjusted EBIT can be reconciled to free cash flows to the firm.

Average forecasts for depreciation and amortization (D&A), capital expenditures (capex) and change in net working capital of leading investment banks were used to demonstrate how Wall Street models future FCFF. Future FCFF were discounted at a WACC of 13%. Most investment banks use the CAPM discussed in Part I, section 3.3.3 to estimate the opportunity cost of equity of a company $i_{E,j}$:

$$i_{E,j} = r_f + \beta_j \left(E(r_M) - r_f \right)$$

Baidu's assets are completely financed by equity; the equity weight is 100%. Cost of equity and weighted cost of capital are therefore identical (Table 5.8).

Table 5.8 Baidu.com, Inc.: WACC assumptions[40]

	Goldman Sachs	Morgan Stanley	Credit Suisse
Risk-free rate r_f	5%	na	4%
Equity risk premium $(E(r_m) - r_f)$	4%	na	6.5%
Beta β_j	2.0	na	1.5
Equity weight w_E	100%	na	100%
Cost of equity $i_{E,j}$	12%	na	13.8%
WACC	12%	13%	13.8%

Baidu's IPO prospectus reveals that American Appraisal, an independent valuator, used a significantly higher WACC of 15% to estimate the fundamental value of Baidu's shares. Unlike the three investment banks, American Appraisal applied a multi-factor model and included a country risk premium of 1.11% and a small size risk premium of 2.86% when estimating Baidu's cost of equity. Using a WACC of 13%, the sum of Baidu's discounted future FCFF during the competitive advantage period is slightly less than USD 300 million. The present value of FCFF during the competitive advantage period is part of Baidu's total enterprise value. In section 5.5 we will discuss how Wall Street calculated Baidu's enterprise value in fall 2005. But before presenting the calculation of Baidu's enterprise value, we will discuss what we call the "financial value driver approach" which can help investors to more realistically model FCFF during the competitive advantage period.

---

[39] We deliberately decided not to capitalize Baidu's operating lease payments as the effect on Baidu's enterprise value would be negligible. Baidu's future minimum operating lease payments are RMB 16.6 million, RMB 5.0 million, RMB 3.7 million and RMB 1.6 million for 2005, 2006, 2007 and 2008, respectively. The present value of future operating lease commitments discounted at a firm's pre-tax cost of debt could be considered as long-term debt. Adjusted operating income equals stated operating income plus current operating lease expenses less depreciation charge for lease assets. The depreciation charge equals the discounted value of future lease commitments divided by the assumed life of capitalized lease assets. Baidu.com, Inc. (2005a), pp. F-21f.

[40] Cost of equity calculated on the basis of the CAPM. Goldman Sachs (2005), p. 22, Morgan Stanley (2005), p. 15, Credit Suisse First Boston (2005), p. 49.

5.4   THE FINANCIAL VALUE DRIVER APPROACH

In the 1960s, George J. Stigler analyzed the rates of return in the US manufacturing industries and noticed:

> ... There is no more important proposition in economic theory than that, under competition, the rate of return on investment tends toward equality in all industries. Entrepreneurs will seek to leave relatively unprofitable industries and enter relatively profitable industries, and with competition there will be neither public nor private barriers to these movements. . . . [41]

The financial value driver approach combines three important economic propositions:

(1) *Under competition returns on capital mean revert to cost of capital*:[42] Companies earning high returns on capital attract competitors. Companies that do not earn their cost of capital, on the other hand, are sooner or later forced to restructure, to return capital to its owners or to file for bankruptcy. As a result, under perfect competition return on capital fades to cost of capital over time. As discussed in section 3.3.2 the length of the competitive advantage period over which a firm can earn a return on capital in excess of cost of capital depends on the sustainability of its competitive advantages or, with others words, how well high returns are protected by "economic moats".

(2) *By definition, returns on capital, operating margins and capital turnover ratios are related*: The DuPont formula allows financial analysts to decompose returns on capital into operating profit margins and capital turnover. Abnormal returns on long-term invested capital can result from abnormal profit margins, abnormal capital turnover ratios or both.

(3) *Expectations on sales and change in invested capital must be consistent*: A company can usually only grow sales if it invests in property, plant and equipment and in net working capital. Revenue growth assumptions must be consistent with forecast capital expenditures and changes in net working capital. Financial analysts typically monitor capex-to-sales and ΔNWC-to-sales ratios to understand the interrelationship between revenues and investment needs.

The financial value driver approach explains the relationship between cost of capital, return on invested capital, operating margins, net sales and long-term invested capital. Empirical evidence suggests that structural differences exist between different industries. Returns on capital, operating margins and capital turnover ratios are often industry specific.[43] The strength of competition depends on the industry in which a specific company operates. In addition, growth prospects of companies operating in the same industry are to some extent similar. Financial analysts therefore usually analyze financial value drivers in an industry context or compare financial ratios of well-defined peer groups of companies.

Conceptually, there are various ways to incorporate the interdependence of financial ratios into FCFF models. A good starting point is to assume that return on capital mean reverts to cost of capital over time under competition. If return on capital is defined as

---

[41] Stigler (1963), p. 54.
[42] Empirical evidence supports the notion that returns on capital mean revert to cost of capital over time. Soliman (2004), p. 5.
[43] Soliman (2004), pp. 25f.

FCFF to invested capital, future FCFF can be predicted by multiplying expected invested capital by expected return on capital. Long-term invested capital at the end of period $t + 1$ equals long-term invested capital at the end of period t plus change in invested capital in $t + 1$. By definition, change in invested capital is capital expenditures (less depreciation) plus change in net working capital (ΔNWC). Return on capital can be decomposed into operating margins and capital turnover (net revenues/long-term invested capital). Proposition (3) requires that expectations on net sales and change in invested capital must be consistent. Figure 5.1 diagrams the relationship between financial value drivers.

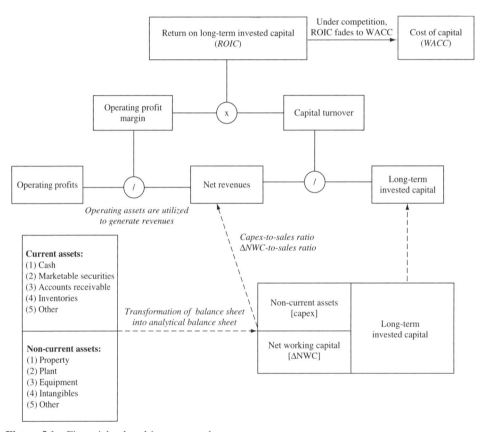

Figure 5.1   Financial value driver approach

To apply the financial value driver approach, long-term invested capital must be estimated. As discussed in section 3.1, estimation of long-term capital requires the transformation of a firm's balance sheet into an analytical balance sheet. In practice, financial analysts usually include current liabilities in net working capital to separate out providers of long-term capital (long-term debt and equity). Table 5.9 reflects the calculation of Baidu's long-term invested capital.

If a company acquires another company, the purchase price is assigned to tangible and intangible assets of the target, if possible. The remaining part of the purchase price is recorded as an intangible asset called goodwill.[44] We included goodwill in invested capital which includes, by definition, all cash invested in the business.

Table 5.9 reveals that the vast majority of net working capital on Baidu's balance sheet was cash. Baidu's asset base increased significantly due to the substantial proceeds from its initial public offering in August 2005. Carefully analyzing invested capital helps to better under-

Table 5.9 Baidu.com, Inc.: long-term invested capital[45]

	in thousands of RMB		in thousands of USD	
	2004	2005	2004	2005
Cash and cash equivalents	200 196	900 593	24 188	111 595
Accounts receivable – net of allowance for doubtful accounts	9645	22 353	1165	2770
Add adj.: allowance for doubtful accounts	627	(4643)	76	(575)
Inventories	0	0	0	0
Add adj.: LIFO reserve adjustment	0	0	0	0
Prepaid expenses and other current assets	2421	10 957	292	1358
Deferred tax assets net of valuation allowance	0	1449	0	179
Total current assets	212 889	930 709	25 721	115 327
Customer deposits	25 990	70 327	3140	8715
Accrued expenses and other current liabilities	21 900	53 137	2646	6584
Deferred revenue	6302	7658	762	949
Deferred income	0	124	0	15
Total current liabilities	54 192	131 246	6548	16 263
Net working capital	158 697	799 463	19 173	99 064
leasehold improvements – gross	1774	6782	214	840
computer equipment and servers – gross	43 924	126 863	5307	15 720
capitalized internal use software costs – gross	5783	6392	699	792
office equipment – gross	2345	3423	283	424
motor vehicles – gross	773	2271	94	282
Fixed assets – gross	54 599	145 731	6597	18 058
less accumulated depreciation	(18 667)	(49 311)	(2255)	(6110)
Fixed assets – net	35 932	96 420	4342	11 948
Payment for land use rights	0	77 200	0	9566
Other depreciating assets – net	1059	0	128	0
Intangible assets – net	12 953	13 303	1565	1648
Add adj.: inflation adjustment	0	0	0	0
Goodwill	0	9287	0	1151
Investments	0	2018	0	250
Deferred tax assets non-current	0	2843	0	352
Add adj.: valuation allowance non-current deferred tax assets	0	1598	0	199
Add adj.: capitalized operating lease	0	0	0	0
Add adj.: capitalized R&D	0	0	0	0
Non-current assets	49 944	202 669	6035	25 114
Long-term invested capital	208 641	1 002 132	25 208	124 178
Long-term invested capital less cash and cash equivalents	8445	101 539	1020	12 583

---

[44] Kieso *et al.* (2004), p. 578.
[45] Baidu.com, Inc. (2005a), pp. F-1 to F-49, Baidu.com, Inc. (2006), pp. F-1 to F-33.

stand a firm's business model. Baidu invested little capital in fixed assets in the past. Servers and computer equipment, the largest item, accounted for only USD 5.3 million in 2004. In fall 2005, analysts were faced with the question whether a company with such a small asset base can generate cash flows which justify a market capitalization of roughly USD 4 billion.[46]

Unlike return on invested capital (ROIC), return on equity (ROE) can be distorted by a firm's choice of capital structure and therefore does not qualify as an appropriate value driver. Return on equity is usually defined as net income divided by (average) common equity.[47] A more appropriate definition of return on invested capital is NOPAT divided by long-term invested capital. NOPAT is net operating profit after taxes where *net* stands for "net of depreciation". Invested capital is defined as the sum of all cash invested in a firm's net assets. Long-term invested capital is the invested capital provided by long-term suppliers of capital.[48] Invested capital is charged with accumulated depreciation as depreciation, a non-cash item, is subtracted from operating earnings to derive NOPAT. Stewart, one of the inventors of the EVA approach, argues that depreciation represents a true economic expense as assets consumed must be replenished before investors receive returns on investment.[49] In Table 5.10 two return on capital ratios are shown: adjusted EBIT $(1 - \tau)$ to long-term invested capital and FCFF to long-term invested capital. The two ratios reflect how efficiently a company uses its long-term invested capital to generate operating earnings and free cash flows.

Invested capital was defined as the sum of all cash invested in Baidu's operating assets over time net of depreciation and amortization. Long-lived assets such as property, plant and equipment are stated at historical costs less depreciation on the balance sheet. Accountants depreciate long-lived assets, not to determine the fair values of these assets, but to allocate their costs to the periods over which assets generate benefits for the company.[50] Book values often represent the best estimates analysts can make to value fixed assets. Estimating the economic value of cash invested in intangible assets like intellectual property, technology or brand names is often not feasible for external analysts. If analysts can formulate estimates superior to accountants on how much cash invested in the company declined or increased in value, adjustments to net asset values should be made. If companies, for example, operate in countries with high inflation, adjustments for inflation must be made to translate historical into current asset prices. In Baidu's case, no adjustments to net asset values were made.

When estimating long-term invested capital, financial analysts typically make several adjustments. Adjustments to operating income and long-term capital must be made consistently. As we deliberately chose not to capitalize R&D expenditures and operating leases when estimating FCFF, we did not capitalize these items when estimating invested capital. Operating leases and R&D expenditures should only be capitalized if capitalized assets have the potential to represent a material part of invested capital.

The financial value driver approach reveals the assumptions implied in Baidu's FCFF valuation. On average, financial analysts at Goldman Sachs, Morgan Stanley and Credit Suisse assumed in fall 2005 that Baidu's revenues would grow at a high, but declining, rate in the next 10 years.

---

[46] Of course, a large part of Baidu's asset base such as its brand name, its technology and its intellectual capital is not adequately reflected on its balance sheet.

[47] Modigliani and Miller (1958), pp. 268–271.

[48] Please note that we included current liabilities consistently in net working capital when calculating (long-term) invested capital, cash flows and weighted average cost of capital.

[49] Stewart (1999), pp. 85f.

[50] Kieso *et al.* (2004), p. 520.

Table 5.10 Baidu.com, Inc.: financial value drivers

STEP 4: Apply the financial value driver approach

in thousands of RMB (if not otherwise stated)	Year 1	Year 2	Year 3	Year 4	Year 5	Year 6	Year 7	Year 8	Year 9	Year 10
	2005E	2006E	2007E	2008E	2009E	2010E	2011E	2012E	2013E	2014E
Expected net revenues	275 609	467 157	735 772	1 077 906	1 465 953	1 869 090	2 261 599	2 668 686	2 988 929	3 287 822
Expected EBIT $(1-\tau)$ adjusted	55 387	125 144	222 648	326 390	485 712	649 413	802 975	924 943	1 075 075	1 208 220
Expected depreciation and amortization	30 667	42 000	52 333	56 000	60 333	65 667	64 500	60 000	62 000	64 000
Expected change in net working capital (ΔNWC) less cash	41 667	46 333	65 000	75 667	78 667	82 667	107 000	113 000	79 000	63 000
Expected capital expenditures (capex)	(81 000)	(65 667)	(92 333)	(113 333)	(140 333)	(158 667)	(180 000)	(251 000)	(204 000)	(224 000)
Expected FCFF	**46 720**	**147 811**	**247 648**	**344 723**	**484 379**	**639 080**	**794 475**	**846 943**	**1 012 075**	**1 111 220**
Implied revenue growth	149%	70%	58%	47%	36%	28%	21%	18%	12%	10%
Implied capex-to-sales ratio	29%	14%	13%	11%	10%	8%	8%	9%	7%	7%
Implied ΔNWC-to-sales ratio	15%	10%	9%	7%	5%	4%	5%	4%	3%	2%
Expected change in net working capital (ΔNWC) less cash	(41 667)	(46 333)	(65 000)	(75 667)	(78 667)	(82 667)	(107 000)	(113 000)	(79 000)	(63 000)
Expected capital expenditures (capex)	81 000	65 667	92 333	113 333	140 333	158 667	180 000	251 000	204 000	224 000
Expected depreciation and amortization	(30 667)	(42 000)	(52 333)	(56 000)	(60 333)	(65 667)	(64 500)	(60 000)	(62 000)	(64 000)
Change in long-term invested capital	8667	(22 667)	(25 000)	(18 333)	1333	10 333	8500	78 000	63 000	97 000
Long-term invested capital	**101 539**	**78 872**	**53 872**	**35 539**	**36 872**	**47 206**	**55 706**	**133 706**	**196 706**	**293 706**
Average long-term invested capital	**54 992**	**90 206**	**66 372**	**44 706**	**36 206**	**42 039**	**51 456**	**94 706**	**165 206**	**245 206**
Implied profit margin [EBIT $(1-\tau)$ adjusted/net revenues]	20%	27%	30%	30%	33%	35%	36%	35%	36%	37%
Implied capital turnover [net revenues/average long-term invested capital]	501%	518%	1109%	2411%	4049%	4446%	4395%	2818%	1809%	1341%
Implied return on capital ratio 1 [EBIT $(1-\tau)$ adjusted/average long-term invested capital]	**101%**	**139%**	**335%**	**730%**	**1342%**	**1545%**	**1561%**	**977%**	**651%**	**493%**
Implied profit margin [FCFF/net revenues]	17%	32%	34%	32%	33%	34%	35%	32%	34%	34%
Implied capital turnover [net revenues/average long-term invested capital]	501%	518%	1109%	2411%	4049%	4446%	4395%	2818%	1809%	1341%
Implied return on capital ratio 2 [FCFF/average long-term invested capital]	**85%**	**164%**	**373%**	**771%**	**1338%**	**1520%**	**1544%**	**894%**	**613%**	**453%**

Operating margins indicate how tightly management controls costs. The cost-to-sales relationship of online advertising is attractive. Capital needs and fixed costs are relatively low and operating leverage therefore high. On average, financial analysts believed in fall 2005 that Baidu's after-tax operating margin would increase from 20% in 2005 to 37% in 2014. The interrelationship between revenues and profitability is obvious: If Baidu decides to expand its marketing and sales force more aggressively to increase its customer base, operating margins will drop. The same is true if Baidu increases R&D expenditures to develop new products and services to attract or maintain customers.

The significant increase in expected FCFF also depends on the assumption that capital expenditures will grow at a much lower rate than sales. The implied capex-to-sales ratio is forecasted to fall from 29% in 2005 to only 7% in 2014. In addition, financial analysts assumed in fall 2005 that net working capital less cash would decrease in each year during the competitive advantage period – mainly because of the strong increase in customer deposits. The analysis of Baidu's implied financial drivers brings to light that financial analysts expected returns on invested capital to stay high for the entire competitive advantage period. Capital turnover measures how efficiently management utilizes invested capital in the generation of sales. The high implied capital turnover ratios shown in Table 5.10 imply that Baidu's management uses a small and extremely scalable asset base very efficiently.

Competitors like Google invest heavily in IT infrastructure. To defend or expand its market share, Baidu could be forced to increase capital expenditures well above the levels forecasted by financial analysts in fall 2005. Baidu's high margins are at risk if competitors with more resources, superior technology and a better reputation enter or increase their presence in the Chinese online advertising market. Table 5.10 reflects only one possible scenario reflecting average expectations of leading investment banks in fall 2005. Using the Monte Carlo method discussed below allows analysts to simulate thousands of possible realizations of the main financial value drivers. When running Monte Carlo simulations, analysts should consider that the main financial value drivers are related.

5.5 FUNDAMENTAL ENTERPRISE VALUE AND MARKET VALUE

The present value of future free cash flows $FCFF_t$ during the competitive advantage period represents only a portion of a firm's total enterprise value. The terminal value captures the cash flows after the explicit forecast period. The sum of the present value of future cash flows during the competitive advantage period and the discounted terminal value, or TV, reflect the fundamental value of a firm's operating assets which are employed to generate revenues and ultimately free cash flows. Some companies have a significant amount of non-operating assets, or NOA,[51] on their balance sheets. The enterprise value, or EV, of a firm includes both the value of operating and non-operating assets:

$$EV = \left[\sum_{t=1}^{T} \left(\frac{FCFF_t}{(1 + WACC_t)^t} \right) + \left(\frac{TV_T}{(1 + WACC_t)^T} \right) \right] + NOA$$

---

[51] To be consistent, the value of a non-operating asset should also be determined by discounting its future cash flows. In practice, however, financial analysts usually add the market value of non-operating assets, if available, to the present value of free cash flows to the firm.

The terminal value represents the value of cash flows after the competitive advantage period. As discussed in section 3.3.4, the perpetuity with growth formula can be applied to calculate terminal values, or TV, if free cash flows to the firm are assumed to grow at a constant rate g_{TV} forever after the competitive advantage period:

$$TV_T = \frac{FCFF_T\,(1 + \overline{g_{TV}})}{WACC_{TV} - \overline{g_{TV}}} \Rightarrow TV_0 = \frac{TV_T}{(1 + WACC_T)^T}$$

Using a $FCFF_T$ in the last year of the competitive advantage period of RMB 1.1 billion, a constant terminal value growth rate of 4%, opportunity cost of capital of 13% and 10% during the competitive advantage period and the terminal value period respectively, leads to a discounted terminal value of RMB 5.6 billion or USD 700 million. Financial analysts typically apply the multiplier method instead of the perpetuity formula to estimate terminal values. Goldman Sachs, for example, derived a terminal value of RMB 9.5 billion by multiplying the present value of expected FCFF in the last year of the competitive advantage period, namely RMB 600 million, by a terminal value multiplier of 16.[52] Analysts at Morgan Stanley multiplied the expected present value of FCFF in the amount of RMB 517 million[53] in the last period of the competitive advantage period first by one plus a terminal growth rate of 4% and then by a multiplier of 11 to derive a discounted terminal value of RMB 5.9 billion or USD 728 million. It is not unusual that the terminal value represents a large part of the total enterprise value.

Table 5.11   Baidu.com, Inc.: terminal value calculation[54]

	Goldman Sachs	Morgan Stanley	Credit Suisse	Perpetuity method
Date of valuation	September 14, 2005	October 27, 2005	September 22, 2005	Fall 2005
Competitive advantage period	2005–2011	2005–2014	2006–2015	2005–2014
Length of competitive advantage period [years]	7	10	10	10
$FCFF_T$ at the end of the competitive advantage period [RMB million]	600	1553	1331	1111
Terminal value exit multiple (FCFF)	16	11		
Terminal growth rate		4%	6%	4%
WACC during competitive advantage period $WACC_T$	12%	13%	13.8%	13%
WACC during terminal value period $WACC_{TV}$				10%
Terminal value [RMB million]	9551			19 261
Present value of terminal value [RMB million]	4603	5914	4908	5674
Present value of terminal value [USD million] at RMB 8.11 per USD	568	728	605	700
Present value of terminal value as % of enterprise value	68%	56%	51%	64%

[52] Goldman Sachs (2005), p. 22.
[53] The present value of expected FCFF in 2014 in the amount of RMB 517 was derived by discounting expected RMB 1553 in 2014 at a WACC of 13% (RMB 1553 × 1.13[9] = RMB 517). Please note that Morgan Stanley discounted FCFF over nine years as they chose to start discounting FCFF in 2006 instead of 2005 as the valuation was made in fall 2005. Morgan Stanley (2005), p. 15.
[54] Goldman Sachs (2005), p. 22, Morgan Stanley (2005), pp. 14f, Credit Suisse First Boston (2005), p. 49.

The enterprise value equals the sum of the present value of FCFF during the competitive advantage period, the discounted terminal value and the value of non-operating assets. Given the assumptions discussed above, we derived a present value of future FCFF during the competitive advantage of USD 299.7 million (RMB 2431 million) and a terminal value of USD 700 million (RMB 5674 million). In addition, Baidu had cash on its balance sheet in excess of USD 111 million (RMB 900 million) after its IPO. As Baidu did not invest the cash to generate higher revenues and ultimately higher cash flows from operations with a larger asset base, cash and cash equivalents should be viewed as a non-operating asset. As a result, Baidu's estimated enterprise value equaled roughly USD 1.1 billion in fall 2005. Table 5.12 shows the enterprise value calculated by Goldman Sachs, Morgan Stanley and Credit Suisse.

Table 5.12   Baidu.com, Inc.: enterprise value calculation[55]

	Goldman Sachs	Morgan Stanley	Credit Suisse
	September 14, 2005	October 27, 2005	September 22, 2005
Present value of FCFF during competitive advantage period [RMB million]	1174	3343	3585
Present value of terminal value	4603	5914	4908
Present value of FCFF during CAP plus present value of terminal value [RMB million]	5777	9257	8494
Value of non-operating assets [RMB million] (cash and cash equivalents)	957	1225	1082
Enterprise value [RMB million]	6734	10482	9575
Enterprise value [USD million]	830	1292	1179

The equity value E is simply the enterprise value less the value of long-term debt D. Long-term debt reported on the balance sheet does not necessarily reflect all obligations made by a company. Baidu's long-term debt is zero. Current liabilities were subtracted from the enterprise value because they were subtracted from current assets to calculate net working capital. Some companies try to hide debt from the balance sheet and lower debt to equity ratios by using off-balance sheet debt. Operating leases and special purpose vehicles are typical examples of off-balance sheet debt. In addition, the amount of reported pension liabilities often understates a firm's true pension burden.[56] Baidu does not promise defined pension benefits but makes contributions to a defined contribution plan and has no obligations beyond making regular contributions to the plan.[57] Like debt, preferred shares are a claim against common equity and must be subtracted from the enterprise value to derive the equity value E. Baidu's outstanding convertible shares were automatically converted into ordinary shares upon completion of the IPO in August 2005.[58] After the IPO, the value

---

[55] Goldman Sachs (2005), p. 22, Morgan Stanley (2005), pp. 14f, Credit Suisse First Boston (2005), p. 49.
[56] Kieso et al. (2004), pp. 1017–1084.
[57] Baidu.com, Inc. (2005a), p. F-21.
[58] Baidu.com, Inc. (2006c), pp. F-27f.

of preferred shares was zero. As long-term debt is zero, Baidu's enterprise value and equity value are identical.

The fundamental value per share equals the equity value divided by the fully diluted number of common shares outstanding:

$$E = EV - D \pm ADJ$$

$$\text{Fundamental value per share} = \frac{E}{\text{\# of shares outstanding}}$$

In fall 2005 analysts at Goldman Sachs, Morgan Stanley and Credit Suisse believed that Baidu's shares were priced for perfection. At the time, Baidu's share price fluctuated around USD 80. Table 5.13 reflects that analysts at Goldman Sachs, Morgan Stanley and Credit Suisse calculated intrinsic values of USD 24, USD 40 and USD 36 per share in fall 2005.

Table 5.13   Baidu.com, Inc.: fundamental value per share[59]

	Goldman Sachs	Morgan Stanley	Credit Suisse
	September 14, 2005	October 27, 2005	September 22, 2005
Enterprise value [USD million]	830	1292	1179
Long-term debt [USD million]	0	0	0
Equity value [USD million]	830	1292	1179
Number of shares outstanding [in million]	34.5	32.3	32.8
Fundamental value per share [USD]	24.1	40	36.0
Share price at date of valuation [USD] (close prior day)	112.25	81.05	80.50

5.6 BAIDU'S SHARE PRICE PERFORMANCE 2005–2007

In fall 2005, Goldman Sachs, Morgan Stanley and Credit Suisse calculated fundamental values per share of USD 24, USD 40 and USD 36 per share, respectively. As Baidu's shares traded well above these intrinsic values, Baidu's shares appeared richly valued in fall 2005. All three investment banks recommended their clients to underweight Baidu's shares in fall 2005. The recommendations proved valuable advice for investors who sold the shares immediately after the IPO or borrowed Baidu's shares and sold them short until February 2006: Baidu's shares lost roughly half of their value in the period August 2005 to February 2006. However, Baidu's share price recovered substantially in the period after February 2006 and traded above USD 143 when we met with Shawn Wang, Baidu's chief financial officer, in Frankfurt on June 15, 2007.

---

[59] Goldman Sachs (2005), p. 22, Morgan Stanley (2005), pp. 14f, Credit Suisse First Boston (2005), p. 49.

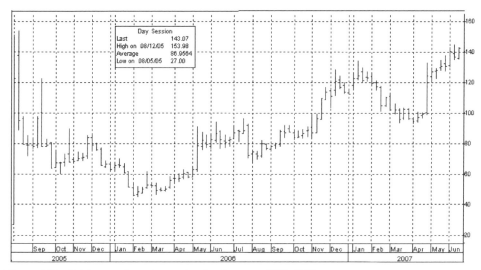

Figure 5.2   Baidu.com, Inc.: share price development 2005–2007

The bar chart in Figure 5.2 shows how quickly Baidu's stock price adjusted when new information emerged. Immediately after Baidu had announced results for its first quarter 2006 beating analysts' expectations, Baidu's shares climbed over 20% in after-hours trading, the biggest increase since its initial public offering on August 5, 2005. Bloomberg reported on May 9, 2006:

> ... Baidu.com Inc., China's most-used search Web Site, said first-quarter profit surged to 35.2 million yuan ($4.4 million) as revenue tripled. The company's U.S. traded shares jumped 24 percent....Baidu.com was expected to post profits of $3.26 million, according to the median estimate of five analysts surveyed by Thomson Financial.... [60]

On July 27, 2006, Baidu announced disappointing financial results for the second quarter 2006. As a result, Baidu's share price declined substantially. Bloomberg reported:

> ... Shares of Baidu.com Inc., owner of China's most-used Internet search engine, plunged 15 percent after the company's third quarter sales forecast lagged behind expectations.... [61]

Baidu's shares changed only marginally immediately after the company announced third and fourth quarter 2006 results which were more or less in line with analysts' expectations.[62] On April 26, 2007, Baidu announced first quarter 2007 results and gave a very bullish outlook for the second quarter of 2007. As a result, Baidu's shares increased dramatically in value:

> ... Baidu.com Inc. (BIDU US) American depositary receipts, each representing one share, jumped $23.13, or 21 percent, to $132.50 in trading after the official close of U.S. exchanges. China's most-used Internet search engine forecasts revenue of $48.9 million to $50.2 million in the second quarter. That topped the average estimate of $43.5 million by analysts in a Bloomberg survey.... [63]

---

[60] Bloomberg (2006a).
[61] Bloomberg (2006b).
[62] Bloomberg (2006c, 2007a).
[63] Bloomberg (2007b).

It is safe to assume that Baidu's share price will continue to be extremely volatile in the future when the company reports results. Whenever new information emerges, financial analysts review their valuation models. Table 5.14 compares the price targets of leading analysts in fall 2005 with their price targets in April 2007.

Table 5.14   Price targets of leading investment banks fall 2005 and mid-2007[64]

		Fall 2005	Mid-2007
Goldman Sachs	Price target	"~ $27; a more aggressive scenario suggests ~ $45"	"new year-end $134 price target"
	Date	14-Sep-05	27-Apr-07
	Share price	USD 112.25	USD 109.37
	Stock rating	Underperform	Neutral
Morgan Stanley	Price target	"DCF value of US$40 per share"	"Our base-case DCF valuation yields a fair value of US$130.9"
	Date	27-Oct-05	27-Apr-07
	Share price	USD 81.05	USD 109.37
	Stock rating	Underweight	Equal-weight
Credit Suisse	Price target	"12-month target price of US$52.0"	"We increased our target price to US$83.0 ..."
	Date	22-Sep-05	27-Apr-07
	Share price	USD 80.50	USD 109.37
	Stock rating	Underperform	Underperform

In June 2007, Baidu's share price traded well above the price targets formulated by leading internet analysts in fall 2005. The development of Baidu's share price, of course, depends on the movement of the overall market. The NASDAQ-100 index increased by 22% from 1589 on September 1, 2005, to 1942 on June 15, 2007. However, the main reason for the positive share price development is the company's stronger than expected revenue growth. In fall 2005, analysts at Goldman Sachs, Morgan Stanley, and Credit Suisse estimated that Baidu's revenues would grow by 137%, 160% and 144% in 2005 and by 71%, 68% and 89% in 2006, respectively.[65] With hindsight, we know today that Baidu's total revenues increased stronger than expected by 171.8% in fiscal year 2005 to USD 39.6 million (RMB 114.9 million) and by 162.5% to USD 107.4 million (RMB 837.8 million) in 2006.[66]

To be fair, forecasting Baidu's revenues is difficult as China's online search market is still at a very nascent stage and online search is growing fast. Baidu's CFO Shawn Wang explained to us in June 2007 that many Chinese companies still use the internet only as yellow pages. As the number of credit cards increase, he sees for the first time early signs of e-commerce developing in China. In the next chapter we demonstrate how analysts can incorporate ranges of possible growth rates into FCFF models instead of point estimates.

---

[64] Goldman Sachs (2005, 2007), Morgan Stanley (2005), Credit Suisse (2005, 2007), Morgan Stanley (2007b).

[65] Goldman Sachs (2005), p. 22, Morgan Stanley (2005), p. 15, Credit Suisse (2005), p. 55.

[66] Baidu.com, Inc. (2006d, 2007a).

Unlike most analysts expected, Baidu did not lose market share but strengthened its position as leading provider of internet search in China in 2006. Baidu's traffic market share increased by 14 percentage points from 48% to 62% in 2006, while Google's market share in China fell from 33% in 2005 to 25% in 2006.[67] The number of Baidu customers is growing fast and customers are spending more money for online advertising on average. Table 5.15 shows that Baidu's revenues are growing rapidly, driven by a strong growth in the number of online marketing customers and increasing revenues per online marketing customer.

Table 5.15 Baidu.com, Inc.: revenue drivers and revenue guidance[68]

	Q2 05	Q3 05	Q4 05	Q1 06	Q2 06	Q3 06	Q4 06	Q1 07
Reporting date	23/08/05	26/10/05	21/02/06	9/05/06	26/7/06	31/10/06	14/02/07	26/04/07
Total net revenues [USD million]	8.4	11.0	14.2	16.9	24.0	30.3	34.8	35.7
Year-on-year growth in total revenues	188.6%	174.4%	167.7%	196.8%	174.9%	169.1%	136.1%	103.3%
Online marketing revenues [USD million]	8.1	10.6	13.8	16.5	23.7	30.1	34.6	35.6
Active online marketing customers	41 248	53 000	63 000	74 000	90 000	102 000	108 000	112 000
Online marketing revenues per online marketing customer [USD]	196.4	200.0	219.7	221.3	260.3	294.8	320.3	323.7
Revenue guidance for next quarter [USD million]	9.6–10.0	12.6–13.1	15.5–16.1	23.0–24.0	30.0–31.0	34.0–35.0	34.0–35.0	48.9–50.2

Arguably most professional investors would agree that revenue and margin expectations are key value drivers of stocks. The Baidu example demonstrates how sales and earnings expectations drive stock prices. The beauty of competitive financial markets is that market participants constantly reassess risk positions when new information emerges. This makes trading in financial markets so exciting – and sometimes expensive. Investors trading in competitive financial markets can observe that stock prices adjust almost instantaneously when new information becomes available. Understanding the movement of stocks is often not easy as many investors do not really adjust their own estimates when new information emerges. Some investors simply buy or sell stocks because they believe that other investors could change their expectations when new information becomes available.[69]

Some investors only look at earnings per share (EPS) data – shown at the bottom of Table 5.16 – and compare price/earnings ratios when companies report. More sophisticated investors apply discounted cash flow models and analyze how changes in expected revenues, expected expenses and expected investment needs affect stock prices. Well-formulated FCFF models enable investors to translate expectations into fundamental or intrinsic values. The problem is not the model. The difficulty is to formulate realistic expectations in an uncertain world. In the next chapter we will explain how investors can incorporate uncertain estimates of their main value drivers into FCFF models.

---

[67] Evolution Securities China (2007), p. 13, Morgan Stanley (2007a), p. 7.
[68] Baidu.com, Inc. (2005b, 2005c, 2006a, 2006b, 2006d, 2007a, 2007b).
[69] Keynes (1997), p. 156.

We updated the data used in the standard FCFF model discussed above after meeting with Baidu's CFO, Shawn Wang, in Frankfurt on June 15, 2007. However, the purpose of the next chapter is not to give a stock recommendation but to explain how to build Monte Carlo FCFF models using Baidu.com, Inc. as a real-world example.

Table 5.16   Baidu.com, Inc.: full year 2005 and 2006 results[70]

	Fiscal year 2005	Fiscal year 2006
[Amounts in thousands of USD, except number of shares and per share data]	Filed June 21, 2006	Filed May 30, 2007
Revenues		
Online marketing services	38 086	106 160
Other services	1469	1199
Total revenues	39 555	107 359
Cost of revenues		
Business tax and surcharges	(2574)	(6642)
Traffic acquisition costs	(2628)	(9633)
Bandwidth costs	(2636)	(5126)
Depreciation of servers and other equipment	(3130)	(6609)
Operational costs	(1848)	(3265)
Share-based compensation expenses	–	(181)
Total cost of revenues	(12 816)	(31 456)
Selling general and administrative	(13 341)	(32 065)
Research and development	(4263)	(10 153)
Share-based compensation	(4160)	–
Provision for doubtful accounts	(533)	–
Total operating costs and expenses	(35 113)	(73 674)
Operating (loss) profit	4442	33 685
Other income		
Interest income, net	1683	5438
Foreign exchange loss, net	(82)	(12)
Other, net	93	537
Total other income (and expenses)	1694	5963
Net (loss) income before taxes and cumulative effect of change in accounting principle	6136	39 648
Income tax expense	(237)	(1570)
Net (loss) income before cumulative effect of change in accounting principle	5899	38 078
Cumulative effect of change in accounting principle	–	590
Net income	5899	38 668
Net (loss) income per share		
Basic	0.30	1.14
Diluted	0.18	1.10
Weighted average number of ordinary shares outstanding		
Basic	19 808 058	33 290 696
Diluted	32 043 888	34 506 594

[70] Baidu.com, Inc. (2006c), p. F-4 and p. 46, Baidu.com, Inc. (2007c), p. F-4 and p. 65. Net (loss) income per share for fiscal 2006 is reported prior to a cumulative effect of change in accounting principle in the amount of USD 0.02 per share.

6
Monte Carlo FCFF Models

6.1 MONTE CARLO SIMULATION: THE IDEA

Economic variables are rarely constant over time. Financial analysts usually have to estimate future realizations of model inputs under uncertainty. As future realizations of economic variables – for example, future growth rates and operating margins – are uncertain, economists are well advised to simulate possible realizations of the input variables of their models to gain an understanding how the uncertain future could possibly look. Monte Carlo simulation is named after the city in Monaco which is known for its roulette tables. Despite its name, the Monte Carlo method was developed in Los Alamos where scientists like John von Neumann worked in the mid-1940s on the atomic bomb and first applied the Monte Carlo method to formulate solutions for the neutron diffusion problem and other questions of mathematical physics.[1] The originator of the Monte Carlo method was Stanislaw Ulam who worked with John von Neumann at the time:

> ... The idea for what was later called the Monte Carlo method occurred to me when I was playing solitaire during my illness. I noticed that it may be much more practical to get an idea of the probability of the successful outcome of a solitaire game (like Canfield or some other where the skill of the player is not important) by laying down the cards, or experimenting with the process and merely noticing what proportion comes out successfully, rather than to try to compute all the combinatorial possibilities which are an exponentially increasing number so great that, except in very elementary cases, there is no way to estimate it. This is intellectually surprising, and if not exactly humiliating, it gives one a feeling of modesty about the limits of rational or traditional thinking. In a sufficiently complicated problem, actual sampling is better than an examination of all the chains of possibilities ... [2]

Monte Carlo simulation can be used to solve high-dimensional differential equations and to calculate the probability of a successful outcome of a game of luck, like solitaire, or more generally of a stochastic process with uncertain realizations, like an investment in the stock market.[3] Today, the Monte Carlo method is not only used in mathematical physics by rocket scientists. Financial economists, for example, apply Monte Carlo simulations to solve option valuation problems as numerical integration can be very time consuming if complex options are involved.[4] Economic variables do not usually depend only on economic processes, but also have a component of randomness. Being intellectually honest, financial analysts can at best determine ranges or *distributions of possible fundamental values* but not exact price targets for stocks as future revenue growth rates, future operating margins, and other inputs

---

[1] Metropolis (1987) and Eckhardt (1987).
[2] Ulam (1991), pp. 196f.
[3] Metropolis and Ulam (1949), pp. 335–337.
[4] Boyle (1977).

which go into DCF models cannot be predicted with certainty. Uncertainty is one of the key characteristics of stock markets. It is surprising that most financial analysts today do not include the uncertainty of their estimates into their valuation models. Financial analysts can learn from the wisdom of Francis Bacon, the English philosopher and statesman:

> ... If a man will begin with certainties, he shall end in doubts, but if he will content to begin with doubts, he shall end in certainties. . . . [5]

Incorporating the uncertainty of the real world into DCF models leads to more realistic solutions as we do not know the model inputs, or more generally the future, with certainty. Financial analysts can incorporate uncertainty into DCF models by using Monte Carlo simulations. The biggest advantage of the Monte Carlo method is its conceptual simplicity. Constructing a Monte Carlo simulation involves only two basic steps:

(1) *Generating (a reasonable amount of) random numbers*: Today, financial analysts do not have to throw coins, draw roulette wheels or conduct other physical experiments to generate random numbers. Most statistical software packages include random number generators which are able to produce large numbers of realizations of a random variable in short periods of time.[6] Ideally, these sequences are as unpredictable as possible. John von Neumann once made a classical remark stating that anybody producing random numbers by applying arithmetic methods is in a state of sin: Random numbers generated by computers are not truly random and hence often referred to as pseudo-random numbers.[7] Mathematicians have developed statistical tests, for example run tests, to examine whether sequences are independently and identically distributed but cannot prove if sequences are truly random.[8]

   According to Bernoulli, the sample average of an infinite sequence of uncorrelated random variables X with the same expected value and variance in all probability converges almost surely to its expected value μ.

$$\lim_{n \to \infty} P\left(\left|\overline{X_n} - \mu\right| < \tau\right) = 1$$

The probability P that the sample average will deviate from its true expected value μ by less than a very small, arbitrarily chosen distance τ is one, if an infinite number of identical random experiments are conducted. Metropolis and Ulam rightly noticed that the estimate will never be confined within given limits with certainty but only with great probability.[9] The Monte Carlo method is often criticized because of its slow convergence rate.[10] Monte Carlo simulations converge at a rate $O(N^{-1/2})$, where N is the number of runs in a Monte Carlo simulation. Increasing the accuracy of a Monte Carlo simulation by a factor of 2 requires an increase in computational effort by a factor of 4.[11] Running a Monte Carlo simulation with 5000 iterations usually yields results which are accurate enough for financial economists. Increasing the number of iterations

---

[5] Francis Bacon (1561–1626) quoted in Savage (1998), p. 52.
[6] A random variable is a stochastic function which assigns a real number to each elementary event.
[7] Jäckel (2002), p. 7.
[8] McLeish (2005), pp. 86–92.
[9] Metropolis and Ulam (1949), p. 336.
[10] The convergence speed can be increased, for example, by variance reduction techniques. Caflisch (1998), pp. 13–42, Jäckel (2002), pp. 77–97 and 111–138.
[11] Caflisch (1998), p. 2.

from 5000 to 20 000 increases the accuracy only by a factor of 2. In most cases, the increase in accuracy is not worth the additional computational effort.

(2) *Transforming random variables to capture the statistical characteristics of the model's input variables*: Investors are usually unable to provide exact point estimates for all input factors of their valuation models. Future revenue growth, operating margins, investment needs and other input factors are uncertain. However, investors can analyze historical distributions of input factors or draw conclusions from past experience. Monte Carlo simulations are typically used if distributions of input factors are more or less well known.[12] Let us assume an investor assumes that an input factor such as the revenue growth rate of a company is normally distributed with a mean μ and a standard deviation σ. The density function of a normal distribution is:

$$f(x) = \frac{1}{\sigma\sqrt{2\pi}} e^{-\frac{(x-\mu)^2}{2\sigma^2}}$$

The normal distribution is a continuous probability distribution widely used by financial economists because of its characteristics described by Abraham DeMoivre and Carl Friedrich Gauss in the eighteenth and nineteenth centuries. The normal distribution is bell shaped and symmetrical about its mean and can be fully described by only two parameters, its mean μ and its standard deviation σ. 68.26% of the area (probability) under the normal curve is included within one standard deviation of the mean, 95.44% within two standard deviations of the mean and 99.74% within three standard deviations. The standard normal distribution is a normal distribution with a mean $\mu = 0$ and a standard deviation of $\sigma = 1$. Provided that $z_1, \ldots, z_n$ standard normally distributed random numbers are generated with a random generator, a normal distribution of n possible realizations of an input factor I can be calculated:

$$I_n = \mu + \sigma z_n$$

For simplicity we assume that the realizations of our input factor I are normally distributed. However, advanced software packages allow investors to choose from a wide range of distributions such as normal, lognormal, uniform, exponential, Weibull, Poisson distributions, etc.[13] Often investors are unable to estimate the parameters of distributions from (a limited number of) historical data, but from experience are able to predict minimum, most likely, and maximum realizations. In these cases they are often best advised to apply simple triangular distributions. The main difference between Monte Carlo FCFF and standard FCFF models is that distributions of possible realizations are used as inputs instead of point estimates. The outcome of a standard FCFF model only reflects the expected fundamental value of a firm. Sometimes, but not always, financial analysts discuss best and worst case scenarios in addition to a most likely scenario in their reports. In contrast to standard FCFF models, Monte Carlo FCFF models show the complete picture: The result of a Monte Carlo simulation is not a single expected fundamental value but the complete probability distribution of all possible fundamental values.[14] Like any other model, the result of a Monte Carlo FCFF model depends on the

---

[12] Jäckel (2002), p. 9.
[13] Jäckel (2002), pp. 9–17, McLeish (2005), pp. 77–162.
[14] Palisade Corporation (2005), p. 29.

quality of its inputs. In the next section we will demonstrate how easy it is to formulate Monte Carlo FCFF models in Excel with @Risk, a widely used software package.

6.2 MONTE CARLO SIMULATION WITH @RISK

In this section we will demonstrate how Excel users can run Monte Carlo simulations to value Baidu's shares with Palisade's @Risk software. @Risk is a sophisticated add-in to Microsoft Excel. The software enables Excel users to run simulations in Excel spreadsheets, an operating environment most people are familiar with. To use @Risk, you first have to install the software. If you do not have @Risk 4.5, you can easily download the software from Palisade's homepage: www.palisade.com. The user guide "@Risk: Guide to Using" explains the full functionality of @Risk in detail. We strongly recommend @Risk's online tutorial. Once @Risk is properly installed, you can start the online tutorial by selecting:

StartMenu/Programs/PalisadeDecisonTools/Tutorial/@RiskTutorial/Risk45.html.

6.2.1 Monte Carlo simulation with one stochastic variable

In our standard FCFF model we used average revenue growth rates g, operating margins m, tax rates τ, and other input factors estimated by leading financial analysts in fall 2005. Table 6.1 shows our standard FCFF model for Baidu.com, Inc. as of June 2007. We updated the data after we met with Baidu's CFO, Shawn Wang, in Frankfurt on June 15, 2007, and used inputs estimated by Morgan Stanley's internet analyst.[15] For the full year 2006, Baidu.com, Inc. generated total revenues amounting to RMB 786 million. Unlike in prior years, Baidu included business taxes and surcharges in costs of revenues instead of netting these charges off against total revenues in 2005.[16] Baidu's revenue growth rates in 2005 and 2006 comfortably exceeded the average top line growth rates estimated by financial analysts in fall 2005. As a result, the intrinsic value jumped dramatically to roughly USD 135 from USD 35. In fall 2005, analysts covering Baidu looked at the company generating USD 13 million *per year*. In 2007, the company produced roughly USD 60 million in revenues *per quarter*. The change in the intrinsic value reflects the transformation of the company. The example shows how sensitive Baidu's fair value is to changes in revenue growth.

Please note that share-based compensation was again added back to adjust operating earnings. As a new or high technology enterprise, Baidu enjoyed substantial tax incentives.[17] Net working capital less cash and cash equivalents declined in the past, mainly because of a strong increase in customer deposits. Like Morgan Stanley, we assumed that Baidu's net working capital will decline until 2015. While net working capital usually increases when a company grows, Baidu benefits from customers helping the company to finance its strong top line growth.

As explained above, the expected present value of future FCFF, or PV(FCFF$_t$), during the competitive advantage period is a function of various inputs:

---

[15] Morgan Stanley (2007b), p. 10, Morgan Stanley (2007a), p. 10.
[16] Baidu.com, Inc. (2006c), p. F-8 and p. 46.
[17] Baidu.com, Inc. (2006c), pp. F-24f.

Table 6.1 Baidu.com, Inc.: updated FCFF model as of June 2007

[In millions of RMB (if not otherwise stated)]	Year 0	1	2	3	4	5	6	7	8	9	10	
For the year ended December 31,	2006	2007E	2008E	2009E	2010E	2011E	2012E	2013E	2014E	2015E	2016E	Broker estimates
Growth in net revenues	163%	96%	64%	48%	36%	29%	25%	23%	21%	17%	13%	
Net revenues	786	1541	2527	3739	5085	6560	8200	10086	12204	14279	16135	Broker estimates
EBIT margin [as % of total revenues]	33%	33%	33%	35%	36%	37%	38%	39%	39%	40%	40%	
EBIT	259	508	834	1309	1831	2427	3116	3934	4760	5712	6454	Broker estimates
Tax on EBIT	12	9	43	215	299	574	728	910	1120	1303	1468	
Tax rate [as % of EBIT]	5%	2%	5%	16%	16%	24%	23%	23%	24%	23%	23%	
EBIT $(1-t)$	247	499	791	1094	1532	1853	2388	3024	3640	4409	4986	Broker estimates
plus share-based compensation	48	63	116	168	269	346	432	531	641	747	847	
EBIT $(1-t)$ adjusted	295	562	907	1262	1801	2199	2820	3555	4281	5156	5833	Broker estimates
D&A	63	164	245	315	368	430	491	554	616	675	729	

Table 6.1 (Continued)

[In millions of RMB (if not otherwise stated)]	Year 0	1	2	3	4	4	6	7	8	9	10	
D&A-to-net revenues	8%	11%	10%	8%	7%	7%	6%	5%	5%	5%	5%	
ΔNWC less cash	90	131	111	100	109	85	64	47	16	(68)	(157)	Broker estimates
ΔNWC less cash-to-net revenues	11%	9%	4%	3%	2%	1%	1%	0%	0%	0%	−1%	
Capex	(194)	(350)	(498)	(660)	(794)	(957)	(1114)	(1268)	(1410)	(1503)	(1545)	Broker estimates
Capex-to-net revenues	−25%	−23%	−20%	−18%	−16%	−15%	−14%	−13%	−12%	−11%	−10%	
FCFF	254	507	765	1017	1484	1757	2261	2888	3503	4260	4860	
Discount factor (WACC):		1.13	1.28	1.44	1.63	1.63	2.08	2.35	2.66	3.00	3.39	
Discounted FCFF		449	599	705	910	1078	1086	1227	1318	1418	1432	
(1) Sum of discounted FCFF		10 221										
(2) Terminal value		24 817										
FCFF in T		1432										
TV growth rate		4%										
TV discount factor (WACC)		10%										
(3) Non operating assets (Cash Q1 2007)		1169										
(4) Long-term debt		0										
Enterprise value (1) + (2) + (3) + (4):		36 207										
RMB/USD		7.72										
Enterprise value in million USD		4690										
Number of shares outstanding (diluted) [in million]		35										
Per share value in USD		135										

(1) expected revenue growth rates g_t,
(2) expected EBIT margins m_t,
(3) expected tax rates τ_t,
(4) expected depreciation & amortization, or $D\&A_t$,
(5) expected changes in net working capital, or ΔNWC_t,
(6) expected capital expenditures, or $Capex_t$,
(7) and the estimated weighted average cost of capital $WACC_t$:

$$PV\,(FCFF_t) = \phi_1\,(g_t,\ m_t,\ \tau_t, D\&A_t,\ \Delta NWC_t,\ Capex_t,\ WACC_t)$$

The terminal value, or TV, represents the value of FCFF after the competitive advantage period. The present value of the terminal value, or PV(TV), is a function of the $FCFF_T$ in the last period T of the competitive advantage period, the WACC during the competitive advantage period, or $WACC_t$, the terminal growth rate g_{TV} and the $WACC_{TV}$ in the stable growth period:

$$PV\,(TV) = \phi_2\,(FCFF_T,\ WACC_t,\ g_{TV},\ WACC_{TV})$$

All of these input factors are highly uncertain. To explain how uncertainty can be incorporated into FCFF models we will assume, initially, that only revenue growth rates g_t are stochastic in nature. All other input factors are still assumed to be deterministic (as shown in Table 6.1). In the standard FCFF we used revenue growth rates of 149%, 70%, 58%, 47%, 36%, 28%, 21%, 18%, 12%, and 10% for the period 2005 to 2014. Of course, in reality even the most knowledgeable analyst does not know with certainty how much revenues will grow in the next 10 years. Formulating a standard FCFF, financial analysts use point estimates as input values. Monte Carlo FCFF models are more realistic than standard FCFF models as probability distributions which describe a range of possible values are used as input values instead of point estimates.

Financial analysts typically use spreadsheets and apply models in discrete time. Revenues are typically assumed to grow in discrete steps, ΔRev_t, over time:[18]

$$Rev_t = Rev_0 + \sum_{t=1}^{n} \Delta Rev_t$$

$$\Delta Rev_t = g_t * Rev_{t-1}$$

Revenue growth rates g_t can be viewed as a set of independent random variables representing draws from a normal distribution with mean μ_t^L and standard deviation σ_t^L:

$$g_t^L = N\,(\mu_t^L, \sigma_t^L)$$

The competitive advantage period, $t = 0, \ldots, T$, is typically decomposed into different stages of a firm's life cycle, $L = 1, \ldots, n$. Stages of high growth are usually followed by periods of more moderate growth.

---

[18] Schwartz and Moon (2000) modeled revenues of internet companies mathematically more elegantly in continuous time and concluded – at the very peak of the internet bubble – that "... depending on the parameters chosen and given high enough growth rates of revenues, the value of an Internet stock may be rational". The quote illustrates that formulating overly sophisticated models does not necessary lead to the right conclusion. Moon and Schwartz (2000), pp. 62 and 74.

Entering probability distributions into Excel models is easy if @Risk is properly installed: Right click on a cell in your spreadsheet and select @*Risk – Define Distribution*. Alternatively, @Risk users can simply click on the "Define Distribution" icon. If we right click on this cell in Excel and choose @*Risk – Define Distribution*, @Risk automatically enters a formula *RiskNormal (mean, standard deviation)* in the selected cell. The @Risk menu allows users to choose from a wide variety of distributions. For illustration purposes, we assume that revenue growth rates are normally distributed and enter 120% and 50% as mean and standard deviation, respectively. On the left hand side of the *Define Distribution* menu, @Risk allows Excel users to enter several arguments. If we enter 95% as *Right P*(robability) value and 5% as *Left P* value, @Risk displays that realized growth rates will vary between 37.8% and 202.2% with a probability of 90% (if a normal distribution with a mean of 120% and a standard deviation of 50% is assumed) (Figure 6.1).

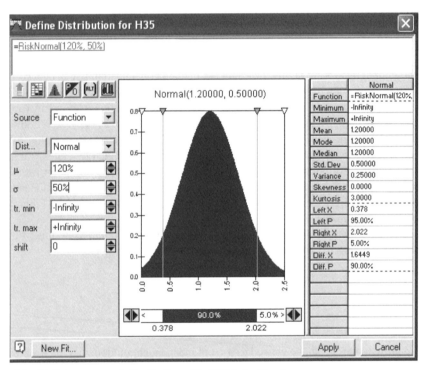

Figure 6.1   Defining a normal distribution with @Risk for Excel

Conceptually, at least two ways exist to define distributions: a *statistical approach* and an *analytical approach*.

(1) *Statistical approach*: Mathematicians have developed statistical tests such as the Anderson Darling test, the Kolmogorov Smirnov test, and the Chi-square test to test if a sample of data originates from a specific distribution. A mathematician would most likely download historical revenues from a trusted source like Bloomberg or Datastream, calculate historical growth rates, and test if historical growth rates follow a specific distribution, for example a normal distribution. If the hypothesis of an underlying normal distribution

is not rejected at a given significance, a mathematician would assume that the sample data is normally distributed and estimate the first two parameters, the mean and the standard deviation, which fully describe a normal distribution.

Unfortunately, in reality financial analysts can often download only a limited amount of meaningful historical data. Historical data is not meaningful, for example, if companies change their business model, restructure, merge with or acquire other companies. For Baidu.com, Inc., only a few data points exist as the company was founded in January 2000.[19] Historical data is also not necessarily representative of the future as revenues, earnings and investment needs depend on the life cycle of a company. Baidu is in a very nascent stage of its life cycle. It is highly unrealistic to believe that Baidu will grow its sales at the same rates as in the past for an extended period of time. Revenues, earnings, and investment needs are also influenced by business cycles. Investors are therefore well advised to differentiate between different stages of a company's life cycle and analyze data, if possible, over complete business cycles.

(2) *Analytical approach*: Financial analysts usually make forecasts not only on the basis of historical data. They usually include past experience and economic insights in their forecasts. Analysts typically visualize historical realizations of input factors in the form of graphs and tables. Visualization helps to better understand how future realizations could *possibly* look. Table 6.2 displays the annual revenue growth rates of Chinese internet companies listed on the NASDAQ National Market.[20]

For comparison, we included the revenue growth rates of Google and Yahoo!. Table 6.2 illustrates that initial high growth periods are usually followed by periods of more moderate growth. The dispersion of growth rates was high for all companies.

Investors typically do not only analyze historical data but also consider a wide range of non-sample information and analyze variables which drive the input factors of their models. To understand business models and industry dynamics, institutional investors meet with managements of companies and sector specialists of investment banks. In Chapter 5 we discussed the *revenue growth driver approach*. Baidu's future revenue growth is driven by factors such as the number of active online customers and average online marketing revenues per active online marketing customer, the expected growth of the Chinese online advertising market and the company's market share.

Some investors argue that forecasting input factors is more an art than a science. Latent ambiguity is arguably the biggest drawback of the analytical approach. Financial analysts typically compare specific companies with a more or less well-defined peer group of companies. Selected peer groups are not necessarily representative for specific companies. Baidu.com, Inc., Sina Corp., Sohu.com, Inc., Netease.com, Inc. and Shanda Interactive Entertainment Ltd. are all Chinese internet companies listed on NASDAQ. However, Baidu is a search engine like Google. Sina, Sohu and Netease are portals offering a wide range of online and e-commerce services and Shanda operates online games in China. In addition, peer groups usually only consist of listed companies which still exist. Peer groups are therefore prone to what financial economists call "survivorship bias". Companies that went out of business are usually not included in peer groups.[21] In the early 1990s, Google competed with companies

---

[19] Baidu.com, Inc. (2005a), p. 1.
[20] In practice financial analysts also monitor quarterly data. Annual data is provided here to save space.
[21] Underperformance is only one of several reasons why companies no longer exist. Companies are often delisted from stock exchanges as a result of acquisitions and mergers.

Table 6.2 Revenue growth rates of a peer group of companies (source: Bloomberg)

in USD million Year ending	Baidu.com, Inc. (BIDU) Revenues	Revenue growth	Sina Corp. (SINA) Revenues	Revenue growth	Sohu.com, Inc. (SOHU) Revenues	Revenue growth	Netease.com, Inc. (NTES) Revenues	Revenue growth	Shanda Interactive Entertainment Ltd (SNDA) Revenues	Revenue growth	Google, Inc. (GOOG) Revenues	Revenue growth	Yahoo!, Inc. (YHOO) Revenues	Revenue growth
31.12.2006	105.1	166%	213	10%	134	28%	277	39%	212	−10%	10605	73%	6426	22%
31.12.2005	39.6	195%	194	−3%	105	1%	200	83%	235	50%	6139	92%	5258	47%
31.12.2004	13.4		200	75%	103	28%	109	67%	157	116%	3189	118%	3575	120%
31.12.2003			114	194%	80	180%	66	145%	72		1466	234%	1625	71%
31.12.2002			39	46%	29	121%	27	749%			440	409%	953 07	33%
31.12.2001			27	88%	13	118%	3	−15%			86	352%	717	−35%
31.12.2000			14	401%	6	268%	4	95%			19	8585%	1110	88%
31.12.1999			3	13%	2	243%	2				0		592	141%
31.12.1998			3		2	243%							245	248%
31.12.1997					0								70	258%
31.12.1996													20	1345%
31.12.1995													1	

Table 6.3 Revenue Growth Forecasts[22]

[in RMB million]

| | Goldman Sachs | | Morgan Stanley | | Distribution | Own estimates | | | | | |
| | 27-Apr-07 | | 27-Apr-07 | | | parameter 1 | | parameter 2 | | parameter 3 | |
						type	value	type	value	type	value
2007–2009											
2007	1545	97%	1539	96%	triangular	min	80%	most likely	100%	max	120%
2008	2694	74%	2526	64%	triangular	min	30%	most likely	70%	max	110%
2009	3921	46%	3728	48%	triangular	min	20%	most likely	60%	max	100%
2010–2012											
2010	–	–	5057	36%							
2011	–	–	6504	29%							
2012	–	–	8125	25%	normal	mean	25%	standard deviation	25%		
2013–2016											
2013	–	–	9979	23%							
2014	–	–	12048	21%							
2015	–	–	14039	17%							
2016	–	–	15917	13%	normal	mean	20%	standard deviation	40%		

[22]Goldman Sachs (2006), Morgan Stanley (2006).

like Alta Vista, Excite, WebCrawler, Lycos, Magellan, Infoseek and HotBot. Most of these companies still exist; however, none of these companies was as successful as Google.[23] The Magellans of the world are usually not part of a peer group. The future will show if Baidu is really the "Google of China".

Table 6.3 displays our revenue growth assumptions. We differentiated between three growth periods: an explicit period (2007–2009), a high growth period (2010–2012) and a period of more moderate growth (2013–2016). Financial analysts typically update their models when companies report results or other relevant information emerges. We compared our revenue estimates with updated forecasts from Goldman Sachs and Morgan Stanley produced in April 2007 after Baidu reported results for the first quarter 2007.

Analysts at investment banks typically use point estimates over multi-year periods. We disagree with this practice. Forecasts over multi-year periods are highly uncertain. The historical dispersion of revenue growth rates of internet companies was high in the past. It is not unusual for internet companies that the standard deviation of growth rates exceeds the mean by a factor of 2.

Investors typically do not think in terms of point estimates, but in ranges of possible values and have an intuitive understanding of minimum, most likely, as well as maximum values. Some investors prefer triangular distributions to normal distributions. To enter a triangular distribution, @Risk users have to select *triang*(ular) instead of *normal* in the *Define Distribution* menu and define minimum, most likely, as well as maximum values. @Risk translates the inputs into a function *RiskTriang(minimum, most likely, maximum)*, when the user selects *Apply*.

@Risk requires that all cells are properly identified. The desired output cell of our Monte Carlo simulation is the intrinsic value per share. To identify an output, select the output cell, click on the "Add Output" icon and define an "output cell name" like "fundamental value". @Risk automatically enters a function in the selected cell: *RiskOutput("fundamental value")* (Figure 6.2).

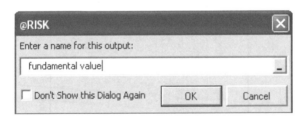

Figure 6.2   Defining output cells with @Risk for Excel

Once all distribution functions have been entered and all outputs identified, simulation settings must be specified by clicking on the "Simulation Settings" icon. We want to run a *Monte Carlo* simulation with *5000 iterations* (Figure 6.3).

Once *Monte Carlo* is activated in the *Simulation Settings* menu, Excel recalculates the spreadsheet each time the user presses the F9 key by drawing possible realizations from the specified input distributions. Fortunately, users do not have to hit the F9 key thousands of times, but simply click on the "Start Simulation" icon to run a Monte Carlo simulation.

---

[23] The "Google Story" is vividly narrated in Vise (2005).

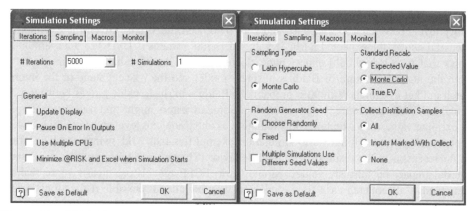

Figure 6.3   @Risk Simulation Settings

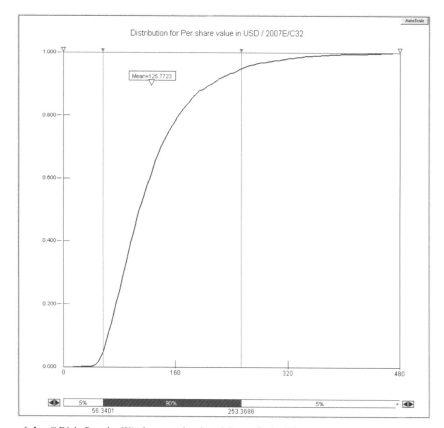

Figure 6.4   @Risk *Results Window* – univariate Monte Carlo FCFF model

The @Risk *Results Window* offers a wide variety of options to display simulation results. Figure 6.4 displays the result of a simulation with 5000 iterations. To chart a cumulative distribution select *Graph – Graph Type – Ascending Cumulative – Line* in the @Risk *Results Window*.

The cumulative distribution shows possible fundamental values on the x-axis and probability levels between 100% (1.000) and 0% (0.000) on the y-axis. Given the assumptions discussed above, the expected intrinsic value of Baidu's shares is USD 125. Our simulation shows that investors should expect huge fluctuations in Baidu's share price in the future given the uncertain nature of Baidu's business model and the nascent stage of the internet search market in China. With 90% probability, Baidu's intrinsic value ranges between USD 56 and USD 253 according to our simulation. Some investors might find it useful to employ the extreme values of a Monte Carlo simulation as entry and exit levels when making investment decisions. Our Monte Carlo simulation exemplifies that wild swings in share prices are not necessarily the result of irrational behavior. Changes of input variables can have a material impact on intrinsic values. Monte Carlo FCFF models are clearly more realistic than standard discounted cash flow models as they include all possible realizations instead of a single "target price". Monte Carlo FCFF models force investors to think in terms of probabilities and help them to make more informed decisions. In reality, not only revenue growth rates but also operating margins, capital expenditures and other input variables are uncertain. In the next section we therefore discuss Monte Carlo FCFF models with several stochastic variables.

6.2.2   Monte Carlo simulation with several stochastic variables

The present value of future cash flows during the competitive advantage period is a function of several input factors:

$$PV\ (FCFF) = \phi_1\ (g_t,\ m_t,\ \tau_t,\ D\&A_t,\ \Delta NWC_t,\ CAPEX_t,\ WACC_t)$$

In section 6.2.1 we have simulated possible realizations of Baidu's future revenue growth rates g. However, in reality not only expected revenue growth rates g but also adjusted EBIT margins m, expected tax rates τ, expected depreciation and amortization as well as future capital expenditures, changes in net working capital and weighted average cost of capital are uncertain. Palisade's @Risk software enables Excel users to build probabilistic models with several stochastic variables. Building a model with several stochastic variables is time consuming as the distributions for each stochastic variable must be defined separately.

Unfortunately, stochastic variables are often not independent. Building realistic Monte Carlo FCFF models requires including the dependence between input variables in the valuation model. Above we have argued that causal relationships exist between our variables. Two relationships are most important:

(1) *Dependence between growth rates and margins*: When revenues grow, expected operating margins often increase as a result of declining average unit costs. Economies of scale result, for example, from lower overhead costs per unit of production, learning effects and more efficient use of technology, capital and labor.

(2) *Dependence between growth rates and investment needs*: A company that wants to grow its revenues usually has to invest in property, plant and equipment and in net working capital such as inventory and receivables. As a result, on the one hand revenue growth rates, capital expenditures and change in net working capital are usually not independent. Clearly, investment needs depend on a firm's business model. A semiconductor company has to invest billions of USD to build a new plant. The business model of a software company, on the other hand, is usually more scalable and requires less investment to grow revenue.

Building a realistic Monte Carlo FCFF model relies on the ability of financial analysts to assess not only the distributions of all input variables but also the dependencies between them. Financial analysts can visualize possible dependence between two stochastic variables, X and Y, by plotting sets of historical realizations (x_i, y_i) on a scatter diagram. Most financial analysts are familiar with correlation coefficients. Correlation – and covariance – measure the degree of linear dependence between two random variables X and Y. Pearson product-moment covariance is defined as:

$$\mathrm{cov}\,(X, Y) = E\,(XY) - E\,(X)\,E\,(Y)$$

If $E(X)$, $E(Y)$ and $\mathrm{var}(X) = \sigma_x^2$, $\mathrm{var}(Y) = \sigma_y^2$ are the expected values and variances of two random variables X and Y, respectively, the linear product-moment correlation r is defined as:

$$r = \frac{\mathrm{cov}\,(X, Y)}{\sigma_x \sigma_y} = \frac{E\,[(X - E\,(X))\,(Y - E\,(Y))]}{\sqrt{E\left[(X - E\,(X))^2\right] E\left[(Y - E\,(Y))^2\right]}}$$

The correlation coefficient ranges in values from -1 to $+1$. $r = +1$ if two variables are perfectly positively correlated, $r = -1$ if two variables are perfectly negatively correlated. Alternatively, the absolute value of the correlation coefficient r can be computed as the square root of the coefficient of determination R^2 which measures the proportion of the total variation in Y explained by a regression of Y on X. If the independent variable X in the linear regression $Y = \alpha + \beta X$ explains 100% of the variation in the dependent variable $Y(R^2 = 1)$, it follows that $r = +1$ if $\beta > 0$ (and $r = -1$ if $\beta < 0$). The correlation coefficient r is a measure of *linear* dependence. Pearson product-moment correlation does not capture non-linear dependence and does not imply causality.[24]

A related number is Spearman's rank order correlation coefficient r_S. Spearman's rank order correlation is typically used when precise data is not attainable. Let n be the number of x_i values and corresponding y_i values. To calculate Spearman's rank order correlations, the x and y values are first ranked in order of their size. Each x_i and y_i is given a rank $j = 1, \ldots, n$ according to its size. If $d_{ij} = j_x - j_y$ are the deviations between the ranks of sets of (x_i, y_i) pairs, Spearman's rank order correlation r_s is given by:[25]

$$r_S = 1 - \frac{6 \sum d_{ij}^2}{n\,(n^2 - 1)}$$

Scientists have argued that it is important to include correlations in Monte Carlo simulations rather than assuming that variables are independent. Correlations can be ignored if linear dependence is weak, if variables have little influence on the outcome or if variables are more or less certain.[26] Incorporating correlations into FCFF models requires that correlation coefficients can be assessed reliably. Correlation coefficients can change over time. Analyzing the causal relationship between variables is a prerequisite of a good economic model.

Financial analysts often estimate future capex-to-sales, ΔNWC-to-sales and D&A-to-sales ratios instead of absolute capital expenditures, change in net working capital and depreciation

[24] Spiegel et al. (2000), pp. 278–327.
[25] Spiegel et al. (2000), pp. 285 and 307–309.
[26] Clemen and Reilly (1999), p. 220.

and amortization levels. Companies can usually grow sales only if they invest in property, plant and equipment and in net working capital. As a result revenues and investments (capital expenditures and change in net working capital) are typically correlated. However, the capex-to-sales, ΔNWC-to-sales and D&A-to-sales ratios are usually more stable over time and less dependent on a company's revenue growth rate. As a result, the correlation between capex-to-sales, ΔNWC-to-sales and D&A-to-sales ratios, on the one hand, and revenue growth rates, on the other hand, is typically very low. We therefore used the following formula to estimate expected FCFF:

$$
\begin{aligned}
\mathrm{FCFF}_t^e = & \left[(\mathrm{Rev}_{t-1} \times (1 + g_t^e)) \times \frac{\mathrm{EBIT}_t^e}{\mathrm{Rev}_t^e} \right] \times (1 - \tau_t^e) \\
& + \left[\frac{\mathrm{D\&A}_t^e}{\mathrm{Rev}_t} - \frac{\mathrm{Capex}_t^e}{\mathrm{Rev}_t} - \frac{\Delta \mathrm{NWC}_t^e}{\mathrm{Rev}_t} \right] \times (\mathrm{Rev}_{t-1} \times (1 + g_t^e)) \pm \mathrm{Adj}
\end{aligned}
$$

The formula is helpful as it "automatically" captures the dependence between revenue growth and investment needs. Using the modified FCFF formula saves a lot of time as the correlation between revenues, on the one hand, and capex-to-sales, ΔNWC-to-sales and D&A-to-sales ratios, on the other hand, is usually very low and can therefore be ignored when formulating Monte Carlo FCFF models.

However, the FCFF formula does not capture the dependence between revenues and margins. It is well known that operating margins typically increase when revenues grow as a result of declining average unit costs ("economies of scale"). @Risk enables Excel users to specify a correlation matrix to capture the pairwise correlations between stochastic variables. Creating a Monte Carlo FCFF model typically requires two steps. First, the distributions for each stochastic variable must be defined. @Risk users can define distributions in the *Define-Distribution* menu. The second step is to specify pairwise correlations. Using @Risk, financial analysts can specify correlations in the *Model Definition Window*. Alternatively, RiskCorrmat() functions can be added to formulas of variables.

@Risk uses a process of rearranging random numbers to induce Spearman's rank order correlation. The method for pairing realizations of independent random variables to induce Spearman's rank order correlation was originally developed by Iman and Conover (1982). Using rearranged sets of paired random numbers ensures that realizations are drawn from correlated distributions. The method leaves the marginal distributions of inputs unchanged and may be used with any type of distribution, i.e. it is a distribution-free approach.[27] Alternatively, so-called copulas can be used to capture the dependence between two variables X and Y. The copula method allows users to specify marginal distributions for stochastic variables and a matrix quantifying pairwise dependences between input variables.[28]

Financial analysts using sophisticated statistical packages like @Risk can incorporate dependencies between input variables into FCFF models without much effort. However, estimating meaningful correlations is difficult if only a few data points are available for single stocks. Calculating correlation coefficients for a peer group of companies operating in the same industry helps financial analysts to better understand industry specific dependencies between inputs such as revenue growth rates and operating margins.[29]

---

[27] Palisade Corporation (2006), Iman and Conover (1982).
[28] Jäckel (2002), pp. 42–57, Clemen and Reilly (1999), p. 209.
[29] Correlation is usually not constant over time and can be viewed as a stochastic process evolving over time. Financial analysts typically apply multivariate GARCH and similar stochastic models in derivatives research. Theoretically, the same approach could be used to model correlation between two sets of fundamental data. Mezrich and Engle (1996).

The Excel sheet *Baidu.xls*[30] reveals our distribution assumptions for all stochastic variables. We compared our forecasts with point estimates made by Morgan Stanley in April 2007.[31] Specifying correlations between stochastic variables is simple if @Risk is properly installed on your PC. To enter a correlation matrix:

(1) Click on the *Display List of Outputs and Inputs* icon to open @Risk's *Model Window*.
(2) Hold the Ctrl key and select the inputs you want to correlate.
(3) Click on the *Define Correlation* icon or right click *Correlate Distributions* to open a correlation matrix.
(4) Enter the desired correlation coefficients in the correlation matrix. Give the matrix a name such as *margins_revgrowth* so that you can identify the matrix later in @Risk's *Model Window*. Click *Apply*.

@Risk automatically enters *RiskCorrmat()* functions to the distribution functions of the selected stochastic variables. To edit the correlation matrix, right click on the correlation matrix in @Risk's *Model Window*. (Figure 6.5)[32]

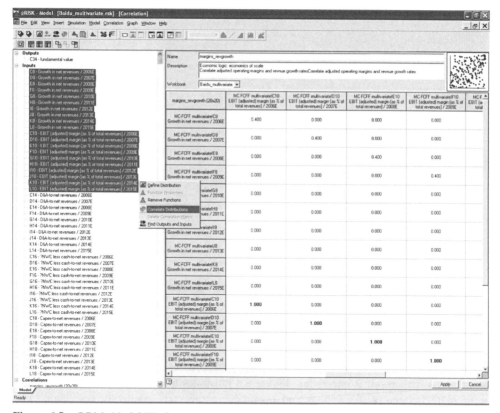

Figure 6.5   @Risk *Model Window*

---

[30] You can download the Excel sheet *Baidu.xls* from our webpage: www.wiley.com/go/equityvaluation.

[31] Morgan Stanley (2007b). Goldman Sachs did not report sufficient long-term forecasts in its company update dated April 27, 2007, which could have been used for comparison. Goldman Sachs (2007).

[32] It is well known that revenues and operating margins are not independent because of economies of scale. We estimated the correlation between revenue growth rates and operating margins in one period, but assumed that the serial correlations of our two input factors over time are zero.

The Excel spreadsheet *Baidu.xls* reflects our assumptions. Operating margins usually increase when revenues grow as a result of economies of scale. We assumed that all other stochastic variables are independent from each other as the correlations between these variables have been negligible in the past. Figure 6.6 displays the result of our Monte Carlo simulation with several stochastic variables and 5000 iterations.

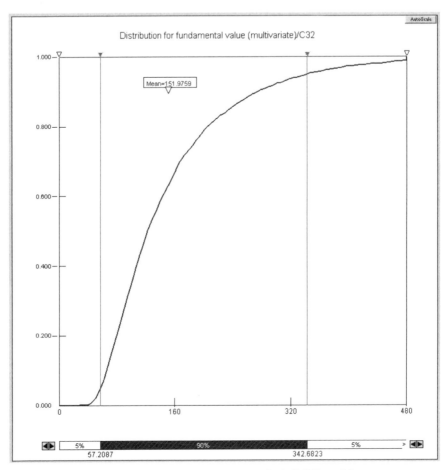

Figure 6.6   @Risk *Results Window* – multivariate Monte Carlo FCFF model

The expected fundamental value of one share of Baidu.com, Inc. is USD 152 given our assumptions. This result is interesting. Figure 6.6 illustrates that extremely high realizations occur more frequently if revenues and operating margins are positively correlated. The figure also shows that substantial upside *potential* for the shares of Baidu.com, Inc. still exists. According to our simulation, the price targets of most investment banks – shown in Table 5.14 – are still conservative.

Modeling fair values helps investors to understand how sensitive intrinsic values are to input changes. We considered different scenarios. The expected intrinsic value per share falls from USD 152 to USD 131 if weighted average cost of capital increases from 13%

to 15%.[33] We followed analysts' conventions and added share-based compensation back to operating earnings. Share-based compensation is an economic cost to shareholders. Like adverse changes in the tax treatment, the dilution effect of share-based compensation was not incorporated in our model.

As discussed above, one of the most important economic propositions states that return on capital fades to cost of capital over time under competition. Analysts at Morgan Stanley implicitly assumed in April 2007 that Baidu's return on invested capital will stay high over the entire forecast period and that Baidu's net working capital will continue to decrease until 2015. Our Monte Carlo FCFF model implies decreasing net working capital, high capital turnover ratios and high ROIC, too. If Baidu's management decides that the company has to invest more in property, plant and equipment or in net working capital to stay competitive, Baidu's favorable capital turnover ratios, its fair value per share and most likely its share price will be adversely affected. Baidu announced that it plans to spend USD 15 million, approximately 8% of its expected revenues in 2007, to enter the Japanese search market. The Japanese search market is dominated by two large players, Yahoo!Japan and Google accounting for 65% and 35% of the market, respectively. The payback of this investment is highly uncertain. If Baidu decides to heavily invest in Japan, its margins and capital turnover ratios will be negatively affected.[34]

Baidu.com, Inc. is an extreme example. The Chinese online market is at a very nascent stage and growing fast. But it is clearly not an isolated case. From the perspective of an equity investor, uncertainty is the rule not the exception. Future realizations of key input variables which go into valuation models can usually not be predicted with certainty. We incorporated the nature of their uncertainty into our valuation model by defining probability distributions reflecting the range and the likelihood of the possible realizations of our input variables. Properly used, Monte Carlo free cash flow models can be useful to investors. The result of a Monte Carlo FCFF model is more realistic than price targets commonly used by most analysts. Monte Carlo FCFF models show the complete picture of all possible outcomes and force investors to think in terms of probability.

6.3   DISCLAIMER

The purpose of Parts I and II of this book is to give an introduction to discounted cash flow models, to explain the economic logic behind the models and to present hands-on examples which illustrate how financial analysts at leading investment banks value stocks. Our intention is, and was, not to provide investment advice. Please do not make investment decisions based on the information presented above:

(1) One of the authors and his employer, an affiliate of Deutsche Bank, do business that relates to companies covered in this book. He buys and (short) sells shares of companies mentioned in this book for various hedge funds and for his personal account. Please assume that conflicts of interest may exist. In fact, you should always assume that investment professionals are guided by self-interest when they write or talk about investments.

---

[33] Risk premia and cost of capital are not constant over time. In Part VIII, Varmaz *et al.* show that fair values can change dramatically if the risk aversion of investors is instable.
[34] Evolution Securities China (2007), pp. 20f, Morgan Stanley (2007b), pp. 6–9.

(2) Never confuse fair values with market prices. We discussed discounted cash flow models to estimate fundamental, intrinsic or fair values. Fundamental values are based on the premise that a company will employ its assets to generate cash flows, will continue its operations and will not liquidate its assets. In reality, the going-concern assumption does not always hold. It is entirely possible that a (strategic) investor will buy Baidu.com (or another company mentioned) and pay a control premium in excess of the expected fair values discussed above. Investors constantly buy and sell shares above or below intrinsic values. Human beings do not act rationally when they make investment decisions. Greedy people constantly buy assets at inflated prices hoping that someone else is stupid enough to pay an even higher price. Anxious people permanently sell shares at distressed levels. After losing a fortune when the South Sea Bubble collapsed, Isaac Newton admitted: "I can calculate the motions of heavenly bodies, but not the madness of people."[35] We believe that shares are priced efficiently in competitive markets in the long run. However, John Maynard Keynes was right when he warned that "the market can stay irrational longer than you can stay solvent".

(3) A valuation is never objective and never timeless. Financial analysts formulate subjective expectations in an uncertain world. Discounted cash flow models are helpful tools to translate subjective expectations into fair values and to analyze value drivers of stocks in a structured way. Smart investors change their forecasts when new information emerges. John Maynard Keynes once allegedly replied to a critic: "When the facts change, I change my mind. What do you do, Sir?" Well, this book was written in 2006/2007. When new information becomes available we will change our forecasts.

---

[35] Isaac Newton, quoted in Malkiel (1990), p. 42.

References

Baidu.com, Inc. (2005a), Prospectus, dated August 4, 2005.

Baidu.com, Inc. (2005b), Baidu announces unaudited results for second quarter of 2005, continued growth and focused investments in Chinese search, August 23, 2005.

Baidu.com, Inc. (2005c), Baidu announces financial results for third quarter of 2005, company reports stronger than expected revenue growth following successful IPO, October 26, 2005.

Baidu.com, Inc. (2006a), Baidu announces fourth quarter and fiscal year 2005 results, company expanded market share in China's rapidly growing search market, February 21, 2006.

Baidu.com, Inc. (2006b), Baidu announces first quarter 2006 results, strong revenue and earnings growth continues, May 9, 2006.

Baidu.com, Inc. (2006c), Form 20-F, filed: June 21, 2006 (period: December 31, 2005).

Baidu.com, Inc. (2006d), Baidu announces second quarter 2006 results, significant growth in customer base and user traffic drives strong revenue and earnings, July 26, 2006.

Baidu.com, Inc. (2006e), Baidu announces third quarter 2006 results, net income increases by over 900% year-over-year, October 31, 2006.

Baidu.com, Inc. (2007a), Baidu announces fourth quarter and full year 2006 results, 2006 annual net income grows 534% year-over-year, February 14, 2007.

Baidu.com, Inc. (2007b), Baidu announces first quarter 2007 results, net income grows 143% year-over-year, April 26, 2007.

Baidu.com, Inc. (2007c), Form 20-F, filed: May 30, 2007 (period: December 31, 2006).

Bloomberg (2006a), Baidu reports 1st-qtr profit surges as sales triple (Update2), May 9, 2006.

Bloomberg (2006b), Baidu shares fall after forecast misses expectations (Update2), July 27, 2006.

Bloomberg (2006c), Baidu third quarter net rises on advertising sales (Update3), November 1, 2006.

Bloomberg (2007a), Baidu quarterly profit rises fivefold on ad sales (Update2), February 14, 2007.

Bloomberg (2007b), Baidu, Microsoft, SanDisk, Sierra, Varian: U.S. Equity Preview, April 26, 2007.

Boyle, P.P. (1977), Options: a Monte Carlo approach, *Journal of Financial Economics*, 4, 323–338.

Caflisch, R.R. (1998), Monte Carlo and quasi-Monte Carlo methods, *Acta Numerica*, 1–49.

Clemen, R.T., and Reilly, T. (1999), Correlations and copulas for decision and risk analysis, *Management Science*, February, 208–224.

Credit Suisse First Boston (2005), Baidu, In search of excellence, Research Report by Wallance Cheung *et al.*, September 22, 2005.

Eckhardt, R. (1987), Stan Ulam, John von Neumann, and the Monte Carlo method, *Los Alamos Science*, Special Issue, 131–137.

Evolution Securities China (2007), Baidu, Research Report by Wendy Huang, June 13, 2007.

Goldman Sachs (2005), Baidu.com, Inc. (BIDU), Research Report by Anthony Noto *et al.*, September 14, 2005.

Goldman Sachs (2006), Company update, Baidu.com, Inc. (BIDU), No upside to revenue and the lock-up will likely pressure shares, Research Note by Anthony Noto *et al.*, July 27, 2006.

Goldman Sachs (2007), Company update, Baidu.com, Inc. (BIDU), Research Note by Anthony Noto *et al.*, April 27, 2007.

Iman, R.L., and Conover W.J. (1982), A distribution-free approach to inducing rank correlation among input variables, *Communications in Statistics*, Vol. 11(3), 311–334.

Jäckel, P. (2002), *Monte Carlo Methods in Finance*, John Wiley & Sons.

Keynes, J.M. (1997), *The General Theory of Employment, Interest, and Money*, Originally published 1936, Prometheus Books.

Kieso, D.E., Weygandt, J.J., and Warfield, T.D. (2004), *Intermediate Accounting*, Eleventh Edition, John Wiley & Sons.

Lang, M. (2004), *Employee Stock Options and Equity Valuation*, The Research Foundation of CFA Institute.

Malkiel, B.G. (1990), *A Random Walk Down Wall Street*, Fifth Edition, Norton.

McLeish, Don L. (2005), *Monte Carlo Simulation and Finance*, John Wiley & Sons.

Metropolis, N. (1987), The beginning of the Monte Carlo method, *Los Alamos Science*, Special Issue, 125–130.

Metropolis, N., and Ulam, S. (1949), The Monte Carlo method, *Journal of the American Statistical Association*, September, 335–341.

Mezrich, J.J., and Engle, R. (1996), How to model correlation; GARCH for groups, Salomon Brothers, Derivatives Research, October.

Miller, M.H., and Modigliani, F. (1961), Dividend policy, growth, and the valuation of shares, *The Journal of Business*, October, 411–433.

Modigliani, F., and Miller, M.H. (1958), The cost of capital, corporation finance and the theory of investment, *The American Economic Review*, June, 261–297.

Morgan Stanley (2005), Baidu.com, Inc., A high class puzzle as high growth meets high price, Research Note by Richard Ji and Jenny Wu, October 27, 2005.

Morgan Stanley (2006), Baidu.com, Inc., 2Q06: When the expectation is sky-high . . . , Research Note by Richard Ji and Jenny Wu, July 27, 2006.

Morgan Stanley (2007a), Baidu.com, Inc., 4Q06: Upgrading to EW-V on softening competition, Research Note by Richard Ji and Jenny Wu, February 15, 2007.

Morgan Stanley (2007b), Baidu.com, Inc., 1Q07: Vigorous outlook ex-cloudy Japanese venture, Research Note by Richard Ji, Jenny Wu and Philip Wan, July 27, 2006.

Mulford, C.W., and Comiskey, E.E. (2002), *The Financial Numbers Game, Detecting Creative Accounting Practices*, John Wiley & Sons.

Palisade Corporation (2005), *@Risk, Guide to Using, Risk Analysis and Simulation Add-In for Microsoft Excel, Version 4.5*, June.

Palisade Corporation (2006), How @Risk creates correlation between inputs – RiskCorrmat() function, http://helpdesk.palisade.com/kb/article.asp?ID=643

PiperJaffray (2005), Baidu.com, Inc., Company note by Safa Rashtchy and Aaron M. Kessler, September 14, 2005.

Porter, M.E. (1998), *Competitive Advantage: Creating and Sustaining Superior Performance, With a New Introduction*, Free Press.

Savage, S.L. (1998), *Insight.xla, Business Analysis Software for Microsoft Excel*, Duxbury Press.

Schilit, H.M. (2002), *Financial Shenanigans, How to Detect Accounting Gimmicks & Fraud in Financial Reports*, Second Edition, McGraw-Hill.

Schwartz, E.S., and Moon, M. (2000), Rational pricing of internet companies, *Financial Analysts Journal*, May/June, 62–75.

Spiegel, M.R., Schiller, J., and Srinivasan, R.A. (2000), *Schaum's Outline of Theory and Problems of Probability and Statistics*, Second Edition, McGraw Hill.

Soliman, M.T. (2004), Using industry-adjusted DuPont analysis to predict future profitability, First draft: May 2002, This version: February.

Stewart, G.B. (1999), *The Quest for Value*, Second Edition, HarperCollins Publishers.

Stigler, G.J. (1963), *Capital and Rates of Return in Manufacturing Industries, A Study by the National Bureau of Economic Research*, Princeton University Press.

Swartz, M. (2004), *Power Failure, The Inside Story of the Collapse of Enron*, Mimi Swartz with Sherron Watkins, First Currency Paperback Edition, April.

Ulam, S.M. (1991), *Adventures of a Mathematician*, Third Edition, University of California Press.

Vise, D.A. (2005), *The Google Story*, Macmillan.

Part III

Beyond Earnings: A User's Guide to Excess Return Models and the HOLT CFROI® Framework[1]

Tom Larsen[2] and David Holland[3]

[1] Credit Suisse Securities, © 2008 David Holland.
[2] Head of Research, Harding Loevner Management, previously Senior Policy Analyst at CFA Institute.
[3] Managing Director at Credit Suisse and co-head of the HOLT Valuation & Analytics Group.

7
Introduction[1]

There is no greater enemy of stock market allocation efficiency than earnings obsession.[2]

While Wall Street feeds on its quarterly earnings obsession, the market, which represents the aggregate opinion of all investors, looks beyond this accounting figure and focuses on assessing the economic performance, or actual cash generation, of companies and industries. If this were not the case, the astute analyst who based his investment decisions on cash flow valuation should be able to systematically beat the market. Since the market is notoriously difficult to beat, it seems reasonable to assume that at least some form of market efficiency encompasses economic performance evaluation.

Although the value of a firm should reflect the present value of the firm's future free cash flow,[3] analysts often act as if earnings are a reliable, quarterly proxy for current cash flow. Is this sensible? A monochromatic focus on earnings ignores the fact that the earnings number is the result of many accounting assumptions that encompass all the financial statements: Income, balance sheet and cash flow. Earnings are normally very different from economic value and free cash flow. The quickest way to pump up earnings is to cut R&D or marketing expenses. Although earnings would dramatically jump, the market would see through this trick and punish the firm for short-circuiting its future. This is where accounting and economics collide.

While the assessment of economic performance starts with the accounting numbers, it must also include the economic effects of the accounting decisions. As recent history has shown, accounting decisions by management may reflect opportunities for earnings enhancement at the expense of value creating economic opportunities.[4] A sound framework should incorporate accounting adjustments to reflect more accurately the economic reality of the firm and its management decisions. If cash flow represents economic honesty and the truth, earnings represent Cerberus guarding the gates of Hades.

So what are the hallmarks of a sound economic performance and valuation model?

- It should systematically identify and remove accounting distortions so that the performance measure mirrors the firm's underlying economics as closely as possible. An accounting model that captures economic reality should start with the firm's assets and liabilities. Income statement items are accounting constructs. Accounting and economic decisions

[1] The authors would like to thank Raymond Stokes, David Reeder and Greg Collett of HOLT for their invaluable assistance reading this part for content and fact checking for errors. Any remaining errors are the responsibility of the authors.
[2] Rappaport (2005).
[3] Under US GAAP and IFRS accounting standards there is no standard definition of free cash flow. However, regardless of definition, most commentators would agree that the future cash flows of the firm form the basis of its value. We will define the cash flows for the CFROI and EP models in this part.
[4] Some of the more notorious examples of putting accounting ahead of economics include Enron, WorldCom, Waste Management, Ahold, and Parmalat.

have become so confused that it is difficult to separate the two although hints often show up as changes in accruals on the balance sheet. On the other hand, some decisions, such as leasing, only place the expense on the income statement, effectively removing the financing decision and asset from the balance sheet. We will show that Cash Flow Return on Investment (CFROI) reverses many accounting distortions and places hidden assets back on the balance sheet.

- The performance measure should mirror standard economic analysis used to evaluate projects and value their anticipated cash flow. It should account for differences between non-depreciating assets and depreciating assets, and take into account asset life. We will show that CFROI is a cross-sectional weighted-average IRR measure. We will also show how the CFROI valuation model reconciles to project economics.

- Inflationary effects should be removed from the performance measure so that results are comparable over time, across borders and across industries. Although inflation is at modest levels in many developed economies in the world today, it has been and remains a distortion. Without adjusting for inflation, trend analysis across years and over borders becomes meaningless. Inflation artificially boosts earnings and accounting returns, which can lead to uneconomic results and decisions. CFROI is a real measure.

- The valuation model should be focused on determining the present value of future cash flow. Cash is king and the only true measure of a firm's value is based on its future cash flow potential. The HOLT CFROI valuation model is a discounted cash flow (DCF) model which allows the flexing of value drivers such as growth, returns and competitive advantage period.

- Competitive forces drive and thrive in market economies. An industrial life cycle should be incorporated into the valuation model to reflect the fact that fortune and high returns fade over time. A key component of the HOLT CFROI valuation model is the notion of an industrial life cycle.

- The overall approach should provide a structured, economic way of thinking and focus on real drivers of value. The HOLT CFROI framework is a total system approach that enables users to compare historical performance to market expectations in an efficient, comprehensive manner. Because CFROI is a real return, it is possible to compare historical returns vs. forecast returns to perform plausibility tests and calibrate investor expectations. It is also possible to compare CFROI against the firm's cost of capital to gauge whether the firm is creating or destroying shareholder value. This is imperative when making and analyzing capital allocation decisions.

Valuations relying extensively on earnings or simplistic accounting-based ratios such as P/E obscure the link between economics and valuation. In fact sophisticated investors realize and take advantage of simplistic valuation models. They recognize that even as people "talk about cash flow . . . they only give it lip service. Our industry is obsessed with earnings, and that's fine with me because people aren't paying attention to measures that give us an informational advantage."[5]

Although financial statement items are increasingly reported at fair value, e.g. employee stock options and derivative instruments, the current financial reporting model is not primarily intended as a model to approximate firm value. If we are not careful to understand the intricacies of the accounting assumptions (timings and accruals) behind the earnings or

---

[5] Gregory Forsythe, director of equity ratings at Charles Schwab Corporation quoted in Bloomberg Markets, February 2007.

accounting ratios, the resulting analysis and valuation will likely be wrong. Earnings and accruals do not represent cash flow. They do, however, represent components of cash flow, albeit sometimes very small components.

Over the past quarter century, there have been a number of attempts to better measure the economics of a company. These measures use accounting as a financial reporting tool, which is what it was originally designed to do. While the financial reporting information may result in obfuscation rather than clarity, these measures attempt to peer through the fog to assess the economic performance and relate that performance to valuation.

Unfortunately, there has been much confusion about the various economic metrics. Some of that confusion may reflect the proprietary nature of the models. Over the years, the proprietors have spent much time marketing the superiority of their particular model over competing models, causing confusion. The purpose of this part is not to side with one model over another but to help alleviate some of the confusion about what these models attempt to do: to measure the economic, not accounting performance of a company, and use that economic insight for purposes of valuation. We encourage analysts to choose the model they are most comfortable using. This part will focus on the two best known models, Economic Value Added developed by Stern Stewart[6] and Cash Flow Return on Investment developed by HOLT Value Associates.[7] While there are numerous other proprietary models, they are primarily derivatives of EVA or CFROI.[8] Because we do not use the precise adjustments recommended by Stern Stewart, the developers of EVA, we employ the more generic term Economic Profit (EP) in this part. Furthermore, the adjustments to CFROI are accurate as of the time of this writing. However, CFROI by definition is a work in progress. As HOLT completes new research, the model will continue to evolve to reflect improved understanding of how markets assess and price stocks.

Most papers written about EP and CFROI focus on EP and contain only a short afterthought on CFROI.[9] This might be because there has been much more written on EP than CFROI so there is more readily available information on that metric. In addition, since the EP model requires that the analyst manually make all of the adjustments necessary to calculate EP, the analyst becomes intimately familiar with the model. On the other hand, the requirement for manual adjustments may result in a mechanical EP calculation using only reported accounting with no effort to untangle the accounting assumptions in order to gain economic insight. The result may enhance transparency, but it certainly does not increase insight. By contrast, the CFROI model is only available to buy-side analysts through the proprietary framework and software provided by HOLT. The software makes all the systematic adjustments as articulated in the framework to calculate CFROI, thereby ensuring the appropriate accounting adjustments for all companies in the database. Since the software package contains a database covering a majority of publicly traded companies around the world,[10] it is rarely necessary

---

[6] EVA® is a registered trademark of Stern Stewart & Co. Further detailed discussions of EVA can be found in Bennett Stewart III (1991). There are numerous other books published that provide information on the EVA concept.

[7] CFROI® is a registered trademark of HOLT, Credit Suisse's corporate performance and valuation service. Further detailed discussions of CFROI can be found in Madden (1999). In 2002, HOLT Value Associates was acquired by Credit Suisse.

[8] Models in the EVA mold are also found under the names Economic Profit (EP) and Shareholder Value Added (SVA). Models in the CFROI mold are also found under the names Economic Margin™ developed by Applied Financial Group, Cash Economic Return developed by LifeCycle Returns, both founded by former employees of HOLT, and Cash Return on Capital Invested (CROCI) developed by Deutsche Bank.

[9] The authors of this part are a former employee of HOLT and a current employee of Credit Suisse. The opinions in this part do not necessarily reflect the opinions of the authors' respective employers.

[10] As of December 2006, the HOLT database contained over 18 000 companies covering 55 countries around the world. All systematic CFROI adjustments occur within the software for all of the companies in the database.

for analysts to roll up their sleeves and manually apply the framework themselves. While this may be regrettable since it risks lowering explicit understanding of the adjustments necessary to calculate CFROI, it does save the analyst time to focus on assessing the economics of the company and its industry, which is what the analyst is ultimately paid to do.

This part begins with a brief discussion of accounting to economics and economics to valuation. It then describes the conceptual framework for CFROI. Next, it provides the explicit adjustments necessary to arrive at the CFROI for Vodafone using the March 2005 Vodafone annual report. Once the CFROI calculation has been detailed, we will undertake the equivalent EP adjustments (where applicable) for Vodafone highlighting the differences between it and CFROI. This will provide a single reference point to understand the similarities and differences between these two metrics. Finally, we conclude with a brief discussion on using both models in valuation.

8

From Accounting to Economics – Part I

Based on the concepts of accrual accounting, to arrive at profit, one includes all of the costs with the revenues incurred for the relevant period, regardless of whether the costs (revenues) involved a cash outlay (inflow) in the period or not. While accrual accounting helps us to understand the matching period between revenues and expenses, management discretion over accrual periods (when the matching occurs) gives it a creative opportunity to improve appearances at the expense of economics. Actual cash outlays frequently occur in different periods than the accrual treatment, resulting in a volatile rift between accounting "profits" and actual cash flow.

In addition to management discretion on accruals, management discretion for creative financing influences the accounting of assets. For example, under certain conditions, the cost of leasing an asset is a direct expense whereas under other conditions it is first capitalized on the balance sheet and then amortized over some period. The accounting for leases affects how the asset flows through the income statement (influencing earnings) and resides on the balance sheet (influencing both assets and debt). Furthermore, when the financing of an asset is debt based (lease or loan), the interest expense explicitly reflects the cost to the firm required by the debt providers. On the other hand, if the asset purchase is with equity (cash), there is no explicit cost to the firm of a required return to the equity providers. Equity is simply what remains after all the liabilities have been paid. There is no place in accrual accounting to recognize that equity investors expect a return just as debt investors do.

The EP and CFROI excess return models[1] attempt to assess the economics of a business: How cash is generated, how the business is financed[2] (regardless of how the accountants might decide to state, or not state, the transaction on the financial statements) and how the business rewards its capital providers. For example, a firm needs assets to operate. How it acquires those assets is a financing decision. The financing decision should not effect the operating economics of the business, though it may effect the financing economics through tax advantages or disadvantages. When leasing an asset, the firm presumably needs that asset. The lease is simply a financing decision. The lease structure, whether capitalized or expensed, affects accounting recognition not operating efficiency. At the

---

[1] These models are called excess return because they recognize that both debt and equity investors impose a cost of capital on the firm. The excess return is that return in excess of the cost of capital. The models are also sometimes referred to as residual income models.

[2] Modigliani and Miller showed that capital structure (i.e. financing of the firm) does not matter in perfect capital markets and in the absence of taxes. MM proposition 1 states, "a firm cannot change the total value of its securities just by splitting its cash flows into different streams: The firm's value is determined by its real assets, not by the securities it issues. . . . MM's proposition 1 allows complete separation of investment and financing decisions." [See Brealey *et al.* (2005), p. 445.] Despite the fact that we do have taxes and do not have perfect capital markets, when analyzing a firm, it is very useful to remember the concept and separate financing from operating decisions and how each impacts the economics of the firm.

extreme, a company like Enron shifted so many items off-balance sheet (assets and debt), so obscuring the true economics (the operating efficiency) of the business, that it was impossible for investors, employees and pundits to understand what was happening until it was too late. The result was massive losses to many of those investors and employees who held shares.

9
From Economics to Valuation – Part I

Another area of confusion between accounting and economics is valuation. Often, once the accounting analysis is complete, an accounting-based valuation ratio is used to estimate value. For example, a P/E ratio relies on earnings and ignores the assumptions to arrive at those earnings as well as the capital represented on the balance sheet to generate those earnings. The earnings figure in no way reflects the quality of the earnings, which is integral to calculating a fundamental P/E ratio. In short, there are so many accounting and forecasting assumptions implicit in a P/E ratio that it is difficult to establish a direct link between accounting and valuation. A robust valuation requires:

- understanding the accounting assumptions;
- correcting and reversing the accounting distortions;
- understanding the economics (strategy, competitive advantage, risks, etc.);
- determining the appropriate forecast assumptions;
- adopting an appropriate valuation approach; and
- performing the valuation.

Even with a sophisticated DCF model, care must be taken when undertaking each of these steps.

EP and CFROI fulfill two key roles: as measures of economic performance and as frameworks for DCF-based valuations. Many commentators mistakenly criticize the ability of management to manipulate these excess return models in a single measurement period at the expense of cash flows in future periods and therefore at the expense of the valuation. These critics miss the point that the metric is both a performance measure and an integral component of a valuation model. Cutting the link between single period performance and multiple period valuation certainly allows for manipulation, even when cash flow is the measure. The link between single period performance and multi-period valuation provides the analyst with a performance baseline[1] from which to recognize the tradeoff between improved current period performance at the potential detriment of future period performance and the resulting valuation.

---

[1] More appropriately, the analyst should use as their performance baseline a trend analysis of previous periods of performance.

10

Where Does Accounting Go Wrong?

It is possible to relate the P/E ratio to a DCF model for a mature, stable firm. Consider the fundamental equation for a P/E multiple below. Its implications illustrate that a simple P/E ratio contains a number of accounting and valuation deficiencies. The forward P/E[1] can be calculated for a firm with constant earnings growth, g, and a constant perpetual return on equity, ROE. The term r_E represents the cost of equity.

$$P/E = \frac{(1 - g/\mathrm{ROE})}{(r_E - g)}$$

Critical readers are doubtless wondering how many firms meet these restrictive conditions. To make matters worse, accounting dependencies and deficiencies are manifold. Earnings and the subsequent ROE can be altered by any number of accounting decisions:

- Asset aging and depreciation policy (changing earnings through the depreciation charge and net assets through accumulated depreciation);
- Leasing of assets (thereby removing the asset from the balance sheet and increasing operating expenses on the income statement);
- Leverage and financial structure (thereby altering the amount of equity on the balance sheet);
- Historical acquisitions and goodwill amortization policy (altering both income statement and balance sheet);
- Timing of expenses and revenue (altering both income statement and balance sheet through the level of accruals).

Note how important ROE is to the P/E ratio. Earnings quality should be an intrinsic consideration when using P/E ratios yet it is rarely mentioned. The lower the ROE, the more it costs to generate earnings growth. If that's not enough to shake the intreprid analyst, ROE is also highly dependent on inflation.

This example illustrates the link between performance measurement and valuation, and how that link can be distorted by using traditional accounting figures such as earnings and ROE. Models that measure economic performance and relate it to valuation correct these accounting distortions.

---

[1] The forward P/E ratio can be derived by substituting the fundamental growth equation, $g = \mathrm{ROE}*(1 - \text{payout ratio})$ or payout ratio $= 1 - g/\mathrm{ROE}$, into the dividend growth model (DGM) which states that the fundamental value per share $P_0 = [\mathrm{EPS}_0 * \text{payout ratio} * (1 + g)]/(r_E - g)$. The result is the forward $P/E = P_0/\mathrm{EPS}_1 = [1 - g/\mathrm{ROE}]/(r_E - g)$. The DGM and the fundamental growth equation are explained in detail in Viebig and Poddig, Part I, Section 3.2 of this book. The forward P/E ratio is also discussed in Damodaran, Part VII, Section 39.4 of this book.

11

From Accounting to Economics: CFROI

11.1 THE BASICS

In order to understand the logic and benefits of the CFROI calculation, let us imagine a simple investment scenario. Suppose you invested $1m in your cousin Greg's home refurbishment business. He asks for an eight-year investment with $800 000 to support the shop and its fittings, and $200 000 for working capital. The shop equipment and fittings are depreciating assets that will need to be replaced after eight years. The working capital will purchase inventory and allow for day-to-day management of the business. You are the sole investor in this business and Greg's salary is an operating expense. He boldly promises that the business will generate a return of greater than 20%.

Since your cousin is a trustworthy character, you leave him to run the business and attend to your other investments. You receive a check for $200 000 every year, which is a 20% return on your original investment. After five years, you decide to pay Greg a visit and check on your investment. When you arrive at his shop, the business seems to be going very well and Greg tells you he expects the business to break through the 20% return barrier.

Greg apologizes for the slow start but confidently tells you that the business earned 20% last year and shows you his forward estimates of the return on net assets (RONA) with returns increasing to 50% (see Table 11.1). After pondering his apology and scratching your head over his rather astounding forecast, you attempt to deconstruct his financial analysis. You ask Greg, "How exactly did you arrive at that 20% return?" Greg answers, "The business earned $100 000 after tax on net assets of $500 000. Next year the return will increase to 25% and we'll really be coining it!"

This enigmatic discussion carries on to the pub where you call a friend who works for an investment bank. He tells you that RONA is highly dependent on reinvestment and depreciation rates. He exclaims that investors are regularly fooled by trying to compare returns on new assets vs. old assets. "The quickest way to increase returns is to cut capex for a few years. It might kill the business, but it'll look like the company is improving on paper and might command a higher price. Don't be fooled by that trick, old chap." You explain this to Greg over a second pint and tell him that the investment banker suggested that they measure the return on gross investment (ROGI), which is the gross cash flow divided by the gross investment (see Table 11.1). Because you are the sole capital provider, the gross cash flow equals the net income plus the depreciation charge, which tallies to $200 000 in this example.

Across the pub, you spot your private banker from Credit Suisse and decide to ask him for a second opinion. He laughs and tells you that he just attended a HOLT seminar where he learned that "you also have to account for asset life, and the split between non-depreciating and depreciating assets when performing a comprehensive company analysis". Now you are at your wit's end and order a final round of drinks to translate the private banker's advice. After declining your kind offer, the Credit Suisse banker calculates an IRR of 13.9%, much lower than the return Greg promised. He explains that the fixed assets will have fully depreciated after eight years and will have little or no residual value. However, the business will be able to liquidate its non-depreciating assets, or working capital, after eight years. This argument makes sense and reminds you of the project analyses you did many years ago studying finance. The private banker then shows you how to calculate the single-period IRR, or CFROI, for every financial year. The CFROI is a constant 13.9% which reconciles to the IRR and makes perfect sense since the business economics have been and are expected to remain constant. You thank the gentleman from Credit Suisse and rightfully stick Greg with the lunch bill.

We hope this example clearly illustrates the problem of performance measurement endemic to all net asset-based ratios. Metrics lie, particularly accounting ratios. Since measurement influences behavior, investors and analysts need to carefully consider management's performance measures and their own. There is no end to the number of examples where inappropriate performance measurement leads to uneconomic behavior. The aim of CFROI is to mirror the IRR economic performance metric as closely as possible. There are four key inputs to IRR: gross investment, gross cash flow, life and salvage value. Their analogs can be found in the CFROI calculation.

Table 11.1 CFROI and other metrics

Year		1	2	3	4	5	6	7	8
Net assets	1000	900	800	700	600	500	400	300	200
Asset life		8	8	8	8	8	8	8	8
Depreciation		100	100	100	100	100	100	100	100
Net income		**100**	**100**	**100**	**100**	**100**	**100**	**100**	**100**
Gross assets		1000	1000	1000	1000	1000	1000	1000	1000
Non-depreciating assets		200	200	200	200	200	200	200	200
Asset life		8	8	8	8	8	8	8	8
Gross cash flow		200	200	200	200	200	200	200	200
RONA		11.1%	12.5%	14.3%	16.7%	20.0%	25.0%	33.3%	50.0%
ROGI		20.0%	20.0%	20.0%	20.0%	20.0%	20.0%	20.0%	20.0%
CFROI		13.9%	13.9%	13.9%	13.9%	13.9%	13.9%	13.9%	13.9%
All amounts in $'000									
Investor's cash flow	−1000	200	200	200	200	200	200	200	400
IRR	13.9%								

Note that many of the terms in this table will be defined later in the text. For the purposes of this example, it is not necessary to understand the precise meaning of each term

11.1.1   Return on net assets (RONA) or return on invested capital (ROIC)

RONA and ROIC measure current dollar net operating profit after tax (NOPAT) divided by historic cost net assets. In year five, when you visit your cousin Greg he calculates the return by dividing $100 of NOPAT by $500 of net assets (NB: NOPAT equals net income in this simple example since there is a single supplier of capital). The result is the nebulous return of 20%. If you had solely relied on Greg's financial statements every year you would have had the misleading impression that he has increased the returns on his business from 11.1% to 20%, when in fact nothing changed in the business except net assets.

11.1.2   Return on gross investment (ROGI)

ROGI improves on RONA by measuring the gross cash flow in current dollars against the gross historical cost. In this example, the year five return is 20% ($200/$1000). With ROGI, management is held accountable for the full investment albeit in historical dollars and management cannot claim success by simply writing-off some bad investments or changing the depreciation policy, thereby improving returns. Other issues with ROGI are that it does not take into account asset composition and life. It will also be distorted by inflation. RONA and ROGI implicitly assume that the business is in steady-state or that the assets are non-depreciating.

11.1.3   Cash flow return on investment (CFROI)

Cash flow return on investment is based on the inflation-adjusted gross investment with two additional requirements: asset life and a split of the gross investment into depreciating (PPE) and non-depreciating assets (working capital). CFROI is a comprehensive metric because it takes the asset life and the asset release at the end of the project into account. Also, the gross investment is marked to current dollars instead of historical cost. CFROI is the single-period, real hurdle rate which, if applied to the stream of cash flows and the non-depreciating asset release, results in a zero NPV project.[1] Stated another way, the present value of the cash flows and non-depreciating asset release exactly equal the investment. In the example above, where no fundamental shifts occur to the economics of the refurbishment business, CFROI remains constant and equals the overall IRR. This result makes perfect sense since it is based on economic principles, not accounting conventions.

As noted, CFROI is conceptually equivalent to an IRR capital investment analysis, except the CFROI calculation is a real number with the effects of inflation accounted for. It is simply the weighted average one-year IRR on all of the firm's projects.[2] Calculating the CFROI/IRR requires four inputs:

- *Present value (PV)* of the investment: Gross investment (GI) in the company adjusted for inflation. Gross investment can be thought of as the gross amount invested in the company.
- *Payment (PMT) or cash flow:* Gross cash flow (GCF) adjusted for inflation and non-cash expenses. GCF is the cash flow generated from the gross investment.
- *Project life (NPER):* Gross asset life estimated by the depreciation expense and total depreciating assets.
- *Future value (FV):* Non-depreciating assets which include working capital (current assets less current liabilities) and other non-depreciating assets such as land and construction-in-progress. The logic is that these non-depreciating assets are released at the end of the project, or reinvested in another project.

---

[1] In Excel spreadsheet terms the RATE function is used where RATE(nper, pmt, pv, fv) is the calculation for IRR, nper equals asset life, pmt equals gross cash flow, pv equals gross investment, and fv equals non-depreciating asset release.
[2] The concept of an IRR project within a firm will be explained in greater detail in Chapter 13.

Figure 11.1[3] is a pictorial representation of the CFROI calculation. If $200 is invested in a four-year project that returns $40 per year and releases $80 from that original $200 investment at the end of year four, the resulting CFROI is 6.36%. In Excel: RATE(nper = 4, pmt = $40, pv = −$200, fv = $80) = 6.36%.

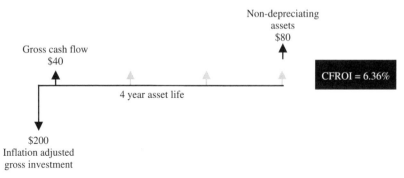

Figure 11.1   CFROI/IRR equivalence

Whether the cash invested is through debt or equity reflects a financing decision that does not effect the calculation.[4]

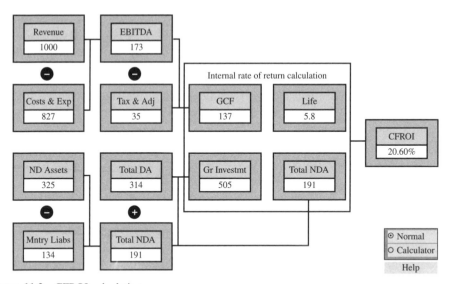

Figure 11.2   CFROI calculation

---

[3] The authors are grateful to HOLT for providing all of the CFROI examples and graphics for this part, including the material to calculate CFROI from an annual report.
[4] In reality since there is a tax advantage to debt, the financing of the firm will affect taxes, which in turn affects gross cash flow, which will have a minor impact on the IRR calculation.

Figure 11.2 shows a graphical presentation of the CFROI calculation for a simple company. In this example, revenue of $1000 generates $137 of gross cash flow.[5] End of year (EOY) gross investment (all asset figures in CFROI are as of year-end) consists of depreciating and non-depreciating assets of $505. The non-depreciating component of gross investment is $191. The life, based on the average life of all depreciating assets in the firm, is 5.8 years. The resulting CFROI calculation is 20.6%. Comparing this CFROI to a cost of capital of 6% results in a positive spread of 14.6%. Thus, the firm is creating value for its shareholders over this one-year measurement period.

11.2 CFROI ADJUSTMENTS USING VODAFONE'S MARCH 2005 ANNUAL REPORT

In this chapter, we discuss the logic behind the accounting adjustments necessary to calculate CFROI. In the HOLT CFROI framework, these adjustments are systematically applied to all firms.[6] Unique or extraordinary events for specific companies may require specific adjustments to those companies.

In section 11.2.1 we provide the equivalent CFROI adjustments (where relevant) to EP as a basis for comparison. Where the adjustments are not relevant, such as the inflation adjustment to CFROI, there will be no adjustments to EP.

11.2.1 Gross investment

Depreciating assets

The first step when calculating gross investment is to separate depreciating and non-depreciating assets. The basic adjustments are as follows:

Depreciating assets

EOY adjusted gross plant (adjusted fixed assets + accumulated depreciation)
+ Inflation adjustment for gross plant
+ Construction in progress
+ Capitalized operating leases
+ Capitalized research and development
+ Inflation adjusted gross plant recaptured
+ Non-depreciating assets (net working capital)
= Gross investment

We will outline the general adjustments for each component of depreciating assets before presenting the specific adjustments for Vodafone. We then present the general components and Vodafone adjustments for non-depreciating assets before showing the calculation of gross investment and moving systematically through each of the other CFROI inputs.

---

[5] The next section describes the process to calculate gross investment, gross cash flow, non-depreciating assets and project life.
[6] The adjustments to Vodafone do not represent every possible adjustment to every possible industry. Rather Vodafone was selected to represent clarity in the more generic and important adjustments in order to allow analysts with or without the HOLT software to understand the concepts behind CFROI.

Adjusted gross plant

When calculating gross plant, the first step is to remove any non-depreciating assets such as land and construction-in-progress, which by definition have not yet entered the depreciating asset base. The reason for the removal is twofold. First, gross plant and depreciation expense are used to calculate the asset life (discussed further below). Including non-depreciating assets in gross plant would distort the asset life calculation. Second, we want to separate depreciating from non-depreciating assets, and both land and CIP are non-depreciating. As discussed in Chapter 11, non-depreciating assets are treated as an asset release for the CFROI calculation. The adjustments to gross plant are:

Adjusted gross plant

Gross plant (fixed assets + accumulated depreciation)
− Land
− Construction in progress
+ Inflation adjustment
= Total adjusted gross plant

Gross plant	Amount	Source
+ Land and buildings	1326	Note 12
+ Machinery and equipment	33 617	Note 12
+ Construction in progress	0	Note 12
+ Tangible and intangible asset imparement (FASB 121)	0	Calculated
Total gross plant	**£34 943**	

Figure 11.3   Vodafone adjusted gross plant (see Appendix 1: Figures A1.3 and A1.4)[7]

Comment: FASB 121 requires the periodic review and impairment of certain long-lived assets and intangibles whenever the carrying amount of the asset may not be recoverable. Any FASB 121 write-downs should be added back to the asset base since they represent shareholder funds expended. As with any other depreciating asset, the FASB 121 write-down should be amortized over the life of the asset.

Adjusted gross plant	Amount	Source
+ Gross plant	34 943	Note 12
− Land	0	Note 12
− Construction in progress	0	Note 12
Total adjusted gross plant	**£34 943**	

Figure 11.4   Adjusted gross plant

---

[7] All financial numbers related to Vodafone in this part are in £m. The numbers can be found in Vodafone's 2005 financial statements and accompanying notes. A copy of all the relevant financial statements and notes can be found in the appendix to this part. The relevant figure in the appendix is referred to in each figure in the text.

Inflation adjustment

Since CFROI is a real number, an adjustment is necessary to remove the effects of inflation. The inflation adjustment to the CFROI calculation restates historical asset costs on the balance sheet to current purchasing units to reflect the change in purchasing power of the monetary units originally used to purchase the assets.

Some critics argue that the inflation adjustment does not reflect the true cost of the asset today and argue that assets should be "fair valued".[8] For example, computers have declined in price over the years and become more powerful. Thus, the inflation-adjusted cost of the computer reflects neither its fair value nor its replacement value. The CFROI calculation is not trying to estimate the fair value investment necessary to replace the assets as of today. It is trying to estimate the investment made in past periods in terms of current purchasing units. For example, assume the firm purchased a computer for $2000 in 2002. In 2005, a computer of equivalent functionality may cost $1500 and be more powerful. However, the firm invested $2000 of investors' funds in 2002. If the computer is still serving its function, the firm is not going to dispose of the 2002 computer and invest $1500 of 2005 dollars for a new computer. The CFROI calculation simply reflects the current dollar value of the 2002 investment in 2005 dollars.

With respect to financial assets or investments held by industrial companies, these are not generally operating assets and there is often a market for these assets or a clear, objective manner in which to value them. In the HOLT CFROI framework, financial assets are stated at their fair value and removed from gross investment for the CFROI calculation. They are added back as investments when performing the firm valuation.

Calculation of the inflation adjustment

The inflation adjustment requires a "delayering" of the asset base. There are four inputs in the delayering calculation: asset life, historic cost, historic growth rate, and a GDP deflator time series.

Imagine a firm that reports gross assets of $2500. Assume the firm began business five years ago and the assets have a five year life. In order to estimate the current purchasing power of those five layers of investments, we must inflation adjust each individual layer. Assume we observe that the firm has grown its gross assets at a nominal average rate of 22.4% over the past five years. We further observe 2% per year average inflation over that time and now have sufficient information to delayer the assets. The calculation is similar to that for sinking fund depreciation. For simplicity's sake, we assume all investment occurs at the end of the year.

The first asset layer in year -4 of $320 results from delayering the reported gross investment of $2500 into an initial capex. In mathematical terms: $2500/((1 + 22.4\%)^5 - 1)*22.4\% = $320 in historical cost. Now that we know the initial asset layer, we simply grow it by 22.4% for each of the next four years to arrive at gross assets of $2500, e.g. year -3 assets $= $320*(1 + 22.4\%) = $392 in historical cost.

To bring the asset layers into current purchasing units, we need to inflation adjust for the number of historic years the asset has been in use. For example, in year -4: $320*(1 + 2\%)^4 = $347 in inflation-adjusted terms, leaving $27 as the inflation adjustment. In year -3, we inflate the asset layer by three years and so on until year zero.

---

[8] The discussion of fair value relates solely to tangible fixed assets in this context and does not include financial assets.

Table 11.2   Asset delayering

	Yr −4	Yr −3	Yr −2	Yr −1	Yr 0	Yr 0 GP
Nominal growth rate	22.4%	22.4%	22.4%	22.4%	22.4%	
Asset layers (capex)	320	392	480	588	719	2500
Inflation	2.0%	2.0%	2.0%	2.0%	2.0%	
Inflation adjustment	26	24	19	12	0	82
Inflation-adjusted gross plant	347	416	500	599	719	2582
Inflation adjustment factor						*1.033*

Thus, a reported gross asset base in year 0 of $2500 with 20% annual real growth and 2% yearly inflation results in the five asset layers represented in Table 11.2 and graphically in Figure 11.5. The inflation adjustment factor in Table 11.2 shows that the reported gross assets receive the equivalent of a 3.3% inflation adjustment. Finally, since growth rates for most companies are volatile from year to year, due to both organic and acquisitive growth, an average growth rate is generally used.

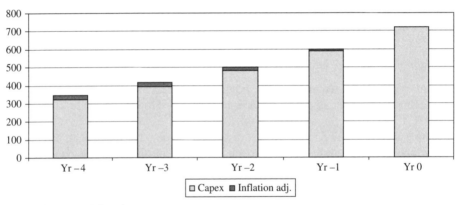

Figure 11.5   Asset delayering

Because of acquisitions and disposals, it is more appropriate to delayer the assets than to try to track them through changes in the reported balance sheet, particularly since many acquisitions are of non-publicly traded companies so there is no disclosure of the gross assets acquired. We will further discuss acquisitions under gross plant recaptured.

Asset light or short asset life firms may have relatively small inflation adjustments. The analyst without access to the HOLT software, which automatically inflation adjusts the assets, may decide to ignore the inflation adjustment. However, be aware that the CFROI calculation is no longer comparable across firms or time. In firms with long-lived assets, the inflation adjustment can reflect a large percentage of the gross investment base. Table 11.3 shows the impact of inflation on assets aged from 5 to 20 years and with inflation rates of 1%, 3% and 5%. While an inflation rate of 3% on a five-year old asset generates a 16% inflation adjustment, that same 3% inflation rate on a 20-year-old asset is over 80%! Firms with long asset lives and low growth rates will receive significant inflation adjustments.

Table 11.3 Impact of inflation on oldest asset layer

Years	Inflation rate	Inflation factor
5	1.0%	5.1%
	3.0%	15.9%
	5.0%	27.6%
10	1.0%	10.5%
	3.0%	34.4%
	5.0%	62.9%
15	1.0%	16.1%
	3.0%	55.8%
	5.0%	107.9%
20	1.0%	22.0%
	3.0%	80.6%
	5.0%	165.3%

Inflation adjusted gross plant	Amount	Source
GP life (GP/depr exp, 3-year median)	8	years
Inflation adjustment factor	1.068	Inflation calculation
Historical growth rate	19.6%	Calculated
Real historical cost	34 943	Per above
Inflation adjustment	2369	Calculated
Inflation adjusted gross plant	**£37 312**	

Figure 11.6 Vodafone inflation adjusted gross plant

The inflation adjustment factor of 1.068 in Figure 11.6 reflects the inflation impact from the individual inflation rates for the eight historic asset layers for Vodafone. Analysts should employ a historic growth rate that is appropriate for the firm in question. Yearly growth rates should be treated suspiciously since growth related to acquisitions can distort the relayering.

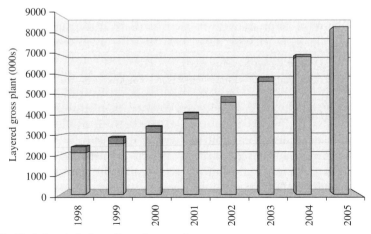

Figure 11.7 Vodafone inflation adjusted gross plant

Capitalized operating leases

Regardless of whether a company accounts for a lease as a financing lease or an operating lease, the use of a lease is fundamentally a financing decision. If the firm did not need the asset, it would not expend funds whether purchased or leased. All operating leases are capitalized onto the balance sheet for the CFROI calculation.

The inputs for capitalizing leases are lease expense, leased asset life (asset life is a good proxy) and the real debt rate. If the company has publicly traded debt, the rate on that debt is a good proxy for the lease debt rate. For companies that do not have publicly traded debt, information on bank loans, or an estimate of the approximate rating of the company if it did have traded debt will work. For example, if the analyst believes the company would be AA rated, use an AA-bond debt rate. Finally, the nominal debt rate should be deflated by the forward expected inflation rate to arrive at the real debt rate.[9]

Table 11.4 presents an example of a capitalized lease calculation given a nominal bond rate of 5%, 2.5% expected inflation, an asset life of 10 years and an annual lease expense of $100. The letters in parentheses reflect the Microsoft Excel inputs for the PV function. In this example, a capitalized lease asset of $878 is added to the balance sheet. It is important to bear in mind that CFROI is based on *gross* investment, thus this calculation estimates the *gross* value of operating leases and may look unfamiliar.

Table 11.4   Capitalizing leases

Nominal bond rate	5.0%
Expected inflation rate	2.5%
Real debt rate (i)	2.4%
Asset life (nper)	10
Lease expense (pmt)	100
Capitalized lease (pv)	878.0

For Vodafone, an additional £9.2 billion is added to the balance sheet to reflect its leased assets.

Capitalized leases	**Amount**	**Source**
Rent expense (pmt)	1337	Note 5
Project life (n - rounded)	8.00	Calculated
Real debt rate (per a corp bond rate)	3.52%	External data
Current £ gross leased property	**£9185**	

Figure 11.8   Vodafone capitalized operating leases (see Appendix 1: Figure A1.5)

Capitalized research and development

Regardless of accounting rules, most analysts consider R&D an economic investment in the firm's future profitability. If the R&D expenditure is not profitable, the firm will experience a growing asset base with no concurrent increase in profitability from the R&D investment, resulting in declining CFROIs.

---

[9] For example, if the nominal bond rate was 5% and expected inflation was 2.5%, the real debt rate would be: $1.05/1.025 = 1.0244$ or 2.4%.

The primary issue for capitalizing R&D is deciding how many years of R&D expenditure to capitalize. Conceptually, companies with long-lived investments or long patent protection periods should capitalize more periods of R&D expense, e.g. pharmaceutical companies. On the other hand, technology companies should use shorter R&D lives since technological innovation results in accelerated obsolescence. While the HOLT software automatically capitalizes R&D based on the firm's industry, analysts should select appropriate R&D lives based on knowledge and analysis.

The capitalization procedure is straightforward. Simply take the R&D expense for each period for which the R&D is capitalized, multiply it by the inflation factor for that period and sum the inflation adjusted R&D expenses. Table 11.5 presents an example for capitalizing R&D with a five-year R&D life. In this example, a capitalized R&D asset of $610 is added to the balance sheet. Please note that because CFROI requires *gross* investment, the aim of this calculation is to estimate the *gross* capitalized R&D.

Table 11.5 Capitalized R&D

Year	R&D expense per I/S	Inflation rate	Inflation factor	Inflation adjusted R&D
Yr −4	100	2.7%	1.11	111
Yr −3	110	2.7%	1.08	119
Yr −2	115	2.7%	1.05	121
Yr −1	125	2.7%	1.03	128
Yr 0	130	2.7%	1.00	130
Infl adj	580			610

As Figure 11.9 shows, an additional £767 million in capitalized R&D is added to Vodafone's balance sheet.

Capitalized R&D (2005, Note 5 and previous years)	Amount	Inflation factor	Inflation adjusted R&D
Telecom R&D life (years)	5		
5-year inflation adjustment factor	1.04		
R&D expense 2001	72	1.11	80
R&D expense 2002	110	1.09	120
R&D expense 2003	164	1.05	173
R&D expense 2004	171	1.02	175
R&D expense 2005	219	1.00	219
Inflation adjusted capitalized R&D	736		**£767**

Figure 11.9   Vodafone capitalized R&D (see Appendix 1: Figure A1.6)

Gross plant recaptured

Frequently, companies make acquisitions during the year. Under purchase accounting rules, net assets of the acquired firm are booked at fair value, which differs from the historic cost of the acquired assets. Since the CFROI calculation relies on historic cost gross investment (the capital providers' funds originally invested), an estimate of that historic cost is needed.

Unfortunately, the original gross investment of the acquired company is rarely available (if a private transaction) or is lost in the transaction disclosure documents.

When information is disclosed about the assets acquired, a good estimate of the historic cost can be made and the difference between fair value and the historic cost can be added back to the gross plant and inflation adjusted. However, lacking such information, we must make a gross plant recaptured estimate. Gross plant recaptured relies on the net plant to gross plant ratio of the acquiring company. Figure 11.10 presents an example of the gross plant recaptured estimate when data relating to the historic cost of the acquired assets is not disclosed.

	Company A	buys	Company B. (not disclosed)	As reported post acquisition Company A	The true post acquisition balance sheet
Gross plant	1000		400	1200	1400
Accumulated depr	500		300	500	800
Net plant	500		100	700	600
Fair value adjustment (assume = net assets)			200		
Net plant/Gross plant ratio	50%		25%	58%	43%
[Net plant]/[NP/GP ratio] =	700	divided by	50%	= 1400	
Less: reported gross plant				1200	
Equal: gross plant recaptured				200	
Adjusted post acquistion Company A					
Gross plant as reported post acquisition				1200	
Plus: Gross plant recaptured				200	
Equal: Adj GP recaptured				1400	
Divided by net plant as reported post acquisition				700	
Equal: Adj NP/GP ratio				50%	

Figure 11.10 Estimating gross plant recaptured

In this example, Company A acquires Company B. Company B was privately held so the true balance sheet has not been disclosed. We do know that pre-acquisition, publicly traded Company A had $1000 in gross plant and $500 in net assets resulting in a net plant to gross plant ratio of 50%. Company A, as reported post acquisition, has $1200 in gross plant and $700 in net assets for a net plant to gross plant ratio of 58%. In order to restore the ratio to 50% (the best guess we have), requires a gross plant recaptured of $200. In reality, while we have correctly estimated gross plant, we have underestimated accumulated depreciation and overestimated the ratio. The final column in Figure 11.10 reflects the true undisclosed gross investment. Finally, the gross plant recaptured is inflation adjusted based on the asset life of the acquiring company.

Acquisitions by Vodafone result in £3.4 billion of gross plant recaptured.

Gross plant recaptured	Amount	Source
Inflation adjustment factor	1.068	per gross plant
Gross plant recaptured	3211	Calculated
+ GP recapture inflation adjustment	218	Calculated
Inflation adjusted gross plant recapture	**£3429**	

Figure 11.11 Vodafone gross plant recaptured

Depreciating assets

After completing all of the adjustments to gross plants, construction-in-progress, capitalized leases, capitalized R&D and gross plant recaptured are added back to arrive at total inflation adjusted depreciating assets, the first input for gross investment.

Vodafone depreciating assets

Depreciating assets	Amount	Source
Inflation adjusted gross plant	37 312	Calculated
+ Construction-in-progress	0	Note 12
+ Capitalized leases	9,185	Note 5
+ Capitalized R&D expense	767	Note 5
+ Inflation adjusted gross plant recaptured	3429	Calculated
Total Inflation adjusted depreciating assets	£50 693	

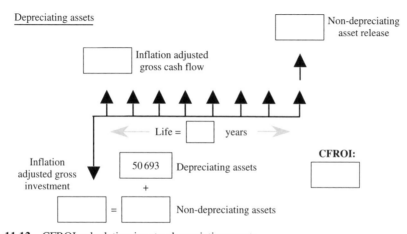

Figure 11.12   CFROI calculation inputs: depreciating assets

11.2.2   Non-depreciating assets

Non-depreciating assets include working capital and other non-depreciating items such as land. Conceptually, non-depreciating assets include:

Non-depreciating assets

Current assets less inventory
 − Current non-debt monetary liabilities
 + Inflation adjusted inventories
 + Inflation adjusted land
 + Other tangible assets
 + Non-depreciating, non-goodwill intangible assets
 = Non-depreciating assets

Current assets less inventory

Unlike EP, the CFROI calculation does not net cash and cash equivalents against debt. While management can certainly use the cash to pay down debt, increase dividends or buy back shares, there is no guarantee that they will do so. Thus, the CFROI calculation holds management responsible for the amount of this low return asset they keep on the balance sheet. However, many analysts will adjust forecast cash levels to those necessary for maintaining operations. The remaining cash is considered "excess". Furthermore, for analytic purposes, it may be useful to adjust historic periods for excess cash when calculating the CFROI in order to better assess the operating returns of the company (not influenced by the low return on cash).

Accounts receivable are generally taken at book value unless the analyst has a contrary opinion regarding the amount of receivables that will ultimately be collected.

Current non-debt liabilities

Non-debt monetary liabilities reflect all current non-interest bearing liabilities (essentially current liabilities excluding anything that carries an interest rate such as short-term debt). For valuation purposes, all interest bearing liabilities are treated as debt and for valuation purposes subtracted from firm value to arrive at the equity value.

Inventory inflation adjustment

In the event that inventory is accounted for according to the last in, first out (LIFO) method, the LIFO reserve will be added to the inventory to more accurately reflect the true cost of the items in inventory. We will further discuss the LIFO reserve section 11.2.4.

Inflation adjusted land

Since land is a non-depreciating asset, it is removed from gross plant and added to non-depreciating assets. However, similar to gross plant, land is inflation adjusted. Unfortunately, land is often only disclosed as part of "land and buildings". In such cases, the "land and buildings" account remains in depreciating assets, unless an estimate can be made of the percentage land represents in the account.

Caution should be exercised when analyzing firms such as home-builders, where land is essentially a component of inventory. In times when land prices are increasing more rapidly than general inflation, inflationary windfall profits can occur. The land inventory will have been sold as part of a finished product, i.e. a house or building, and will need to be replaced with new land that has been rising in price faster than general inflation. In these instances, the analyst needs to understand how inventory wavers in relation to inflation and contributes to profitability.

Other tangible assets

Since no information is generally available regarding the age or depreciability of these assets, they are placed in non-depreciating assets. If such information is available, these assets should be placed in the accounts where they most appropriately belong.

Non-depreciating assets are the second input for the gross investment calculation and an input for the CFROI calculation.

A word on non-depreciating non-goodwill intangible assets

The 3G adjustment in Figure 11.13 reflects an estimate of the non-impaired value of Vodafone's 3G licenses. 3G spectrum was auctioned off in Europe with great fanfare at inflated prices. Since that time, wireless companies have begun to impair their 3G assets. The 3G adjustment in non-depreciating assets reflects an estimate of the operating component of this asset. Further discussion of this issue can be found in section 11.3.

Non-depreciating assets	Amount	Source
Current assets less inventory	9268	B/S, Note 15
+ Current non-debt liabilities	(14 445)	B/S, Note 17
Net monetary assets	**−£5177**	
Land	0	Note 12
Land inflation adjustment factor	1.068	per gross plant
Inflation adjusted land	**0**	
Net monetary assets	(5177)	
+ Inventory	430	B/S
+ Inflation adjusted land	0	B/S
+ Other tangible assets	2096	Note 15
+ Prepaid pension	(9)	Note 32
+ 3G adjustment	4275	Calculated
Total inflation adjusted non-depreciating assets	**£1615**	

Figure 11.13 Vodafone non-depreciating assets (see Appendix 1: Figures A1.7–A1.11; the 3G adjustment will be discussed in further detail below)

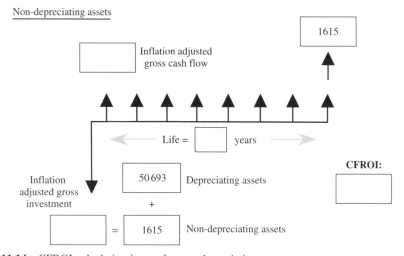

Figure 11.14 CFROI calculation inputs for non-depreciating assets

With more and more companies acquiring assets such as intellectual property, patents, brands, databases and electronic spectrum, additional research is needed into the costs, returns and asset lives of these non-goodwill intangibles, which function as operating assets. Some of these assets, such as patents or trademarks, have legal protection for a finite period. The period of protection is akin to a depreciation or amortization life and such assets should be treated as depreciating. However, other intangible assets are in a true sense non-depreciating. An obvious example is radio spectrum. Radio spectrum does not wear out and although governments generally grant spectrum for a limited period, it is rare that a company has ever had its spectrum license revoked.

Another example of a non-depreciating asset might be classic films or songs. The cost of producing a James Dean movie or a Beatles album bears no relation to the value of such assets today. Even if the original cost had been capitalized it would have long ago been fully depreciated. Thus, if a reliable value (usually related to a sale) can be placed on these assets, one might consider them non-depreciating. The digitization of music and film makes this non-depreciating argument ring even louder. Songs that were popular generations ago are readily available at the click of a mouse on sites such as iTunes and it costs next to nothing to store them.

Gross investment	Amount	Source
Total inflation adjusted non-depreciating assets	1615	Calculated
Total inflation adjusted depreciating assets	50 693	Calculated
Inflation adjusted gross investment	**£52 308**	

Figure 11.15   Vodafone gross investment

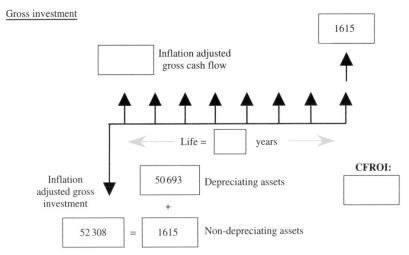

Figure 11.16   CFROI calculation inputs for gross investment

Depreciating plus non-depreciating assets result in the gross investment input for the CFROI calculation.

11.2.3   Project life

Since CFROI is equivalent to the weighted average return on all of a firm's projects, an essential part of the CFROI calculation is the project life. There are three inputs into the project life calculation: adjusted gross plant project life, capitalized lease project life, and capitalized R&D project life:

Gross plant project life

The project life for gross plant is simply:

$$\text{Life} = \frac{(\text{Adjusted gross plant} + \text{Gross plant recaptured})}{\text{Depreciation}}$$

For companies that have made acquisitions, the depreciation expense represents a blend of gross plant purchased to support operations and acquired gross plant. Thus, it is necessary to include both adjusted gross plant and gross plant recaptured in the numerator. As discussed above, land is excluded from this calculation because it is a non-depreciating asset and construction in process is excluded because it has not yet entered the depreciating asset base and therefore does not yet have an associated depreciation charge. Finally, to avoid unusual project lives, i.e. the depreciation expense may reflect a partial year, a three-year median project life is used.

Gross plant project Life		Amount	Source
Adj gross plant		34 943	Calculated
+ Gross plant recaptured		3211	Calculated
Adj gross plant for asset life		38 154	Calculated
Depreciation expense		4528	Note 12
Gross plant project life = (38 154/4528)		**8.4**	
Three-year median GP project life			
	2003	8.6	
	2004	8.0	
	2005	8.4	
Three-year median GP project life		**8.4**	

Figure 11.17   Vodafone gross plant project life (see Appendix 1: Figure A1.12)

Capitalized leases

Leased assets generally consist of a similar asset mix as capital assets. If the leased assets have a different known asset life than that of gross plant, it should be used.

Capitalized R&D

The capitalized R&D project life is the same as the number of years R&D is capitalized. The capitalization period should reflect the analyst's opinion given the company and industry.

Calculating the depreciating asset project life

When calculating the firm's project life a harmonic mean of the three asset classes is used. A weighted average does not properly account for the life of each asset class. Figure 11.18 demonstrates two methods for calculating the project life. For the purposes of this example, we have assumed that capitalized leases have a different life than fixed assets.

- *Implied depreciation (column c)*: Calculate the implied depreciation based on asset life and historic cost (column b/column a).
- *Asset life cycle (column d)*: Calculate the asset life cycle. To understand the concept of the asset life cycle, consider two assets, one with a six-year life and one with a three-year life. During the course of the six-year life of the first asset, there will be two three-year life assets used. Conceptually, the three-year asset will cycle through twice during a single cycle of the six-year asset. To calculate the asset life cycle, take the maximum life of all the assets in column a, and divide that by the life of the specific asset in question. For example, the maximum life is 12 years for fixed assets. The asset life cycle for capitalized leases is 1.5 given their eight-year life. One and a half capitalized lease assets are used during the life of the fixed asset.
- *Asset life cycle investment (column e)*: Calculate the asset life cycle investment (column d ∗ column b). For example, for every 12 year, $5000 investment in fixed assets, three cycles of capitalized R&D at $2000 are invested for a total capitalized R&D investment of $6000.
- *Weighting (column f)*: Calculate the weighted average of column e, the average asset life cycle investment for each asset.
- *Harmonic mean (column g)*: Calculate the mean. The weighting (column f) multiplied by life (column a).
- *Total*: Sum column g to arrive at the project life.
- *Alternate method:* Alternatively, it is possible to skip the calculations in columns d through g and calculate the project life via implied depreciation. Simply take the sum of the historic costs (column b) and divide by the implied depreciation (column c) to arrive at the same answer. Columns d through g provide an alternate means to explain the concept of asset life cycles.

When calculating project life for companies that report using an accelerated depreciation method, analysts should refer to the footnotes for the asset lives of the various asset categories. From the footnote information, an implied depreciation and project life can be

Asset	a Life	b Historic cost	c Implied depreciation	d Asset life cycle	e Asset life cycle investment	f Weighting	g Harmonic mean
Fixed assets	12	5000.0	416.7	1.0	5000.0	32.3%	3.9
Capitalized leases	8	3000.0	375.0	1.5	4500.0	29.0%	2.3
Capitalized R&D	4	2000.0	500.0	3.0	6000.0	38.7%	1.5
Total		10 000	1292		15 500		7.7
Harmonic mean			7.7				

Figure 11.18   Calculating the project life

Total project life	Asset value	Life	Implied depreciation
Inflation adjusted gross plant + GP recaptured	40 741	8.4	4835
Operating leases	9185	8.4	1090
Capitalized R&D	765	5.0	153
Sum of depreciating assets	50 691		6078
Blended asset life using implied depreciation = (50 691/6078)		8.34	
Asset life used for CFROI calculation (rounded)		**8.30**	

Figure 11.19   Vodafone project life, using the implied depreciation method

calculated. Relying on accelerated depreciation to calculate project life will result in an artificially low life and an underestimated CFROI.

Based on the harmonic mean of the asset lives, we can input the CFROI project life.

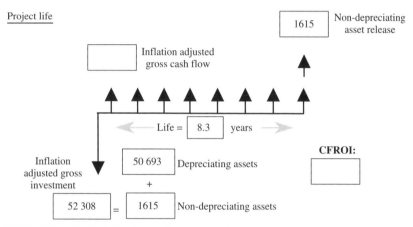

Figure 11.20   CFROI calculation inputs for project life

11.2.4   Gross cash flow

Gross cash flow measures the gross cash flow generated from the firm's operating assets and represents the final input for the CFROI calculation.

Gross cash flow

Net income after tax
+ Depreciation and amortization
+ Interest expense
+ Rental expense
+ R&D expense
+ Monetary holding gain (loss)
+ FIFO profits
+ Pension expense (FASB 87)
+ Minority interest
± Special items (after tax)
= Inflation-adjusted gross cash flow

Net income after tax

Unlike EP where an adjustment for taxes is undertaken to reflect the operating return on the unlevered firm, CFROI makes no such adjustment in arriving at gross cash flow. EP and other measures recalculate taxes in order to unlever the firm. The cash savings from the interest tax shield is reflected in a tax-advantaged cost of debt, which is part of the discount rate. CFROI recognizes the tax advantage of debt in the gross cash flow and calculates a weighted average cost of capital that rises (rather than falls) as debt rises. In other words, the tax savings from debt are recognized in the gross cash flow (the numerator of the CFROI equation) while the riskiness of debt is recognized through a rising cost of capital (the denominator) when performing the DCF analysis.

Depreciation and amortization

Depreciation and amortization are added back as non-cash items.

Interest expense

Interest expense is added back to net income since we are calculating the return to all capital providers. The interest tax shield from debt remains in net income to reflect the tax advantage to cash flow of debt financing. As debt increases, the firm's risk increases and this is recognized through a higher cost of capital.

Rental expense

Since rental expense represents a financing decision, it is added back to net income and capitalized on the balance sheet as described in detail in section 11.2.1. For valuation purposes, a debt value of capitalized leases is added to debt and equivalents. Along with all other debt and equivalents, it is subtracted from the firm value to arrive at the equity value. The tax advantage of rental expense is treated similarly to interest expense.

R&D expense

R&D expense is added back to net income since it is treated as a capital expenditure. It is capitalized on the balance sheet as described in section 11.2.1.

Net monetary holding gain (Loss)

The monetary holding gain simply reflects the impact of inflation on monetary assets during the course of the year.
   The calculation is:

   Beginning of year (BOY) net monetary assets
   less beginning of year (BOY) net monetary liabilities
   times change in the GDP deflator

   Low inflation in many of today's industrialized countries results in a minor adjustment.

Monetary holding gain (loss)	Amount	Source
Current assets less inventories – BOY	11 311	B/S, Note 15
+ Current non-debt liabilities – BOY	(12 972)	B/S, Note 17
Net monetary assets (liabilities) – BOY	(1661)	
× % change in GDP deflator	2.2%	External data
Monetary holding gain (loss)	**37**	

Figure 11.21   Vodafone net monetary holding gain (see Appendix 1: Figures A1.7 and A1.8)

FIFO profits

The FIFO inventory method more accurately captures the replacement cost of inventory on the balance sheet in an inflationary environment (the newest assets remain on the balance sheet and the oldest assets are sold and expensed through cost of goods sold on the income statement). However, the LIFO method more accurately captures the cost of inventory sold. Since many companies do not account for inventory under the LIFO method, the CFROI calculation makes an inflation adjustment to inventory. The FIFO profits calculation is:

BOY inventory balance
times percent of FIFO inventory (if all inventory is on FIFO this is 100%)
equals FIFO inventory
times change in the PPI
equals FIFO profits

If all inventory is accounted for using LIFO, no adjustment is necessary.

FIFO profits	Amount	Source
inventory book value – BOY	458	B/S
× % of inventory using FIFO	100%	B/S
FIFO inventory	458	Calculated
× % change in PPI	−2.5%	External data
FIFO profits	**(11)**	

Figure 11.22   Vodafone FIFO profits (see Appendix 1: Figure A1.9)

Pension expense

Pension expense comes from the pension footnote and is net of service cost and pension cost. Pension debt is added to debt and equivalents for valuation purposes. However, in the case of a pension surplus, this is not added to the value of the company, since these funds rightfully belong to the pension holders.

Minority interest

Any minority interest is added back.

Special items

Any special items are added back. The special item must first be tax adjusted to account for the impact on cash flow, before it is added back.

Gross cash flow	Amount	Source
Net income after tax	(7540)	I/S
+ Depreciation and amortization	19 598	Notes 5, 13
+ Interest expense	995	Note 7
+ R&D expense	219	Note 5
+ Rental expense	1337	Note 5
+ Monetary holding gain (loss)	37	Calculated
+ FIFO profits	(11)	Calculated
+ Pension (net of total service cost and pension cost)	17	Note 32
+ Minority interest	602	I/S
+ Associate and JV income	(2215)	I/S Notes 3, 10
± Special items (after tax @ 30%)	(293)	Note 4 and I/S
Total inflation adjusted gross cash flow	**£12 745**	

Figure 11.23   Vodafone gross cash flow (see Appendix 1: Figures A1.13–A1.21)

11.3   CFROI CALCULATION FOR VODAFONE

CFROI calculation	Amount
Inflation adjusted depreciating assets	50 693
Inflation adjusted non-depreciating assets (FV)	1615
Inflation adjusted gross investment (PV)	52 308
Inflation adjusted gross cash flow (pmt)	12 745
Project life (nper)	8.30
CFROI calculation [Exel function=rate(nper,pmt,pv,fv)]	**18.6%**

Figure 11.24   CFROI calculation

After calculating gross cash flow, we have all of the inputs for the CFROI calculation. The result of the calculation is a CFROI of 18.6%. Is this CFROI good or bad? Comparing Vodafone's CFROI against its real discount rate of 5.4% (as calculated by HOLT and discussed in further detail below), we can see that Vodafone has a positive spread of 13.2% above its cost of capital. This return would place Vodafone well within the top 20% of industrial returns.[10]

In the CFROI approach, the CFROI represents the weighted average return on the projects that encompass the firm. In a sense we are viewing the firm as a single project; however, the firm is assumed to be ongoing. We are simply measuring management's ability to generate returns on the assets currently in place in the company. When we get to the section

---

[10] Analysis based on the HOLT database of over 18 000 company returns.

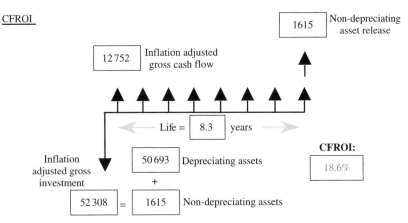

Figure 11.25   CFROI calculation

in which we use CFROI for valuation purposes, we will explain how the firm replaces the project (assets) currently in place with future projects (capex and/or acquisitions). It will also become clear how management may trade improved performance in a current period for better or worse performance in future periods. From a valuation perspective, this simply reflects the trading of cash flows between one period and another and the resulting valuation.

11.4   A COMMENT ON GOODWILL

Goodwill is the amount in excess of book value paid for an acquisition. The goodwill may reflect the value of a brand or a sustainable competitive advantage. The astute reader may have noticed that there is no place in the CFROI calculation for goodwill, yet it is on the books and it does reflect an expenditure of shareholder funds. How does CFROI hold management accountable for goodwill?

CFROI is designed to measure the economic profitability of the operating business; the cash generated against the cash invested. While goodwill is certainly an expenditure of shareholder funds, it is not an operating asset. Management has the ability to improve the return on operating assets. Managers can improve margins by cutting costs, or improve asset efficiency by generating more revenue from operating assets. However, management can do nothing to make goodwill either more or less efficient. Because it represents an excess over the book value of the assets, it can only be a drag on the returns of the business.

CFROI as a measure of the operating return of the business is a measure operating managers can influence. In order to judge senior management's ability to acquire businesses (hold them accountable for the goodwill from acquisitions), a transaction CFROI is calculated. The transaction CFROI calculation requires two steps:

(1) The transaction CFROI ratio = Gross investment/(Gross investment + Goodwill)
(2) Transaction CFROI = Transaction CFROI ratio * "Operating" CFROI

Transaction CFROI	Amount	Source
Gross Investment	52 306	Calculated
Total intangibles	99 718	Notes 11, 13
Net goodwill written off	256	Calculated
Non-goodwill intangibles (3G licenses)	(4275)	Calculated
Total intangibles	**95 699**	
Transaction CFROI ratio (GI/(GI + intangibles))	35.3%	Calculated
CFROI	18.6%	Calculated
Transaction CFROI (Transaction CFROI ratio * CFROI)	**6.6%**	**Calculated**

Figure 11.26   Vodafone transaction CFROI (see Appendix 1: Figure A1.22)

Since the transaction CFROI represents the amount of operating return lost due to the cost of acquisitions (acquisition price > net book value) the transaction CFROI is less than CFROI. Analysts should assess how the ratio between the two changes over time. For example, Figure 11.26 shows that while Vodafone generates an operating CFROI of 18.6% (13.2% positive spread), all of Vodafone's acquisitions result in a transaction CFROI of 6.6% (1.2% positive spread). Clearly, management has transferred a significant amount of wealth to the shareholders of the acquired companies, i.e. they paid high premiums.

Comments: The £4275 impairment of non-goodwill intangibles for Vodafone reflects a 30% charge based on general comments from the industry on the overpayment of 3G licenses. Under IFRS, companies are required to undertake an impairment test yearly on such assets. We would expect to start seeing better estimates of the value of such assets in future annual reports.

The trends of CFROI and transaction CFROI provide useful insights. For example, Figure 11.27 presents the returns for Vodafone, represented by the stacked bars (the lower light part of the bar reflects transaction CFROI: CFROI with goodwill. The upper, dark part

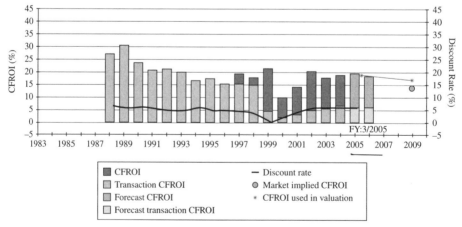

Figure 11.27   Vodafone CFROI and transaction CFROI

of the bar reflects CFROI: the return on the operating business). In 1999, Vodafone acquired Mannesmann. Both Vodafone and Mannesmann were high return businesses as reflected in the 21.4% CFROI. However, because Vodafone acquired Mannesmann at a large premium, the transaction CFROI dropped to 4.4% (the 17% difference reflects value transferred to Mannesmann shareholders). Vodafone still earned a 25 basis point positive spread because of the very low cost of capital during the tech bubble. In 2001, Vodafone paid a high premium for its 3G licenses. Because the 3G asset was not yet producing anything, CFROI fell to about 9.7% and transaction CFROI fell slightly below the cost of capital at the time. Since 2001, the CFROI of the operating company has improved to as high as 20.3% and 18.6% as of March 2005. An important point is that although Vodafone paid a premium for Mannesmann and its 3G licenses, it has managed those acquisitions to greater operating returns (CFROIs).

From Accounting to Economics: Economic Profit

12.1 THE BASICS

Unlike CFROI, which calculates a return on investment via an IRR calculation, EP measures the absolute amount of wealth creation in a given year. EP is the residual profit left after subtracting a capital charge from the net operating profit after tax (NOPAT). The capital charge is made on the capital employed by the firm bearing in mind that both debt and equity investors demand a return on their investment.[1]

The first step in calculating EP is to calculate NOPAT (net operating profit after tax):

Revenue
− Cost of goods sold (COGS)
− Selling, general and administrative costs (SG&A)
− Depreciation
+ Other operating income
= EBIT (earnings before interest and taxes)
* (1 − Cash tax rate)
= NOPAT

The next step is to calculate the cost of capital, based on the firm's capital structure. In its simplest guise (without considering accounting adjustments), the invested capital used in calculating the capital charge is:

Fixed assets
+ Current assets
− Current liabilities
= Invested capital

The calculation of invested capital is often based on the average capital to reflect the fact that NOPAT is earned during the course of the year, while the balance sheet reflects a point in time. For valuation purposes (discussed in more detail below), the opening invested capital is used for the capital charge.

Since NOPAT is the operating profit to the firm's capital providers, a weighted average cost of capital (WACC) based on the relative market weights of debt and equity in the firm's capital structure should be used:[2]

---

[1] See Bennett Stewart III (1991), for a further detailed discussion of all possible accounting adjustments to EVA and the logic behind these adjustments. Unfortunately, many practitioners from financial analysts to corporate managers simply calculate EVA from the accounting numbers, somewhat leaving the "economic" out of EVA.

[2] See Brealey *et al.* (2005), pp. 218, 503–504.

$$\text{WACC} = \% \text{ Debt} * \text{Cost of debt} * (1 - \text{Corporate tax rate}) + \% \text{ Equity} * \text{Cost of equity}$$

Generally, the cost of equity is calculated using the CAPM model, where:

$$\text{Cost of equity} = \text{Risk-free rate} + \beta *(\text{Equity risk premium})$$

The capital charge and subsequent EP can then be calculated from the following equations:

$$\text{Capital charge} = \text{WACC}^* \text{ Average invested capital}$$
$$\text{EP} = \text{NOPAT} - \text{Capital charge}$$

The EP calculation is presented graphically in Figure 12.1. In this example, we assume revenue of $1000, EBIT is 12% of revenue, the corporate tax rate is 33% and average assets are $494. Finally, we assume a 10% WACC.

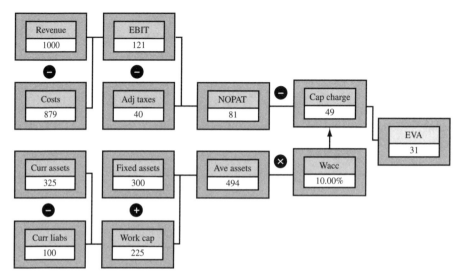

Figure 12.1   EP calculation

It is beneficial to calculate the return on invested capital (ROIC) for benchmarking purposes and understand the firm's performance relative to its cost of capital.

$$\text{ROIC} = \frac{\text{NOPAT}}{\text{Invested capital}}$$

For valuation purposes, the ROIC should be based on the opening capital. The calculation is generally based on the average capital when assessing corporate performance. EP can be calculated from:

$$\text{EP} = (\text{ROIC} - \text{WACC}) \times \text{Invested capital}$$

Firms that beat their cost of capital have a positive EP and are considered wealth creators. Firms whose returns fall below their cost of capital have a negative EP and are condemned with the appellation of wealth destroyer.

At this stage, it is worthwhile to consider the connection between EP measurement and valuation.

$$\text{Firm value} = \text{Invested capital}_0 + \sum_{n=1}^{N} \frac{\text{EP}_n}{(1 + \text{WACC})^n}$$

If a firm is expected to generate positive EPs into the future, its enterprise value should exceed its book value. A useful multiple to consider is the firm's market value divided by its book value (MV/BV) as represented by the invested capital. The basic components of the firm's market value are its market cap and market value of debt. A MV/BV multiple that is greater than one implies that the market is expecting the firm to create value and produce positive EPs. A value of less than one implies that wealth destruction and negative EP flows are expected. Note that when returns are expected to remain in line with the firm's cost of capital, its enterprise value should equal the invested capital and it should trade at a multiple of one. It is highly beneficial to understand the market's future EP expectations when comparing multiples and making investment decisions.

12.2   CAVEATS

There are a number of subtle issues to consider when using EP. In many textbooks goodwill is generally considered part of the invested capital. Three approaches can be pursued:

- Include net goodwill in the invested capital. In this case, the amortization charge should be included as an expense in the NOPAT calculation.
- Include gross goodwill in the invested capital. The draconian approach is to hold management perpetually responsible for all goodwill spent. In this case, the amortization charge should *not* be included as an expense in the NOPAT calculation.
- Exclude goodwill from the invested capital and the amortization charge from NOPAT. Goodwill treatment in this case is similar to that of the CFROI framework.

Including goodwill in the invested capital can lead to confused results for firms with a high level of goodwill on their balance sheets. It might be insightful to note that management made a wealth destroying acquisition and include goodwill in the capital, but it is of little help in measuring the performance of operating managers or the firm's operating assets. It also makes benchmarking an almost hopeless task.

Although it is insightful to calculate the firm's EP based on all capital employed, we recommend that only the operating and non-goodwill capital is considered in the evaluation of the firm's operating performance and valuation. Comparability will be greatly enhanced. In our experience, it is often best to value the firm on an organic basis and to value acquisitions separately. Future acquisitions are difficult to forecast and the ultimate concern is whether future acquisitions are positive NPV projects or not. A brief list of other considerations includes:

- *Intangible assets*: It is sensible to treat intangible assets that are cash generative as part of the invested capital. If so, the amortization charge should be part of the NOPAT calculation.
- *Operating vs. non-operating investments*: If investments are operating they should be treated as invested capital and the income associated with them should be part of the

NOPAT calculation. Non-operating investments should be excluded from invested capital and the value of the market value of these investments added back for the purposes of valuation.

- *Current liabilities so large as to result in negative invested capital*: This will benefit the company's EP but will result in a negative ROIC, which is counter-intuitive and of little benchmarking value. Dell is an example of a firm that uses its creditors to successfully fund its growth and operations.
- *Forecasting the cash tax rate*: It is generally sensible to ramp the cash tax rate to the corporate tax rate or a normalized tax rate over the life of an explicit forecast.

12.3 EP ADJUSTMENTS USING VODAFONE MARCH 2005 ANNUAL REPORT

According to Bennett Stewart in his book *The Quest for Value,* there are some 160 possible accounting adjustments to EP. However, the most important adjustments are relatively standard, and similar to CFROI. The primary exception is that EP, as a nominal number, requires no inflation adjustment. Using the CFROI adjustments for Vodafone, we show the equivalent adjustments for EP, where appropriate.

12.3.1 Balance Sheet

Probably the most important systematic adjustments to the balance sheet are to capitalize R&D and lease expense. As in the CFROI framework, R&D is an investment and leasing reflects a financing decision.

Adjusted net working capital
+ Net fixed assets
+ Net intangible assets
+ Operating investments
+ Capitalized leases
+ Capitalized R&D
= Invested capital

Because it is a nominal number and based on the firm's net assets, EP does not require the detailed inflation adjustments or gross plant recaptured of the CFROI calculation.

Adjusted Net Working Capital

Calculating the adjusted net working capital is straightforward. First, consider whether the firm has excess cash. Damodaran argues for the removal of all cash from working capital since one can value cash by counting it and estimate its return by observing the risk-free rate.[3] However, many analysts will leave an amount of operating cash in current assets and subtract what they consider surplus from the asset base for the EP calculation. For simplicity, we have followed Damodaran's suggestion and classified all cash in Vodafone's accounts as surplus thereby removing it from the asset base. If the firm accounts for its inventory on

---

[3] See Damodaran, http://pages.stern.nyu.edu/~adamodar/

a LIFO basis, the LIFO reserve should be added back. Finally, we have moved accounts receivable (debtors) falling due in more than one year from current assets to other long-term assets to remain consistent with the CFROI calculations. Figure 12.2 presents the working capital adjustments for Vodafone.

Working capital	2004	2005	Source
Current assets	13 149	11 794	B/S
− Debtor's amounts falling due more than one year	1380	2096	B/S
− Cash	5790	3666	B/S
+ LIFO reserve	0	0	
= Adjusted current assets	5979	6032	
Non-interest bearing current liabilities	12 972	14 445	Note 17
Net working capital	(6993)	(8413)	

Figure 12.2 Working capital adjustments (see Appendix 2: Figure A2.1)

Tangible and Intangible Assets

We use net property, plant and equipment as reported but adjust goodwill to reflect the total amount of intangible fixed assets, less the CFROI adjustment for 3G licenses, plus the total goodwill in associates and accumulated goodwill amortization to hold management accountable for all shareholder funds expended for acquisitions. Although this does not affect the standard EP calculation, we believe it is a useful exercise to separate goodwill intangibles from non-goodwill intangibles in order to assess the amount of operating intangible assets versus goodwill. The dominance of goodwill, accounting for almost 79% of Vodafone's net fixed assets, will have a significant effect on the company's returns as discussed above. We will revisit this issue and strip out the goodwill for forecasting and valuation purposes below. We will also exclude investments from the EP balance sheet before calculating invested capital below, as these are not considered operating assets. However, we will add investments back for purposes of valuation later in this part.

Fixed and intangible assets	2004	2005	Source
Net property, plant and equipment	18 083	18 398	B/S
Net goodwill (less net other intangible assets)	107 498	95 443	B/S, Notes 11, 13
Accumulated goodwill amortization	53 883	68 515	Notes 11, 13
Net other intangible assets	4275	4275	HOLT adj
Investments	4124	3996	B/S, Note 13
Other operating assets	1380	2096	B/S
PV of operating leases	2172	2435	Calculated
Net capitalized R&D	350	439	Calculated
Fixed assets	191 765	195 597	

Figure 12.3 Fixed and intangible asset adjustments (see Appendices 1 and 2: Figures A1.2, A2.1, A2.2. Note: net goodwill = 99 718 (per Figure A1.22) less net other intangible assets of 4275 = 95 443)

Two adjustments require further discussion, capitalization of operating leases and R&D.

Capitalized Leases

Since leasing is a financing decision, we recommend capitalizing lease expenses. The standard methodology for capitalizing leases is to calculate the present value of the operating lease commitments as disclosed in the footnotes.[4] As Figure 12.4 shows, Vodafone discloses its operating lease commitments for the next 5 years and all years beyond year five. The first step for capitalizing operating leases is to estimate the average cost of Vodafone debt (see Appendix 2, Figure A2.3). Since Vodafone borrows money throughout the world, we could undertake a currency adjusted weighted average debt rate. However, since the debt rate should be based on the same currency as the forecasts, a credit analysis of Vodafone's UK debt is sufficient. Our credit analysis results in an average interest rate of 6.0% on Vodafone's UK debt obligations.

To calculate the present value of the lease commitments, we discount the first five years at 6.0%. Since we do not know the timing of lease payments beyond year 5, there is insufficient information to estimate the present value of this residual period without the help of some assumptions. First, we need to estimate the embedded lease commitment period beyond year 5 by taking the beyond year 5 total and dividing it by the average lease commitment (£1132/£388 = 2.9 years).[5] We divide £1132 by 3 to get the estimated yearly lease commitment of £377 for years 6 through 8. These lease commitments are then discounted at 6%. The total value of capitalized operating leases is £2435. A similar analysis for 2004 yields an average UK debt rate of 6.0%, and a present value of lease commitments of £2172. The resulting mid-year present value of operating lease commitments for purposes of the EP calculation is £2304.

Weighted average VOD interest rate 2005 Operating lease payments due	6.0% Commitment	Discount factor	PV of lease commitments
First year	630	0.94	595
Second year	406	0.89	362
Third year	352	0.84	296
Fourth year	299	0.79	237
Fifth year	255	0.75	191
Beyond fifth year	1132	0.67	755
Present value of lease payments			2435
Estimated years embedded beyond year 5 (rounded)	3		
Average lease payment beyond year 5	377		
Average PV of operating leases 2004–2005			2304
Implied interest on operating leases @	**6.0%**		**137**

Figure 12.4   Capitalized leases (see Appendix 2: Figures A2.3 and A2.4)

We note that when capitalizing leases for CFROI, we start with the reported lease expense per the income statement of £1337, while under EP we start with the reported lease obligation due within one year of £630. One may question why these two numbers are so different. First, the reported lease obligation reflects the minimum amount owed over the coming year.

---

[4] See Damodaran, http://pages.stern.nyu.edu/~adamodar/pc/oplease.xls, see also Peterson and Peterson (1996), pp. 14–15.
[5] The average of the lease commitments for years 1–5 is £388. We round 2.9 years to 3.0 years.

Second, lease expense reflects what was actually paid over the just ended year. This expense may include more than the minimum obligation due to the way the lease is structured. In addition, the March 2005 Vodafone annual report states that the operating lease expense includes "fixed line rentals" which is probably a metering charge.

Capitalized R&D

Capitalized R&D is the mid-year adjusted sum of R&D expenses for the previous five years less an accumulated amortization charge, based on a five-year life. To calculate the mid-year adjusted amortization expense, take the average of the current and previous year R&D expense and divide by the life. As Figure 12.5 shows, in 2005, the calculation is: $((219 + 171)/2)/5 = £39$ (this amount is used as part of the total amortization charge in the NOPAT calculation below). The Total amortized R&D 2005 of 22 is calculated as follows: $(1 - 0.5)$ to reflect the mid-year of the R&D expended, divided by the R&D life of five years and the R&D expense of 219 or $(1 - 0.5) * (219/5) = 22$, the amortization expense for the capitalized R&D expense for 2005. The final column, Net capitalized R&D, is simply the difference between the R&D expense and the R&D amortization, and reflects the amount of R&D added to the balance sheet in 2005.

Capitalized R&D (2005, Note 5 and previous years' notes)	Amount	Amortization (mid-year adjusted) 2005	Total amortized R&D 2005	Net capitalized R&D
Telecom R&D life (years)	5			
R&D expense 1999	37			
R&D expense 2000	46			
R&D expense 2001	72	12	65	7
R&D expense 2002	110	18	77	33
R&D expense 2003	164	27	82	82
R&D expense 2004	171	34	51	120
R&D expense 2005	219	39	22	197
Capitalized R&D as of 2005	**736**	**130**	**297**	**439**
Capitalized R&D as of 2004	*563*	*99*	*213*	*350*

Figure 12.5   Capitalized R&D (see Appendix 1: Figure A1.16)

Besides calculating the annual amortization charge, it is also necessary to calculate the cumulative amortization in order to calculate the net capitalized R&D. Details are provided in Figure 12.5.

Total investors' funds

Total investors' funds for calculating EP are equal to net working capital plus fixed and intangible assets less investments (which are added back to equity value in the valuation). The analyst should decide if investments are operating or non-operating and then treat any income from investments in a consistent manner. For Vodafone, we remove investments from the asset base and add them back to the valuation.

Total investors' funds	2004	2005	Source
Net working capital	(6993)	(8413)	B/S
Fixed and intangible assets	191 765	195 597	B/S, Notes 11, 13
Less investments (added back at valuation)	4124	3996	B/S, Note 13
Invested capital for EP calculation	**180 648**	**183 188**	
Surplus cash	5790	3666	B/S
Total invested capital	**186 438**	**186 854**	
Average invested capital (excluding surplus cash)		**181 918**	

Figure 12.6   Total investors' funds

Net operating profit after tax	2004	2005	Source
Sales	33 559	34 133	I/S
− COGS	15 352	15 813	Note 5
− Sales, general and administrative	5656	5440	Note 5
= EBITDA	12 551	12 880	
− Depreciation and amortization	19 667	19 598	Notes 5, 13
= EBIT	(7116)	(6718)	
+ R&D expenses	171	219	Note 5
− Amortization of capitalized R&D	99	130	Calculated
+ Goodwill amortization	15 305	15 070	Notes 5, 13
+ Implied interest expense of capitalized operating leases	130	137	Calculated
Adjusted EBIT	**8390**	**8579**	
+ Change in LIFO reserve	0	0	
+ Change in other reserves	0	0	
NOPBTA	**8390**	**8579**	
Cash tax rate calculation			
Income tax expense	2866	2835	I/S
− Change in deferred taxes	576	330	Note 21
= Cash tax expense	2290	2505	
As reported pre-tax income	(5335)	(4103)	I/S
− Special items	125	297	I/S, Note 4
+ Goodwill amortization	15 305	15 070	Notes 5, 13
= Adjusted pre-tax income for tax calculations	9845	10 670	
Cash tax rate (cash taxes/adjusted pre-tax income)	23.3%	23.5%	
Cash taxes	1952	2014	
NOPAT	**6439**	**6565**	
NOPAT margin	*19.2%*	*19.2%*	

Figure 12.7   NOPAT calculation (see Appendices 1 and 2: Figures A1.1–A1.21 and A2.5–A2.10. Note: pre-tax income excludes an exceptional tax credit of 599 (Figure A2.8) which is included in special items). The cash tax rate reflects cash taxes paid after adjusting for special items

12.3.2   Net operating profit after tax (NOPAT)

To calculate NOPAT, start with net sales as reported in the income statement, remove depreciation, amortization and any special items from cost of goods sold and SG&A, as shown in Figure 12.7. Subtract D&A to arrive at EBIT. To calculate adjusted EBIT add the R&D expense less R&D amortization (see Figure 12.5) and the implied interest on capitalized operating leases (see Figure 12.4). Since income associated with investments (which were removed from the balance sheet above) is after the EBIT line, no further adjustments are necessary. If there is a LIFO reserve, add it back as well as any changes in other reserves to reflect a source or use of cash. To calculate cash taxes paid, work out the cash tax rate and multiply it by the net operating profit before taxes (NOPBTA) to arrive at NOPAT. While the inflation adjustments may be the most complicated part of the CFROI calculation, capturing and adjusting for the tax implications of interest, non-operating items and deferred tax liabilities may be the most complex part of the NOPAT and EP calculation. Because gross goodwill will be included in the invested capital, the goodwill amortization charge will not be treated as an operating expense in the NOPAT calculation.

12.3.3   Economic profit

To calculate EP, multiply average invested capital by the cost of capital and subtract that amount from NOPAT. While the discount rate relevant for CFROI is a real rate, for EP it is a nominal rate. We estimate a nominal WACC of 7.8% as reflected in Figure 12.8.

WACC calculation	
Debt and debt equivalents	15 823
Market cap	78 322
Cost of debt	6.0%
Cost of equity	8.5%
Marginal tax rate	30%
WACC	**7.8%**

Figure 12.8 Weighted average cost of capital calculation. The tax rate for the WACC calculation reflects the statutory marginal tax rate for the company and may differ from the cash tax rate in the NOPAT calculation which reflects tax benefits, tax deferrals or reversals of previous deferrals. In the case of Vodafone, the cash tax rate, reflecting actual cash taxes paid differs from the statutory tax rate.

Finally, Figure 12.9 shows Vodafone's EP calculation for 2005. Due to all of the goodwill on the balance sheet, the company earned a negative EP.

EP	2005
Sales	34 133
NOPBTA	8579
Cash tax rate	23.5%
NOPAT	6565
NOPAT margin	19.2%
BOY invested capital	180 648
Average invested capital	181 918
EP (calculated with the average invested capital)	(7577)
EP (calculated with BOY invested capital)	(7478)
Discount rate (WACC)	7.8%
ROIC (NOPAT/average invested capital)	3.6%

Figure 12.9 EP calculation

12.3.4   EP or CFROI?

How can Vodafone have a negative EP and a positive CFROI? Remember, CFROI distinguishes between operating capital in the form of fixed assets and non-goodwill intangibles and goodwill. Management can improve the efficiency of operating capital. Management cannot improve the efficiency of goodwill. Goodwill acts as deadweight on capital efficiency. It is value transferred to shareholders of companies acquired.

By contrast, EP does not distinguish between operating capital and goodwill putting it into the same basket. Thus, management is held responsible for all shareholder funds spent, but cannot be judged on how well they are managing the operating business. The number to compare ROIC to is transaction CFROI, which does include goodwill. The transaction CFROI for Vodafone is 6.6%, which is near the company's real cost of capital of 5.5%, versus a nominal spread on a return on invested capital (ROIC) of 3.6% against a 7.8% nominal cost of capital. In Chapter 13, we use an operating EP in which we have removed goodwill from the balance sheet. By removing goodwill, we follow the CFROI methodology and focus on valuing operating assets.

Which measure is better? EP is generally easier to calculate and communicate. It is also an absolute amount. These attributes make it effective for compensation programs and corporate performance communication. On the other hand, it is susceptible to inflation and accounting distortions. It is also dependent on the amount of capital employed. EP proponents see this as a strength of the model because returns as a percentage value and growth do not incorporate the magnitude of value created. They argue that large companies with low (albeit positive spread) returns may look less attractive than small companies with high returns. These commentators believe that by converting the percentage ROIC into an absolute monetary sum, the amount of capital at work is incorporated into the comparison.[6]

While this is a useful perspective for the operating manager (more capital at work creates more value in a positive spread business), we believe it risks distorting the analysis from the perspective of the investor. While it is advantageous to earn a positive spread on a larger capital base, this advantage may result in overlooking those smaller high return companies that deploy less capital. For example, as long as Wal-Mart earns a positive spread on its capital resulting in a positive EP, Wal-Mart's huge capital base will give it a large EP. A small retailer may earn a larger spread above the cost of capital, it may have many growth opportunities, but unless it can deploy as much capital as Wal-Mart, it is at a disadvantage when comparing EPs. What does matter is that a positive spread business with growth opportunities can allocate capital to capture those growth opportunities. While the larger company may create more absolute value, the small company may create more value per share. From the investor's perspective it is the per share growth in value that matters not the growth in total EP. The ability to identify positive spreads and growth opportunities is important.

When ranking companies by EP, larger companies tend to end up at the top of the list, while smaller companies, which may have better operating returns but less capital deployed, end up farther down the list. We believe that separately assessing the return-discount rate

---

[6] See, for example, Dobbs and Koller (2005), p.20. "One disadvantage of ROIC and growth, however, is that neither incorporates the magnitude of the value created, so a small company or business unit with a 30 percent ROIC seems more successful than an enormous company with a 20 percent return. We use economic profit to convert ROIC into a dollar metric so that we can incorporate the size of the value created into comparisons with other companies."

spread as well as the value of growth opportunities overcomes this disadvantage for the investor.

CFROI provides more insight into the differences between returns on the operating capital of the company and its acquisition goodwill. In addition, with its inflation adjustments, it allows for benchmarking across time and country borders. As a percentage, it also allows for benchmarking among firms regardless of size (as discussed in the previous paragraphs). ROIC and NOPAT margin allow for benchmarking, but these metrics are sensitive to inflation, asset age and asset mix, which limits their utility. CFROI and EP are more likely to be directionally different with firms that have particularly old or new assets combined with long asset lives. Over time, the CFROI calculation using gross investment and asset life is able to detect a decline in asset efficiency (declining CFROI) as assets age. Use of net assets in EP often leads to the opposite result. If assets age more quickly than their efficiency declines, we risk facing the scenario of a rising EP against declining asset efficiency. Such analysis would be particularly difficult in the presence of acquisitions and divestitures. Inconsistencies between CFROI and ROIC decrease as the level of non-depreciating assets in the asset composition increases. For fixed asset intensive companies and industries, the differences can be striking and CFROI is the preferred metric.

From Economics to Valuation – Part II

13.1 GENERAL RULES

Before discussing valuation, it is useful to highlight the general rules for using CFROI or EP when assessing potential paths for future value creation.

When EP is positive, the firm has created wealth for its equity shareholders in the period measured equal to the EP. Thus, there are two key questions to ask when using EP:

- Does the firm generate positive EP?
- If EP is positive, can the firm grow the business and increase EP?

When assessing CFROI there are three key questions to ask:

- What is the CFROI level?
- What is the cost of capital?
- Given the CFROI spread (CFROI less the cost of capital), should the firm grow or contract?

A frequent criticism of both CFROI and EP is that management can trade future CFROIs or EPs for current CFROIs or EPs. The tradeoff requires the rejection of future positive return projects since they would negatively impact current period earnings and potentially both EP and CFROI. In other words, management decides to trade future higher cash flows for current period cash flow and earnings.

13.2 MARKET VALUE ADDED

EP attempts to address this shortcoming by looking at market value added (MVA). MVA is simply the spread between the market value of the firm and its book value. If management is making short-term decisions to increase current period EP to the detriment of long-term decisions, the MVA should drop. However, an accurate assessment of what is implied in the market value can make the judgment of management actions difficult. A good metric to look at in this case is MVA/EP.

13.3 CFROI

Figure 13.1 presents a framework to assess the three CFROI questions above.

(1) When CFROI > the cost of capital (a positive spread), grow the business, or lacking growth opportunities, maintain or improve CFROI.
(2) When CFROI = the cost of capital (neutral spread), growth neither creates nor destroys value, therefore management should focus on improving CFROI through improving either margins and/or asset utilization.

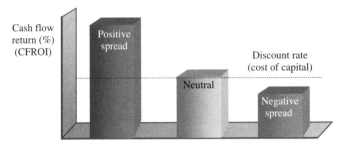

Figure 13.1   CFROI growth versus operating improvement rules

(3) When CFROI < the cost of capital (negative spread), exit from low return businesses and focus on improving CFROI, either through improved margins and/or asset utilization. Growth destroys value.[1]

It is worth repeating that both CFROI and EP should be used in a twofold manner: as a single period measure of performance and as a starting point for valuation. Thus, if management chooses to trade future CFROIs or EPs for higher current CFROIs or EPs, not only will they break the above general rules, but the present value of the firm's future cash flows will decline, thus negatively impacting its valuation.

13.4   A WORD ON DEBT

As mentioned, both EP and CFROI recognize the Modigliani and Miller insight that financing decisions do not change value in the absence of taxes.[2] The EP capital charge and EP valuation require the analyst to unlever the levered firm. As described above, NOPAT reflects the operating profit to the unlevered firm, while the tax shield from debt is recognized in the weighted average cost of capital, the mechanical weakness of this approach is that the cost of capital can be minimized by employing 100% debt financing (debt is cheaper than equity and has a tax advantage). Firms do not use 100% debt financing because as the level of debt rises, the risk of financial distress also increases. The standard weighted average cost of capital calculation does not recognize an increasing debt level as an increasing risk to the firm.[3] Analysts should carefully consider the cost of debt and equity at different levels of debt when discounting future cash flows. The cost of debt is not constant.

CFROI recognizes the tax advantage of debt by leaving the impact of the tax shield in the gross cash flow when the benefit is earned. Interest expense is added back to net income when calculating gross cash flow, but the income tax paid is not adjusted. CFROI does not tax adjust the cost of debt in the weighted average cost of capital calculation. The market derived cost of capital calculation used with CFROI allows for an increasing cost of capital as the level of debt and risk of financial distress increase. In other words as debt increases, the interest tax shield increases, but this is offset by a rising cost of capital.

---

[1] There is an obvious exception to the negative spread rule. Start-up firms or firms undertaking new lines of business might have negative spreads. Returns and sales growth are expected to increase as the business matures.
[2] See Chapter 8, note 12.
[3] See Damodaran at http://pages.stern.nyu.edu/~adamodar/ for a discussion of how to adjust for this problem.

13.5   VALUATION

With the accounting distortions "cleaned up", both CFROI and EP are more closely aligned to actual cash flow generation. The next step is to take advantage of that alignment to estimate future value creation or cash flows through projected EPs or CFROIs.

We will discuss the general framework using CFROI in valuation first, followed by the general framework for an EP-based valuation.[4]

13.5.1   CFROI valuation: General framework

Given the same adjustments and forecasts, a valuation using discounted EP or free cash flow ("FCF") streams will result in the same value while a CFROI valuation will generally result in a different value. The difference relates to how the excess return (above or below the cost of capital) in the residual period is calculated and how the asset base is calculated. A schematic showing the key drivers and components of the CFROI valuation model is diagrammed in Figure 13.2. Before going into more detail, we must first understand how to calculate cash flows within the CFROI framework.

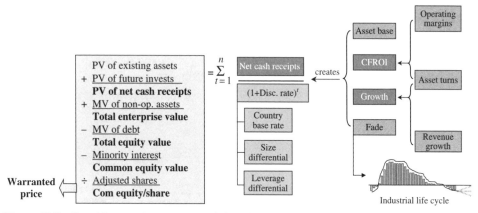

Figure 13.2   Key drivers and components of the HOLT CFROI valuation model

13.5.2   Understanding project returns

Before calculating cash flows, we should step back to the concept of capital budgeting and the IRR of a project. We demonstrated that a firm's asset base can be represented as a series of asset layers. Since cash flow generation is a function of the asset base in place, each asset layer can be thought of as an individual project generating a distinct cash flow. Conceptually, we can think of a firm making an investment in a project at the beginning of the year and earning the return on that investment at the end of the year. CFROI is simply the weighted average return of all the individual projects.

---

[4] The purpose of this chapter is to introduce the analyst to the concepts of the valuation framework. Detailed descriptions of how all the numbers in the examples were arrived at are beyond the scope of this part. Further discussion of CFROI valuation can be found in Madden (1999). Further information on EP valuations can be found in Stewart (1991).

To better understand project returns, let us imagine Kelly, a young entrepreneur, who lives near the beach and decides to open a business to rent boogie boards to tourists. Kelly's business will consist of renting boogie boards and selling condiments such as suntan lotion and sodas. In order to start her business, Kelly buys two boogie boards at $30 each and $10 worth of condiments for a gross investment of $70. Kelly's business plan assumes the boogie boards will last four years and between rentals and condiment sales, her business will generate $20 of cash flow per year. At the end of year 4, the boogie boards (depreciating assets) will need replacement while the condiments (inventory or non-depreciating assets) will still have a value of $10. The IRR for this project using the Excel rate function is: RATE(nper = 4, pmt = $20, pv = −$70, fv = $10) = 10.1%.

Now suppose that Kelly believes she has an opportunity to expand her business with the same economics. Figure 13.3 graphically depicts the business if Kelly opens an additional rental stand over each of the next four years. After the fourth layer of investment the business will have one project (boogie board rentals) starting its last year of life and one project starting its first year of life. With this simple example, the weighted average return, the CFROI, will exactly match the project ROI of each of the four individual boogie board rental stands, i.e. RATE(nper=4, pmt=$80, pv=−$280, fv=$40) = 10.1%.

Figure 13.4 illustrates the remaining cash flows from Kelly's boogie board business with a full complement of rental stands. Assuming we have the four layers of investment in place, i.e. the fourth boogie board stand has just opened; we expect to have a gross cash flow of $80 generated during year 4 and an inventory of $40. However, at the end of year 4 we retire the oldest boogie boards and release the inventory (non-depreciating assets) of $10 resulting in a gross cash flow plus NDA release of $90. Three boogie board stands now remain (year 5) with a gross cash flow of $60, generated in the following year and a further

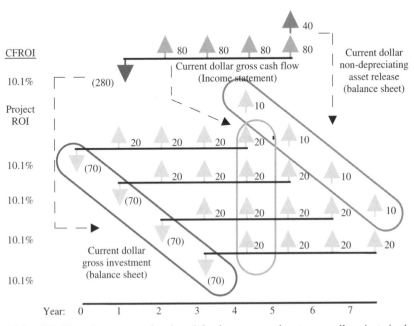

Figure 13.3   CFROI as the cross-sectional, weighted-average cash return on all projects in the firm

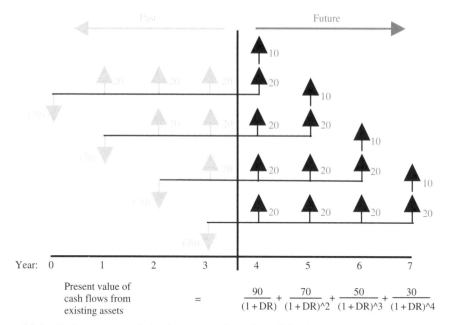

Figure 13.4 Cash return on existing investment (asset layers) in place

inventory release of $10 to give a gross cash flow plus NDA release of $70 and so on until the last layer of investment retires as shown in Figure 13.4.

13.5.3 The residual period

If Kelly's boogie board business were to close down after the fourth investment in boogie boards retires at the end of year 7, the value of the business would simply represent the cash flow generated as each asset layer (set of boogie boards) winds down plus the inventory release, less the investment made each year. We refer to this value as the value of existing assets.

However, from a firm valuation perspective, we are not interested in only the projects currently in place but the whole business going forward through time. Assume at the end of year 4, Kelly believes she can expand. Based on a market study by JB Consultants, she finds she can replace the oldest boogie boards with new improved Hawk boards which travel faster on the waves and handle gnarly cutbacks. Kelly expects she can rent the improved boogie boards at a higher price and that customers will use them longer resulting in additional purchases of suntan lotion and sodas.

If gross investment has increased to $85, or an incremental increase of $15, that increase reflects the split between incremental NDA and incremental or "growth capex". To estimate the split between non-depreciating condiments and depreciating boogie boards we look at the ratio of NDA and gross investment from the original business or $10 divided by $70, which equals 14.3%. Thus, an incremental $15 investment results in a split between NDA of $12.1 ($85*14.3%) and depreciating assets of $72.9 ($85 − $12.1). Replacement capex is equal to the $60 original boogie board cost plus "growth capex" of $12.9, the incremental cost for the improved boogie boards. Since total NDA equals $12.1, incremental NDA equals $2.1 for the additional condiments resulting in a total growth in gross investment of $15. Kelly estimates with the higher rental fees and greater condiment sales, she can now generate $24 in gross cash flow versus the $20 with the old boogie boards.

Unfortunately, although Kelly believes she can grow her business by attracting more customers and selling more sodas, her study also suggests that her high returns will attract competition. Although her gross cash flow will increase, that increase results in a lower projected IRR for the project of 9.7%. Figure 13.5 shows the effects on the business if competition comes in and forces returns and growth down.

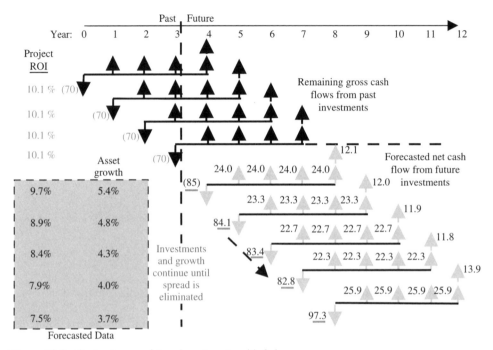

Figure 13.5   Cash return on future investments with fade

As investors, we can only see the CFROI of the whole business, not the results of the individual projects. Thus, as investors we would expect to see the following end of year 5 information: life = 4, gross investment = $295.0 ($70.0*3 + $85.0), gross cash flow = $84.0 ($20.0*3 + $24.0), NDA = $42.1 ($10*3 + $12.1). In Excel terms: RATE(nper=4, pmt=84.0, pv= − 295.0, fv=42.1) = 10.0% (versus the 10.1% CFROI as of end of year 4).

The CFROI of the business has declined slightly. However, we do not mind returns declining as long as the incremental returns remain above the cost of capital. What we do not see (as shown in Figure 13.4) is that the project ROI (IRR) on the latest boogie board investment is 9.7%, while the original projects continue to generate IRRs of 10.1% and this is what is pulling the overall CFROI down to 10%. In this simple example, we have modeled returns to decline. In the real world, the IRRs of individual projects will change from year to year and the returns for future projects may increase resulting in a rising CFROI.

However, our modeled decline in forecasted CFROI introduces an important concept into the residual calculation; that of competition and fade. Basic micro-economics teaches us that superior returns attract competition which drives down profitability. In a free and fair market, competition will continue to exert pressure on excess returns until they are competed away and economic profits become zero. Thus, while we may model rising CFROIs in our explicit forecast period, in the residual period, CFROIs fade. The fade reflects competition whittling away excess returns until the firm only covers its cost of capital (CFROI = discount rate). When there are no excess returns, economic profit equals zero, future project NPVs equal zero and the IRR equals the cost of capital. The rate of fade should reflect the competitive advantages and environment of the firm being analyzed. The fade rate is a key valuation driver and requires careful consideration.

Net cash receipts

While we have shown how to calculate the CFROI for this project, we have not discussed the actual cash flows, or net cash receipts, that are to be discounted. Net cash receipts reflect the gross cash flow less investment (capex plus change in working capital). In our example, gross investment of $295.0 is the asset base in place at the end of year 4 which generates the cash flows in year 5 mentioned above. Thus in year 4 we have the additional investment layer of $85.0 of which $12.1 is inventory. We retire the first project layer of $70.0 (of which $10.0 is an inventory release). Gross assets therefore rise by $15.0 ($85.0 – $70.0) of which $2.1 is inventory ($12.1 – $10.0).

To summarize, in year 4 we have investment of $85.0 (including additional NDA of $12.1) an NDA release of $10.0 plus a gross cash flow of $80.0 (four layers of $20.0) to yield an NCR of $5.0. The $24 of gross cash flow from the expanded business will start in year 5.

For valuation purposes, $5.0 represents year 4 net cash receipt for discounting. Notice that the capex consists of two components: replacement capex which is the cost of the original boogie boards and condiments of $70 (assuming there is no inflation, so the cost remains the same) plus growth capex which is the incremental cost of the improved boogie boards and additional condiments of $15.0. Since a firm cannot grow until it replaces retiring assets, growth reflects only that component of capex which enlarges the business, in this case $15.0 or 5.4% ($295/$280 – 1). Figure 13.6 presents the NCR calculation from start-up through year 8 for Kelly's boogie board rental business.

Year	0	1	2	3	4	5	6	7	8
Gross investment	−70.0	−140.0	−210.0	−280.0	−295.0	−309.1	−322.5	−335.3	−347.6
Growth capex		−70.0	−70.0	−70.0	−15.0	−14.1	−13.4	−12.8	−12.3
Replace retired assets					−70.0	−70.0	−70.0	−70.0	−85.0
Gross cash flow		20.0	40.0	60.0	80.0	84.0	87.3	90.0	92.3
NDA release for year					10.0	10.0	10.0	10.0	12.1
Growth in assets	−70.0	−70.0	−70.0	−70.0	−15.0	−14.1	−13.4	−12.8	−12.3
Replace retired assets					−70.0	−70.0	−70.0	−70.0	−85.0
Net cash receipts	−70.0	−50.0	−30.0	−10.0	5.0	9.9	13.9	17.3	7.2

Figure 13.6   Net cash receipt calculation

Analysts often fail to account for asset retirement and replacement and underestimate the level of capex required to fund growth. This can lead to serious problems when forecasting and valuing a firm.

13.5.4   CFROI residual period approach

Although the value of the explicit period cash flows in an FCF, EP or CFROI forecast should be the same (the impact of nominal versus real cash flows and discount rates should not change the present value), the value of the residual period will most likely differ. In a standard EP or FCF model, the residual period typically employs the Gordon growth model (also known as the dividend discount model) and often in a highly questionable manner.[5] There is an important conceptual difference between the Gordon growth model and a fading CFROI residual.

The Gordon growth model takes into account the rate at which cash flow is growing and the cost of capital at which to discount the growing cash flow. However, if there is a spread between the returns and discount rate (CFROI not equal to the discount rate or EP not equal to zero), that spread is locked in for eternity. As the cash flow grows, the spread over the cost of capital persists *ad infinitum*.[6] By contrast, the CFROI valuation model reflects the expectation of competition gnawing away excess returns. In other words, in each period of the residual, the business grows, just as in the Gordon growth model. However, the excess spread between the firm's returns and the cost of capital declines or fades. In addition, as the firm grows, additional growth becomes more difficult, so the growth rate also fades. This industrial life cycle concept is presented in Figure 13.7 and is an integral part of the HOLT CFROI valuation algorithm and framework.

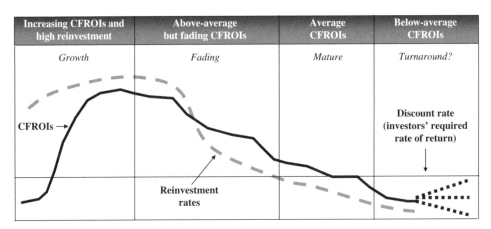

Figure 13.7   The industrial life cycle concept. Firms trade at a premium to book value when attractive returns and growth are expected. As growth opportunities dry and competition erodes high returns, firms transition from a wealth creating stage to a mature stage. Successful firms "beat fade" and find new markets and ways to sustain high returns. Unsuccessful firms and highly competitive industries watch their returns fade to or below the cost of capital. Firms that are meeting their cost of capital should trade at their book value

---

[5] The basic equation for the Gordon growth model is $CF_1/(r-g)$, where CF_1 is the next projected cash flow, g is the growth rate and r is the discount rate. The forward cash flow should be normalized. For a complete discussion of the Gordon growth model, see Stowe *et al.* (2002), pp. 55–83.

[6] CFROI residual growth rates fade to a long-term level of 2.5%, similar to long-term real economic growth. The growth rate for the Gordon growth model should reflect a long-term sustainable growth rate. It must also be less than the discount rate. Unfortunately, analysts often spend much time preparing their explicit forecasts, but very little time considering the appropriate long-term sustainable growth rate. Since the residual value has a large impact on the DCF value and the residual growth rate a big impact on the Gordon growth calculation, it is essential that considerable thought go into this number.

Finally, HOLT research has found that real economic returns as represented by CFROI have remained relatively stable around the world at 6% and this serves as the mean reverting value. Within the HOLT framework, a real (ex inflation) market-derived discount rate is based on an assumption that the overall market is fairly valued.[7] Individual company discount rates are calculated from a fair value market algorithm.[8] Once CFROI equals the discount rate, the firm neither creates nor destroys value and the NPV of future growth is zero; the firm is only meeting its investors' demanded long-term cost of capital. At that point, the value of the firm is simply the present value of cash flow generated from the wind down of the existing assets.

The primary drawback to the CFROI residual calculation is that it is much more involved than the simple Gordon growth formula. It requires calculating returns, growth and retirements at a fading rate, for a sufficient period that the CFROI-discount rate spread narrows to zero. In addition, the discount rate calculation requires a regression of all companies in the market for which the discount rate is based. If the Gordon growth model is the eternal optimist with its oft embedded assumption of eternal wealth creation, then the life cycle fade is the pragmatist and embodiment that gravity is a universal force. The CFROI fading residual reflects the reality that competition forces excess returns towards zero. If management successfully "beats fade", we would expect to see shareholder value created through a rising share price. We strongly recommend that analysts spend a great deal of their time thinking about the industries and firms where fade can be delayed by innovation and superior management, or where it will be accelerated by disruption and mismanagement. Understanding long-term market expectations is crucial to success.

13.5.5 Economic profit valuation: General framework

Although both EP and CFROI discount future cash flow, due to the residual calculation, a CFROI valuation will generally result in a different value from an EP valuation. However, an EP valuation should result in the same value as an FCF valuation, although the recognition of value (cash flow vs. residual profit flow) is different. While an FCF valuation forecasts explicit cash flows for a certain period, an EP valuation forecasts NOPAT, capital charge and EP for each period of the explicit forecast. The Gordon growth model is typically applied to both EP and FCF models for the residual period.

Let's try to make the mathematics more apparent. The explicit forecast lasts N years in the valuation equations below. When using the Gordon growth model, it is imperative that the EP and FCF in the first year of the terminal period are calculated. Growth and returns have to remain constant in the terminal period for this equation to be valid.

FCF valuation:

$$\text{Terminal value} = \frac{\text{FCF}_{N+1}}{(\text{WACC} - g)}$$

---

[7] Even if the analyst does not agree with the overall market fair value assumption, this assumption can provide some interesting insights. For example, while the long-term discount rate has remained stable around 6%, during the tech bubble, we could observe market derived discount rates below 3%. The astute analyst would not see these low discount rates as a failure of the market derived methodology, but as an indication of market exuberance. In hindsight, we can see that reversion to mean discount rates was a stronger force than the new sustainably high return technology and service economy we had supposedly entered! Chalk one up for gravity.

[8] The result of the Credit Suisse-HOLT discount rate calculation is that one-half of all companies in a market are more expensive than their share price and one-half less expensive than their share price, given the default growth, return and fade assumptions built into the framework.

$$\text{Value} = \sum_{i=1}^{N} \frac{\text{FCF}_i}{(1 + \text{WACC})^i} + \frac{\text{FCF}_{N+1}}{(\text{WACC} - g)(1 + \text{WACC})^N}$$

EP valuation:

$$\text{Terminal value} = \frac{\text{EP}_{N+1}}{(\text{WACC} - g)}$$

$$\text{Value} = \text{Invested capital}_0 + \sum_{i=1}^{N} \frac{\text{EP}_i}{(1 + \text{WACC})^i} + \frac{\text{EP}_{N+1}}{(\text{WACC} - g)(1 + \text{WACC})^N}$$

The EP model has aesthetic advantages. For example, if a firm is perennially meeting its cost of capital, its EP will remain zero and its value will be equal to the invested capital, or book value. The level of FCF is highly dependent on growth and has no intrinsic information about wealth creation. A firm that is beating its cost of capital and growing will have a negative FCF if growth exceeds ROIC. This is not a bad thing if the growth capex is invested in projects that generate returns above the cost of capital. In order to characterize the terminal year, we:

- Grow the last explicit NOPAT by a terminal growth rate.
- Subtract a terminal year capital charge (residual period opening capital * cost of capital) to calculate the initial terminal period EP.

The present value of the EP stream and residual are added to the opening invested capital to arrive at firm value. Debt and debt equivalents are subtracted from firm value to arrive at equity value.

Analysts often unwittingly assume that high returns continue *ad infinitum* in their DCF valuations. A useful model to employ is to assume that all incremental investment in the terminal period has a constant return on incremental invested capital (ROIIC). If NOPAT is assumed to grow at a constant rate of g in the terminal period, the value of the terminal period can be estimated from the equation:[9]

$$\text{Terminal value} = \frac{\text{NOPAT}_{N+1}(1 - g/\text{ROIIC})}{(\text{WACC} - g)}$$

Note that for the case where ROIIC is assumed to be equal to the cost of capital, WACC, the equation reduces to the simple expression:[10]

$$\text{Terminal value}_{\text{ROIIC}=\text{WACC}} = \frac{\text{NOPAT}_{N+1}}{\text{WACC}}$$

Following the same fade concepts in the CFROI residual, it is possible to forecast a fading EP where ROIC declines until it equals the cost of capital and EP equals zero. A closed-form terminal value can be calculated from the expression:

$$\text{Terminal value} = \frac{\text{EP}_{N+1}}{(\text{WACC} + f)}$$

---

[9] See Viebig and Poddig, Part I, Section 3.3.4 in this book and Copeland *et al.* (2000), pp. 269–271.
[10] Damodaran (2002), p.313.

If the assumption is made that the terminal EP stream will fade to zero at an exponential decay rate of f, then this equation is valid. Note that a rate of 10% would correspond to a characteristic time of 10 years. The fade rate f can range from 0% (no fade) to 100% (instantaneous fade). As a point of interest, this equation is equivalent to calculating the terminal value of a perpetual EP stream that drops to zero after $1/f$ years. The firm value is:

$$\text{Value} = \text{Invested capital}_0 + \sum_{i=1}^{N} \frac{\text{EP}_i}{(1 + \text{WACC})^i} + \frac{\text{EP}_{N+1}}{(\text{WACC} + f)(1 + \text{WACC})^N}$$

13.6   VALUATION OF VODAFONE

In this section, we demonstrate that an EP and FCF valuation result in the same value while a CFROI valuation results in a different value.

Before we begin the EP valuation, we recalculate EP based on operating capital (excluding goodwill) which is presented in Figure 13.8. Notice the significant impact on EP of removing the £95.4 billion of goodwill! The result of this adjustment is now a positive operating EP of £5 billion and an ROIC of 34.1% (versus a negative EP of £9.7 billion and ROIC of 2.7% when goodwill is included as described in Chapter 12). One result of removing goodwill from the operating asset base is that EP and ROIC are now directionally similar to CFROI.

Figure 13.9 presents a simple forecast for Vodafone using the following assumptions:

- Six-year forecast to demonstrate that there is nothing sacred about five-year forecasts.
- Sales growth of 1.7% rising to 3% in the terminal year.
- Flat margins throughout the forecast period.
- R&D expense remains stable at 0.6% of sales and is capitalized with a five-year life.

Total investors' funds	2004	2005	Source
Net working capital	(6993)	(8413)	
Operating fixed and intangible asset adjustment			
Fixed assets per original EP calculation	191 765	195 597	
Net goodwill	107 498	95 443	B/S, Notes 11, 13
Goodwill amortization	53 883	68 515	Notes 11, 13
Investments (added back at the valuation)	4124	3996	B/S, Note 13
Operating fixed and intangible assets	26 260	27 643	
Operating invested capital	**19 267**	**19 230**	
Surplus cash	5790	3666	B/S
Total invested capital	25 057	**22 896**	
BOY invested capital		19 267	
Average invested capital		**19 248**	
NOPAT		6565	
EVA (calculated with the average invested capital)		5068	
EVA (calculated with BOY invested capital)		5067	
Discount rate (WACC)		7.8%	
ROIC (NOPAT/average operating invested capital)		34.1%	

Figure 13.8   Operating EP (calculated without goodwill)

- The tax rate rises along a smooth curve from 23.5% in the last fiscal year (2004–March 2005 annual report) to the UK marginal tax rate of 30% at the end of the forecast period.
- Working capital remains flat at −24.6% of sales.[11]
- Capital expenditures as a percent of sales remain flat at 14.3%.
- Capitalized leases grow at the same rate as that of net PPE.

	Mar-04	Mar-05	Mar-06	Mar-07	Mar-08	Mar-09	Mar-10	Mar-11
Vodafone forecasts	**2003**	**2004**	**2005**	**2006**	**2007**	**2008**	**2009**	**2010**
Sales	33 559	34 133	34 717	35 311	35 915	36 529	37 154	37 789
Sales growth		*1.7%*	*1.7%*	*1.7%*	*1.7%*	*1.7%*	*1.7%*	*1.7%*
R&D expense	171	219	223	227	230	234	238	242
R&D expense (as a % of sales)	*0.5%*	*0.6%*	*0.6%*	*0.6%*	*0.6%*	*0.6%*	*0.6%*	*0.6%*
EBITDA	12 551	12 880	13 100	13 324	13 552	13 784	14 020	14 260
EBITDA margin	*37.4%*	*37.7%*	*37.7%*	*37.7%*	*37.7%*	*37.7%*	*37.7%*	*37.7%*
Depreciation	4362	4528	4749	5087	5369	5581	5703	5713
Amortization	15 305	15 070	0	0	0	0	0	0
NOPBTA	8390	8579	8558	8422	8352	8361	8468	8695
Cash tax rate	*23.3%*	*23.5%*	*24.6%*	*25.7%*	*26.7%*	*27.8%*	*28.9%*	*30.0%*
NOPAT	**6439**	**6565**	**6455**	**6261**	**6119**	**6035**	**6020**	**6086**
NOPAT margin	*19.2%*	*19.2%*	*18.6%*	*17.7%*	*17.0%*	*16.5%*	*16.2%*	*16.1%*
NOPAT growth		*2.0%*	*−1.7%*	*−3.0%*	*−2.3%*	*−1.4%*	*−0.3%*	*1.1%*
Balance sheet assumptions								
Net working capital (as a % of sales)	*−20.8%*	*−24.6%*	*−24.6%*	*−24.6%*	*−24.6%*	*−24.6%*	*−24.6%*	*−24.6%*
Net working capital	−6993	−8413	−8557	−8703	−8852	−9004	−9158	−9314
Operating cash (as a % of sales)	*17.3%*	*10.7%*	*10.7%*	*10.7%*	*10.7%*	*10.7%*	*10.7%*	*10.7%*
Operating cash	5790	3666	3729	3792	3857	3923	3990	4059
Capex (as a % of sales)	*13.4%*	*14.3%*	*14.3%*	*14.3%*	*14.3%*	*14.3%*	*14.3%*	*14.3%*
Total capex	4508	4890	4974	5059	5145	5233	5323	5414
Net PPE	18 083	18 398	18 622	18 593	18 369	18 022	17 642	17 343
Operating intangible assets (3G license)	4275	4275	4275	4275	4275	4275	4275	4275
Other long-term assets	1380	2096	2122	2118	2093	2053	2010	1976
Capitalized R&D	350	439	632	803	929	1020	1037	1055
Capitalized leases	2172	2435	2465	2461	2431	2385	2335	2295
Operating invested capital	**19 267**	**19 230**	**19 559**	**19 547**	**19 245**	**18 752**	**18 142**	**17 630**

Figure 13.9   Vodafone six-year forecast

While the Vodafone annual report, which acts as the base year, is dated March 2005, we have used a year naming convention in which March 2005 is represented as fiscal year 2004 in the analysis. All historical and forecast fiscal years are one year less than the March year-end calendar date for the Vodafone annual report.

---

[11] The purpose of this forecast is simply to demonstrate the equivalence of an EP and DCF valuation and the difference to a CFROI valuation. It is not intended to be a realistic forecast. For example, a more realistic assumption related to working capital would be for it to move from negative to positive at the end of the forecast period.

Figure 13.10 presents the EP and FCF forecast and valuation, and demonstrates the equivalence of these two methods. The result of both of these forecasts is a valuation for Vodafone of £1.67. Notice that the EPs for discounting use BOY capital since this is the asset base upon which the NOPATs are generated. Residual period nominal growth for both the EP and FCF models is 3%, which represents long-term nominal growth. This value is often linked to long-term inflation or nominal GDP growth. We use the Gordon growth model to estimate the value of the residual period.[12]

	2004	2005	2006	2007	2008	2009	2010
NOPAT	6565	6455	6261	6119	6035	6020	6086
Invested capital	19 230	19 559	19 547	19 245	18 752	18 142	17 630
ROIC (BOY)	34.1%	33.6%	32.0%	31.3%	31.4%	32.1%	33.5%
Growth	−0.2%	1.7%	−0.1%	−1.5%	−2.6%	−3.3%	−2.8%
Free cash flow	6602	6127	6272	6422	6528	6630	6598
Free cash flow % growth	95.0%	−7.2%	2.4%	2.4%	1.7%	1.6%	−0.5%
Discount rate factor		0.93	0.86	0.80	0.74	0.69	0.64
PV of FCFs		5685	5401	5131	4840	4561	4212

EP	5068	4962	4742	4601	4540	4563	4678
Discount rate (WACC)	7.8%	7.8%	7.8%	7.8%	7.8%	7.8%	7.8%
Discount factor		0.93	0.86	0.80	0.74	0.69	0.64
PV of EP		4604	4084	3676	3366	3140	2986

DCF constant growth residual valuation

Long-term growth rate	**3.0%**
WACC	**7.8%**
Sum PV of future cash flows	29 831
Free cash flow $T+1$	5740
PV of TV	76 894
Total EV	**106 725**
Net debt (cash)	12 157
Gross debt	12 005
Operating lease debt	2435
Operating cash	3666
Excess cash	0
Other long-term liabilities	1383
Book value of investments	
Market value of investments	16 278
Minorities	2818
Theoretical market capital	**108 028**
No. of shares	64 596
DCF value per share	**1.67**

EP constant growth residual valuation

Long-term growth rate	**3.0%**
WACC	**7.8%**
Sum PV of EPs	21 856
EP $T+1$	4900
PV of TV	65 638
PV 2005 BOY capital	19 230
Total EV	**106 725**
Net debt (cash)	12 157
Gross debt	12 005
Operating lease debt	2435
Cash	3666
Other long-term liabilities	1383
Book value of investments	
Market value of investments	16 278
Minorities	2818
Theoretical market capital	**108 028**
No. of shares	64 596
DCF value per share	**1.67**

Figure 13.10   FCF and EP valuation

[12] Mathematically, the free cash flow terminal value reflects terminal NOPAT = £6086*(1 + 3%) = £6296 and terminal invested capital = £17 630*(1 + 3%) = £18 159 and free cash flow = NOPAT less change in invested capital, or £6269 − (£18 159 − £17 630) = £5740. The present value of the terminal value = £5740/(7.8% − 3%)*0.64 = £76 894. The EP terminal value reflects the same terminal NOPAT as the free cash flow model less the BOY capital times the capital charge (£6086 − (£17 630*7.8%) = £4900). The present value of the EP terminal value equals £65 638(= £4900/(7.8% − 3%) * 0.64); see Figures 13.9 and 13.10

For the EP valuation, reported 2004 EOY capital (BOY capital for the 2005 forecast) is added to the valuation to reflect the investors' funds in capital at the beginning of the forecast period. While the FCF and EP valuations measure value differently (free cash flow vs. EP), they are measuring the same economics. Both rely on the same forecasts, resulting in the same asset base and the same Gordon growth model terminal value assumptions. Thus, both result in the same valuation.

To arrive at equity value, we subtract debt and equivalents (including our calculation of operating lease debt which is equal to our operating lease asset) and other long-term liabilities from the firm valuation. We add cash and equivalents, which we had removed from the asset base for the operating EP calculation. In cases where investments are not assumed to be an operating asset, use the book value of investments if no information about market value is available. If such information exists, i.e. the investments are in known publicly traded companies, use market value instead of book value. Finally, we subtract minority interest to arrive at equity value.

If we have a view on the return on incremental invested capital (ROIIC) in the terminal period, the terminal value can be calculated from the expression:[13]

$$\text{Terminal value} = \frac{\text{NOPAT}_{N+1}\left(1 - {}^{g}\!/\text{ROIIC}\right)}{(\text{WACC} - g)}$$

where g represents the long-term NOPAT growth. A conservative approach would be to set the ROIIC equal to WACC, thus imposing the condition that all incremental investments in the terminal period do not generate economic value.

For an EP valuation, the equation can also be written as:[14]

$$\text{Terminal value} = \frac{\text{EP}_{N+1}}{\text{WACC}} + \frac{\text{NOPAT}_{N+1}\left({}^{g}\!/\text{ROIIC}\right)(\text{ROIIC} - \text{WACC})}{\text{WACC}(\text{WACC} - g)}$$

In the case of Vodafone, this lowers the valuation to £0.88 as demonstrated in Figure 13.11!

It should be clear by this point that a CFROI valuation and an EP/FCF valuation will differ due to the residual value calculation, i.e. Gordon growth versus fading residual. Usually, the EP/FCF valuation will result in a higher value than the CFROI because of the perpetual spread in the terminal period.

However, as is demonstrated in Figure 13.11, the fading EP/FCF valuation results in a much lower value than the CFROI valuation as reflected in Figure 13.12. A key reason for the difference is due to the calculation of the asset base, which generates future cash flows and is the basis for the CFROI calculation. In the EP/FCF valuation, the asset base reflects net assets, while in the CFROI valuation it reflects gross investment (although both are adjusted to remove goodwill). The results from these two very different asset bases and economic treatments are different sets of cash flow forecasts and thus different valuations. Because CFROI is a more comprehensive measure of economic performance than EP, the CFROI and net cash receipt forecasts should provide a more reliable economic representation of Vodafone's operating performance even when EP is assumed to fade at a similar rate as in this example.

[13] Copeland *et al.* (2000), pp. 269–271.
[14] Copeland *et al.* (2000), p.272.

DCF fading valuation	
Long-term growth rate	**3.0%**
WACC	**7.8%**
Fade rate	**10.0%**
PV of explicit FCFs	29 831
Sum PV of future cashflows	25 534
PV of terminal value (yr 100)	96
Total EV	**55 461**
Net debt (cash)	12 157
Gross debt	12 005
Operating lease debt	2435
Operating cash	3666
Excess cash	0
Other long-term liabilities	1383
Book value of investments	
Market value of investments	16 278
Minorities	2818
Theoretical market capital	**56 764**
No. of shares	64 596
DCF value per share	**0.88**

EP fading valuation	
Long-term growth rate	**3.0%**
WACC	**7.8%**
Fade rate	10.0%
PV of explicit EPs	21 856
Sum PV of future EPs	14 375
PV of terminal value (yr 100)	0
PV 2005 BOY capital	19 230
Total EV	**55 461**
Net debt (cash)	12 157
Gross debt	12 005
Operating lease debt	2435
Cash	3666
Other long-term liabilities	1383
Book value of investments	0
Market value of investments	16 278
Minorities	2818
Theoretical market capital	**56 764**
No. of shares	64 596
DCF value per share	**0.88**

Figure 13.11   EP and FCF fading valuation

Valuation results	**2005**
PV of existing assets	73 434
NPV of future investments	9683
+ Market value of investments	16 278
Total economic value	**99 396**
− Debt and equivalents	19 015
− Minority interests	2192
Warranted market Capital	**78 189**
Shares outstanding	64 596
Warranted share price (GBP)	**1.21**
Closing price	1.21
% upside	−0.2%

Figure 13.12   Vodafone CFROI valuation

Figure 13.13 presents the relative wealth chart for our Vodafone CFROI-based valuation. The top panel presents the CFROIs which remain stable around 15% (the light part of the bar reflects transaction CFROIs including goodwill) over the forecast period. These CFROIs begin to fade at a 10% rate beyond the six-year forecast toward 6%. The bottom panel presents real asset growth (operating assets excluding goodwill), which tales off at the end of the six-year forecast (and will fade up toward a real long-term economic growth of 2.5%).

13.7   EP OR CFROI?

What are the differences between metrics when performing valuations?

CFROI allows us to assess the "quality" of our forecasts. Overly optimistic forecasts, which are often the result of many minor optimistic assumptions summing to an unrealistic

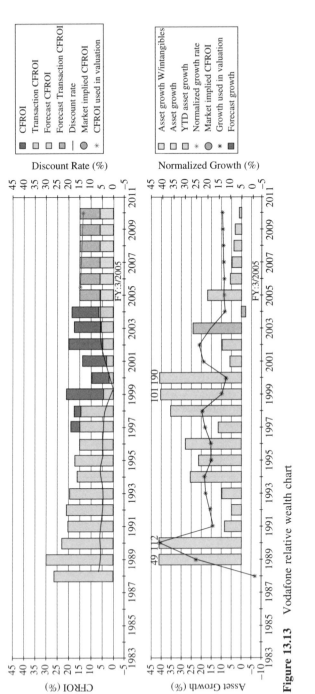

Figure 13.13 Vodafone relative wealth chart

forecast, result in the classic hockey stick-shaped forecast. By observing the trend of the CFROI forecast, we can visually see the plausibility of the forecast assumptions. Because CFROI is a real measure, it is easy to perform benchmarking studies over time and across borders within the HOLT ValueSearch software. This is extraordinarily powerful when reviewing company forecasts and investigating market-implied expectations. Benchmarking EP levels is not particularly insightful and ROIC can be distorted by inflation and asset age, which limits its utility. Treatment of goodwill confuses matters further.

A CFROI forecast, due to the nature of the IRR calculation, explicitly takes into account asset retirements. A company cannot grow until it replaces retired assets. Thus, the analyst must forecast sufficient capex to cover both growth and retirements. There is no explicit way to adjust for this in an EP framework.

EP suffers the same drawback as a standard FCF valuation: the risk of locking in an excess return spread between the firm's returns and its cost of capital in the residual period. The result will often be an excessive valuation of the residual period. A CFROI-based valuation ensures that any excess return fades away in the residual period.

13.8   A FINAL WORD

The motivation behind the development of CFROI, EP and other "economic" metrics was to overcome accounting deficiencies and create a framework in which a historic analysis links to a forward-looking forecast and valuation. This part focused on the mechanics. Once the mechanics are learned, the challenge is to internalize the framework in order to uncover insights. Insights come from a full understanding of the company and its environment. Analysts should be able to answer the following questions:

- How will sales growth, margins and asset turns trend going forward?
- What is the relationship between the company, its suppliers, customers, employees and competitors?
- How do these expected trends and company relationships match up with management comments about the company?
- How do answers to the previous questions support the company's strategic position and general strategic goals?
- Does the firm have a sustainable competitive advantage and do answers to the preceding questions support the maintenance of that advantage?
- Can shares be purchased at a reasonable price?

The ability to answer these questions within an internally consistent framework to arrive at an unbiased valuation should help identify attractive investment opportunities. An improved understanding of a firm's economics will help the analyst break free from the earnings obsession and focus on connecting a firm's strategic position with its future cash flow generation and true economic value. Strategy *and* valuation need to be considered before investment. Investment in a superior company with highly optimistic market-implied expectations is an invitation to underperform.

Appendix 1
Vodafone Financial Statements and Relevant Notes for CFROI Calculation

Consolidated Profit and Loss Accounts for the years ended 31 March

	Note	2005 $m	2005 £m	2004 £m	2003 £m
Group turnover	3				
– Continuing operations		64,470	34,133	32,741	28,547
– Discontinued operations		—	—	818	1,828
		64,470	34,133	33,559	30,375
Operating (loss)/profit	3, 4, 5				
– Continuing operations		(10,018)	(5,304)	(4,842)	(5,052)
– Discontinued operations		—	—	66	(243)
		(10,018)	(5,304)	(4,776)	(5,295)
Share of operating profit/(loss) in joint ventures and associated undertakings		2,253	1,193	546	(156)
Total Group operating loss					
Group and share of joint ventures and associated undertakings	3	(7,765)	(4,111)	(4,230)	(5,451)
Exceptional non-operating items	6	25	13	(103)	(5)
– Continuing operations		25	13	(44)	20
– Discontinued operations		—	—	(59)	(25)
Loss on ordinary activities before interest	3	(7,740)	(4,098)	(4,333)	(5,456)
Net interest payable and similar items	7	(1,141)	(604)	(714)	(752)
Group		(742)	(393)	(499)	(457)
Share of joint ventures and associated undertakings		(399)	(211)	(215)	(295)
Loss on ordinary activities before taxation		(8,881)	(4,702)	(5,047)	(6,208)
Tax on loss on ordinary activities	8	(4,224)	(2,236)	(3,154)	(2,956)
Group tax on loss on ordinary activities before exceptional tax		(4,339)	(2,297)	(2,866)	(2,624)
Share of joint ventures and associated undertakings		(1,016)	(538)	(288)	(332)
Tax on loss on ordinary activities before exceptional tax		(5,355)	(2,835)	(3,154)	(2,956)
Exceptional tax credit		1,131	599	—	—
Loss on ordinary activities after taxation		(13,105)	(6,938)	(8,201)	(9,164)
Equity minority interests		(1,031)	(546)	(753)	(593)
Non-equity minority interests		(106)	(56)	(61)	(62)
Loss for the financial year		(14,242)	(7,540)	(9,015)	(9,819)
Equity dividends	9	(5,020)	(2,658)	(1,378)	(1,154)
Retained loss for the Group and its share of joint ventures and associated undertakings	23	(19,262)	(10,198)	(10,393)	(10,973)
Basic and diluted loss per share	10	(21.51)¢	(11.39)p	(13.24)p	(14.41)p

Figure A1.1   P&L

Balance Sheets at 31 March

	Note	Group 2005 $m	Group 2005 £m	Group 2004 £m	Company 2005 £m	Company 2004 £m
Fixed assets						
Intangible assets	11	157,647	83,464	93,622	—	—
Tangible assets	12	34,750	18,398	18,083	—	—
Investments		38,248	20,250	22,275	94,027	106,177
Investments in associated undertakings	13	36,639	19,398	21,226	—	—
Other investments	13	1,609	852	1,049	94,027	106,177
		230,645	122,112	133,980	94,027	106,177
Current assets						
Stocks	14	812	430	458	—	—
Debtors: amounts falling due after more than one year	15	3,959	2,096	1,380	83	87
Debtors: amounts falling due within one year	15	10,581	5,602	5,521	76,655	65,540
Investments	16	1,541	816	4,381	28	—
Cash at bank and in hand		5,384	2,850	1,409	—	53
		22,277	11,794	13,149	76,766	65,680
Creditors: amounts falling due within one year	17	(28,024)	(14,837)	(15,026)	(90,425)	(95,679)
Net current liabilities		(5,747)	(3,043)	(1,877)	(13,659)	(29,999)
Total assets less current liabilities		224,898	119,069	132,103	80,368	76,178
Creditors: amounts falling due after more than one year	18	(23,387)	(12,382)	(12,975)	(9,174)	(9,271)
Provisions for liabilities and charges	21	(8,598)	(4,552)	(4,197)	—	—
		192,913	102,135	114,931	71,194	66,907
Capital and reserves						
Called up share capital	22	8,095	4,286	4,280	4,286	4,280
Share premium account	23	98,754	52,284	52,154	52,284	52,154
Merger reserve		186,853	98,927	98,927	—	—
Capital reserve		—	—	—	88	88
Own shares held	23	(9,672)	(5,121)	(1,136)	(5,085)	(1,088)
Other reserve	23	1,188	629	713	629	713
Profit and loss account	23	(97,628)	(51,688)	(43,014)	18,992	10,760
Total equity shareholders' funds		187,590	99,317	111,924	71,194	66,907
Equity minority interests		3,712	1,965	2,132	—	—
Non-equity minority interests	24	1,611	853	875	—	—
		192,913	102,135	114,931	71,194	66,907

Figure A1.2   Balance sheet

12. Tangible fixed assets

	Land and buildings £m	Equipment, fixtures and fittings £m	Network infrastructure £m	Total £m
Cost:				
1 April 2004	1,214	5,979	23,371	30,564
Exchange movements	9	57	(37)	29
Additions	126	1,690	3,250	5,066
Disposals	(23)	(274)	(419)	(716)
31 March 2005	1,326	7,452	26,165	34,943
Accumulated depreciation and impairment:				
1 April 2004	293	3,640	8,548	12,481
Exchange movements	4	27	–	31
Charge for the year	86	1,144	3,298	4,528
Disposals	(10)	(184)	(301)	(495)
31 March 2005	373	4,627	11,545	16,545
Net book value:				
31 March 2005	953	2,825	14,620	18,398
31 March 2004	921	2,339	14,823	18,083

Figure A1.3   Land and buildings

12.Tangible fixed assets

	Land and buildings £m	Equipment, fixtures and fittings £m	Network infrastructure £m	Total £m
Cost:				
1 April 2004	1,214	5,979	23,371	30,564
Exchange movements	9	57	(37)	29
Additions	126	1,690	3,250	5,066
Disposals	(23)	(274)	(419)	(716)
31 March 2005	1,326	7,452 **+** 26,165		34,943
Accumulated depreciation and impairment:		**=**		
1 April 2004	293	3,640 **33,617** 8,548		12,481
Exchange movements	4	27	–	31
Charge for the year	86	1,144	3,298	4,528
Disposals	(10)	(184)	(301)	(495)
31 March 2005	373	4,627	11,545	16,545
Net book value:				
31 March 2005	953	2,825	14,620	18,398
31 March 2004	921	2,339	14,823	18,083

Figure A1.4   Machinery and equipment

5. Operating loss

Operating loss has been arrived at after charging/(crediting):

	2005 £m	2004 £m	2003 £m
Staff costs (see note 31)	2,293	2,331	2,278
Depreciation of tangible fixed assets:			
Owned assets	4,467	4,181	3,783
Leased assets	61	181	196
Goodwill amortisation	12,929	13,095	11,875
Impairment of intangible and tangible fixed assets	315	–	485
Amortisation of other intangible fixed assets	412	98	53
Research and development	219	171	164
Advertising costs (including applicable staff costs)	864	990	902
Bad debt expense	224	209	193
Operating lease rentals:			
Plant and machinery	37	98	78
Other assets including fixed line rentals	1,300	1,254	1,269
Own costs capitalised attributable to the construction or acquisition of tangible fixed assets	(301)	(290)	(207)

Figure A1.5   Rental expense

5. Operating loss

Operating loss has been arrived at after charging/(crediting):

	2005 £m	2004 £m	2003 £m
Staff costs (see note 31)	2,293	2,331	2,278
Depreciation of tangible fixed assets:			
Owned assets	4,467	4,181	3,783
Leased assets	61	181	196
Goodwill amortisation	12,929	13,095	11,875
Impairment of intangible and tangible fixed assets	315	–	485
Amortisation of other intangible fixed assets	412	98	53
Research and development	219	171	164
Advertising costs (including applicable staff costs)	864	990	902
Bad debt expense	224	209	193
Operating lease rentals:			
Plant and machinery	37	98	78
Other assets including fixed line rentals	1,300	1,254	1,269
Own costs capitalised attributable to the construction or acquisition of tangible fixed assets	(301)	(290)	(207)

Figure A1.6   R&D expense for capitalized R&D calculation

	Note	Group 2005 $m	Group 2005 £m	Group 2004 £m	Company 2005 £m	Company 2004 £m
Current assets						
Stocks	14	812	430	458	–	–
Debtors: amounts falling due after more than one year	15	3,959	2,096	1,380	83	87
Debtors: amounts falling due within one year	15	10,581	5,602	5,521	76,655	65,540
Investments	16	1,541	816	4,381	28	–
Cash at bank and in hand		5,384	2,850	1,409	–	53
		22,277	11,794	13,149	76,766	65,680

15. Debtors   Cash & ST Invest (2005) = 3,666

	Group 2005 £m	Group 2004 £m	Company 2005 £m	Company 2004 £m
Due within one year:				
Trade debtors Receivables = 2,768	2,768	2,593	–	–
Amounts owed by subsidiary undertakings	–	–	76,303	65,098
Amounts owed by associated undertakings	23	17	–	–
Taxation recoverable	268	372	37	–
Group relief receivable Other current assets =	–	–	43	132
Other debtors 23 + 268 + 413 + 2.130 = 2.834	413	491	272	310
Prepayments and accrued income	2,130	2,048	–	–
= Net Monetary Assets (2005) = 3,666 + 2768 + 2834 = 9,268	5,602	5,521	76,655	65,540

Net Monetary Assets (2004) = 4,381 + 1,409 + 5,521 = 11,311

Figure A1.7   Current assets less stocks (inventory)

17. Creditors: amounts falling due within one year

Current Non-debt Liabilities (2004) = 15.026 – (42+2.000+12) = 12.972

	Group 2005 £m	Group 2004 £m	Company 2005 £m	Company 2004 £m
Bank overdrafts	47	42	–	–
Bank loans and other loans	332	2,000	15	956
Finance leases	13	12	–	–
Trade creditors Accounts Payable	2,897	2,842	–	–
Amounts owed to subsidiary undertakings	–	–	88,710	93,553
Amounts owed to associated undertakings	9	8	–	–
Taxation + Income Tax Payable	4,759	4,275	–	–
Other taxes and social security costs	332	367	–	–
Other creditors + Current liabilities =	444	741	4	71
Accruals and deferred income 9 + 332 + 4.619 + 1.395 =	4,619	4,011	301	371
Proposed dividend	1,395	728	1,395	728
	14,837	15,026	90,425	95,679

= Current Non-debt Liabilities (2005) = 2.887 + 4.759 + 6.799 = 14.445

Figure A1.8   Current non-debt monetary liabilities

	Note	Group 2005 $m	Group 2005 £m	Group 2004 £m	Company 2005 £m	Company 2004 £m
Current assets						
Stocks	14	812	430	458	–	–
Debtors: amounts falling due after more than one year	15	3,959	2,096	1,380	83	87
Debtors: amounts falling due within one year	15	10,581	5,602	5,521	76,655	65,540
Investments	16	1,541	816	4,381	28	–
Cash at bank and in hand		5,384	2,850	1,409	–	53
		22,277	11,794	13,149	76,766	65,680

Figure A1.9   Stocks (inventory)

15. Debtors

	Group		Company	
	2005 £m	2004 £m	2005 £m	2004 £m
Due within one year:				
Trade debtors	2,768	2,593	–	–
Amounts owed by subsidiary undertakings	–	–	76,303	65,098
Amounts owed by associated undertakings	23	17	–	–
Taxation recoverable	268	372	37	–
Group relief receivable	–	–	43	132
Other debtors	413	491	272	310
Prepayments and accrued income	2,130	2,048	–	–
	5,602	5,521	76,655	65,540
Due after more than one year:				
Trade debtors	49	37	–	–
Other debtors	122	76	–	–
Prepayments	384	302	–	–
Deferred taxation (note 21)	1,541	965	83	87
	2,096	1,380	83	87
	7,698	6,901	76,738	65,627

Figure A1.10   Other tangible assets

32. Pensions

Fair value of the assets and liabilities of the schemes

	UK			Germany			Japan			Other			Total		
	2005 £m	2004 £m	2003 £m	2005 £m	2004 £m	2003 £m	2005 £m	2004 £m	2003 £m	2005 £m	2004 £m	2003 £m	2005 £m	2004 £m	2003 £m
Bonds	105	89	56	115	104	–	–	1	–	6	4	7	226	198	63
Equities	418	345	208	54	51	–	–	1	–	52	33	27	524	430	235
Other assets	105	–	–	12	10	107	2	–	1	5	3	4	124	13	112
Total fair value of scheme assets	628	434	264	181	165	107	2	2	1	63	40	38	874	641	410
Present value of scheme liabilities	(619)	(457)	(383)	(213)	(192)	(180)	(30)	(35)	(127)	(148)	(122)	(126)	(1,010)	(806)	(816)
FRS 17 assets/(deficits)	9	(23)	(119)	(32)	(27)	(73)	(28)	(33)	(126)	(85)	(82)	(88)	(136)	(165)	(406)
Related deferred tax (liabilities) /assets	(2)	7	36	13	11	30	12	14	53	32	30	30	55	62	149
Net FRS 17 surplus/(deficit)	7	(16)	(83)	(19)	(16)	(43)	(16)	(19)	(73)	(53)	(52)	(58)	(81)	(103)	(257)
Analysed as:															
Assets	7	–	–	2	–	–	–	–	–	–	–	–	9	–	–
Liabilities	–	(16)	(83)	(21)	(16)	(43)	(16)	(19)	(73)	(53)	(52)	(58)	(90)	(103)	(257)

Figure A1.11   Prepaid pensions

12. Tangible fixed assets

	Land and buildings £m	Equipment, fixtures and fittings £m	Network infrastructure £m	Total £m
Cost:				
1 April 2004	1,214	5,979	23,371	30,564
Exchange movements	9	57	(37)	29
Additions	126	1,690	3,250	5,066
Disposals	(23)	(274)	(419)	(716)
31 March 2005	1,326	7,452	26,165	34,943
Accumulated depreciation and impairment:				
1 April 2004	293	3,640	8,548	12,481
Exchange movements	4	27	–	31
Charge for the year	86	1,144	3,298	4,528
Disposals	(10)	(184)	(301)	(495)
31 March 2005	373	4,627	11,545	16,545
Net book value:				
31 March 2005	953	2,825	14,620	18,398
31 March 2004	921	2,339	14,823	18,083

Figure A1.12   Depreciation expense

78 Financials

Consolidated Profit and Loss Accounts for the years ended 31 March

	Years ended 31 March		
	2005 £m	2004 £m	2003 £m
Turnover			
Mobile telecommunications	**33,184**	31,915	27,847
Other operations	**1,108**	2,128	3,540
Less: turnover between mobile and other operations	**(159)**	(484)	(1,012)
	34,133	33,559	30,375
Total Group operating loss	**(4,111)**	(4,230)	(5,451)
Mobile telecommunications(a)	**10,875**	10,729	9,170
Other operations(a)	**29**	20	11
	10,904	10,749	9,181
Goodwill amortisation	**(14,700)**	(15,207)	(14,056)
Exceptional operating items	**(315)**	228	(576)
Exceptional non-operating items	**13**	(103)	(5)
Net interest expense	**(604)**	(714)	(752)
Taxation	**(2,236)**	(3,154)	(2,956)
Loss on ordinary activities after taxation	**(6,938)**	(8,201)	(9,164)
Loss for the financial year	**(7,540)**	(9,015)	(9,819)

Figure A1.13 Net income

5. Operating loss

Financials 89

Operating loss has been arrived at after charging/(crediting):

	2005 £m	2004 £m	2003 £m
Staff costs (see note 31)	**2,293**	2,331	2,278
Depreciation of tangible fixed assets:			
Owned assets	**4,467**	4,181	3,783
Leased assets	**61**	181	196
Goodwill amortisation	**12,929**	13,095	11,875
Impairment of intangible and tangible fixed assets	**315**	–	485
Amortisation of other intangible fixed assets	**412**	98	53

13. Fixed asset investments

Associated undertakings

Financials 97

	Group £m
Share of net assets:	
1 April 2004	3,075
Exchange movements	(41)
Share of retained results excluding goodwill amortisation	152
Share of goodwill amortisation	(42)
31 March 2005	**3,144**
Capitalised goodwill:	
1 April 2004	18,151
Exchange movements	(173)
Acquisitions (note 25)	5
Goodwill amortisation	(1,729)
31 March 2005	**16,254**

= Depreciation and Amortization = 4,467 + 61 + 12,929 + 412 + 1,729 = 19,598

Figure A1.14 Depreciation and amortization

Financials 91

7. Net interest payable and similar items

	2005 £m	2004 £m	2003 £m
Parent and subsidiary undertakings:			
Interest receivable and similar income	(602)	(592)	(666)
Interest payable and similar charges:			
Bank loans and overdrafts	49	46	133
Other loans	677	820	921
Tax liabilities	261	215	55
Finance leases	8	10	14
	995	1,091	1,123
Group net interest payable	393	499	457
Share of joint ventures:			
Interest payable and similar charges	–	–	8
Share of associated undertakings:			
Interest receivable and similar income	(16)	(7)	(24)
Interest payable and similar charges	227	222	311
	211	215	287
Share of joint ventures and associated undertakings net interest payable	211	215	295
Net interest payable and similar items	604	714	752

Figure A1.15   Interest expense

5. Operating loss

Financials 89

Operating loss has been arrived at after charging/(crediting):

	2005 £m	2004 £m	2003 £m
Staff costs (see note 31)	2,293	2,331	2,278
Depreciation of tangible fixed assets:			
Owned assets	4,467	4,181	3,783
Leased assets	61	181	196
Goodwill amortisation	12,929	13,095	11,875
Impairment of intangible and tangible fixed assets	315	–	485
Amortisation of other intangible fixed assets	412	98	53
Research and development	219	171	164
Advertising costs (including applicable staff costs)	864	990	902
Bad debt expense	224	209	193
Operating lease rentals:			
Plant and machinery	37	98	78
Other assets including fixed line rentals	1,300	1,254	1,269
Own costs capitalised attributable to the construction or acquisition of tangible fixed assets	(301)	(290)	(207)

Figure A1.16   R&D expense

5. Operating loss

Financials 89

Operating loss has been arrived at after charging/(crediting):

	2005 £m	2004 £m	2003 £m
Staff costs (see note 31)	2,293	2,331	2,278
Depreciation of tangible fixed assets:			
Owned assets	4,467	4,181	3,783
Leased assets	61	181	196
Goodwill amortisation	12,929	13,095	11,875
Impairment of intangible and tangible fixed assets	315	–	485
Amortisation of other intangible fixed assets	412	98	53
Research and development	219	171	164
Advertising costs (including applicable staff costs)	864	990	902
Bad debt expense	224	209	193
Operating lease rentals:			
Plant and machinery	37	98	78
Other assets including fixed line rentals	1,300	1,254	1,269
Own costs capitalised attributable to the construction or acquisition of tangible fixed assets	(301)	(290)	(207)

Figure A1.17   Rental expense

32.Pensions continued
Pension disclosures required under SSAP 24

During the year ended 31 March 2005, the total amount charged to the profit and loss account in respect of all the Group's pensions plans was £95 million (2004: £79 million, 2003: £95 million), as analysed below:

	2005 £m	2004 £m	2003 £m
Defined benefit schemes:			
United Kingdom	31	31	24
Germany	5	7	12
Japan	28	10	32
Other	8	6	5
Net pension charge: Defined benefit schemes	72	54	73
Net pension charge: Defined contribution schemes	23	25	22
Total amount charged to the profit and loss account	95	79	95

	UK 2005 £m	UK 2004 £m	Germany 2005 £m	Germany 2004 £m	Japan 2005 £m	Japan 2004 £m	Other 2005 £m	Other 2004 £m	Total 2005 £m	Total 2004 £m
Operating profit:										
Current service cost	37	32	6	8	5	10	30	44	78	94
Past service cost	–	–	–	–	–	–	–	1	–	1
Total charge to operating profit	37	32	6	8	5	10	30	45	78	95
Finance costs/(income):										
Interest cost	26	22	9	9	1	1	6	6	42	38
Expected return on pension scheme assets	(31)	(22)	(8)	(5)	–	–	(3)	(2)	(42)	(29)
Total (credit/charge to finance (income)/costs	(5)	–	1	4	1	1	3	4	–	9
Total charge to loss before taxation	32	32	7	12	6	11	33	49	78	104

= Pension adjustment = 95 – 78 = 17

Figure A1.18   Pension expense

Consolidated Profit and Loss Accounts for the years ended 31 March

	Note	2005 $m	2005 £m	2004 £m	2003 £m
Net interest payable and similar items	7	(1,141)	(604)	(714)	(752)
Group		(742)	(393)	(499)	(457)
Share of joint ventures and associated undertakings		(399)	(211)	(215)	(295)
Loss on ordinary activities before taxation		(8,881)	(4,702)	(5,047)	(6,208)
Tax on loss on ordinary activities	8	(4,224)	(2,236)	(3,154)	(2,956)
Group tax on loss on ordinary activities before exceptional tax		(4,339)	(2,297)	(2,866)	(2,624)
Share of joint ventures and associated undertakings		(1,016)	(538)	(288)	(332)
Tax on loss on ordinary activities before exceptional tax		(5,355)	(2,835)	(3,154)	(2,956)
Exceptional tax credit		1,131	599	–	–
Loss on ordinary activities after taxation		(13,105)	(6,939)	(8,201)	(9,164)
Equity minority interests		(1,031)	(546)	(753)	(593)
Non-equity minority interests		(106)	(56)	(61)	(62)
Loss for the financial year		(14,242)	(7,540)	(9,015)	(9,819)
Equity dividends	9	(5,020)	(2,658)	(1,378)	(1,154)

Figure A1.19   Minority interest

Consolidated Profit and Loss Accounts for the years ended 31 March   78 **Financials**

	Note	2006 $m	2005 £m	2004 £m	2003 £m
Group		(742)	(393)	(499)	(457)
Share of joint ventures and associated undertakings		(399)	(211)	(215)	(295)
Loss on ordinary activities before taxation		(8,881)	(4,702)	(5,047)	(6,208)
Tax on loss on ordinary activities	8	(4,224)	(2,236)	(3,154)	(2,956)
Group tax on loss on ordinary activities before exceptional tax		(4,339)	(2,297)	(2,866)	(2,624)
Share of joint ventures and associated undertakings		(1,016)	(538)	(298)	(332)

3. Segmental analysis   **Financials** 85

			Mobile telecommunications					Other operations		Total
	Germany £m	Italy £m	UK £m	Other EMEA £m	Americas £m	Asia Pacific £m	Total £m	Germany £m	Other EMEA £m	Total Group £m
Year ended 31 March 2006:										
Share of operating profit/(loss) in associated undertakings	–	–	–	337	890	4	1,231	–	(38)	1,193
Total Group operating (loss)/profit	(5,161)	(1,522)	745	719	859	221	(4,139)	65	(37)	(4,111)
Exceptional non-operating items	–	–	–	(10)	3	20	13	–	–	13
(Loss)/profit on ordinary activities before interest	(5,161)	(1,522)	745	709	862	241	(4,126)	65	(37)	(4,098)
Total Group operating (loss)/profit	(5,161)	(1,522)	745	719	859	221	(4,139)	65	(37)	(4,111)
Add back:										
– Goodwill amortisation	6,824	3,779	230	2,349	788	729	14,699	1	–	14,700
Subsidiaries	6,824	3,779	230	1,369	–	726	12,928	1	–	12,929
Associates	–	–	–	980	788	3	1,771	–	–	1,771

Associates & JV income = (211) + (538) + 1,193 + 1,771 = 2,215

Figure A1.20   Associates and JV income

4. Exceptional operating items   88 **Financials**

	2005 £m	2004 £m	2003 £m
Impairment of intangible and tangible fixed assets	(315)	–	(485)
Contribution tax	–	351	–
Reorganisation costs	–	(123)	(91)
	(315)	228	(576)

Consolidated Profit and Loss Accounts for the years ended 31 March   78 **Financials**

	Note	2006 $m	2005 £m	2004 £m	2003 £m
Total Group operating loss					
Group and share of joint ventures and associated undertakings	3	(7,765)	(4,111)	(4,230)	(5,451)
Exceptional non-operating items	6	25	13	(103)	(5)
– Continuing operations		25	13	(44)	20
– Discontinued operations		–	–	(59)	(25)
Loss on ordinary activities before interest	3	(7,740)	(4,098)	(4,333)	(5,456)
Net interest payable and similar items	7	(1,141)	(604)	(714)	(752)
Group		(742)	(393)	(499)	(457)
Share of joint ventures and associated undertakings		(399)	(211)	(215)	(295)
Loss on ordinary activities before taxation		(8,881)	(4,702)	(5,047)	(6,208)
Tax on loss on ordinary activities	8	(4,224)	(2,236)	(3,154)	(2,956)
Group tax on loss on ordinary activities before exceptional tax		(4,339)	(2,297)	(2,866)	(2,624)
Share of joint ventures and associated undertakings		(1,016)	(538)	(298)	(332)
Tax on loss on ordinary activities before exceptional tax		(5,355)	(2,835)	(3,154)	(2,956)
Exceptional tax credit		1,131	599	–	–

= Special Item = -315 + 13 + 599 = 297 less 3.90 (13 * 30% tax rate) = 293

Figure A1.21   Special items

11. Intangible fixed assets

	Goodwill £m	Licence and spectrum fees £m	Financials 95 Total £m
Cost:			
1 April 2004	130,377	15,063	145,440
Exchange movements	2,737	244	2,981
Acquisitions (note 25)	1,757	–	1,757
Additions	–	124	124
Disposals	(52)	–	(52)
31 March 2005	134,819	15,431	150,250
Accumulated amortisation and impairment:			
1 April 2004	51,597	221	51,818
Exchange movements	1,323	7	1,330
Amortisation charge for the year	12,929	412	13,341
Impairment	315	–	315
Disposals	(18)	–	(18)
31 March 2005	66,146	640	66,786
Net book value:			
31 March 2005	68,673	14,791	83,464
31 March 2004	78,780	14,842	93,622

13. Fixed asset investments
Associated undertakings

	Financials 97 Group £m
Capitalised goodwill:	
1 April 2004	18,151
Exchange movements	(173)
Acquisitions (note 25)	5
Goodwill amortisation	(1,729)
31 March 2005	16,254

= Total Intangibles = 83,464 + 16,254 = 99,718

Figure A1.22   Intangible assets

Appendix 2

Additional Notes from Vodafone Annual Report for EP Calculation

	Note	Group 2005 $m	Group 2005 £m	Group 2004 £m	Company 2005 £m	Company 2004 £m
Current assets						
Stocks	14	812	430	458	–	–
Debtors: amounts falling due after more than one year	15	3,959	2,096	1,380	83	87
Debtors: amounts falling due within one year	15	10,581	5,502	5,521	76,655	65,540
Investments	16	1,541	816	4,381	28	–
Cash at bank and in hand		5,384	2,850	1,409	–	53
		22,277	11,794	13,149	76,766	65,680

Cash& ST Invest (2005) = 3,666

17. Creditors: amounts falling due within one year

	Group 2005 £m	Group 2004 £m	Company 2005 £m	Company 2004 £m
Bank overdrafts	47	42	–	–
Bank loans and other loans	332	2,000	15	956
Finance leases	13	12	–	–
Trade creditors **Accounts Payable**	2,897	2,842	–	–
Amounts owed to subsidiary undertakings	–	–	88,710	93,553
Amounts owed to associated undertakings	9	8	–	–
Taxation **+ Income Tax Payable**	4,759	4,275	–	–
Other taxes and social security costs	332	367	–	–
Other creditors **+ Current liabilities =**	444	741	4	71
Accruals and deferred income **9 + 332 + 4,619 + 1,395 =**	4,619	4,011	301	371
Proposed dividend	1,395	728	1,395	728
	14,837	15,026	90,425	95,679

= Current Non-debt Liabilities (2005) = 2.887 + 4.759 + 6.799 = 14.445

Figure A2.1 Working capital

11. Intangible fixed assets

	Goodwill £m	Licence and spectrum fees £m	Financials 95 Total £m
Cost:			
1 April 2004	130,377	15,063	145,440
Exchange movements	2,737	244	2,981
Acquisitions (note 25)	1,757	–	1,757
Additions	–	124	124
Disposals	(52)	–	(52)
31 March 2005	**134,819**	**15,431**	**150,250**
Accumulated amortisation and impairment:			
1 April 2004	51,597	221	51,818
Exchange movements	1,323	7	1,330
Amortisation charge for the year	12,929	412	13,341
Impairment	315	–	315
Disposals	(18)	–	(18)
31 March 2005	**66,146**	**640**	**66,786**
Net book value:			
31 March 2005	**68,673**	**14,791**	**83,464**
31 March 2004	78,780	14,842	93,622

13. Fixed asset investments
Associated undertakings

Financials 97

	Group £m
Capitalised goodwill:	
1 April 2004	18,151
Exchange movements	(173)
Acquisitions (note 25)	5
Goodwill amortisation	(1,729)
31 March 2005	**16,254**

Net Goodwill = 83,464 + 16,254 = 99,718
Goodwill amortization = 66,786 + 1,729 = 68,515

Figure A2.2 Goodwill and goodwill amortization

VOD notes due (Note 18)	Interest rate	Amount 2005 (£M)	% of UK loans	Weighted avg UK interest rate
Japanese yen bond due 2006	0.83%	15		
Japanese yen bond due 2006	1.78%	126		
Euro bond due 2006	5.40%	275		
Euro bond due 2006	5.75%	1029		
US dollar bond due 2006	7.50%	116		
US dollar bond due 2007	4.16%	79		
Japanese yen bond due 2008	2.58%	127		
US dollar bond due 2008	3.95%	264		
Euro bond due 2008	4.63%	517		
Euro bond due 2008	5.50%	33		
Sterling bond due 2008	6.25%	249	22.72%	1.42%
Sterling bond due 2008	6.25%	158	14.42%	0.90%
US dollar bond due 2008	6.65%	132		
Euro bond due 2009	4.25%	1301		
Euro bond due 2009	4.75%	568		
Japanese yen bond due 2010	2.00%	128		
Japanese yen bond due 2010	2.28%	126		
Japanese yen bond due 2010	2.50%	127		
US dollar bond due 2010	7.75%	1435		
US dollar bond due 2013	5.00%	526		
Euro bond due 2015	5.13%	342		
US dollar bond due 2015	5.38%	481		
Euro bond due 2018	5.00%	513		
US dollar bond due 2018	4.63%	263		
Sterling bond due 2025	5.63%	246	22.45%	1.26%
US dollar bond due 2030	7.88%	390		
Sterling bond due 2032	5.90%	443	40.42%	2.38%
US dollar bond due 2032	6.25%	260		
Total (UK bonds)		**1096**	**100%**	**6.0%**

Figure A2.3 Vodafone creditor analysis – Note 18

26. Commitments

Operating lease commitments

Commitments to non-cancellable operating less payments are analysed as follows:

	2005			2004		
	Land and buildings £m	Other assets £m	Total £m	Land and buildings £m	Other assets £m	Total £m
In respect of leases expiring:						
Within one year	99	91	190	79	97	176
Between two and five years	146	91	237	147	85	232
After five years	170	33	203	136	42	178
Payments due:						
Within one year	415	215	630	362	224	586
In more than one year but less than two years			406			366
In more than two years but less than three years			352			295
In more than three years but less than four years			299			256
In more than four years but less than five years			255			218
Thereafter (more than five years)			1132			1016
			3074			2737

Figure A2.4   Operating lease commitments

5. Operating loss

	2005 Total[m] £m	2004 Continuing operations £m	Discontinued operations £m	Total £m	2003 Continuing operations £m	Discontinued operations £m	Total £m
Group turnover	34,133	32,741	818	33,559	28,547	1,828	30,375
Cost of sales	(20,753)	(18,986)	(475)	(19,461)	(16,910)	(986)	(17,896)
Exceptional operating items	–	351	–	351	–	–	–
Other cost of sales	(20,753)	(19,337)	(475)	(19,812)	(16,910)	(986)	(17,896)
Gross profit	13,380	13,755	343	14,098	11,637	842	12,479
Selling and distribution costs	(2,031)	(2,065)	(14)	(2,079)	(1,863)	(20)	(1,883)
Administrative expenses	(16,653)	(16,532)	(263)	(16,795)	(14,826)	(1,065)	(15,891)
Goodwill amortisation	(12,929)	(13,095)	–	(13,095)	(11,875)	–	(11,875)
Exceptional operating items	(315)	(123)	–	(123)	(91)	(405)	(496)
Other administration expenses	(3,409)	(3,314)	(263)	(3,577)	(2,860)	(660)	(3,520)
Total operating expenses	(18,684)	(18,597)	(277)	(18,874)	(16,689)	(1,085)	(17,774)
Operating loss	(5,304)	(4,842)	66	(4,776)	(5,052)	(243)	(5,295)

SG&A = 2,031+16,653-12,929-315 = 5,440

Figure A2.5   Selling, general and administrative expenses

5. Operating loss

	2005 Total £m	2004 Continuing operations £m	2004 Discontinued operations £m	2004 Total £m	2003 Continuing operations £m	2003 Discontinued operations £m	2003 Total £m
Group turnover	34,133	32,741	818	33,559	28,547	1,828	30,375
Cost of sales	(20,753)	(18,986)	(475)	(19,461)	(16,910)	(986)	(17,896)
Exceptional operating items	–	351	–	351	–	–	–
Other cost of sales	(20,753)	(19,337)	(475)	(19,812)	(16,910)	(986)	(17,896)
Gross profit	13,380	13,755	343	14,098	11,637	842	12,479

Operating loss has been arrived at after charging/(crediting):

Financials 89

Cost of sales = 20.753-0-4.467-61-412 = 15,812

	2005 £m	2004 £m	2003 £m
Staff costs (see note 31)	2,293	2,331	2,278
Depreciation of tangible fixed assets:			
Owned assets **Depreciation = 4,467+61 = 4,528**	4,467	4,181	3,783
Leased assets	61	181	196
Goodwill amortisation	12,929	13,095	11,875
Impairment of intangible and tangible fixed assets	315	–	485
Amortisation of other intangible fixed assets	412	98	53
Research and development **R&D = 219**	219	171	164
Advertising costs (including applicable staff costs)	864	990	902
Bad debt expense	224	209	193
Operating lease rentals:			
Plant and machinery	37	98	78
Other assets including fixed line rentals	1,300	1,254	1,269
Own costs capitalised attributable to the construction or acquisition of tangible fixed assets	(301)	(290)	(207)

Figure A2.6   Cost of sales and depreciation

5. Operating loss

Financials 89

Operating loss has been arrived at after charging/(crediting):

	2005 £m	2004 £m	2003 £m
Staff costs (see note 31)	2,293	2,331	2,278
Depreciation of tangible fixed assets:			
Owned assets	4,467	4,181	3,783
Leased assets	61	181	196
Goodwill amortisation	12,929	13,095	11,875
Impairment of intangible and tangible fixed assets	315	–	485
Amortisation of other intangible fixed assets	412	98	53

13. Fixed asset investments
Associated undertakings

Financials 97

	Group £m
Share of net assets:	
1 April 2004	3,075
Exchange movements	(41)
Share of retained results excluding goodwill amortisation	152
Share of goodwill amortisation	(42)
31 March 2005	3,144
Capitalised goodwill:	
1 April 2004	18,151
Exchange movements	(173)
Acquisitions (note 25)	5
Goodwill amortisation **Amortization = 12,929 + 412 + 1,729 = 15,070**	(1,729)
31 March 2005	16,254

Figure A2.7   Amortization

4. Exceptional operating items

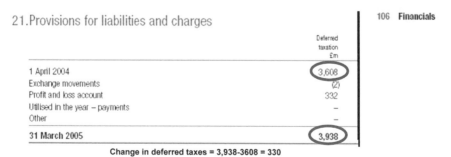

	2005 £m	2004 £m	2003 £m
Impairment of intangible and tangible fixed assets	(315)	–	(485)
Contribution tax	–	351	–
Reorganisation costs	–	(123)	(91)
	(315)	228	(576)

Consolidated Profit and Loss Accounts for the years ended 31 March

	Note	2005 $m	2005 £m	2004 £m	2003 £m
Total Group operating loss					
Group and share of joint ventures and associated undertakings	3	(7,765)	(4,111)	(4,230)	(5,451)
Exceptional non-operating items	6	25	13	(103)	(5)
– Continuing operations		25	13	(44)	20
– Discontinued operations		–	–	(59)	(25)
Loss on ordinary activities before interest	3	(7,740)	(4,098)	(4,333)	(5,456)
Net interest payable and similar items	7	(1,141)	(604)	(714)	(752)
Group		(742)	(393)	(499)	(457)
Share of joint ventures and associated undertakings		(399)	(211)	(215)	(295)
Loss on ordinary activities before taxation		(8,881)	(4,702)	(5,047)	(6,208)
Tax on loss on ordinary activities	8	(4,224)	(2,236)	(3,154)	(2,956)
Group tax on loss on ordinary activities before exceptional tax		(4,339)	(2,297)	(2,866)	(2,624)
Share of joint ventures and associated undertakings		(1,016)	(538)	(288)	(332)
Tax on loss on ordinary activities before exceptional tax		(5,355)	(2,835)	(3,154)	(2,956)
Exceptional tax credit		1,131	599	–	–

= Special Item = -315 + 13 + 599 = 297

Figure A2.8   Special items

7. Net interest payable and similar items

Financials 91

	2005 £m	2004 £m	2003 £m
Parent and subsidiary undertakings: Tax on interest expense = 602 * (25.2% marginal tax rate) = 250.4			
Interest receivable and similar income	(602)	(592)	(666)
Interest payable and similar charges:			
Bank loans and overdrafts	49	46	133
Other loans	677	820	921
Tax liabilities	261	215	55
Finance leases	8	10	14
	995	1,091	1,123

Figure A2.9   Tax on interest income

21. Provisions for liabilities and charges

106   Financials

	Deferred taxation £m
1 April 2004	3,608
Exchange movements	(2)
Profit and loss account	332
Utilised in the year – payments	–
Other	–
31 March 2005	3,938

Change in deferred taxes = 3,938-3608 = 330

Figure A2.10   Change in deferred taxes

References

Stewart, G.B., III. (1991), *The Quest for Value*, HarperCollins Publishers.

Brealey, R.A, Myers, S.C., and Allen, F. (2005), *Principles of Corporate Finance*, 8th Edition, McGraw-Hill Irwin.

Copeland, T., Koller, T., and Murrin, J. (2000), *Valuation: Measuring and Managing the Value of Companies*, Third Edition, John Wiley & Sons.

Damodaran, A. (2002), *Investment Valuation*, Second Edition, John Wiley & Sons.

Dobbs, R., and Koller, T. (2005), Measuring long-term performance, McKinsey Quarterly, Special Edition: *Value and Performance*, 17–27.

Madden, B. (1999), *CFROI Cash Flow Return on Investment Valuation: A Total System Approach to Valuing the Firm*, Butterworth-Heinemann.

Peterson, P.P., and Peterson, D.R. (1996), *Company Performance and Measures of Value Added*, The Research Foundation of the Institute of Chartered Financial Accountants.

Rappaport, A. (2005), The economics of short-term performance obsession, *Financial Analysts Journal*, 61(3), May/June, 77.

Stowe, J.D., Robinson, T.R., Pinto, J.E., and McLeavey, D.W. (2002), *Analysis of Equity Investments: Valuation*, United Book Press.

Part IV

Morgan Stanley ModelWare's Approach to Intrinsic Value: Focusing on Risk-Reward Trade-offs[1]

Trevor S. Harris[2], Juliet Estridge[3] and Doron Nissim[4]

---

[1] Morgan Stanley, © 2008 Trevor Harris.
[2] Managing Director and Vice Chairman at Morgan Stanley.
[3] Vice President at Morgan Stanley.
[4] Associate Professor and Chair of the Accounting Department at Columbia Business School.

14

Introduction

Our approach to valuation analysis evolved as we grappled with integrating classical economic and finance principles with the practical realities of what is observable, measurable, understandable and relevant to users. The result is an approach that many traditionalists will consider to be heretical, especially as we argue against the illusion of precision they often strive for.

Our conceptually based formal model employs commonly recognized forecast elements[1] to establish one or more measures of the "intrinsic" value (IV) of a company for use by investors and company managers. We have designed the model to be flexible so it can rely on a few key inputs or incorporate additional detailed information that relates to the key drivers of a company's performance and hence IV. IV is rarely expected to be equal to the actual stock price, but comparing a set of plausible values to price allows us to challenge our own ideas or expectations and, as investors, to assess the gap between price and IV in terms of a risk-reward trade-off.

The notion of IV we are solving for is best expressed by Warren Buffett:

> Intrinsic value is an all important concept that offers the only logical approach to evaluating the relative attractiveness of investments and businesses. Intrinsic value can be defined simply: It is the discounted value of the cash that can be taken out of a business during its remaining life. . .
>
> . . . When the stock temporarily overperforms or underperforms the business, a limited number of shareholders – either sellers or buyers – receive outsized benefits at the expense of those they trade with.[2]

There are several core principles we have incorporated into the IV model and its application:

- *Price and risk of a security is driven by information and investors' interpretation (or intuition).* We can, and do, use market price or volatility measures as indicators to inform our analysis, but stock prices are not the key driver of value. The value of a business is driven by its economic fundamentals, which can vary through time, but the company's stock price will vary for a number of reasons besides the company's activities. It is commonly understood, but bears repeating, to note that on most days, the intraday volatility of any company's stock price has little to do with changes in the company's fundamentals, and more to do with other factors driving supply and demand of the security. These other factors are important to investing but usually should not be incorporated into estimates of IV. A simple example of this is when a company is added to a key benchmark index like the

---

[1] These include revenue or revenue growth, operating costs or margins, net operating assets or operating asset turnover, net borrowing costs, leverage, and returns of capital or payout ratios. We will define these more explicitly later in this part.
[2] Buffett (1998) p. 187.

S&P 500. Funds that operate with this index as a benchmark performance criterion will usually have to acquire the stock of the added company and excess demand will force up the price for a short period of time.

• *The idea that we can get an exact measure of intrinsic value of a company at any point in time is an "illusion of precision".* A single measure of a company's (intrinsic) value is unlikely to equal its stock price for more than a few minutes, at best. Any measure of a firm's value should be seen as an expected value within a distribution of alternative outcomes. Our approach focuses on identifying the present value of expected outcomes, considering the value of alternative plausible outcomes (not just a random simulation), and then analyzing the investment risk-reward trade-off by comparing these to current and historic market prices. Ideally we would also consider the other factors driving prices.

The higher the rate of profitability a company earns, the harder it is to sustain these levels over time, unless the company has significant, and sustainable, barriers to entry. Analogously, negative rates of profitability cannot be sustained indefinitely; eventually the company has to "die", if it generates losses indefinitely.

The more new capital a company invests, the more difficult it is to earn high rates of profitability on this new capital, at least over time. The dilemma for companies that have very high return on net operating assets (invested capital) is that the income or free cash being generated can rarely be reinvested at similar high rates of return, especially after the early growth stages (recent examples are Cisco, Microsoft or Google).

• *Long-term industry growth rates are hard to sustain much above national (or global) growth levels.* But, the dynamics and flexibility of companies to redefine the "industry" or products, means that some (albeit not many) companies can "grow" at "abnormal" rates for longer than many long run valuation models traditionally assume. Companies like our own (Morgan Stanley) or Goldman Sachs are classic cases where traditional underwriting and advisory work have evolved to incorporate risk intermediation, proprietary trading and other profitable businesses. Understanding the quality of management is critical to assessing whether and how current profitability can be sustained or grown. Good managers also adapt to new environments allowing excess profitability to persist longer than simple industry decay models usually assume.

• *Attempting to measure a precise cost of capital is futile.* Debates rage on about "correct" measures of risk-free rates, beta, the equity risk premium, single vs. multifactor models, the appropriate measure of market return, and the role of leverage. As most of us know, practical measures of these are approximations at best, so trying to get exact measures has little practical payoff. Moreover, depending on how we deal with certain market risk (e.g. exchange rates) and specific uncertainty in our forecasts, we need to ensure we are not "double-counting" the risk in our discount rate. In calculating a company's IV, we believe directional or relative measures are usually sufficient. To obtain an initial starting point, we recommend using a required return on equity of 3 to 4% above government bond yields and then refine the measure as necessary. While the company's IV should be based on a market-based measure cost of capital, for any investor the required rate of return may be different. So an investor's required return can vary for a variety of reasons, including investment horizon, portfolio mix, loss sensitivity, size of position and investment mandate and alternative investment opportunities. We leave it up to each individual to define the required rate of return (cost of capital), and use a backward induction approach to estimate a market-implied cost of equity, and weighted average cost of capital (WACC).

With these core principles in mind, we begin our measurement of IV by trying to understand the key drivers of a firm's income-generating ability. To do this we have to understand revenues, operating costs, operating assets and liabilities, funding costs and funding sources, and how these change and interact over time. By ensuring that we retain the integrated logic of the accounting relationships that link these elements, we become largely agnostic about the specific focus of the valuation model. So we can equally solve for dividend discount (DDM), discounted cash flow (DCF) or residual income valuation (RIV) models. That said, we often find more traditional estimations of DDM or DCF to be flawed because the cash flow or "dividend" is difficult to measure, and the measurement problem is usually exacerbated by the approximations made for the usually critical "terminal value". Thus, if we had to choose one "starting point", we would always choose a residual income approach (a representation of the present value of economic rents). In our view, CFROI-, CROCE-, and EVA®-based valuations are all nuances around the basic logic of residual income valuation.

In the rest of this part, we describe how we organize the basic model inputs into a framework to better forecast future profitability, then develop the conceptual foundation of our valuation model. With these building blocks, we show how we apply the model in actual companies. Finally, we provide some empirical evidence confirming the logic of the framework we are using.

15
Linking Fundamental Analysis to the Inputs of the Valuation Model

To measure intrinsic value we start by estimating the cash that *can be taken out* of a business during its remaining life. To illustrate our approach, we follow a logical process, starting with a new business.

At the inception of a business, a company gets funding from the owners (shareholders) and often from other lenders who give them fixed terms of repayment, hence becoming obligations or debt of the corporation. Managers of the business use this (cash) funding to purchase or hire resources (e.g. equipment, goods and services), take actions to transform the resources and then resell the "new" products or services to customers, usually at a higher price. The customers (hopefully) pay the company for their purchases, and this cash is usually first used to service the company's obligations, before it goes to the owners.

Over time, the managers have to decide how to use any excess or "free" cash. They could return the cash to the owners, in which case we no longer have to consider its future use. But if they choose to retain the cash, then we have to consider how it is going to be used in the future. The first question is what do the managers need to spend to sustain the current level of business, and what is the source of funding for this. Then we ask what else they need or will spend to generate growth in the business, and how profitably they can do this. If there is demand for the company's products or innovations, there is often a need to spend on incremental operating resources to have the products to sell. The free cash from past activities may or may not be sufficient to meet these needs; if not, we look to additional sources of funding. This cycle continues through time, and so we refer to it as the "cycle of life" of a business (see Figure 15.1). To estimate an intrinsic value we usually have to look beyond a single cycle, despite the fact that the set of possibilities and uncertainty of outcomes increases (not to be confused with risk from pricing volatility) with time.

The cycle of a company represented in Figure 15.1 includes thousands, or millions, of transactions, actions and decisions, and it is rarely possible to have access to or to use all these data. So there has to be some organizing principle for transforming the real economic activity into summary measures that give investors an ability to assess how well their resources are being used by the managers, and what to expect going forward. This is what an accounting measurement system does. It provides a set of organizing principles and measurement approaches that are combined with descriptions to give a summary of the economic resources and obligations at a point in time, and how these change with the firm's activities over time. It is important to note that a particular set of generally accepted accounting principles (GAAP) may do a good or bad job of reflecting the economic reality, but there has to be a system to organize the data if it is to be useful.

Figure 15.2 illustrates how the core components of the "cycle of life" can be presented in terms of "stocks" and "flows" of resources and obligations that net to reflect the owners'

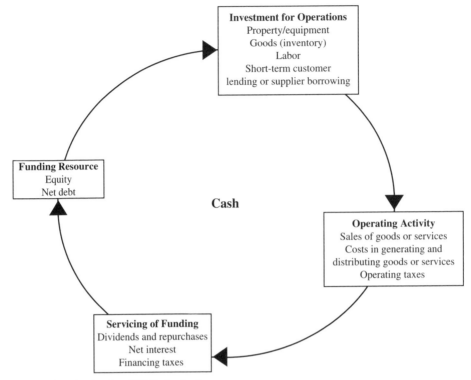

Figure 15.1   The "cycle of life" of a business

wealth. We also indicate the key accounting labels. Figure 15.3 then expands this to reflect more traditional financial reporting measures. The key point is that *all* the financial statements are interlinked, so to estimate future performance and the resulting income or cash flow meaningfully we have to retain the links.

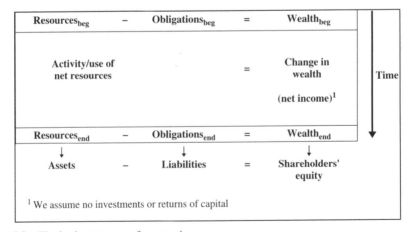

Figure 15.2   The basic structure of accounting

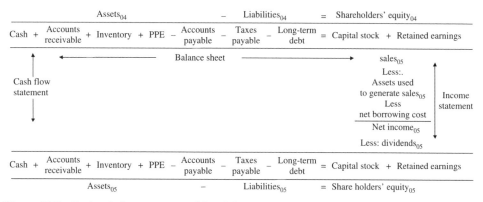

Figure 15.3 Basic relations among traditional financial statement

It is worth reiterating that our goal is to understand and estimate the economic activity of the company through time so we can assess its value. An analogy we have used is to think of the business as a never-ending movie, where the outcomes are uncertain. At any point in the movie we can take a snapshot of the current state of the business (the balance sheet), while the (moving) picture of what happened over time (the movie up to now) is the income statement (or in some cases a cash flow statement).

If the movie is a clear portrayal of "reality", we can use this information to guess what's coming next. Each frame or report summarizes a lot of action, and it "works" as information if the viewer can interpret and integrate what he sees.

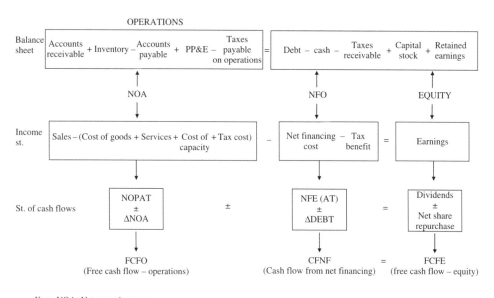

Key: NOA: Net operating assets
     NFO: Net financial obligations
     NOPAT: Net operating profit after tax
     NFE (AT): Net financial expense (after tax)

Figure 15.4 Rearranging the financial statements to reflect the "cycle of life"

For many of us, the inadequacy of current accounting regulations, the complexity of real businesses, and our inability to absorb and integrate all the data create challenges in translating the data and information we have into a useful model. But progress is being made. The key starting point is to provide an organizing framework that more closely aligns with the cycle of life of a business and that allows for varying levels of disaggregation in the areas that drive value creation of a business.

So what is our organizing framework? The initial distinction is to separate clearly operating from funding activities. This is simple in concept, but quite complicated in practice. To start we rearrange the traditional format of financial statements to reflect this split (Figure 15.4).

We use the aggregate measures illustrated in Figure 15.4 in describing the conceptual foundation of our valuation models, and then extend the organizing framework to show how we can select the level of disaggregation we choose, depending on the key drivers of value and the information available to us.

16

Our Valuation Framework

In this chapter we go through the conceptual logic behind our valuation model. (Readers who are familiar with the foundations of valuation theory, or those who are more interested in the practical applications, can skip to the next chapter.)

Intrinsic value is the discounted present value of cash we can take out of the company in the future. For anyone who has calculated the value of a simple bond, the calculation should sound very familiar. For those who have not, Figure 16.1 shows the calculation for a bond issued at a premium.

A bond has a two-year life. Its face value, to be paid at the end of the two years, is $1000. It has an annual coupon (cash payment) of 12% ($120), and the required rate of return (discount rate) is 10%.

$$\text{Value}_{Today} (V_0) = \frac{120}{(1+0.1)^1} + \frac{120}{(1+0.1)^2} + \frac{1000}{(1+0.1)^2} = \$1032.8 \tag{1}$$

Figure 16.1   The basis of all valuations – a fixed payments case

The intrinsic value of the bond is higher than the face ("book") value because it generates and pays out a return in excess of the market's (investor's) required rate of return.

In this simple case, there is no uncertainty about the earnings and cash flows (assuming no bankruptcy risk), so the only ambiguity about the value could be in the discount rate. Consider the situation where all other investment opportunities of similar risk that are available to you offered an 8% return. You would view the value to be higher than $1033 (actually closer to $1070) and would view this investment as a bargain. If your investable assets were large enough, you could bring down the "market" discount rate, but in reality, few investors are that big, even with borrowing. So even in this trivial case, there are scenarios under which individual investors can have different "intrinsic values" for the same underlying cash flows.

The simple fixed payments case is easily converted to a conceptual valuation of a company. Remember that IV from an owner's perspective is the present (discounted) value of expected future net cash payments *to the shareholders*:

$$V_0 = \frac{D_1}{(1+k_e)^1} + \frac{D_2}{(1+k_e)^2} + \ldots \infty \tag{2}$$

Where: V_0 = value today (time = 0) of shareholders' (equity) capital,
D_t = net dividends (net of contributions and returns of equity capital) at time t,
k_e = cost of equity capital

Equation (2) represents the pure dividend discount model (DDM), and assumes a constant discount rate (more on this later). To link this back to business and financial statements refer back to Figure 15.4, and note that D is the same as free cash flow to equity holders (FCFE).

In practice, most explicit forecasts extend 2–5 years into the future, so we have to consider how to deal with the long period to infinity. If the last forecasted period is 4 years out and at that point the dividend is "fixed" we can capitalize D_4, to obtain the value

$$V_0 = \frac{D_1}{(1+k_e)} + \frac{D_2}{(1+k_e)^2} + \frac{D_3}{(1+k_e)^3} + \frac{D_4/k_e}{(1+k_e)^3} \qquad (3)$$

In practice, a constant, flat dividend is rare. An extension of this simple case assumes that dividends always grow at a single growth rate (g), then:

$$D_t = D_0(1+g)^t \qquad (4)$$

and by substituting equation (4) into (3), we get

$$V_0 = \frac{D_1}{k_e - g} \qquad (5)$$

also known as the Gordon growth model.[1]

The main application of this model, in practice, is found in an earnings-multiple-based valuation model. If a company always pays out a fixed percentage of what it earns, $(p = $ payout ratio) $D_t = pE_t$, and earnings grow at the constant rate g.

Then it is simple to substitute pE_1 into the Gordon growth model,

$$\text{i.e. } V_0 = \frac{pE_1}{k_e - g} \qquad (6)$$

A special case of this is where all (new) investments earn k_e, payout ratios equal 1 or there is zero growth, in which case we would get:

$$V_0 = \frac{E_1}{k_e} \qquad (7)$$

This should start to look familiar to many people. If price (P) was equal to V (value) then we could rewrite (7) as $\frac{P_0}{E_1} = \frac{1}{k_e}$. So benchmark $\frac{P}{E}$s for stable companies are approximately equal to one divided by the cost of equity capital. Life would be simple if we could stop here, but in practice constant payouts or growth rates are virtually never found. Still worse, if managers have good investment opportunities they should pay little or no dividends. The extreme case in practice is Warren Buffett's Berkshire Hathaway which, to shareholders' delight, has not paid a dividend since he took it over. So putting 0 into the DDM or Gordon growth models would not yield a meaningful answer for a stock that was recently valued at $100 000 per share. But the accounting relations in Figure 15.4 allow us to get a more useful and interesting result, even for Berkshire Hathaway.

---

[1] Note that with $g = 0$, equations (3) and (5) are equal.

Recall that D in the DDM is the free cash flow (FCF) to equity holders, but FCFEquity $(D_1) = $ FCFOperations [FCFO] $-$ CF from Net Financing [CFNF].
Substituting into the DDM, we get:

$$V_0 = \left[\frac{FCFO_1}{(1+k_o)} + \frac{FCFO_2}{(1+k_o)^2} + \dots \infty \right] - [\text{Present value of } CFNF_{1\to\infty}] \qquad (8)$$

k_o is the cost of operating capital or weighted average cost of capital (WACC) at time t.

Equation (8) is the traditional discounted cash flow (DCF) model. Conceptually, DCFs are a great way to go, but in our experience, DCFs are often *not* the best starting point to estimate IV in practice. The reasons for this view, which may seem like heresy, are quite simple and not a surprise to most people who have calculated DCFs in practice. Free cash flows are actually very hard to measure, and distinguishing between FCF from operations and net financing is extremely difficult in practice. To see this, consider one of our favorite examples, defined benefit pension plans. GM is well known to have massive obligations for pension and other post employment benefits. In 2003, it raised approximately $19bn in debt at a cost a little above 7% (about $1.4bn) and contributed the cash to its pension funds. The expected return on these pension assets was 9%, and the resulting income ($1.7bn) was reported in operating labor costs (as an offset to other labor costs) and so most practitioners treated the $1.7bn as both operating income and operating cash flow.[2] There are several issues to consider: First, the actual return and expected return are rarely the same; in 2003 and 2004 the return was well over 10%, so what is the real operating (or even financing) cash flow? Second, if we leave the $1.7bn as FCFO and the cost of debt (approx. $1.4bn) is in CFNF, do we feel comfortable our discount rates will appropriately reflect the relative risks so that we do not create a fictional "arbitrage" value? Third, projecting these pension-related "cash flows" 3–5 years out is hard enough, but how should we treat these in the terminal value period? There are no simple answers to these questions, but to believe we can get precise estimates of operating cash flow in such cases is naïve.

A somewhat similar issue is the treatment of employee stock options. Some people argue that employee stock compensation expense is a "non-cash" charge, but if we eliminate this cost, where and when is this transfer of value reflected in a DCF (assuming they are exercised)? We will review later how we treat these items, in our ModelWare measures. For now, the main point is that you should not be deluded into believing you can get precise measures of cash flow for use in a DCF. Stated differently, cash flows from reported numbers rarely reflect cash flow to the company that could be distributed to shareholders.

Another big issue with DCFs is that successful companies are often spending operating cash for future growth. Consider the cases of US retailers Kohl's and Target. As we see in Table 16.1, from 2000 through 2004 there were several periods of negative FCFO using reported numbers.

In 2005, and using Morgan Stanley analyst current forecasts for 2006 and 2007, the FCFOs turn positive. The reason FCFO is negative in the earlier years is that the companies were investing in inventories, property and equipment, and in Target's case they also lent more to customers. The negative FCFO was from funding growth, yet if we were doing a

---

[2] In addition, under current US GAAP, the $19bn contribution would also be reported as part of cash flow from operations.

Table 16.1 Free cash flow from operations 2000–2007e

		2000	2001	2002	2003	2004	2005	2006e	2007e
Kohl's	Reported	(438)	(56)	(81)	10	(15)	121	167	2471
	ModelWare	(831)	(218)	(391)	(425)	(229)	(744)	56	1905
Target	Reported	1092	76	(646)	(1011)	652	3687	823	862
	ModelWare	912	(94)	(846)	(1274)	417	4430	546	702
Sears Hldg	Reported	–	–	–	–	–	(4253)	3554	2389
	ModelWare	–	–	–	–	–	(3348)	3053	2558

DCF for Kohl's at the beginning of 2000, with a 3–5 year forecast (based on actuals), we would have as a starting point:

$$V_0 = \frac{(438)}{(1+k_0)} + \frac{(56)}{(1+k_0)^2} + \frac{(81)}{(1+k_0)^3} + \frac{10}{(1+k_0)^4} + \frac{(15)}{(1+k_0)^5} + \ldots ?? \qquad (9)$$

We do not have to discuss what the right WACC is to realize this is a tough valuation to make credibly. We could "fix" the DCF by getting the "right" terminal value, but what basis is there to choose a terminal value? In practice, people start creating proxies to obtain positive measures of terminal period operating cash flow, like EBITDA, and then use a multiple of this measure to calculate a terminal value. This approach may give a positive value but it has no conceptual, or frankly, logical basis, and as we have argued for some time, EBITDA is not and never will be a measure of operating cash flow.[3]

Even if we can calculate the DCF of the operating business, to get an intrinsic value that can be compared to a stock price, we have to deduct the value of financial obligations. Another rarely discussed concern with the DCF model in equation (8) is that in practice getting a consistent measure is not trivial. Using accounting-based models, we can calculate the PV of the cash flows from net financing, but in practice many people use a book value of "debt" and other items not in operations, or when available a market measure of debt. Neither choice is what the conceptual model specifies. Going back to our GM pension case, if we treat the funding of the pensions and the net assets or obligations as financing in nature, as we do in ModelWare at Morgan Stanley, then we have to ensure consistency in the measures used in the operating and financing components, as the "risk" of the auto operations is not the same as the "risk" (or return) of pension assets and obligations. The latter is affected by uncertainty of the expected payments to beneficiaries, the relevance of discount rates used, and the inherent risk when pension assets and obligations are not "matched".

The relevance of making a distinction between operating and financing to effectively reflect the intrinsic value of a business using a DCF (or other multi-period calculations) can be seen with the case of leased resources used in operations. To understand a company's ability to generate income or positive cash flow we need to evaluate the operating capacity of a business. So for retailers, deciding the size and location of the stores and the nature of fixtures and fittings is critical to operating success, so all these operating assets must be considered, regardless of how they are financed. If they are leased this may create strategic optionality, but this is still primarily a funding decision and should be reflected as such.

---

[3] See Harris (2002).

Another classic case is the airline business, where for many years the bulk of the fleet in some airlines was leased and not reflected on the balance sheet with financing costs treated as part of operating rental payments.[4] In ModelWare we treat all leases as financing of the underlying asset. This adjustment (together with pensions) is the main cause of the difference between the ModelWare and Reported FCFO for Kohl's and Target in Table 16.1. Note that the lower FCFOs reflect the investment in operating capacity for the future. Which cash flow (reported or ModelWare) reflects the economic operations of the business, that proponents of a conceptually based DCF would require? We believe the ModelWare numbers are closer to economic reality, but even proponents of DCFs as precise measures of IV have rarely made these adjustments in practice.

In sum, we want to emphasize two main points from the discussion. First, most DCF calculations are going to be imprecise, and frequently DCFs cannot even facilitate useful calculations. Second, it is a "stretch" of reality to believe that because the input is called "cash flow" we have resolved the practical measurement problems espoused in criticisms of accrual measures like earnings. Even carefully constructed valuation approaches like CFROI, which is based on discounting "net cash receipts" with a "cash in/cash out perspective", do not, and cannot, measure real cash. In describing CFROI, Madden himself says: "It is important to note that cash flows from operating activities . . . is not the cash flow concept used in either the calculation of net cash receipts or CFROIs. *We accept the principles of accrual accounting for measuring economic performance.*"[5]

We have shown some practical problems with the DDM and DCF models, but is there an alternative? We believe the answer is yes. There is no conceptual distinction; rather, the difference arises in improved clarity and precision in relating the measure of intrinsic value to the way companies perform and how we generate estimates and scenarios about future outcomes.

Before formally developing the conceptual model, we want to give you a sense of why we find the practical aspects so compelling. If you ask yourself how you decide what price to pay for any good or service, it is basically a price that is less than (or, at worst, equal to) the value you expect to receive. In the case of the bond in Figure 16.1, we pay more than face value because the coupon pays higher than our required rate of return. The same logic can be applied to a company. If we have a book (or "face") value of the underlying business, then the intrinsic value of the company will be higher than this book value as long as the rate of return on the book value is higher than our required rate of return. The exact amount higher will be the discounted value of that extra return through time. The excess return is also known as: economic rent, residual income, "abnormal" earnings, economic value added, and probably a myriad of other terms. There is no "magic" to the generic approach. But, with this basic idea we can begin to ask questions about the sources of profitability and why, or how, the profitability will persist, grow or improve in ways that link directly to both the underlying business (the "cycle of life" in Figure 15.1), and the financial statements, which are still the primary financial information about the company (see Figures 15.3 and 15.4).

We will be more specific about how we relate the business to the value, but first we develop the formal model.

---

[4] "Pan European retailers-not made to measure: an apples-to-apples look at Europe's clothing retailers" (with European Retail Team), Morgan Stanley Dean Witter, November 2, 1998, "Global Airlines: flight to quality" (with Global Airlines Team), Morgan Stanley Dean Witter, October 13, 1998.
[5] Madden (1999), p. 108. Emphasis added.

The relationship among net dividends (D), earnings (E) and shareholders' equity (B), is shown in Figures 15.3 and 15.4 and can be represented as:

$$B_1 = B_0 + E_1 - D_1 \tag{10}$$

which states that ending equity = beginning equity + current earnings − net return of capital. Rearranging (equation (10)) to state it in terms of dividends gives:

$$D_1 = B_0 + E_1 - B_1 \tag{11}$$

By adding and subtracting the cost of equity times beginning equity ($k_e B_0$), we can state earnings in terms of residual income:

$$E_1 = k_e B_0 + \underbrace{(E_1 - k_e B_0)}_{\text{Residual income}} \tag{12}$$

Substituting (12) into (11) allows us to define dividends in terms of residual income,

$$D_1 = B_0(1 + k_e) + (E_1 - k_e B_0) - B_1 \tag{13}$$

which we can then substitute into our DDM model in Figure 16.1, to give

$$V_0 = B_0 + \sum_{t=1}^{\infty} \frac{E_t - (k_e \times B_{t-1})}{(1 + k_e)^t} = B_0 + \sum_{t=1}^{\infty} \frac{(\text{ROE}_t - k_e) \times B_{t-1}}{(1 + k_e)^t} \tag{14}$$

Where ROE_t is the return on equity, calculated as E_t / B_{t-1}.

Equation (14) states that the (intrinsic) value of a company is its book value today plus the sum of the discounted economic rents, that is the present value of excess profitability, defined as the excess of its income relative to cost of equity, times each period's invested capital. In its restated form on the right of (14) the valuation approach is even easier to interpret. The intrinsic value to a shareholder is greater than its stated book value of equity, if a company can earn a return on its invested (capital) in excess of the required return on this capital. We like to think of the residual income valuation[6] (RIV) model in (14) as "bond math" applied to a company, where the ROE is analogous to the coupon.

While RIV in equation (14) is estimated at an equity level, splitting RIV into operating and financing components is straightforward in concept. The logic is best understood in the context of our reorganized financial statements in Figure 15.4, and the basic accounting equation.

Shareholders equity (B_1) = Net operating assets (NOA_1) − Net financial obligations (NFO_1)

So

$$V_0 = V_0^{NOA} - V_0^{NFO} \tag{15}$$

---

[6] See further discussion of the residual income model at the end of this part.

Given our split of earnings into the operating and financing components it is simple to show the components of (15), in residual income equivalent of equation (14).

$$V_0^{NOA} = \text{NOA}_0 + \sum_{t=1}^{\infty} \frac{(OI_t - k_{ot}\text{NOA}_{t-1})}{(1+k_{ot})^t} = \text{NOA}_0 + \sum_{t=1}^{\infty} \frac{((\text{RNOA}_t - k_{ot}) \times \text{NOA}_{t-1})}{(1+k_{ot})^t} \quad (16)$$

$$V_0^{NFO} = \text{NFO}_0 + \sum_{t=1}^{\infty} \frac{(\text{NFE}_t - k_{dt} \times \text{NFO}_{t-1})}{(1+k_{dt})^t} = \text{NFO}_0 + \sum_{t+1}^{\infty} \frac{((\text{NBC}_t - k_{dt}) \times \text{NFO}_{t-1})}{(1+k_{dt})^t} \quad (17)$$

Where: k_{ot} is the cost of invested (operating) capital at time t, equal to WACC.
k_{dt} is the cost of debt capital
NBC_t is the % net borrowing cost at time t, defined as net financing expense as a percent of beginning period net financial obligations.

Equations (15) to (17) show how we can disaggregate the equity-based RIV into two separate activities, operating and funding, a first step in a sum of the parts valuation. This logic can easily be extended to any segment of a company's business for which we can obtain relevant profitability and invested capital data. The problem in practice is that current financial reporting systems do not make clear separations between operating and funding activities, and even less clear are distinctions across additional segments. But, by using the logical connection of the accounting model shown in Figures 15.2 to 15.4, we can relate the underlying transactions and activities of a business to the valuation model, subject to data constraints. The following section demonstrates our approach using Sears Holdings as a real example.[7]

---

[7] We use Sears Holdings for several reasons. The current company was created by the combination of Sears and Kmart, two large but troubled retailing companies in the US. So it is impossible to rely on historical data to impute meaningful forecasts. In addition, since the combination, investors have had very different views of the company's future prospects, and the company gives no guidance. We can discuss how views on IV do not necessarily change even while the price has been changing, as we engaged in a discussion with investing clients at a conference in October 2005. At the time our analysts IV estimate for the "base case" was around $125. We performed our own upside and downside cases using the scenarios laid out in Sears Holdings Corporation "Focus on the customer", Morgan Stanley Equity Research, September 9, 2005, and derived a high case around $160 and a low case around $80.

17

Linking Business Activity to Intrinsic Value:
The ModelWare Profitability Tree

As discussed earlier, to determine an intrinsic value of a company we need to understand how it operates and funds its activities, in its "cycle of life". We illustrated how this is partially reflected in reported financial statements, and how these can be rearranged to better align with the economic activity (Figures A2.1 through A2.4). We then developed the basic conceptual approach to valuation, showing how DDM, DCF and RIV are conceptually consistent, but practically RIV has distinct advantages. One of the primary advantages is that the inputs to the valuation calculation are the elements of the business and the financial reporting system that are observable and serve as the starting point in forecasting future performance of a business. This basic linkage is the "Profitability Tree" shown in Figure 17.1.

For a variety of reasons, including the way people are taught, and because analysts have become so focused on forecasting a company's quarterly (reported) earnings, we see forecast models built on standard financial reporting formats, with a strong focus on

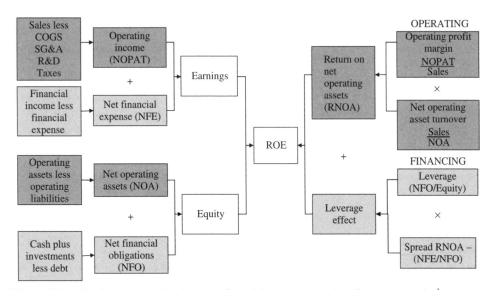

Figure 17.1   The basic connection between financial statements and performance metrics[1]

[1] Source: Morgan Stanley Research, "The apples to apples earnings monitor", Trevor Harris, December 10, 2000.

revenue growth, followed by working through each element in the financials. The left-hand side of the basic Profitability Tree shows how the balance sheet and income statement, reclassified to separate operating and financing elements, flow into the ROE measure used in RIV or the operating and financing valuations in equations (16) and (17). Reclassifying traditional financial reporting elements to an operating and financing split is not a simple exercise. For example, we already discussed (for DCFs) how operating leases and pensions or other post-employment benefits (OPEBs) will distort profitability measures if not split into their operating and financing components, but there are many other examples.[2] However, the current presentation in financial statements into assets and liabilities or revenues and expenses, especially if not reclassified, does not, in our view, facilitate thoughtful analysis of the future activities of a business from an intrinsic value perspective. Instead, when considering multi-period forecasts for estimating IV we try to address a core set of questions:[3]

(1) Is current earnings (and free cash flow) feasible and sustainable?
(2) What are the primary sources of expected growth and does the company have the necessary resources to achieve this?
(3) Is there potential operating leverage and how sustainable is it?
(4) How effectively does the company manage its capital structure?
(5) If new capital is being invested, is it required to sustain the business or is it for real growth, and can it generate a marginal return in excess of its marginal cost?
(6) What are the risks associated with these expectations?

How do the accounting treatments used by the company impact our answers to questions (1) through (6)?

In addressing these questions and creating forecasts of future performance (not what next quarter's reported earnings will be), it is usually more appropriate to use the underlying profitability drivers that lead to value creation. Stated differently, what can managers do to enhance intrinsic value for shareholders? We believe the basic elements of this are growth, capital (operating and funding) efficiency, productivity enhancement, and value accretive investment. The key metrics to capture and model these elements are shown on the right-hand side of the Profitability Tree in Figure 17.1.[4] ROE has four pillars: operating margin, net operating asset turnover, the proportion of debt financing and the spread between what a dollar of new capital funded from debt can earn as it is put to use, and what it costs to fund the borrowing. Note that these metrics are derived from the same elements on the left side of the Profitability Tree, but allow for a more logical connection to how value is created and to answering the questions we pose.

To better understand this assertion let's consider how we begin to address questions (1)–(6) for Sears Holdings. Figure 17.2 shows the Sears Holdings 2006 (FYE January 2007) basic profitability tree.

---

[2] A more detailed discussion can be found in Harris et al. (2004).

[3] These questions should be considered within the context of the key principles outlined at the beginning of this note.

[4] Some people initially believe that Figure 17.1 is the "DuPont formula", but there is an important distinction. The traditional DuPont formula is: $ROE = \frac{Net\ Income}{Sales} * \frac{Sales}{Assets} * \frac{Assets}{Equity}$. Comparing this to the profitability tree, you can see the split between operating and financing is not in the DuPont formula. The value creating attributes of the operating and funding businesses are very different so combining them limits our insights. Consider cash rich companies like Cisco where more than 40% of total assets was cash and short-term financial investments, as of fiscal year end 2006, and more than 50% in 2005. An improved asset efficiency from reducing cash has different value implications than an equivalent improvement from getting more revenue with fewer operating assets.

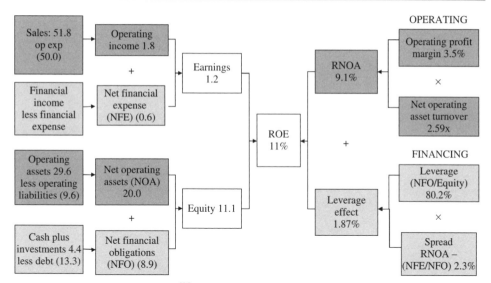

Figure 17.2   The Profitability Tree^{SM} for Sears Holding for fiscal year Jan 2006

Fiscal 2007 ModelWare net income for Sears Holding is expected to be $1.37bn on a revenue of $50.7bn. If we assume that cost of equity is 8.5%,[5] that next period earnings are sustainable and that there is no value accretive growth beyond then, we can apply a simple earnings multiple (equation (7)) to get a value of $16.1bn or approximately $103.6 per share. The stock price at the end of September 2006 has been around $160 per share, suggesting that the market is assuming, not only that the current earnings will be sustained, but that there will be a significant amount of growth. The next step is to consider what growth is already factored into current price, which also helps us to think through questions (1)–(6), and how aligned price is with intrinsic value. Figure 17.3 describes the steps.

The first element we look for is where the growth is coming from and if there is potential operating leverage. Good managers of companies seek to expand operating margins by increasing sales without increasing fixed costs and/or with reducing variable costs. Ways to do this include increasing prices with limited reduction of quantities sold, getting scale benefits off an existing cost base, moving to higher margin products, getting fixed costs down, finding new products or services to offer (scope benefits) and reducing fixed costs. Good fundamental analysis focuses on these points. In Sears' case, the primary value proposition from the merger was to obtain operating leverage via cost efficiency, which has been achieved to date, despite negative overall sales growth.

Most companies require operating resources and capital to generate sales. For example, Sears requires stores, inventory, equipment and potentially receivables to generate sales. But if it can maintain or improve sales with relatively little new investment in these elements then it improves its value. For example, in looking for value creation, analysts focus on changes in "same store" sales to monitor operating asset efficiency and potentially margin improvement (from leveraging the fixed cost of the stores and staff). Reduced days inventory

---

[5] Using a basic CAPM model as a starting point, with a 4.5% 10-year government bond rate, a 4% equity premium and a current beta of 0.98 (per Bloomberg) we get an 8.5% cost of equity capital.

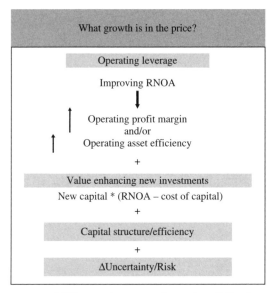

Figure 17.3   The key sources of difference between price and capitalized current earnings

on hand (especially relative to days payable outstanding) is another indicator of potential asset or cost efficiency.[6] These are measures of performance that great companies focus on and are used by investors as indicators of "earnings quality". Revenue growth with sustainable operating leverage can be a powerful force in creating intrinsic value, as should be apparent by integrating a built out profitability tree and RIV (equations (14)–(17)).

But revenue (and income) growth can also be created by investing in new operating assets or businesses. When Kmart purchased Sears, the acquiring company's sales nominally increased from 2004 to 2005 by approximately 150%, but we clearly should not consider this revenue growth to create value or to be priced in the same way as growth in same store sales, as $11bn was spent to acquire the new revenue. Growth from investment creates value when the return on new investment exceeds the cost of the new capital, that is, when the new operating assets generate positive residual income. In addition, as described in one of our core principles, over time new investments tend to earn lower rates of marginal returns, as the most profitable opportunities tend to attract initial investments.

To make this idea a little more tangible, consider the following question. Assume Sears' earnings per share grew by $2, of which $1 was from operating leverage that will be sustained and $1 was from investing $1bn in new stores. Should each dollar of EPS growth improve Sears' intrinsic value equally? Your answer should be NO, as the operating leverage is fully accretive to value, but only the earnings above the cost of the new investment generate incremental value to shareholders. In testing this notion empirically, we found that on average in the US, from 1988 through 2002, there was a significantly higher value (approximately 3×) placed on operating income growth from operating leverage than on growth from new investments (Harris and Nissim, 2004).

---

[6] We discuss many of these ratios and their relevance to understanding value creation in Harris and Huh (2000).

So in our analyses we try to understand the direction and sources of growth from a company's operating activity. One simple way to consider this is by looking at the trends of operating margins and operating asset turnover (efficiency) both over time and relative to peers. Figure 17.4 shows these trends for Sears (SHLD), Target (TGT) and Kohl's (KSS) in the "profitability map" (Harris and Huh, 2000).[7]

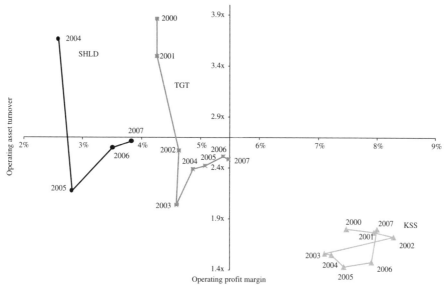

Figure 17.4   Profitability map[8]

There are three things to focus on when glancing at the profitability maps.

(1) *Evaluate the direction over time.* Moving to the upper right (northeast) is preferred as it reflects both margin and efficiency improvement, and can justify higher valuations (relative multiples). For Sears we see that in fiscal year Jan 2005, the first year of the combined company, the operating margin (OM) was 2.8% and the operating asset turnover (OpATO) was 2.2 times so the RNOA of 6.1% was close to the cost of (operating) capital at that time. Nevertheless, despite declining revenue growth rates expected in 2006 and 2007 both OM and OpATO improve raising RNOA. The trajectory is good.[9]

(2) Look for inflection points in the trends and evaluate what is causing them.

[7] Harris first created the profitability map in 2000 when trying to understand whether the high valuations of companies during the late 1990s could be justified by fundamental valuation analysis. In this analysis, he showed that the high valuations could be justified by companies who could get operating margins and operating efficiency to grow simultaneously (Harris and Huh, 2000), which is easily illustrated in a profitability map that has operating asset turnover on the vertical axis and operating margins on the horizontal. Highly valued companies should generally be heading towards the northeast.
[8] Source: Company data, Morgan Stanley Research.
[9] Our experience, based on anecdotal evidence, is that most analysts have positive biases in their expectations about revenue, OM and OpATO trends. In addition, investors tend to extrapolate these trends too easily by applying a perpetuity notion to recent trends. This behavior can lead to a deviation between stock prices and IV.

(3) Consider the OM and OpATO and their trends relative to competitors and try to understand if and what the economic justification is for this. For example, looking at Figure 17.4 we see that Kohl's is a higher margin lower operating asset turnover business than Sears and Target, this is partly because they have a higher concentration of apparel in their product mix.

The discussion of what growth is in the price and how this extends to intrinsic value has focused on the operating components. In considering what future growth is already in the price, we identify two other broad categories in Figure 17.2. Despite classical finance theory, we believe that in practice there is value to be created by increasing efficiency in the way a company funds its operating activity. A practical anecdote may help convince skeptical readers. The simplest case is the fact that many companies have "excess" cash. As stated earlier, in 2006 Cisco has more than 40% of its total assets in cash and short-term financial investments. There is no question that the financial assets currently earn less than Cisco's investments in operating activities. There are at least three likely reasons why Cisco (and many other companies) hold excess cash. First, they want liquidity reserves to meet fixed costs during unexpected downturns, i.e. as a hedge against uncertainty or to allow for speed in making acquisitions. Second, is that a significant portion of the cash is held outside the US, having been "earned" by its non-US subsidiaries. If the cash is distributed back to the US and out to shareholders, it is likely to trigger a tax charge because of US tax rules so there is some unrecognized tax opportunity cost. A third reason, which we have argued for many years, is that companies that utilize employee stock options as a means of paying and motivating their employees will be hesitant to pay dividends, as holders of unexercised options lose the value of the capital that is returned via a dividend. Another example of a funding choice that is inconsistent with conceptual economic efficiency is evidenced in that most companies in the US that have funded defined benefit pension plans continue to fund and invest these funds inefficiently from a shareholder's perspective (Moore, 2006).

So if you accept that, while arguably rational, these financing choices are not made from a simple efficient market, zero net present value perspective, how should we factor them into our valuation analysis? A standard approach is to assume they have been dealt with in the discount rates used (WACC), or to assume that the book value of these financial assets and liabilities proxy for their market values. Therefore, if we can value the operating business (using DCF or the residual operating income model) we can get the IV by subtracting book value of debt. To accept this argument assumes a level of precision in measures like risk-free rates, equity risk premia, beta and market efficiency that makes no practical sense. While our thinking on this is far from fully developed, we believe it is useful to analyze the value of the financing activity as if it were a separate line of business. This forces us to think through the value and risk of a company's funding strategy. Note that if we truly believe that the concepts of corporate finance apply in practice, we should be able to get this analysis to yield a value that is equal to the "book" value of debt used in a WACC calculation and a cost of debt equal to its discount rate. As anyone who has done such an exercise knows, this is usually not plausible.

But there is another point that argues in favor of analyzing a company's funding activity for IV. If Sears can generate an RNOA of at least 9% (as our analyst expected in 2006), and it can borrow at say 6% on an after tax basis, why would it not borrow and invest more? Just asking this question and exploring the alternatives (e.g. that current stores are at full capacity, incremental investments earn lower RNOA, etc.) help us better address the sources and sustainability of value creation.

The final consideration relating to what growth is in the price (Figure 17.3) is changes in perceived differences in uncertainty or risk.[10] The idea behind this broad category is that when we analyze a company we usually (implicitly or explicitly) consider a range of alternatives and end up with measures that reflect an expected value, but not certainty. So in Sears' case Morgan Stanley analyst Greg Melich expects revenue to go down based on a macro view of demand and Sears' available floor space, products and customer base relative to its competitors. He also raises questions about whether the investment (or lack thereof) in the stores creates short-term efficiency but longer-term problems. Greg's set of views are represented in his forecasts for 2006 to 2010. As time evolves, he will get new information and will revise his expectations even though nothing fundamental in the business needs to have changed. The price reflects a market view, which could reflect a different set of expectations to Greg's about the fundamentals of the business but the price can also be impacted by issues that have nothing to do with these fundamentals. Our favorite anecdote of this was from the "Apples-to-Apples" report on Global Telecoms (Harris with Global Telecom Team, 1998). Based on our analysis at the time it was clear that the price exceeded any plausible measure of intrinsic value. Yet we agreed with the analyst's view that the stock would still outperform the local market for a period of time. The reasoning was rational. There was significant uncertainty about the Japanese economy and in particular the level of bad debts in the banks and companies, what it would mean for credit, for asset values and consumption. Yet, in this flood of uncertainty, the one beacon of safety was the nationalized telecom company, where receivables were short-dated, the product was a "necessity" and for a while there were regulated barriers to entry. For investors who had to invest in Japanese equity, NTT was a clear safe haven. Thus, for a time the excess demand was likely to continue to drive up the price of NTT's stock. The catalyst for any price reversal was reduced uncertainty about the bad debt problem and the economy more generally, not a change in the company's own business activities.

---

[10] Mauboussin (2006) makes an interesting observation about differences between risk and uncertainty.

18

ModelWare's Intrinsic Value Approach

The logical train of reasoning we have been outlining links financial statement information and a firm's key profitability metrics to the elements of the conceptual valuation models. In this chapter, we demonstrate the links more explicitly by illustrating the approach we have adopted in ModelWare, and describe how we apply the conceptual foundation in practice.

To illustrate what we are doing we use Sears Holdings with a hypothetical valuation as of the date of writing.[1] Although not ideal for illustrating some aspects of the model, we choose Sears because it is a newly created company with no meaningful history, the company does not give guidance about its strategy, and investors have had widely differing views of the intrinsic value of the company. The price volatility over the last 16 months reflects this difference. Figure 18.1 shows the basic components that go into the valuation model and the intrinsic value measure at the start of the year and one year later. The key inputs to the model are as follows:

(1) We start with at least one year of history and any number of years of "explicit" forecast (usually from an analyst) of operating revenue, operating margin (or expenses), net operating assets (or OpATO), net financial expense, leverage, total return of capital (or dividends and share repurchases payout). While these are the only necessary items to incorporate into the model, we assume that if a forecast exists then one or more of these components will have elements that are more granular in the forecast. For example, in Sears' case the analyst team has significant detail behind the revenue forecasts including stores, size of stores, revenue per square meter, with variations based on the brand and type of products sold, and so on.

(2) Within ModelWare all components should be tagged with an XML-like[2] tag based on a taxonomy we have developed, so that no matter how granular the detail, there will be a consistent aggregation within, and across, industries as to what is included in each core calculation. Tables A.1 and A.2 in the Appendix show the definitions and some of our idiosyncratic treatments. We will discuss a few of these in detail in the next chapter, but the key is that the system allows for tagged elements to be as flexible and extensible as the user wants because the calculation rule is determined in a fully extended profitability tree, thus ensuring the logical consistency of the earnings, balance sheet and cash flow components.

---

[1] All this information should be viewed as hypothetical and should not in any way be used or seen as an investment recommendation.

[2] As XBRL (eXtensible Business Reporting Language) taxonomies evolve we are using these tags (or mapping to them) where possible to facilitate the speed of update and integration of reporting data into the database.

Intrinsic value per share (current)	**127.31**
Intrinsic value per share (in 12 months), cum dividends	**138.14**
Current Price	*160.38*

Cost of equity	8.5%
Implied WACC	7.4%
Long-term RNOA on new investments	9.5%
Long-term ROE on new investments	12.2%
Specific forecast period (years)	**6**
Years to reach steady-state growth	**25**

	History	Morgan Stanley analyst published estimate					Model	Steady state
	2006	**2007**	**2008**	**2009**	**2010**	**2011**	**2012**	**(2031)**
OPERATING								
Operating revenue	51 813	50 732	50 008	49 132	48 592	48 400	49 126	
Growth		*−2.1%*	*−1.4%*	*−1.8%*	*−1.1%*	*−0.4%*	*1.5%*	*4.0%*
Operating expenses	50 000	48 796	48 145	47 324	46 833	46 686	47 386	
NOPAT	1813	1937	1862	1808	1758	1715	1740	
NOPAT margin	*3.5%*	*3.8%*	*3.7%*	*3.7%*	*3.6%*	*3.5%*	*3.5%*	
Net operating assets	19 073	18 310	18 687	18 253	17 864	17 769	18 036	
Net operating asset growth	*−4.6%*	*−4.0%*	*2.1%*	*−2.3%*	*−2.1%*	*−0.5%*	*1.5%*	
Operating asset turnover	*2.59*	*2.66*	*2.73*	*2.63*	*2.66*	*2.71*	*2.72*	
RNOA	*9.1%*	*10.2%*	*10.2%*	*9.7%*	*9.6%*	*9.6%*	*9.6%*	
FCF operations	2724	2700	1485	2242	2147	1810	1628	
Present value of FCFO	2537	2343	1201	1689	1507	1183	992	
Residual income (operating)	347	537	519	437	419	404	402	
Present value of residual income (operating)	323	466	419	329	294	264	245	
FINANCING								
Net financial expense (income)	527	516	377	378	379	380	272	
Borrowing costs	8.8%	9.6%	7.8%	7.0%	6.8%	7.2%	5.0%	*5.0%*
Financing spread	0.2%	0.6%	2.3%	2.6%	2.8%	2.4%	4.6%	
Dividends and net repurchase	1550	1550	1750	2000	1500	1500	1398	
Dividend and net repurchases payout	*127.9%*	*113.5%*	*122.7%*	*145.6%*	*113.2%*	*116.6%*	*97.8%*	
Net debt (cash)	5379	4817	5359	5539	5313	5432	5667	
Change in net debt	*−39.5%*	*−10.5%*	*11.3%*	*3.4%*	*−4.1%*	*2.2%*	*4.3%*	
Leverage (net debt/equity)	*50%*	*46%*	*52%*	*57%*	*55%*	*58%*	*60%*	*60%*
Other non-operating expense (income)	74	56	59	56	54	48	48	
Minority interest and other	2923	2923	2923	2923	2923	2923	2923	
Net income	1212	1365	1426	1374	1325	1287	1269	
Shareholders' equity	10 771	10 570	10 405	9791	9628	9414	9464	
ROE	*11.3%*	*12.7%*	*13.5%*	*13.2%*	*13.5%*	*13.4%*	*13.5%*	
Present value dividend and net repurchase	1435	1329	1389	1470	1021	945	712	
Residual income (equity)	688	488	739	553	554	516	516	
Present value of residual income (equity)	637	418	587	407	377	325	301	

Figure 18.1 The key inputs and results from ModelWare IV applied to Sears Holdings as of September 2006[3]

---

[3] Refer to Morgan Stanley published research by Gregory Melich *et al.* "Sears Holdings Corporation: what's next for SHLD", August 21, 2006.

(3) The valuation model has potentially four "stages":

(a) The first stage uses the data from an analyst's detailed model. However, many people feel uncomfortable modeling details beyond a few years, so this period is rarely more than 3 to 5 years. This is the detailed "explicit" stage. In Table A.1, we show the ModelWare defined calculations of the key inputs to the valuation from analysts' detailed 5-year forecast for SHLD that was made in mid-2006.[4] To be clear, there is a much more detailed (tagged) analyst's model underlying these aggregated measures.

(b) For a business that is not at a steady rate of growth, or has an operating cycle that is greater than the period the analyst has forecast, or for which you want to test out certain scenarios, there is a desire (and even a need) to forecast trends or strategic options for a number of additional years without fully detailed models. To facilitate this limited but still "explicit" analysis, the current ModelWare IV tool allows the user to specify any or all of the key metrics identified in point 1, for as long as the user desires, without having to link it to the underlying complexity in the analyst's full model. For illustration purposes, we have extended the forecast period by one year. Anecdotally we have found having this ability facilitates thinking through what likely growth rates, margins and leverage (payout) make economic sense. This second stage is not necessary. However, because we have incorporated the ability to explicitly adjust the key components that drive the valuation, from the first forecast period, we are also able to easily perform explicit scenario analyses. As we see in Figure 18.1, the valuation using the analyst's forecasts is $127, far below the current price, which has been varying around $160. We can adjust any element of the model's inputs to assess alternative forecasts. For example, we could simply increase revenue growth, but this is not assumed to automatically create operating leverage. Because we require integrity in the model's key inputs and we want to force users to consider where the value is being derived from (per Figure 17.3) we initially hold operating margin and operating asset turnover constant so revenue growth creates operating cost and operating asset growth. The user has to explicitly select the source of operating leverage or efficiency. This is in contrast to most analyses where revenue growth often is assumed to be "free", especially with respect to investments in net operating assets. Given the way most models are constructed, analysts do not automatically consider the investment required to generate revenue growth. For example, without pricing power, revenue growth can only be generated by increased volumes, but in any business (goods or services) there are volume constraints on existing capacity. Yet revenue growth from pricing power requires no new investment in plant or inventory but some investment in receivables. Analogously, declining sales lead to some reduction in costs and NOA but usually not in any way that is symmetric to an equivalent increase in sales. Anecdotally, over the years, we have observed that the majority of analysts' forecasts, even those with slow or negative sales growth, assume constantly improving operating asset turnover, often at high rates of increase. Efficiency improvements are often possible, but rarely are they as large or as frequent as assumed. The ModelWare IV tool

---

[4] We remind readers that all data used is intended to be for illustrative purposes only, and should not be considered in any way as investment advice.

allows the user to adjust the defaults sequentially so revenue growth, cost or asset efficiency are not automatic but can be incorporated. The key point is that there is a necessary economic logic to driving value creation (see Figure 17.3), and we want to encourage users of an IV application to consider these rather than just assuming such operating leverage is automatic. The flexibility to adjust the key elements includes creating an ability to quickly model an acquisition scenario (discussed later).

(c) The third stage is the "transition" period between the last date of any detailed forecast (from points 3(a) and 3(b)) and a point in time in the future when the company reaches a steady state of revenue growth without operating leverage improvement. The key inputs are a set of assumptions about what will happen when the company reaches a "steady state". Given the core principles we outlined in Chapter 14, we assume that a company cannot grow revenue above an industry (and eventually economy-wide) growth rate at some point in time in the future (when steady state is reached). So, we have to choose that level and how long it will take to get there.

Clearly, the answer differs by company and industry. A company that is small with a low market share, but has products in demand and a pipeline of new products, will take a long time to get to steady state; many successful biotech companies could fit into this category. On the other hand, a company that has mature products and little prospects for growth, is essentially already in steady state, many food companies like Heinz would be recent examples of this. A company that is already large with a dominant market share in its industries will have difficulty growing in any single market. In some of these cases (e.g. GE in the US) the company finds growth by constantly moving into new products, sectors and markets, so that commonly used short "fade rates" tend to understate the true value of these companies. In addition, if a company has a product for which demand is expected to remain strong and there are high barriers to entry, then it can sustain high RNOAs and ROEs for long periods, as long as it does not reinvest its earnings or free cash flows (CocaCola has been an example of this). If a company has a continuous policy of conservative accounting, like expensing all R&D, then NOA and equity are understated and ROE will remain high even when in steady state. This does not mean we advocate capitalizing and amortizing R&D, as this just creates another error in the amortization process, but we just need to take care not to assume an unrealistically low "terminal" ROE or RNOA. In steady state, we also require the user to assume constant cost of borrowing and leverage rates.

In Sears' case, at the time of writing our analyst assumed declining sales over his full 5-year forecast period. This cannot continue indefinitely so we hypothetically assume revenue will reverse trend in the 6th year and converge linearly toward a nominal revenue growth of 4% over 25 years. We assume a reinvestment of net operating assets, in steady state, which is equal to the revenue growth rate because once a company is in steady state, there is no new operating leverage to be gained. (Note, we are talking about setting a steady state level of revenue growth, not of RNOA or ROE.) For Sears, we set leverage at the level in the last period of explicit analysis and the borrowing cost at a level that assumes that the company will not invest significant liquid assets at rates significantly below the cost of debt.

The final steady state input is important. Recall that one of our key principles is that it is difficult for new investments of capital to earn high rates of return. The last input we require is an estimate of what the rate of return on new capital (net operating assets or equity) will be once the company is in steady state. The answer depends on a variety of factors, but a natural starting point would be to fix the ROE on incremental investments close to the cost of equity, or to set the RNOA on incremental NOA to the level of steady state WACC. Given that we require a steady state leverage and cost of borrowing, once we have determined the steady state RNOA or ROE, the other is easily calculated, so the choice of ROE or RNOA is not critical. Note that even if the steady state RNOA (ROE) is set equal to WACC (cost of equity), this does not mean that the aggregate RNOA or ROE will converge to this level at the steady state period (or indeed any time after that) as this rate is only applied to the new investments of capital. In practice, we could set the steady state values based on various historical trends, and algorithmic starting points can easily be derived. In general, we believe that the combination of information and intuition are important advantages and that an IV application should allow individuals to incorporate their intuition and test out alternative possibilities. When setting the expected rate of return on new investments, factors to consider include the amount of capital one assumes the company will reinvest in steady state, and the degree of conservatism in the accounting. If a company is paying out most of its income (free cash) to shareholders, then the new investment will be small, and marginal RNOA can remain higher. The source of change in NOA is also important. For example, if it is from growth in marginal receivables the return will be different than if it is from a new plant or purchase of patent.

The rate of return on new investments is important because we make a critical distinction in our model between the existing business and new investments. Once the user completes the explicit analysis of operating margins and asset efficiency, we assume that the operating margins stay steady through the period to steady state. Once these steady state variables are set, we linearly adjust the revenue growth rates from the last period of explicit analysis (end of years chosen for 3(b)) to the steady state growth rate over the number of years required to reach steady state. We similarly adjust the RNOA on new investments during this transition period. These two assumptions allow us to estimate operating profit margin, total (versus incremental) RNOA, new investments in NOA, and operating asset turnover, each period through to when the company is expected to reach steady state.[5]

(d) The last stage is the convergence period that occurs after the company reaches its steady state. Essentially, we apply the same logic as in the "transition" period, except that now the key inputs revenue growth, leverage and cost of borrowing are fixed. But, unlike typical terminal multiples, we retain the core principle that separates the profitability of the existing business from the profitability of new investments of capital. As a result there is no terminal period; rather, we allow the calculation to continue to the point where the incremental present value becomes too small to matter.

---

[5] Over time we can and may test the empirical validity of alternative patters for revenue growth and RNOA on new investments of capital and refine the application of the model. But as we do not believe a precise estimate is ever possible, we do not think this will yield much improvement.

Table 18.1   Summary of RNOAs through first 10 years of "forecasts" for Sears and Kohl's[6]

Forecast year	1	2	3	4	5	6	7	8	9	10
	2006	2007	2008	2009	2010	2011	2012	2013	2014	2015
SHLD	6.13%	9.07%	10.15%	10.17%	9.68%	9.63%	9.60%	9.60%	9.61%	9.61%
KSS	10.65%	11.66%	14.39%	14.57%	14.24%	14.04%	13.83%	13.65%	13.49%	13.36%

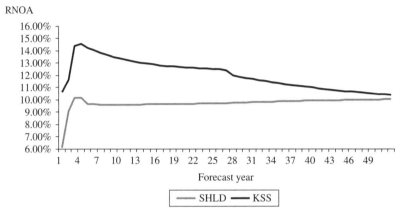

Figure 18.2   Summary of RNOA through time

Table 18.1 and Figure 18.2 illustrate how the four stages interrelate for SHLD and KSS. From 2006 to 2010 we have the RNOA forecasts that were made from detailed analysts' models. Figure 18.2 shows how the pattern starts to "converge" after 2011 through to steady state (year 25) and then beyond that in KSS, one can see a second less steep slope. To the casual observer, it may seem unlikely that a company will experience such a steep increase in profitability for 5 to 6 years and then a pattern of constant decline, yet this is implicitly what exists in any traditional long-run valuation model that does not allow for exponential growth long into the future. Futhermore, Harris and Nissim (2004) found that for US firms, for the period from 1988 to 2002, ROEs tended to follow a quadratic function of reversion to the mean displaying a pattern not dissimilar to what we see post the explicit period. To the extent we feel uncomfortable with the analyst's explicit forecasts or we want to introduce an alternative pattern of adjustment this is relatively straightforward, in our application using the process described in 3(b). Similarly, sensitivity to the steady state can also easily be "tested" by considering plausible alternative assumptions.

To reiterate, there is no perfect single answer, but, the valuation model is driven by sound economic principles, and we provide additional graphical outputs to facilitate a user's comfort with the valuation. These are shown as Figures 18.3 and 18.4. Figure 18.3 a "waterfall" chart, is broken into four partitions.

---

[6] Source: Morgan Stanley estimates and hypothetical forecasts.

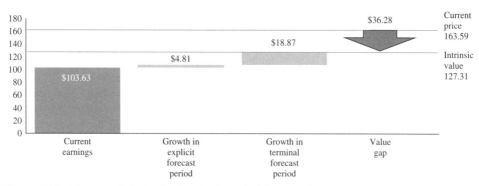

Figure 18.3   The waterfall of valuation for Sears Holdings as of September 2006

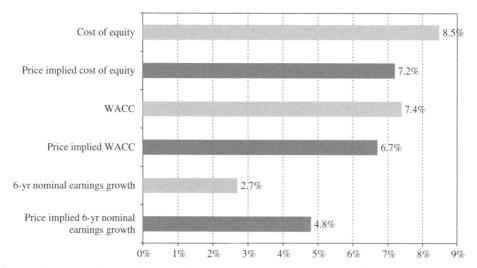

Figure 18.4   Analysis of price implied variables of valuation for Sears Holdings as of September 2006

The first "bar" reflects the value if the current business is sustained at its current level with no value-additive growth. This value can be obtained by capitalizing current earnings by the cost of equity (equation (7)), or summing the book value of equity and capitalizing residual income (using the cost of equity). In SHLD this is $103.6 of the $127.3 intrinsic value (in Figure 18.3). The second "bar" reflects the incremental value created in the explicitly modeled period (in SHLD's case in Figure 18.2 and Table 18.1, the period through 2011). This can be based on incremental residual income or capitalized incremental earnings adjusted for dividends, and represents $4.8 of the $127.3 intrinsic value (in Figure 18.3). It is so small because our analysis assumes very little incremental value creation in the explicit period with declining sales offset by operating leverage improvement but an RNOA not much above the cost of capital. The third "bar" represents the period beyond the explicit period identifying the percentage of value represented by our "transition" and "convergence" periods, and is $18.9 out of the $127.3. The reason this is "high" is that we are allowing an assumption that SHLD's revenue growth will increase back to an economy standard of 4%, and that all new capital invested earns slightly above the cost of capital. Clearly, given the past and expected performance, sustainable revenue growth may be seen as high, but, unlike traditional multiple-based terminal value calculations such as in a DCF, we understand the source of the perceived value creation and can perform *explicit* sensitivity analysis to make revenue lower or adjust return on new capital. The final "bar" reflects the gap between the actual price and the intrinsic value and challenges us to think about what we might be missing that the market price is reflecting, which we partially address in Figure 18.4. The core logic behind Figure 18.3's waterfall chart is to demonstrate a level of comfort with the valuation, as we move to the right on the horizontal axis the level of detailed analysis decreases, and potential uncertainty increases. So, subject to our comfort with the sustainability of the current level of earnings (profitability), the more value that is reflected in the earlier periods (to the left), the stronger would be our conviction in the measure of intrinsic value.

To provide additional "heuristics" to help users gauge a level of comfort with the assumptions in the forecasts and valuations, we consider how our assumptions compare to price-implied equivalents. We illustrate this in Figure 18.4 in which we provide summary statistics of both the models' assumed cost of capital (equity and WACC) and rates of earnings growth over the explicit forecast period, and the price implied equivalents of these measures assuming a shift in the relevant "curve".

Therefore, as we see in Figure 18.4, if we assume our forecasts and model assumptions are correct, the price implied cost of equity is 7.2% vs. the 8.5% we used. An investor can always decide that this rate is sufficient if the forecasts are considered "low" and the rate is higher than alternative investment opportunities. Alternatively, if the discount rate of 8.5% is considered appropriate or necessary, we show that the 6-year earnings growth would need to be 4.8% vs. the 2.7% in the forecast model. The user can decide whether this is plausible to justify the price.

As previously discussed, we do not believe price will equal intrinsic value for more than a few minutes, if ever. Consequently, to understand the risk-reward trade-off an investor is taking, it is useful to compare the price path over some period, with the measure of intrinsic value. With these inputs, Figure 18.5 reflects the basic (single scenario) "risk-reward" chart provided in ModelWare's IV application.

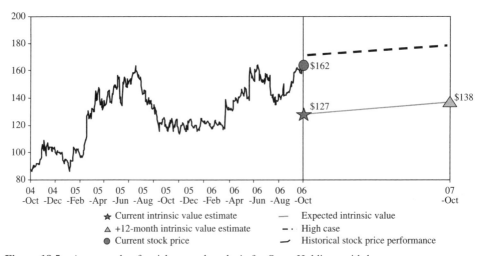

Figure 18.5   An example of a risk-reward analysis for Sears Holdings with base case

But if the gap between price and a reasonably calculated intrinsic value is as large as we see for SHLD in Figures 18.3 and 18.5, we have to ask ourselves, what scenario could the market be pricing in that we have not forecasted? As an analyst, this does not mean we have to redo our explicit detailed model; rather it leads us to question what alternative scenario(s) the market is considering.

SHLD is an interesting example because it was created when Eddie Lampert, a highly successful investment manager who controlled K-Mart, acquired Sears and began a process of restructuring, creating operating leverage through increased efficiency in inventory and property management as well as improved cost controls. A year before writing this note we had analyzed upside and downside cases for a client conference when the price and estimated intrinsic values were around $125. Aggressive assumptions of synergy, selling and repositioning some stores and restructuring based on our analysts' most optimistic assumptions gave an upside value around $160, while the downside was closer to $80. This is clearly a wide range, and we found clients with strong views on all sides. Notably, in this case historical performance was of little direct use as the combined firm was different and the acquisition introduced a very different style of management. The flexibility of our intrinsic value tool allowed us to contemplate and analyze some interesting scenarios. However, that was a year ago. Today our analysts' basic view has not changed, neither has the basic intrinsic value as expected profitability improvements are reflected in the forecasts, and there has been little change in these over a year. So what other scenario is "in the market"? The most frequently mentioned possibility in the financial press is a possible large acquisition of a competitor like The Gap (GPS).[7] We perform a hypothetical "acquisition" by taking the forecasts for GPS and combining it with the SHLD information shown in Figure 18.1, to see what it does to IV. We assume a 20% premium over the current market price of GPS, that it is partly funded by equity ($10bn of the $26bn price), and that there are limited synergies after year 1. The result is shown in Figure 18.6. Perhaps unsurprisingly, we get close to the recent market price that has been around $160. Comparing Figures 18.1 and 18.6, we see the impact on revenue growth, operating margins, operating asset efficiency and leverage. We performed this analysis in less than 30 minutes and can relate the value, 74% of which is in the first 6 years of the forecasted value, to explicit profitability and reinvestment measures, increasing our comfort with the plausibility of the scenario.

Naturally, we can derive other scenarios,[8] but each should be tied to explicit adjustments from the primary analysts' starting point. Then investors can decide which scenarios they perceive to be plausible. Figure 18.7 shows our risk-reward chart with the $127 intrinsic value and the $163 acquisition scenario, with past price movement and the 12-month forward values from the evaluations. The risk-reward chart allows investors or portfolio managers to decide where the risk-reward trade-off lies based on their beliefs about the company's prospects. For example, if they own the stock, they can decide if they want to sell as it has reached a "high" case, or "keep it" as the momentum is still directionally upward. In the latter case, as it moves above a bullish scenario they could buy a put option to protect downside risk or sell a covered call to get some additional upside (the price of the call), etc. If the investor was considering buying the stock at this level of around $160, there may still be upside, but clearly it is a riskier investment than it was at our conference a year before

---

[7] For example, see "Heard on the street", *Wall Street Journal*, September 16, 2006.
[8] Another approach to generate scenarios is described in Viebig and Poddig in Part II of this book.

Intrinsic value per share (current)	161.58
Intrinsic value per share (in 12 months), cum dividends	**175.32**
Current price	*160.38*

Cost of equity	8.5%
Implied WACC	7.7%
Long-term RNOA on new investments	10.0%
Long-term ROE on new investments	11.8%
Specific forecast period (years)	**6**
Years to reach steady state growth	**25**

	History		Morgan Stanley analyst published estimate				Model	Steady state
	2006	**2007**	**2008**	**2009**	**2010**	**2011**	**2012**	**(2031)**
OPERATING								
Operating revenue	51 813	66 732	67 008	68 132	68 592	69 400	70 788	
Growth		*28.8%*	*0.4%*	*1.7%*	*0.7%*	*1.2%*	*2.0%*	4.0%
Operating expenses	50 000	62 862	63 055	64 248	64 751	65 583	66 895	
NOPAT	1813	3870	3953	3884	3841	3817	3893	
NOPAT margin	*3.5%*	*5.8%*	*5.9%*	*5.7%*	*5.6%*	*5.5%*	*5.5%*	
Net operating assets	19 073	49 077	44 040	44 311	44 217	44 479	44 786	
Net operating asset growth	*−4.6%*	*157.3%*	*−10.3%*	*0.6%*	*−0.2%*	*0.6%*	*0.7%*	
Operating asset turnover	*2.59*	*1.36*	*1.52*	*1.54*	*1.55*	*1.56*	*1.58*	
RNOA	*9.1%*	*7.9%*	*9.0%*	*8.8%*	*8.7%*	*8.6%*	*8.7%*	
FCF operations	2724	(26 134)	8990	3613	3935	3555	3586	
Present value of FCFO	2537	(24 243)	7736	2884	2914	2442	2285	
Residual income (operating)	347	2401	174	493	429	412	468	
Present value of residual income (operating)	323	2210	108	358	285	253	270	
FINANCING								
Net financial expense (income)	527	572	1219	839	738	648	576	
Borrowing costs	8.8%	9.6%	5.5%	5.5%	5.5%	5.5%	5.3%	5.0%
Financing spread	0.2%	−1.7%	3.5%	3.3%	3.2%	3.1%	3.4%	
Dividends and net rep	1550	(10 000)	964	896	1524	2031	3114	
Dividend and net repurchases payout	*127.9%*	*−308.4%*	*36.0%*	*30.0%*	*50.0%*	*65.1%*	*95.3%*	
Net debt (cash)	5379	22 156	15 249	13 416	11 786	10 957	11 081	
Change in net debt	*−39.5%*	*311.9%*	*−31.2%*	*−12.0%*	*−12.1%*	*−7.0%*	*1.1%*	
Leverage (net debt/equity)	*50%*	*92%*	*59%*	*48%*	*40%*	*36%*	*36%*	35%
Other non-operating expense (income)	74	56	59	56	54	48	48	
Minority interest and other	2923	2923	2923	2923	2923	2923	2923	
Net income	1212	3242	2675	2989	3049	3121	3269	
Shareholders' equity	10 771	24 013	25 724	27 817	29 342	30 432	30 587	
ROE	*11.3%*	*30.1%*	*11.1%*	*11.6%*	*11.0%*	*10.6%*	*10.7%*	
Present value dividend and net repurchase	1435	(9217)	550	750	1022	1150	1503	
Residual income (equity)	688	2327	634	802	684	627	682	
Present value of residual income (equity)	637	2144	539	628	494	417	418	

Figure 18.6 The key inputs and results from ModelWare IV applied to a hypothetical combination of Sears holdings and the GAP as of September 2006

when the intrinsic value and price were closer together around $125. Another way to use our intrinsic value and risk-reward analysis would be for investors who are able to patiently wait for attractive value investing opportunities. Just as investors can follow momentum as prices move up, there are many cases where bad news is overdiscounted, and the market price moves below a low profitability downside scenario. When the price overshoots the downside case, the risk-reward trade-off may shift to the reward side. A case in point was analysis we did with our media analyst in 2004 on Cox Communications, a US cable operator. The market was discounting the stock, presumably because of conservative depreciation policies following a large capex cycle and concerns about the competitive landscape. Our analyst had detailed projections and analyses highlighting that the capacity cost required to sustain the business, and plausible mixes of revenue growth. We used this to calculate measures of IV for high, expected, and low cases. The market price fell to our low case IV and the family who were the primary shareholders and management did a management buyout, clearly perceiving that the market had overdiscounted the value of the business.

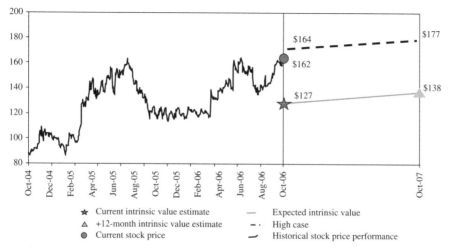

Figure 18.7   An example of a risk-reward analysis for Sears Holdings with two scenarios

This process of analysis will not be new to most readers. What we consider as a key difference is that the scenario generation, if done properly, is not based on a multiple of earnings, sales or cash flow, nor is it a result of adjusting terminal assumptions or cost of capital. Rather, the scenarios can be directly related to explicit product revenues, costs, net operating assets or funding choices. Ideally, these will also be considered keeping in mind the sources of uncertainty. So in the case of Sears Holdings, the focus will be on potential acquisition targets as well as revenue and cost trends; in the Cox case, it was capex trends, and competition from telecom companies and content on the web. In sum, the focus is on linking the business activity (economics) to the numbers and valuation and not relying on "magical" formula or conceptually sound models or concepts where the quest for precision causes us to ignore the inherent measurement problems in all over inputs.

19
Treatment of Key Inputs

It is easy for us to argue that we should focus on the real economics of business activities, but the reality is that we have to deal with the information we have in financial statements and other sources of data. So how do we make this transition between what we have and what we need? The development of our IV model is a continuous process. For example, we have not incorporated some complex adjustments to the economically "right" answer, because we sense that analysts and investors are uncomfortable with the concepts and "overengineering" a solution may not help investors, as price discovery (incorporation of the underlying economic reality into price) is unlikely in a medium-term horizon.

This again may seem to be heretical, but to illustrate our point, consider the case of employee stock options (ESOs). Current accounting rules require companies to expense a cost based on a grant date option price and a vesting period. We view (and treat) the cost as a "cash-equivalent" compensation cost with the offset being a "loan" from the employee, and hence an obligation of the company and its shareholders. The loan is "funded" with an equity instrument. So the operating expense is the compensation cost, as without an option we assume there would be a compensation substitute (cash or shares or . . .). However, we also believe that economic cost to shareholders includes the "mark-to-market" of the "obligation" through time until the option is exercised. Therefore, the total economic expense from grant date to exercise date is the difference between the share price at date of grant and the price at the date of exercise. To capture this in IV requires at a minimum a complex estimation of the stock price at the date of exercise, the expected time of exercise for given grants, careful analysis and monitoring of option grant and exercise patterns, and what is expensed and captured in the measurement of diluted shares outstanding through time. Having "built" such a program into one version of IV we chose to leave it out for now as it is not clear whether the complexity provides more precision in our estimates. To understand this more without going through the details, we often emphasize to our analysts and investing clients that the more difficult and even meaningful measurement problem surrounding ESOs is not the measurement on grant date, but the impact on future dilution if the company is successful. We suggest that companies are well aware of this problem and try to mitigate some of the opacity by using a share repurchase program to neutralize the impact of exercised ESOs on shares outstanding. This raises a related question of how to treat the issuance and repurchase of shares from exercise of ESOs.[1] For now, we treat the expense of ESOs as an operating cash flow, and do not systematically deal with the ESO exercise issues. However, as ModelWare IV continues to evolve we expect to modify the current application, especially for sectors where ESOs are significant, like biotech.

---

[1] A related issue is the allocation of the value to the current shares and options outstanding. The treasury stock approach in EPS is supposed to deal with this, but that calculation has an earnings focus.

There are many other areas where we have made choices in how we adjust the classification or measurement of reported items, to better reflect the economic drivers and the operating versus funding split, highlighted in Figure 17.1. Rather than go through all of these in laborious detail, we have summarized our approach to the basic measures in Table A.1, and then describe the issue and our approach to some of the standard problems in Table A.2. We reemphasize that our approach considers the expected economic impact of a potential adjustment, and whether there is sufficient information disclosed to make an adjustment. As we look forward, we increasingly seek information outside the financial reporting system to supplement what financial statements and notes provide.

Having explained our approach to measuring the inputs to the numerator of the IV calculation the last critical point to discuss is our treatment of the cost of capital (equity and WACC).

20
The Cost of Capital

As discussed, we view obtaining precision in the estimated cost of equity or WACC as practically insoluble and of more use as a theoretical construct. This is not to say we do not want some bounding of the discount rate. However, we strongly believe that we cannot choose a discount rate without considering the decision context and the degree to which we have incorporated uncertainty in the measure we are discounting. In addition, consider some of the practical issues with each of the key components of traditional measures of the cost of capital.[1]

20.1 RISK-FREE RATE

The typical risk-free rate people start with is a liquid government bond of a medium- to long-term duration. Therefore, in the US we often saw people using 30-year Treasuries until the market shifted to the 10-year bond being the most liquid. When we do global research, especially in markets where local government bond markets are underdeveloped or where the local government bonds are risky, then we have a problem. But this is not the only issue.

Why are we using a single rate rather than a yield curve? If a company earns a significant portion of its wealth creation in the next 3 years, say from a blockbuster product, do we really want to discount these values (residual income, dividend or cash flow) using a long-duration bond rate? Furthermore, a portfolio manager has to make a decision about where to invest the funds "today", so the benchmark alternative can be a short-term yield. There are obviously counterarguments. However, we have observed anecdotally that, in economic environments with ample liquidity, limited economic uncertainty other than geopolitical risk and no foreseeable positive or negative shocks in sectors or regions where the pools of liquidity can go, companies with strong profitability and little growth have still been priced at high values relative to traditional long-duration rates. Yet, if we use the full government bond yield curve the intrinsic value is much closer to the price.

Would we adjust the discount rate constantly as government bonds trade in an active market, and, if so, wouldn't we have to adjust the numerator as well? Ultimately, such models can be built, but it is not clear what advantage there would be to this level of precision given how many other variables are being estimated. Thus, when we choose a rate, we tend to look at the most recent average rate over a 3-month period unless there is a known structural shift in rates.

---

[1] The points raised in the discussion on cost of capital reflect hundreds of discussions with analysts, academics and both corporate and investing clients over the years.

20.2 EQUITY RISK PREMIUM

The number of hours we see spent on this topic has to be disproportionate to its usefulness. The basic conceptual point is how much of a premium the market (investors) demand to compensate for the additional risk of equity over the risk-free rate. Clearly, with equity as the residual claimant on the firm's resources, it is riskier than other funding sources. Yet, this is precisely what we are trying to capture with the estimation in the numerator of the intrinsic value analysis, so are we double counting the uncertainty if we include the risk premium in both the numerator and denominator? Assuming there is some acceptance of the argument then the answer depends on where you choose to deal with the uncertainty. For the market as a whole, the risk premium is estimated from various measures of market volatility. However, here again there are some basic questions. If we are valuing the company's intrinsic value, why do we care about short-term pricing volatility? Note that most people are quite happy to use 10-year bonds to estimate the risk-free rate and then use an equity risk-premium based on short-term price volatility. In fact, one of the reasons for differences in estimation of the equity risk premium is the duration of the return period and how the return itself is calculated. But again, should business managers operate and make strategic decisions using costs of capital based off short-term price volatility, or should they consider how uncertain and volatile their operating performance is? We can surmise that one of the advantages that Warren Buffett and other deep value long-term investors have is that they focus on the uncertainty of the business and not the idiosyncrasies that cause volatility in "Mr. Market". In general, we use an equity risk premium (ERP) of 4% as a starting point.[2]

20.3 BETA-ESTIMATION

To estimate a cost of equity explicitly requires some measure of beta, the coefficient that indicates the correlation between a company's stock return and the market's return. Those of you who have looked up different sources will usually find widely varying estimates of a company's beta at any point in time. Some of the issues that impact the estimation are:

- The "market" measure used, for example, is the DAX, the best market measure for Germany. Should it be the S&P 500, the Russell 2000 or any other index for the US market? The choice affects the measure of beta.
- What is the appropriate return period to use in the estimation, daily, weekly or monthly, and for how many months or years? If you have a typical holding period for stocks of 3 years, do you really care about daily volatility? Should the period be just historical or predictive too?

The set of questions goes on, so to argue that any one measure of beta is precise is meaningless. For an investor or analyst using ModelWare's intrinsic value approach we recommend selecting the cost of equity capital that represents the required rate of return at the time of the valuation, and conditional on the amount of uncertainty they have reflected in their forecasts. In general, for estimating a more general IV for corporations in the US, we start with an 8 to 8.5% cost of equity in the current market environment. To get a more specific measure we recommend a starting measure that uses an average predicted beta over

---

[2] The equity risk premium is also affected by taxes so in the US the ERP should have gone down after the Tax Act of 2003, which changed the rate of tax on capital gains.

a period of time (say a quarter or 6 months), and an equity risk premium of around 4%. We add the product of these to a risk-free rate that is a reasonable benchmark in the market again averaged as described above. In all cases, we prefer to also look at the price-implied cost of equity and evaluate whether this is reasonable in the context of our investment alternatives.

Having a cost of equity is potentially sufficient to estimate ModelWare IV with the DDM or residual income equity approaches. However, we question whether the cost of equity should be constant over time. The question seems more acute when we have been constantly changing leverage, and when we calculate the weighted average cost of capital. In principle, the cost of equity adjusts with changing leverage to offset the impact of changes in the weights of equity and debt used in calculating WACC. However, the principle is based on a theoretical (and precise) measure of beta and assumes we can measure the market value of debt, neither of which is true in practice. In our minds, the most troublesome aspect of the calculation is holding the WACC constant when we have clearly defined leverage ratios and costs of debt based on our ModelWare adjusted numbers. Therefore, we effectively adjust each period's WACC to incorporate the cost of debt and the weighting factors for debt and equity each year. But as this is hard to present, we provide a single measure which represents the weighted average of all the individual annual WACCs. The single measure of WACC is most useful to indicate whether the forecasts reflect an average net debt or net cash position. In the latter case, the WACC is higher than the cost of equity. While this has been true for many companies recently, it should not be generally true and often suggests the forecasts have allowed a cash build-up by the company that will depress the intrinsic value.

More generally, we reemphasize that the discount rate should not be viewed as a precise measure, and suggest that companies and investors would be better off focusing on their forecasted performance and inferring the implied cost of capital relative to a price.

21
Summary and Conclusions

The intrinsic value tool we have built in ModelWare relies on a sound conceptual framework and some key operating principles, and it utilizes the logical relations that exist in the traditional accounting model. As a result, we can derive equivalent measures of intrinsic value using DDM, DCF or RIV models. However, we focus on the critical performance measures that can be disaggregated back to the traditional financial indicators, such as revenue, operating costs, net operating assets and leverage. As existing accounting practices introduce measurement errors relative to the underlying economic reality, we introduce a series of adjustments in the underlying measures before incorporating them into our valuation calculations. However, all our measures are estimates, including a cost of capital, so we argue that investors and analysts probe alternative outcomes and provide at least three scenarios to assess the risk-reward trade-offs between price and these scenarios.

We find that analysts, investors and corporate managers have been led to believe they can estimate a precise cash flow measure that overcomes the measurement problems in accrual accounting. Then, whether it is called a cash flow return on investment, a discounted free cash flow, a cash return on capital employed or some cash-based economic value added, they sometimes believe that the resulting cash-based valuation is "correct". If you get nothing else out of this note, we hope at the least you will appreciate that all of these measures are actually accrual based and are not really cash, and that you should not suffer from an "illusion of precision" in any single measure of intrinsic value.

Appendix

Table A.1 ModelWare valuation: definition of key measures[1]

Measure	What's measured	ModelWare approach
Operating revenue (OpR)	Value of sales (revenue) generated from ongoing operating activity used as the primary source of growth	For historical measures we generally accept the local GAAP revenue recognition principles, although we appreciate that the principles chosen can distort (or be used to distort) the comparability of reported revenue. In general, there is insufficient disclosure to standardize adjustments, but where there is information, we have incorporated some adjustments. Specifically, we exclude sales or volume discounts, any excise or similar value-added taxes, and standard allowance for bad debts, and include royalty and license income. For companies with financial services as operating activity, classify fees and net interest income on the net book (net operating assets) as operating revenue. For forecasts, ideally the revenue is built up from more fundamental data using product or sector volume and price information.
Operating expense (OpE)	Costs incurred in ongoing operating activities, but excluding the costs of funding those operating activities	Data not available in most jurisdictions for ideal presentation of cost components (cost of materials, labor, capacity, research, services, marketing and distribution), so we aggregate cost of goods sold, research and development, selling, marketing and distribution, general and administrative costs, and any other costs consumed in operations. Where there is ambiguity about a cost, we consider it an operating expense.

[1] This exhibit is adapted from Harris *et al.* (2004).

Table A.1   (Continued)

Measure	What's measured	ModelWare approach
NOPAT (net operating profit after tax)	The *after tax* income from operating activities	Our basic approach includes all revenue and expenses that relate to operating activity, but we also adjust for certain items like unconsolidated associate company income when there is no proportional consolidation and the associated companies are integrally linked to the operations of the investor company (Coca Cola and its investee bottlers, e.g. Coca Cola Enterprises, is an example). We eliminate the funding elements of pension and OPEB costs and adjust for operating leases by treating them as equivalent to purchased assets financed with a loan (see below). We charge taxes by applying a "statutory" tax rate (inclusive of federal, state and local taxes plus any other "permanent" adjustments) to the taxable components.
NOPAT margin	The percentage of revenue generated as operating profit. It is used when considering the extent to which revenue growth is sustaining (can sustain) profitability, and the degree of cost efficiency that leads to improved profitability	We calculate the NOPAT margin as NOPAT divided by operating revenue times 100. In the absence of information to reflect proportional consolidation (our preferred method), we classify as operating certain investments in associate companies accounted for under the equity method. As a result, the operating margins will be relatively higher, because there is no specific revenue associated with these investments, but the income is in NOPAT. In practice, we have found that analysts have a reluctance to treat equity investments as operating unless there is a clear link. When using NOPAT margins, it is often important to use a statutory rate rather than an "effective" tax rate. Otherwise, the tax component, which is often affected by financing activities, can distort the underlying operating performance that is of interest. Another alternative is to use pre-tax operating profit (PTOP) but then we have to incorporate taxes as a separate component or activity. We choose to use a post-tax measure of operating margin because we think it is a more appropriate measure of sustainable profitability in the absence of financing decisions.
Net operating assets (NOA)	A firm's net resources needed to run the operations of the business and generate the operating revenue. It does not consider the specific source of external funding. This is analogous to the invested capital that the company is using to run its core business	ModelWare looks to the assets (resources) and liabilities (obligations) that are actively managed in generating operating revenues and expenses. This is often most easily achieved by identifying what is strictly financing and what is clearly non-operating in nature. If there is doubt, we usually assume that the asset or liability is operating. Where data is available, ModelWare NOA include any unrecognized premium from past mergers and acquisitions, either from transactions treated as pooling (or uniting) of interests, or from previously amortized or written-off goodwill, where material. ModelWare NOA include the remaining implied book value of capitalized non-cancelable operating leases, but exclude any pension surplus or deficit, which is treated as financing. ModelWare NOA include the book value of investments in associated companies that are integrally related to the other operating activities of the firm.

ModelWare NOA include assets that are securitized but remain "managed" or used by the company; ModelWare reverses the securitized assets and puts them back "on the books", as if they were collateralized borrowing. In reality, disclosures do not always provide enough information to correctly add back such securitized items.

ModelWare NOA generally excludes cash because there is no meaningful way to identify what cash is "needed" to operate a business. In addition, in many countries, operating cash is actually a "bank overdraft" or line of credit which many people view as clearly "debt" or financing. Cash management is also an activity usually undertaken by the treasurer's office, and under our criteria, this is financing. However, in rare cases where the operating cash is "known" we allow it to be included as part of the "working capital" of the operating business.

In financial services companies, the managed investments and "cash" balances, deposits, loans, and leases are treated as operating assets or liabilities.

| Operating asset turnover (OpATO) | The revenue generated per unit of operating capital, or investment in net operating assets.   This is used to reflect the efficiency in the use of resources and expected source of operating leverage. | OpATO is operating revenue divided by beginning of period NOA. We acknowledge that we could use an average measure to incorporate the impact of large investments of NOA made during a period, but our starting point remains the beginning of period NOA.

As we classify certain investments in associate companies accounted for under the equity method as operating, OpATO will be relatively lower as there is no specific revenue associated with these investments, and the investment is included in NOA. Note that this is the opposite effect to the operating margin.

The decision as to which net assets to include when calculating OpATO can be controversial, and we describe some of the detail above. But the simple answer for most items is to consider which assets or obligations are being used to generate the operating revenue in the numerator. A practical approach is also to consider those assets or obligations that are not financing in nature, that is, those managed by the finance and treasury managers, and any other accounts that are clearly non-operating. All other accounts can then be considered as operating. |
| Net financial income/ (expense) (NFE) | Cost or income from assets or obligations designated as financing; typically activities under the jurisdiction of senior financial officers such as treasurer, CFO, finance director. | Traditional interest and dividend income on financial investments, and interest expense on financial obligations, are the most common components of NFE. We include preferred dividends as we consider preferred stock a financial obligation. We isolated those items considered financing in nature to avoid potential distortions from including income and costs of all non-operating items (e.g. minority interest and investments in non-operating associates) as financing. Where known, we include FX transaction gains and losses reported in earnings as part of NFE, even if these result from exposure of trade receivables and trade payables, as the decision to carry the foreign exchange risk is a financing decision. |

Table A.1   (Continued)

Measure	What's measured	ModelWare approach
		We treat gains/losses on net monetary items resulting from price-level adjustments as financing costs. When inflation plays a large role, these gains and losses reflect an offset to the inflationary effect of monetary items that are reflected in the interest rates applied. For now, we exclude gains/losses from foreign currency translation adjustments (included in other comprehensive income or statement of total recognized gains and losses), even though these are financing costs and often result from loans deemed part of net invested capital. Companies do not provide enough information to facilitate meaningful forecasts, and historical translation adjustments are not split between debt and equity financing. Currently we net the cost of financing obligations and the income on financing assets. The net reflects financing strategies by companies, for example, with both large obligations and cash and marketable securities. This mix is usually a conscious decision about funding operations and growth, in light of strategic choices for capital raising (or return of capital to shareholders). We recognize there are advantages to considering financial assets separately from obligations and may build this in future versions of the model. However, we have found that equity analysts generally pay little attention to where they put cash, so netting reduces the error caused by this.
Borrowing cost	The cost of (return on) net financial obligations (assets)	Borrowing cost is net financial income (expense) divided by beginning of period net financial obligations.
Net debt	The net financial resources of the businesses. Any net obligation reflects the borrowed funds and the extent of a company's leverage of equity to fund operating activity	In ModelWare, net debt includes all borrowings, debt from capitalized operating leases, net pension obligations, cash and financial investments, and preferred "equity". We also include other interest-bearing liabilities in net debt. In particular, asset retirement obligations and nuclear decommissioning costs that are recorded at present values and then accreted at the discount rate through time will be treated as debt. We net financial assets against borrowings. The decision of whether to leave resources in cash and investments or to pay down debt or return the capital to shareholders is a decision about cash management and capital structure. We also based our classification of financing items on what we would expect a finance director, chief financial officer or treasurer to be responsible for in a typical situation. See further discussion of NOA. We treat net pension obligations as financing. As discussed under operating and net financing expense, we believe that the decision of when to fund and how to invest funds related to pensions and other post-employment benefits is a pure financing decision. A company could have paid the cash when "earned" and insured the future payment stream. Its choice not to go this route is a financing choice.

We treat preferred stock as debt and not equity. The difference between most preferred stock and debt is that in the former, the coupon and yield is paid in the form of a dividend, but this is economically analogous to junior subordinated debt. In contrast, owners' equity is the recipient of residual profitability and bears first losses. To us, the nominal form of payment is not the best distinguishing feature. If the preferred shares were participating preference shares (a rare occurrence today), we would be more inclined to classify them as equity, depending on the nature of the participation rights.

We do not treat minority as debt. Our initial thought was to include minority as debt, and we view it as more debt-like than equity. But minority shareholders participate in or own a share of the financial obligations of a subsidiary, so to treat them as pure debt seemed inappropriate. Our conclusion was to treat them as "other non-operating liability".

Leverage	Leverage is the ratio of debt funding relative to equity funding. It is used to assess both risk and efficiency of the capital structure.	We calculate leverage as net debt divided by shareholders' equity, ensuring that the period for which they are measured (beginning or ending) is consistent for both measures. We measure leverage relative to shareholders' equity and not assets or net operating assets. As we see in the Profitability Tree in Figure 17.1, ModelWare creates calculations that facilitate a clear mapping from the individual accounts to profitability ratios. Leverage based on equity facilitates this decomposition. We also decompose other non-operating items relative to equity, which allows us to see all forms of funding. If the other non-operating items are net assets, then the leverage based on net operating assets would not convey the real funding from net debt. However, we also calculate debt/capital to reflect the proportion of debt relative to other funding sources. While the use of leverage is theoretically value-neutral, we believe that in practice, capital structure can matter and create value. For example, General Electric has for many years effectively borrowed at low nominal interest rates and invested this capital in businesses with higher RNOA, effectively creating wealth for its shareholders.
Other non-operating income (expense)	Income statement amounts that are clearly neither operating nor financing in nature.	We include all items that are clearly not operating or financing in nature. Common items included are income from associate companies accounted for as equity investments that are unrelated to operating activities and minority interests. These are incorporated in our calculation of intrinsic value.
Other non-operating assets (liabilities)	Balance sheet amounts that are clearly neither operating nor financing in nature.	We include all items that are clearly not operating or financing in nature. Common items included are associate companies accounted for as equity investments that are unrelated to operating activities and minority interests. We also include dividends payable, a category that exists in some countries.

Table A.1   (Continued)

Measure	What's measured	ModelWare approach

Share-holder's equity	The equity or net asset value attributable to the common shareholders (owners) of the business.	ModelWare takes an ordinary or common shareholder (proprietary) perspective and so includes only those amounts that relate to these shareholders. Consequently, shareholders' equity includes the share capital accounts, treasury stock (or any investment in own shares), other reserves, other comprehensive income, and retained earnings. Preferred or "mezzanine" equity is treated as debt. In some cases, especially in financial services companies, we allow for an adjustment of material unrecognized gains or losses on investments.
		
		    We treat treasury stock or investment in own shares as negative equity rather than an asset. It has long been held that companies cannot trade in their own shares and generate gains and losses in them or report them as resources. While it is true that some shareholders may be perceived as having "gained" if shares are repurchased at a lower price than where they are reissued, this would always be at the expense of other shareholders, so considering all shareholders, there is no real gain or loss.
		
		    For financial services companies where operations include trading securities, we view the distinction between available-for-sale and trading as artificial. As a result, for these companies we include incremental unrealized gains and losses on available-for-sale securities in operating income.

Free cash flow from operations (for DCF)	The cash flows generated (or used) by a company's operating business, before taking into account funding.	For the forecasted periods, free cash flow from operations (for DCF) starts with NOPAT and subtracts any increase in NOA. ModelWare captures all cash flows associated with operations, not just those changes in "current" assets and liabilities. So expenditures on capacity (PP&E) or indefinite-life intangibles identified as operating are included despite their classifications as investments in some local GAAP.

Table A.2   ModelWare intrinsic value's approach to selected adjustments

	Problem	What we did	How we did it
Operating Leases	Global accounting rules require some leases to be classified as "operating", forcing the lease payment to be treated as an operating expense and leaving leased assets and liabilities unrecognized.	Leasing is simply a choice of how to finance assets used in operating activity. It is impossible to make a meaningful judgment about how efficiently or profitably the company is relative to competitors, or even relative to prior periods, unless all operating resources are included. Therefore, where operating leased assets are significant, we capitalize and treat them as if purchased at lease inception.	In the income statement, we eliminate the lease (rental) charge from OpE and include a depreciation charge in OpE and an interest charge in NPE based on the implied interest rate and principal outstanding each period. In growth phases and a lease's early stages, operating expenses tend to fall, but interest costs rise, so net income is lower. This reverses at the end of any given lease.

		We then depreciate them over the lease life. Analogously, we recognize the financing obligation and costs.	On the balance sheet, we add the capitalized lease to NOA and net debt, which are only equal at the inception and completion of the lease. We treat the addition of new leases as "capex" in FCFO, offset by an increase in debt.
Post-retirement benefits	In the US and certain other jurisdictions, the financing components of post-retirement expense are incorporated in operating costs. It is trivial for companies to create operating income from financing costs by borrowing and then investing the cash raised into the pension. This confuses asset management returns with normal operating activity. Historically, the smoothing of actuarial changes and investment gains/losses has created unrecognized assets/liabilities, but new global accounting rules are changing this.	Where post-retirement benefits are significant, we ensure that the costs are appropriately classified as operating or financing and that the economic obligation is reflected in the balance sheet, as part of leverage.	In the income statement, we eliminate interest costs on pension obligations, returns on pension assets and actuarial adjustments from OpE when material and reclassify them as NFE. On the balance sheet, we adjust for historical unrecognized amounts in net debt and equity (net of taxes).
Taxation	A company's reported tax expense includes a complex combination of cash, accrued and deferred taxes on operating, financing and other non-operating items, including items that never flow through earnings. Deficiencies in current disclosures limit one's ability to clearly separate these components.	We consider the annual statutory tax rate that a company would be expected to pay, weighted for the share of operations in each region in which it operates. The statutory rate changes as the mix of regions or regional rates change.	In the income statement, we allocate taxes to NOPAT and NFE by applying the statutory rate to the relevant pretax measures. The balance of actual taxes is reflected in other non-operating income (expense).

Table A.2   (Continued)

Measure	What's measured	ModelWare approach	
			On the balance sheet, we attempt a similar split, separating deferred taxes based on where the underlying balance sheet amounts are categorized. As with all items, where there is doubt we would default to operating. The one area in which we systematically split out a financing component of deferred tax is for those deferred taxes associated with pensions and post-employment benefits, as these are clearly separated and often material.
One-time items	One-time items can obscure performance measures and hinder the ability to forecast the sustainable portion of earnings.	We eliminate one-time items at analysts' discretion, as there is no simple rule as to what is "recurring". We focus on forecast data, and good analysts tend to be consistent in excluding historical items from forecast costs, margins, etc. If we see a cost recurring we do not allow it to be reflected as one-time.	In the income statement, we eliminate one-time items from OpE or NFE as appropriate, in order to facilitate better forecasts. However, we do incorporate one-time items in our valuation by adding (subtracting) them in the calculation of residual income.
In cash flow, we include the cash flow associated with one-time items in FCFO.
Inventory accounting	Inventory accounting can vary from company to company in some regions.	We choose to adjust to FIFO for comparability and simplicity. Replacement cost is the best measure of ongoing cost, and LIFO is closest to this, especially in times of rapid price change. However, we lack the data to transform FIFO into LIFO. And with the IASB move to FIFO the LIFO data should be scarcer.	The difference between FIFO and LIFO inventory is usually disclosed, so on the balance sheet, we add back this LIFO reserve to the inventory, and hence it is part of NOA.
On the income statement, we take the change in this amount and include it in OpE. This is not just driven by our comparability objective but also because the distortion to inventory values is cumulative and generally higher than any single year's adjustment to earnings.

Goodwill and intangibles assumed to have "indefinite" life	Equity may be understated due to unrecognized goodwill from poolings or from previous amortization and non-impairment write-offs.	We capitalize all goodwill to better understand how profitably managers have invested shareholders' funds, and to observe whether these returns exceed the required return – not in a single year but over time. This distinction is important because initially, profitability will be lower and often below the cost of capital, as the cumulative amount of purchased future profitability is recognized immediately. We want to highlight organic versus acquisition-based growth.	On the balance sheet, we add all goodwill back to NOA and equity. In the income statement, we exclude goodwill amortization and amortization of intangible assets assumed to have an "indefinite" life from operating expenses. Such amortization is double-counting costs if a firm is sustaining its franchise. If it is not, then we would expect an impairment charge.
R&D and IPR&D	If acquired R&D relates to specific products; it should be treated as acquired products, not R&D.	Non-recurring or one-time acquired R&D is deemed part of an acquisition premium and not expensed but treated as part of goodwill. The recurring portion is equivalent to outsourced R&D and expensed.	ModelWare does not capitalize R&D and amortize it over some period. On a global cross-sector basis, it is too arbitrary. There are some valid arguments for R&D capitalization, but adjustments are too subjective (limited detail on underlying products in research, shrinking payback periods for R&D investments, arbitrary amortization periods). So by capitalizing and amortizing we may get a more comparable ROE or ROIC but we introduce measurement error in the amortization period.
Stock options and other share-based expense	The cost of labor is distorted in various countries by the use of share-based payments that are not recognized as costs or expenses. While in other countries, such as the US, current accounting rules require companies to expense a cost based on a grant date option price and a vesting period.	Options and other share-based compensation should be treated as a "cash-equivalent" compensation cost with the offset being a "loan" from the employee, and hence an obligation of the company and its shareholders. The loan is "funded" with an equity instrument.	In the income statement, we include option and other share-based compensation expense in OpE. In cash flow, we treat the option and other share-based compensation expense as if it were a cash outflow in FCFO and do not systematically deal with the ESO exercise issues. However, as ModelWare IV evolves we expect to modify the current application, especially for sectors where ESOs are significant, like biotech.

Table A.3   Residual income model: questions and answers

Many people, when first seeing a residual income model, question why this model is any better than other valuation models. Questions that we hear include:

Book value and earnings are distorted by accounting measurement problems, being based on a mix of historical costs and market or fair values, so how can they be relevant or useful?	One of the benefits of RIV is that it combines measures of both the shareholders' invested capital and a measure of the return on that capital through time. So, as long as the logical connection between the two is retained, there is no problem. On a stand-alone basis, book value of equity or ROE by itself can be a poor measure in valuation, but combining them through time is useful. Consider the case of goodwill from acquiring another company. If goodwill is capitalized, equity goes up and ROE for the initial periods will be lower than if goodwill is written off. But if there is any value created from the acquisition, we should see an improving return on net operating assets and equity, as there is a "fixed" invested capital relating to the goodwill. If the goodwill is written off immediately it can seem as if there are "free" revenue and earnings growth and improved profitability. But it becomes hard and often impossible to sustain these high levels of ROE, particularly on the marginal reinvested capital. The actual intrinsic value will be the same in both cases, just the pattern of B_0 and related residual income will change. When goodwill is capitalized B_0 (ROE_1) will be relatively high (low) and ROE should begin to rise. If goodwill is written off immediately, we have the opposite effect. In ModelWare we have capitalized goodwill but do not amortize it as we believe this provides us the information to understand what reported revenue and earnings growth has already been "paid for", so it forces us to think where value accretive growth comes from. A similar logical reasoning process can be used for any measurement issue, because one of the merits of a well-specified accounting model is the continuous "settling up" or reconciliation of earnings and equity (net assets), as indicated in Figures 15.2 to 15.4.
The terminal value problem has not been eliminated in RIV.	This is true, although there has been academic work on how to derive an appropriate terminal value measure in RIV.[2] We describe our approach, which mitigates the problem, when going through an example of our application, but there is another advantage to RIV over DCF or DDM models. In many cases, the majority of the actual computed value in an RIV is in the combination of invested capital and residual income through the explicit forecast period, even with the usual 3–5 years forecast period, especially if this covers an operating cycle. So the terminal value problem is less distortive.
Valuations are still sensitive to estimates of cost of equity.	Again this is true but the sensitivity is much lower than for a typical DCF or DDM model. One reason for lower sensitivity in RIV is that in RIV the measure being discounted is smaller than FCFO in most cases, and as noted already the impact of any terminal value is also smaller. But another benefit we have observed in practice is that we find that people using RIV consider the cost of capital more carefully because they are comparing it to the return on capital (ROE) in calculating residual income (equation (12)). The practical advantage of analyzing returns on capital to costs of capital is that it allows the investor/analyst to be consistent in where the business risk is being incorporated, the performance measure or the cost of capital (required return).

---

[2] See Ohlson and Zhang (1999)

The RIV model in equation (14) is specified at the equity level, so does not deal with the point we emphasize in the "cycle of life", and earlier discussions, that it is important to split operations from financing.

Increasing leverage and improving operating performance can both enhance ROE but they have different value implications. We believe it is critical that to understand and value businesses, you need to consider each operating business, with financing considered separately. However, we do not believe in the "illusion of precision" and if you want a quick estimate of IV, especially to get a reasonableness test, then RIV at the equity level is often better than alternatives like EV/EBITDA ratios. A second point is that we believe that if we are estimating the intrinsic value of the company as the cash that can be distributed to shareholders in the future we need to focus on the metrics after payment (expensing) of financing costs and taxation, as these costs are paid out (charged) before shareholders get the residual net assets or cash. So as a quick starting point, earnings and equity are reasonable.

References

Buffett, W.E. (1998), *The Essays of Warren Buffett: Lessons for Corporate America*. L.A. Cunningham (ed.). The Cunningham Group.

Harris, T.S. (2002), Debunking the cash flow myths, Morgan Stanley, July 3.

Harris, T.S. with European Retail Team (1998), Pan European retailers – not made to measure: an apples-to-apples look at Europe's clothing retailers, Morgan Stanley Dean Witter, November 2.

Harris, T.S. with Global Imaging Team (1998), Global Airlines: flight to quality, Morgan Stanley Dean Witter, October 13.

Harris, T.S., and Huh, E.H. (2000), Valuing and measuring a technological edge, Research Report, Morgan Stanley Dean Witter, October 10.

Harris, T., and Nissim, D. (2004), Convergence trends for profitability and payout, Working Paper, Columbia Business School, December.

Harris, T.S., Huh, E.H., and Fairfield, P.M. (2001), The Apples to Apples[SM] earnings monitor: gauging profitability on the road to valuation, Morgan Stanley Dean Witter, December 8.

Harris, T.S. *et al.* (2004), ModelWare (ver 1.0): a road map for investors, Morgan Stanley, August 2.

Mauboussin, M.J. (2006), Interdisciplinary perspectives on risk, Legg Mason Capital Management, August 15.

Madden, J.B. (1999), *Cash Flow Return on Investment (CFROI) Valuation: A Total System Approach to Valuing the Firm*, Butterworth-Heinemann Finance.

Moore, J.F. (2006), Back to black (and Tepper too), PIMCO, September.

Ohlson, J.A., and Zhang, X.-J. (1999), On the theory of forecast horizon in equity valuation, *Journal of Accounting Research*, Vol. 37, No. 2, Autumn.

Part V
UBS VCAM and EGQ Regression-based Valuation[1]
David Bianco[2]

[2] Strategist, email: david.bianco@ubs.com

22

Introducing "EGQ" – Where Intrinsic Methods and Empirical Techniques Meet

The Global Valuation & Accounting Group at UBS Investment Research has developed a system to faithfully combine DCF-based intrinsic valuation methodologies with important relative valuation considerations using linear regressions. The key to this next level in valuation is a metric that the group at UBS calls the Economic Growth Quotient (EGQ).

EGQ is a measure of a company's value-added growth potential. Quantifying value added growth potential is an analytical challenge that the group believes is best approached by focusing on a company's ability to generate incremental economic profits. The group believes that the most significant determinant of a company's observed valuation relative to its peers, or other companies of similar systematic risk, is the market's outlook for the company's ability to generate incremental economic profits over both the near and distant future. The empirical evidence presented later in their valuation regressions using EGQ as the independent variable support this concept.

Incremental economic profit projections require operating performance forecasts based upon rigorous fundamental analysis of the company and its industry – operating forecasts that capture both the growth potential of a business and the investments required to support that growth. The valuation experts at UBS believe that the best framework for making such forecasts is a discounted cash flow model with economic profit calculations accompanying each future year's free cash flow estimate. UBS Investment Research uses a globally standardized discounted cash flow and economic profit projection model for this purpose. This model is called the UBS Value Creation Analysis Model or "UBS VCAM" and it is available for clients to download from the UBS equity research website.[1]

The UBS VCAM is an intrinsic valuation model based on the well-established principles of discounted cash flow and economic profit analysis. VCAM uses operating forecasts from databases populated by UBS research analysts for companies covered by the firm. UBS analysts cannot directly enter free cash flow or economic profits forecasts into the system, instead VCAM uses analyst forecasts for important operating items like revenue, operating profits, taxes, working capital and capital expenditures to calculate future free cash flows and economic profits to ensure consistent calculations and to promote a thought process that focuses on the fundamentals of the business in a context most familiar to investors. Transparency of assumptions was a crucial VCAM design element.

More details regarding VCAM and how it reconciles DCF and economic profit-based valuation methodologies will be explained later in this part. But what is important to

---

[1] The Value Creation Analysis Model (VCAM) is discussed in Bianco *et al.* (2006). Financial economists have applied regression-based models for many years to explain valuation multiples, see for example: Whitbeck and Kisor (1963), Bower and Bower (1970), Malkiel and Cragg (1970), and Bell (1974).

understand upfront is that in addition to calculating DCF-based share value estimates, VCAM also calculates EGQ estimates for companies using incremental economic profits projections derived from analyst operating forecasts. EGQ is a ratio that represents the present value of all future economic profits above current economic profits relative to the present value of existing profits (NOPAT) valued in perpetuity. Because EGQ is based upon an explicit DCF and future economic profit model, EGQ is a single metric that accurately captures the collective interaction of all four economic profit dynamics. Using EGQ as the independent variable in valuation regressions is in our view the key to faithfully combining intrinsic and relative valuation methodologies.

Regressions can be a very powerful valuation tool. They help identify and quantify factors that determine real world company valuations. For instance, EGQ regressions capture the real world effect of relative attractiveness. Peer companies compete for investor capital, the most undervalued and overvalued shares will be the first to attract investor attention. EGQ regressions also provide a powerful visual summary of layered alpha opportunities in the market, clearly separating stock selection from industry allocation decisions in a way that facilitates long/short strategies (buy companies under the regressed line, sell those above the line). Furthermore, regressions can help the most devout intrinsic minded investors read the market for highly controversial intrinsic valuation factors like appropriate cost of capital or economic profit fade rates. However, many popular valuation regressions are based on incomplete variables and can be very misleading. This chapter will explain how to properly employ regression-based valuation techniques in a way that is conceptually consistent with intrinsic valuation principles.

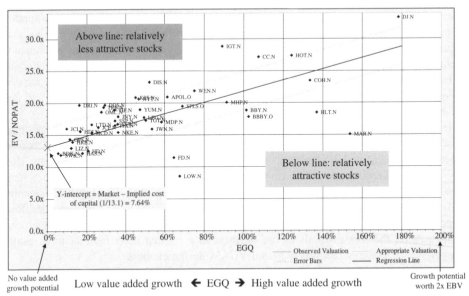

Figure 22.1   EGQ regression valuation explained: S&P 500 Consumer Discretionary Sector, August 2006,[2] (Source: UBS VCAM)

---

[2] Bianco and Burkett (2006), p. 3.

23

A Quick Guide to DCF and Economic
Profit Analysis

Here, we review the precepts of DCF and economic profit analysis and explore some issues
to consider when using discounted cash flow/economic profit analysis (DCF/EPA)-based
valuation models such as VCAM.

23.1 POWERFUL ANALYTICAL FRAMEWORKS, BUT NOT A COMPLETE SOLUTION

Discounted cash flow/economic profit analysis (DCF/EPA) is a DCF model with accompanying ROIC and economic profit calculations for each forecast year.[1] DCF/EPA analysis
provides an effective framework for evaluating whether economic value will be enhanced
under certain assumptions.

Forecasting the future to estimate current share values is really an exercise in estimating the
probability of a variety of possible outcomes rather than a specific estimate. Investors must
look into the near and distant future and make assumptions regarding how the economics and
fundamentals of an industry/business will affect all elements of the DCF/EPA framework
on a probability weighted forecast scenario basis.

We believe DCF/EPA models are very useful analytical tools. In particular, these models
can:

(1) Identify valuation discrepancies between conventional valuation methodologies;
(2) Gauge the effectiveness of capital utilization;
(3) Reveal and quantify the differing means of creating value for various indus-
    tries/companies;
(4) Help signal market expectations; and
(5) Provide effective frameworks for various scenario and share value sensitivity analysis.

23.2 DYNAMICS OF ECONOMIC PROFIT ANALYSIS

Companies increasing shareholder value generate economic profit growth. There are several
financial drivers of future economic profits, or what we will call "value dynamics". This
guide examines each of these value dynamics.

---

[1] For an introduction into DCF models see Viebig and Poddig in Part I of this book. The EPA framework is also discussed in
Larsen and Holland in Part III of this book.

Economic Profit (EP):
Profit less period cost of capital = (ROIC − WACC) × Invested Capital

---

Economic Value Added (EVA®) = PV of all future Economic Profits

$$= \sum_{n=1}^{VCH-1} PV\,[EP_n] + PV\left[\frac{EP_{VCH}}{WACC}\right]$$

Corporate value:
Current invested capital + EVA® = PV of all future Free Cash Flows

Figure 23.1   Value dynamics[2]

As will become evident, value and value creation can only be accurately measured when all of these value dynamics are examined collectively and that is the objective of VCAM and EGQ.

23.3   "UNADULTERATED EVA"

There are four principal value dynamics in economic profit analysis:

- Changes in returns on invested capital (ROIC).
- Changes in the cost of capital (WACC).
- Changes in the invested capital base (IC).
- Changes in the number of future years during which the first three value dynamics can interact to generate incremental economic profits. This is the competitive advantage period (CAP) or value creation horizon (VCH).

It is important to recognize that sound economic profit analysis, particularly valuation, is not based on retrospective or even near-term-only forecasts. EVA® is often mistakenly simplified to a one-period economic profit measure.[3] A well-designed EVA®-based valuation framework should reflect the impact on share value of near-term sacrifices for long-term benefits.

23.4   VALUE DYNAMIC 1: ROIC

Return on invested capital (ROIC) is perhaps the most widely scrutinized value dynamic. ROIC is a profitability measure that considers a company's profit per sales dollar as well as the capital required to generate each sales dollar. ROIC is comprised of two components: NOPAT and invested capital.

ROIC = NOPAT/Invested capital

ROIC is critical when comparing the profitability of different companies. As depicted below, high margins are not necessarily indicative of high returns. Examining margins without the associated capital base used to generate the profits is incomplete and especially flawed when done across industries.

---

[2] Bianco and Burkett (2006), p. 17.
[3] The EVA approach is also discussed in Part III of this book.

	Company A	Company B
Sales	$1000	$10 000
EBIT	$100	$500
Operating Margin	**10%**	**5%**
Taxes	$40	$200
Invested Capital	$1200	$3000
ROIC	**5%**	**10%**

Figure 23.2 Focus on ROIC, not just profit margins[4]

ROIC can be boosted by increasing NOPAT or decreasing invested capital, but an ongoing increase in cash flow only comes from increasing NOPAT.

ROIC can also be expressed as $= (\text{NOPAT/Sales}) \times (\text{Sales/Invested capital})$

or ROIC $=$ Profits margins $\times$ Invested capital turnover

NOPAT $=$ Net operating profit (less) adjusted taxes:

NOPAT $=$ EBIT $+$ Goodwill amortization $-$ Unlevered operating taxes

NOPAT $=$ Unlevered free cash flow $+$ Change in invested capital

The drivers of NOPAT are probably the most scrutinized of all value-dynamic drivers, as they are all income statement factors that also influence earnings estimates. The factors that influence operating costs (excluding goodwill amortization and including taxes) are the determinants of NOPAT.

An important realization regarding NOPAT is that it is equivalent to unlevered (adjusted as if the company had no debt) free cash flow when the firm has reached "steady state", which is the assumed condition at the end of the forecast horizon. At that stage, capital expenditures will be equivalent to depreciation and working capital needs should remain constant as it is assumed that the firm has exhausted its growth opportunities or its competitive advantages.

23.5 VALUE DYNAMIC 2: INVESTED CAPITAL

Invested capital is derived from a company's balance sheet and can be calculated via an operating or financing approach.

Operating Approach	=	**Financing Approach**
Current assets		Short-term notes
Less NIBCLs*		Current LT debt
Net working capital		Long-term debt
Net PP&E		Deferred liabilities
Other assets		Shareholders' equity
Invested Capital	=	**Invested Capital**

Figure 23.3 Calculating invested capital[5]

---

[4] Bianco and Burkett (2006), p. 18.
[5] Note: * NIBCLs $=$ Non-interest-bearing current liabilities.

Although invested capital is a component of value dynamic 1 (the denominator in ROIC), it is often forgotten that it is a value dynamic by itself. Just as profit margins fail to measure true profitability without being held relative to an invested capital base, ROIC alone fails to measure value creation without being held to an invested capital base. ROIC/WACC is only part of the economic profit calculation, factoring in the size of the capital base is critical.

	(ROIC-WACC)	$\times$	**Invested Capital**	$=$	**Economic Profit**
Company A	25%–10%	$\times$	$2000	$=$	$300
Company B	15%–10%	$\times$	$10\,000	$=$	$500

Figure 23.4 Equivalent ROIC/WACC spreads applied to different capital bases[6]

Companies with an equivalent return on invested capital do not necessarily possess the same potential for value creation. Maintaining a high ROIC becomes increasingly difficult as the invested capital base increases. Some enterprises have small investment opportunities that offer high returns, and others may have large investment opportunities with more modest returns.

23.6   VALUE DYNAMIC 3: WACC

Although research on the cost of capital may be among the most detailed of all the value dynamics, it remains one of the most contentious topics in the EPA framework. We outline the standard theory and mechanics behind estimating a company's cost of capital below. Our advice to investors is to use a cost of capital that makes sense and then use sensitivity analysis to make certain the investment conclusion holds within a reasonable range of differing rates.[7]

Market value weighted cost of capital:

$WACC = K_e \times \frac{E}{V} + [K_d \times (1 - t)] \times \frac{D}{V}$

Cost of equity (K_e)

Capital Asset Pricing Model (CAPM):

$K_e = R_f + \beta \times ERP$

Cost of debt (K_d)

$K_d = $ *weighted average market borrowing rate*

where

E = *market value of equity*

D = *market value of debt*

V = *market value of enterprise* $(= E + D)$

t = *tax rate*

R_f = *long-term risk-free rate of return (10-year US Treasury note yield to maturity)*

β = *measure of sensitivity of returns to the market*

ERP = *equity risk premium = expected equity market return less risk free rate*

Figure 23.5 Components of WACC calculation

---

[6] Bianco and Burkett (2006), p. 20.
[7] WACC are discussed in more detail by Viebig and Poddig in Part I section 3.3.3 of this book.

23.7   VALUE DYNAMIC 4: THE VALUE CREATION HORIZON

In theory the competitive advantage period (CAP), or what we usually refer to in the VCAM as the value creation horizon (VCH), is the number of future years economic profits are expected to increase from changes in the first three dynamics. The CAP/VCH is also an estimate of the market's willingness to be far-sighted and consider such continued economic profit growth as being visible.

This practical theoretical distinction means that the CAP/VCH does not decay merely from the passing of years. Rather, changes in the CAP/VCH only occur from shifts in a company's competitive positioning and long-term growth prospects as assessed from the current moment in time.

We believe companies in the same industry tend to have similar CAPs. Macro industry characteristics such as barriers to entry, rivalry among competitors, threat of substitute products, and power of suppliers or customers greatly influence a company's ability to earn economic profits. CAPs exceeding the industry average typically belong to companies with exceptionally strong brands, proprietary technology/processes, etc.

The CAP/VCH is probably the hardest of all valuation assumptions to substantiate. Competitive environments are in a constant state of change, and small changes in factors that influence today's environment may have a dramatic impact on the future. The market adjusts its CAP/VCH estimate as incremental information offering insight into the future emerges.

23.8   COMBINING ALL FOUR VALUE DYNAMICS: EGQ

We believe all four value dynamics must be considered concurrently to accurately estimate a company's future value-added growth potential. Combining all the value dynamics requires both a forward-looking and multi-period capability. Economic profit, while the most comprehensive profit metric for any one period, suffers from being based only on one period.

This is why we created VCAM and its EGQ measure. In addition to considering the interaction of changes in ROIC, WACC and the invested capital base in any single forecast year, VCAM's EGQ accounts for the interaction of the first three value dynamics over the entire forecast horizon.

EGQ is comparable across all companies because it considers the differing collective interaction of all four principal value dynamics. EGQ is based on and will always be consistent with incremental value creation analysis from a DCF/EPA model. Until EGQ, no one metric fully captured a company's incremental value creation potential.

23.8.1   EGQ vs. PVGO

Investors may recognize our concepts of incremental value creation (IVC) and EGQ as something similar to PVGO (present value of growth opportunities). PVGO, when expressed as a percentage, typically refers to the portion of a company's observed enterprise value (EV) that is greater than its economic book value.

$$\text{PVGO as } \% \text{ of EV} = [\text{Observed EV} - (\text{NOPAT/WACC})]/\text{Observed EV}$$

The main conceptual difference between PVGO and EGQ is that EGQ is based on explicit operating forecasts to estimate a company's value-added growth potential, whereas PVGO is solved for using observed market EV. Market implied PVGO is a good measure of market expectations, which can be meaningfully compared to one's own expectations using EGQ.

EGQ represents the value of IVC relative to economic book value (EBV) rather than total enterprise value. This difference in calculation from PVGO is done to prevent scaling distortions in linear regressions. Thus, to compare an explicitly estimated company EGQ to its market implied PVGO, EGQ must be converted to express the explicitly estimated IVC relative to the firm's estimated total EV.

23.8.2   The search for the ultimate valuation methodology

For reasons explained throughout this report, we believe EGQ[8] valuation regressions represent an important addition to intrinsic valuation theory and accepted methodologies. We certainly think expert valuation practitioners can benefit from using this analysis as part of their process. Most investors, even many professionals, are unlikely to have the time or resources to construct and maintain such complicated valuation systems. Nevertheless, we think a good understanding of the concepts underlying EGQ valuation regressions is likely to help any investor make better decisions.

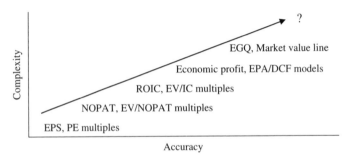

Figure 23.6   Valuation Metric Theory

---

[8] EGQ = IVC/EBV. The formula is discussed in more detail in section 25.1.

24

Regression-based Valuation

Regressions can be a powerful valuation tool. They help identify and quantify factors that determine company valuation. Because regression lines minimize the distance from all X, Y observation points they generally split the universe of observations into two parts, that being above and beneath the line. This characteristic makes regression valuation inherently relative. Said differently, a regression will always identify some attractive and some unattractive companies. This is very different from DCF or intrinsic-based valuation methods, which can deem all examined companies as attractive or unattractive.

The challenge in properly using regressions for company valuation lies in identifying an independent variable that robustly explains observed valuations of differing companies. Most regression-based attempts to explain observed valuations, typically expressed as PE or EV multiples, use company characteristics such as growth or cost of capital as the independent (explanatory) variable. A classic example is the PEG ratio, which is calculated by dividing the company's observed PE with an estimate of its EPS growth rate. Other company characteristics or factors can be used, one of the more popular being ROIC/WACC. As we will explain, we believe that none of the factors, including ROIC/WACC, commonly used by either fundamental or quantitative investors is capable of robustly explaining observed valuations. For this reason we created a new metric, the Economic Growth Quotient (EGQ), a metric based on and conceptually consistent with DCF analysis, designed to be used as the independent variable in regression-based valuation.

Once a robust independent variable is constructed, such as our EGQ metric from the UBS VCAM (a standardized DCF model), regression-based valuation can elevate a DCF model from being a single company valuation methodology to a disciplined stock selection and sector allocation framework. Because regression-based valuation will always be relative, investors can use regressions to clearly separate stock selection from sector or industry allocation decisions. In effect, regression-based valuation can help DCF-minded investors pursue a layered alpha strategy. First, choose which companies to own within an industry and then decide whether to underweight or overweight the industry. Regressions can even help with style preference decisions, such as value vs. growth.

Beyond the ability of EGQ-based regressions to value companies on a relative basis, using intrinsic DCF analysis on each company as the point of comparison, EGQ regressions have the ability to read the market. The empirical nature of regressions allows EGQ regressions to be used to reveal market assumptions for controversial DCF inputs such as cost of capital or appropriate forecast horizons. Later in the report we discuss how using EGQ regressions as an empirical tool can result in what we call emergent valuation. But our favorite thing about regression valuation is that it is visual. Regressions allow investors to examine the valuation of numerous companies in a picture.

UBS Economic Growth Quotient

25.1 THE EGQ CALCULATION

The UBS Economic Growth Quotient (EGQ) is a measure of a company's economic profit growth potential. It is calculated as the present value of all the company's projected future economic profits incremental to the current level divided by the present value of the company's current earnings valued in perpetuity. This ratio compares value attributable to the company's future growth to that derived from its business already in place.

In the UBS Value Creation Analysis Model (VCAM), we refer to the present value of all future incremental economic profits as incremental value creation (IVC) and the present value of a company's current after-tax operating earnings valued in perpetuity (NOPAT/WACC) as economic book value (EBV).

$$EGQ = IVC/EBV$$

$$VCAM \text{ DCF estimated enterprise value} = IVC + EBV$$

If a company has an EGQ of 100%, then half of its estimated intrinsic enterprise value is attributable to its expected economic profit growth, as the present value of its forecasted incremental economic profits would be equivalent to its current earnings valued in perpetuity. An EGQ of 300% would indicate that forecasted economic profit growth is worth three times the value of EBV. EGQ can be either positive or negative, theoretically with no limit.

25.2 EGQ SPECIAL ATTRIBUTES

25.2.1 A complete metric

EGQ is based on and designed to agree with DCF and economic profit analysis. EGQ does this by reflecting the collective interaction of all four principal value dynamics: return on invested capital (ROIC), weighted average cost of capital (WACC), invested capital (IC) and the value creation horizon (VCH). It is only when all four of these principal value dynamics are considered collectively that economic profit and DCF-based valuations are equal.

25.2.2 Not influenced by the current capital base

EGQ is a measure of future economic profits that strips out base level economic profits – EGQ represents only incremental EVA®. Because EGQ is based on marginal economic profits, it is not influenced by a firm's current invested capital base. EGQ is only influenced by future changes in profit compared to future changes in the invested capital base. Unlike total economic profit, EGQ can be fairly compared across different companies without making elaborate (often contentious and still incomplete) balance sheet derived invested capital adjustments for the effects of historical inflation, asset write-downs, accumulated goodwill amortization, restructuring and other special charges, etc.

25.2.3   Limited sensitivity to the assumed cost of capital

Most DCF value estimates or economic profit measures are extremely sensitive to the cost of capital assumption. However, because EGQ relates the value of economic profit growth to the value of current earnings in perpetuity it has limited sensitivity to the assumed cost of capital.

$$\text{WACC} \downarrow \Rightarrow \frac{\overbrace{\text{PV (incremental EP)}\uparrow}^{\text{IVC}}}{\underbrace{\left(\text{NOPAT}\big/\text{WACC}\right)\uparrow}_{\text{EBV}}} \approx \begin{array}{c} \text{EGQ} \\ \text{unchanged} \end{array}$$

Figure 25.1   EGQ's muted sensitivity to the assumed cost of capital[1]

Although a lower WACC would cause a higher value for the IVC, it would also cause a higher value for the EBV. There is only a muted influence from changes in WACC in this part of calculating EGQ from the differing present value of near versus distant growth in incremental economic profits. Investors may recognize this as the duration effect. Thus, while EGQ does exhibit sensitivity to cost of capital assumptions owing to the duration effect and also if there are invested capital base changes, its sensitivity is very modest compared to that of DCF values or economic profits. Provided the initial cost of capital assumption is a reasonable estimate (preferably CAPM based), EGQ will very reliably measure a company's value-added growth potential relative to its EBV without distortions caused by moderately incorrect cost of capital assumptions.

25.2.4   Comparable across companies of different size

EGQ, as a ratio rather than a dollar value like economic profit, is better compared across companies of different sizes. It is inappropriate to attempt to adjust economic profits for company size by simply examining the economic profit margin (ROIC/WACC). Economic profits are already adjusted for size by the capital charge, and a large company generating large economic profits deserves credit for significantly enhancing wealth on a large scale. Determining the appropriate multiple on its current earnings is a separate analysis altogether,

---

[1] Bianco and Burkett (2006), p. 6.

one that depends on the company's prospects for future economic profit growth relative to the value of current earnings – that is what EGQ does.

25.2.5   Explains observed multiples on flows like earnings or cash flow

EGQ explains why some companies trade at premium earnings multiples, whereas most economic profit measures only attempt to explain multiples on book value. Valuation incorporates the worth of a firm's invested capital and current earnings, but it must also consider what the firm will do in the future.

26
UBS EGQ Regression Valuation

26.1 INTRINSIC MEETS RELATIVE VALUATION

Using EGQ as the independent variable in a valuation regression is based on our thesis that differences in observed valuation multiples of companies similar in systematic risk are mostly driven by differences in the market's expectation for each company's value-added growth potential. We define value-added growth as incremental economic profits. Incremental economic profits are future increases in economic profit beyond the level currently earned.

Estimating incremental economic profits requires forward-looking analysis of a company's potential to grow its business and, importantly, the investments required to support that growth. We think the best framework for quantifying and testing such forecasts is a hybrid DCF and future economic profit model, such as the UBS Value Creation Analysis Model (VCAM).

DCF-based valuation produces "intrinsic" values, and a DCF estimated intrinsic value will be either higher or lower than the observed market value. While this stand-alone valuation is important, such an approach can suffer when all companies examined are screening as intrinsically attractive or unattractive. The benefit of using an EGQ regression is that it identifies which companies are the most attractive and the most unattractive using DCF analysis and intrinsic values as the basis of comparison. Using an observed valuation multiple as the dependent variable, and EGQ as the independent variable, companies beneath the regression line are relatively attractive investments, while companies above the regression line are relatively unattractive investments.

Another benefit of using EGQ valuation regressions is that the accuracy of the company's relative attractiveness, as delineated by the regression line, relies on a correct relative ordering of each company's forecasted growth and required investments, not necessarily the exact nominal operating forecasts for each company. We believe this helps alleviate concerns some investors have with the accuracy of long-term forecasts as required for DCF valuation. However, the accuracy of the nominal growth forecasts does influence the regression's assessment (y-intercept) of overall group attractiveness. EGQ regressions assume that companies have a similar cost of capital, thus only compare companies in the same sector or industry, i.e. those with similar systematic risk.

We think most investors would agree that a company's real world valuation does not exist independently from the real world valuations of other companies, particularly those in the same industry or peer group. EGQ regression valuation for one firm is influenced by the current market valuations of its peers. We believe this is an appropriate and necessary consideration as similar companies compete for investor capital. Thus, regressions based on our EGQ metric combine the most useful aspects of intrinsic and relative valuation.

26.2   EGQ REGRESSIONS: RELATIVE VALUATION THEATER

The linear formula regressed from company EGQs and their respective current EV/NOPAT multiples can be used to value companies. We call this regressed linear formula the market value line (MVL). The MVL assigns appropriate *relative* EV/NOPAT multiples and share values to each company based on its EGQ. MVL assigned valuations capture a company's DCF estimated intrinsic value per its EGQ and then adjusts that intrinsic value to reflect the existence of other peer companies also with observed intrinsic to market value discrepancies.

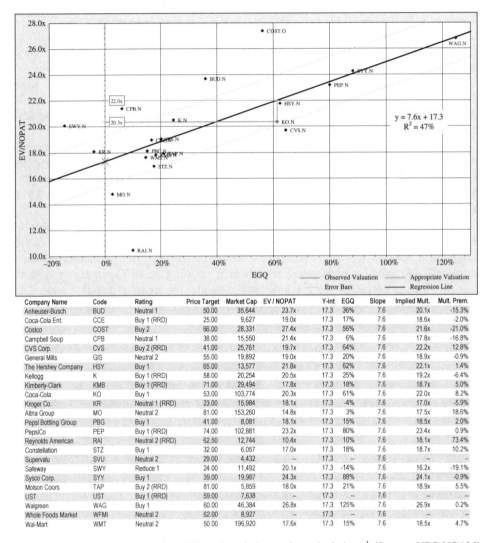

Company Name	Code	Rating	Price Target	Market Cap	EV / NOPAT	Y-int	EGQ	Slope	Implied Mult.	Mult. Prem.
Anheuser-Busch	BUD	Neutral 1	50.00	35,644	23.7x	17.3	36%	7.6	20.1x	-15.3%
Coca-Cola Ent.	CCE	Buy 1 (RRD)	25.00	9,627	19.0x	17.3	17%	7.6	18.6x	-2.0%
Costco	COST	Buy 2	66.00	28,331	27.4x	17.3	56%	7.6	21.6x	-21.0%
Campbell Soup	CPB	Neutral 1	38.00	15,550	21.4x	17.3	6%	7.6	17.8x	-16.8%
CVS Corp.	CVS	Buy 2 (RRD)	41.00	25,761	19.7x	17.3	64%	7.6	22.2x	12.8%
General Mills	GIS	Neutral 2	55.00	19,892	19.0x	17.3	20%	7.6	18.9x	-0.9%
The Hershey Company	HSY	Buy 1	65.00	13,577	21.8x	17.3	62%	7.6	22.1x	1.4%
Kellogg	K	Buy 1 (RRD)	58.00	20,254	20.5x	17.3	25%	7.6	19.2x	-6.4%
Kimberly-Clark	KMB	Buy 1 (RRD)	71.00	29,494	17.8x	17.3	18%	7.6	18.7x	5.0%
Coca-Cola	KO	Buy 1	53.00	103,774	20.3x	17.3	61%	7.6	22.0x	8.2%
Kroger Co.	KR	Neutral 1 (RRD)	23.00	15,984	18.1x	17.3	-4%	7.6	17.0x	-5.9%
Altria Group	MO	Neutral 2	81.00	153,260	14.8x	17.3	3%	7.6	17.5x	18.6%
Pepsi Bottling Group	PBG	Buy 1	41.00	8,081	18.1x	17.3	15%	7.6	18.5x	2.0%
PepsiCo	PEP	Buy 1 (RRD)	74.00	102,881	23.2x	17.3	80%	7.6	23.4x	0.9%
Reynolds American	RAI	Neutral 2 (RRD)	62.50	12,744	10.4x	17.3	10%	7.6	18.1x	73.4%
Constellation	STZ	Buy 1	32.00	6,057	17.0x	17.3	18%	7.6	18.7x	10.2%
Supervalu	SVU	Neutral 2	29.00	4,432	--	17.3	--	7.6	--	--
Safeway	SWY	Reduce 1	24.00	11,492	20.1x	17.3	-14%	7.6	16.2x	-19.1%
Sysco Corp.	SYY	Buy 1	39.00	19,987	24.3x	17.3	88%	7.6	24.1x	-0.9%
Molson Coors	TAP	Buy 2 (RRD)	81.00	5,859	18.0x	17.3	21%	7.6	18.9x	5.5%
UST	UST	Buy 1 (RRD)	59.00	7,638	--	17.3	--	7.6	--	--
Walgreen	WAG	Buy 1	60.00	46,384	26.8x	17.3	125%	7.6	26.9x	0.2%
Whole Foods Market	WFMI	Neutral 2	62.00	8,927	--	17.3	--	7.6	--	--
Wal-Mart	WMT	Neutral 2	50.00	196,920	17.6x	17.3	15%	7.6	18.5x	4.7%

Figure 26.1   EGQ regression with MVL assigned share value calculations,[1] (Source: UBS VCAM)

---

[1] Bianco and Burkett (2006), p. 8.

26.3   EGQ REGRESSIONS: A LAYERED ALPHA FRAMEWORK

- Stock selection: Buy stocks beneath the line, sell above the line.
- Sector allocation: $1/y$-intercept is the market offered return on the group.
- Style preference: Slope $>$ y-intercept signals market preference for growth.

26.4   *Y*-INTERCEPT INDICATES COST OF CAPITAL

The EGQ regressed market value line (MVL) is algebraically expressed by its slope and y-intercept. The slope represents how much the market is paying for growth, specifically how many EV/NOPAT multiple points per 100% EGQ. The y-intercept is a reflection of the market's offered return on the group. It can be thought of as the market implied cost of capital for the companies in the regression. This implied cost of capital or IRR on the group is $1/y$-intercept.

The EGQ regression identifies the cost of capital ($1/y$-intercept) that best explains the observed valuations of all the companies respective of their projections for value-added growth. If a company's EGQ is 0% (no value-added growth potential) then its EV/NOPAT multiple would be determined solely by the y-intercept, as the intrinsically appropriate multiple is 1/CoC, which is the same as the y-intercept.[2]

26.5   SLOPE VS. *Y*-INTERCEPT INDICATES STYLE

The slope of the MVL relative to the y-intercept reflects the market's preference for high vs. low growth companies (as projected for each company in the estimates underlying EGQ) or in style terms, growth vs. value. If the slope of the MVL is materially higher than the y-intercept, the market is exhibiting a growth preference for the group of companies in the regression. If the slope is materially lower than the y-intercept, there is a value preference. If the two values are reasonably close there is no material style preference.

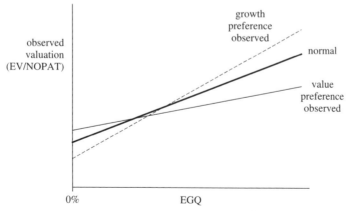

Figure 26.2   Market value lines with value or growth preferences[3]

---

[2] Provided certain adjustments are made to account for the perpetual sustainability of any economic profits embedded in NOPAT as well as any earnings quality distortions from depreciation provisions based on historic asset costs, it can be appropriate to capitalize NOPAT at the real cost of capital or 1/(CoC-inflation).

[3] Bianco and Burkett (2006), p. 9.

Because we designed the EGQ metric to be consistent with DCF valuation, EGQ regressions represent a linear relationship in which the slope and the y-intercept theoretically should be equal. For example, a company with an EGQ of 100% should have a valuation twice that of a company with an EGQ of 0%, which would result in the company's EV/NOPAT multiple being two times the y-intercept. This is because an EGQ of 100% means that the company's growth is worth as much as its current earnings in perpetuity. Therefore, if the MVL slope is not equal to the y-intercept in observed reality, it signals a style preference.

We believe style preference in the market is an understandable and rational phenomenon. We think it is reasonable for the market to curb its valuations for growth companies in uncertain and risky environments as the anticipated profit growth may be at risk to downward revision. Similarly, we think it reasonable for the market to push multiples higher during more visible and optimistic periods. Perhaps style can be thought of as the market's way of expressing doubt in the accuracy of prevailing expectations or the underlying EGQ estimates.

26.6   EMERGENT VALUATION

Intrinsic valuation + Relative valuation = "Emergent valuation"

Intrinsic or DCF/EPA derived valuations, as produced by VCAM, are an integral component of the overall valuation process owing to their methodical nature and focus on all future cash flows available to investors and risk adjusted opportunity cost of capital. But we believe the relative or observed nature of the EGQ regression is a significant and very valuable advancement to such intrinsic frameworks, as it incorporates other proximate competing investment opportunities available to investors and it can help reveal and incorporate market valuation factors that intrinsic valuation frameworks often neglect.

We believe some of these market factors include prevailing discount rates not equivalent to CAPM estimates, the relative effect that current market valuations of similar companies have on each other, the market's preference for growth vs. value, and industry-specific issues common to the group (M&A activity, litigation, etc.). In addition, the relative approach of the EGQ valuation system helps mitigate share value sensitivity to some of the more contentious assumptions in the DCF/EPA framework, such as the value creation horizon and aspects of the terminal value calculation like the economic profit fade rate.

26.7   WHY REGRESS EGQ VS. EV/NOPAT?

The y-axis in EGQ regressions represents the market's current multiple on NOPAT based on one-year forward projections. We choose EV/NOPAT for two reasons. First, we needed to express company valuations in relative rather than nominal terms to allow comparisons across different-sized companies, multiples are most commonly used to enable such comparisons. Second, we believe EV/NOPAT multiples are the most accurate for comparing relative valuations.

Enterprise value represents the value of a firm independent of its capital structure. It includes all interest-bearing net debt (less cash) along with the market's value of equity. Enterprise value eliminates the unequal leveraging effect to earnings for companies with different capital structures.

NOPAT only includes proceeds for financial claimholders (equity and debt). Unlike the more popular EV/EBITDA multiples, NOPAT is calculated after the company's tax provision which represents cash that belongs to the government and not financial claimholders (tax rates differ across companies). Also, EBITDA does not properly account for differences in

D&A levels across companies – this makes EBITDA a very poor measure to use across industries. Physical capital intensive companies/industries will have a greater proportion of their EBITDA by D&A than companies/industries without many physical assets. Because D&A does not belong to financial claimholders (it is a provision set aside to maintain assets), comparing relative valuations based on EV/EBITDA across industries can be very misguided.

NOPAT, when properly calculated, also excludes tax benefits from the deductibility of interest expense (interest tax shields), which makes NOPAT a profitability measure completely independent of corporate capital structures.[4]

Finally NOPAT is not influenced by unequal degrees and/or timing of capital expenditures across differing companies. While some criticize NOPAT for assuming that depreciation and non-goodwill amortization correctly approximate a company's maintenance capex needs, we note that we have not found this assumption to be overly stretched for US companies complying with GAAP standards. Furthermore, an adjustment to NOPAT can be easily made, if necessary, to account for inadequate or excessive D&A provisions.

26.8   THINK OPPOSITE WHEN UNDER THE *X*-AXIS

For companies with negative earnings, the world of EGQ regressions gets turned upside down. For companies with negative earnings, the more negative EGQ the stronger a company's growth prospects. Accordingly, it is the negative earnings companies above the line that are attractive. This is opposite to that of normal EGQ regression lines, which typically plots within the top two quadrants.

While the details of coordinate geometry can be a bit confusing, it is reassuring that EGQ regressions are mathematically and graphically robust enough to handle companies with negative earnings. EGQ regressed lines used for valuation correctly account for companies with negative earnings without any adjustments. For example, a company with negative earnings today (negative EV/NOPAT), but with strong growth prospects from that level (a negative EGQ, because the positive PV of IVC is divided by the negative current NOPAT) has positive share value, as negative times negative is positive.

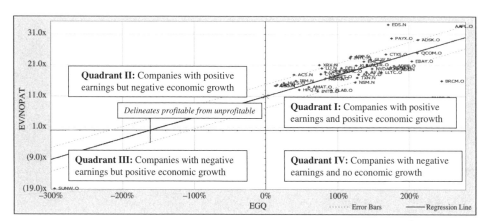

Figure 26.3   Companies under the line in quadrant III are relatively unattractive,[5] (Source: UBS VCAM)

---

[4] The calculation of NOPAT is discussed in more detail in Viebig and Poddig, Part I, section 3.3.2, and Larsen and Holland, Part III, in this book.
[5] Bianco and Burkett (2006), p. 12.

Understanding Regressions

27.1   KEY TAKEAWAYS

- A low R-squared does not mean the model is flawed.
- Statistically significant observed relationships do not ensure causality.
- Interpreting regressions hinges on the nature of underlying observations.

There are a handful of key statistics used to describe linear regressions. Two of these define the line itself: The slope (beta) and y-intercept (alpha). Some statistics describe the "fit" or explanatory power of the model: R (correlation coefficient) and R-squared (the coefficient of determination). Other important statistics measure the precision or reliability of the model and its estimates under normal conditions, such as standard errors and t-statistics.

   We use the calculation of a stock's beta, per the traditional CAPM approach, to estimating cost of equity, to frame our discussion of the key statistical measures related to linear regression analysis.

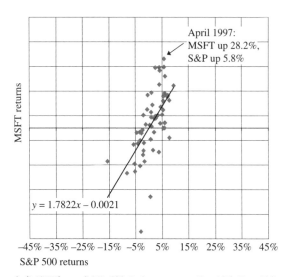

Figure 27.1   Microsoft (MSFT) vs. S&P 500 Index returns: Jan '96–Dec '00

   Figure 27.1 shows monthly Microsoft returns (on the vertical y-axis) plotted against monthly total returns of the S&P 500 Index (on the horizontal x-axis). It is common practice in regression analysis to present the dependent variable on the y-axis and the independent variable on the x-axis. Keep in mind that a regression equation only captures the degree of common variation among variables; correlation does not necessarily imply causality. For

---

Monthly returns of Microsoft vs. the S&P 500
January 1996–December 2000

Equation being estimated

$r_{MSFT} = \alpha + \beta r_{S\&P} + \varepsilon$

Resulting estimate (regression line):

$r_{MSFT} = -0.0021 + 1.7822\, r_{S\&P}$

Key statistics	
The regression line	
Beta (slope of the line)	1.782
Alpha (y-intercept)	−0.002
The explanatory power of the model	
Correlation coefficient	0.6229
R-squared (coefficient of determination)	38.8%
The accuracy of the estimates	
Standard error (of beta)	0.294
t-Statistic (= beta/standard error)	6.063

Figure 27.2   Regression results – MSFT market model

example, there is a strong positive relationship between the number of firefighters that fought a blaze and the damage caused by a fire. This does not mean the firefighters caused the damage. Figure 27.2 presents the estimated linear equation and major statistics calculated to assess the observed relationship.

27.2   THE LINE – WHAT IS THE RELATIONSHIP?

27.2.1   Slope (beta)

Slope refers to the change in Y for every one-unit change in $X (\Delta Y/\Delta X)$. If the plotted line is at exactly a 45° angle, this implies that when X rises by some amount, Y rises by the same amount, and the slope is one. The slope of a regressed line is formally called beta, and the y-intercept is formally called alpha. Sometimes the slope is called m and the y-intercept is called b, as in the linear equation: $y = mx + b$ (where $m =$ beta and $b =$ alpha).

We constructed Figure 27.1 with the x- and y-axes on the same scale, to show the steepness of the line. Microsoft's beta is 1.78, meaning that during the selected historical period, when the S&P 500 is up 1%, Microsoft is up 1.78% on average, and when the S&P is down 1%, Microsoft is down 1.78% on average. Because MSFT and the S&P tend to move in the same direction, MSFT's beta is positive (as are nearly all stocks). Beta, in the context of this regression, is a measure of systematic or market risk, which is how sensitive a company is to the market or really the macroeconomic conditions that affect the market overall (aka undiversifiable risk). A beta of less than one indicates that the stock was less sensitive to such macro conditions than the overall market. Stocks in non-cyclical sectors typically have betas less than one.

27.2.2   y-Intercept (alpha)

The y-intercept is where the estimated regression line crosses the vertical axis; the expected value of the dependent variable (y-axis) when the independent variable (x-axis) is zero. In the case of a market model, the y-intercept also indicates actual performance relative to performance predicted by the model. An-alpha greater than zero indicates the stock performed better than expected during the regression period and an alpha of less than zero means the stock performed worse than expected. Microsoft performed almost exactly as predicted by our model, as its alpha is slightly greater than zero. In theory, long run alphas should be zero, otherwise there would be arbitrage opportunities from going long positive alpha securities (those that always perform better than expected) and shorting negative alpha securities. If one ran this regression for every stock in the market, the average alpha should be zero, because on average the market cannot perform better or worse than itself.[1]

27.3   THE EXPLANATORY POWER OR STRENGTH OF THE RELATIONSHIP

27.3.1   Correlation coefficient (R)

A measure of common variation between two variables is the correlation coefficient (R). Correlation can range from −1 to 1, and will always have the same sign as beta. It indicates how strong the linear association is between the two variables. For example, if every time the S&P moved up by a certain amount, MSFT always moved up by a set multiple of that amount, R would equal 1 (this is perfect correlation). If R equaled zero, it would mean that there was no relationship; knowing what happened to the S&P would give you no indication whatsoever of MSFT's returns. The actual R in our example is 0.62, indicating a strong positive relationship between MSFT and S&P 500 returns.

27.3.2   Coefficient of determination (R-squared)

R-squared is literally the square of R (correlation coefficient squared). This is why it has to be a positive number between 0 and 1 (because R is always between −1 and 1). R-squared measures how much of the variation in the dependent variable is "explained" by variation in the independent variable. It measures how well the regressed line fits the observations. An R-squared of 100% means all observations fall exactly on the regressed line; 0% indicates no relationship. In our MSFT example, almost 39% of the variation in MSFT returns can be attributed to variation in market returns. Put differently, most MSFT volatility is firm specific, but 39% of total volatility is systematic and related to market volatility. For a market model, an R-squared of 30% is very common, though it might appear low when compared to regressions of other types. There are many stock specific

---

[1] Sharpe and Alexander (1990), p. 222, define a security's alpha as "the differences between its expected return and an appropriate (equilibrium) expected return". A security is mispriced relative to an equilibrium model if it has a nonzero alpha. The Capital Asset Pricing Model (CAPM), a widely used equilibrium model, requires that *excess returns* above the risk-free rate are applied. The CAPM is discussed in Viebig and Poddig, Part I, section 3.3.3 in this book.

factors in stock returns, but our estimate of beta still has high statistical significance (see below).

For EGQ regressions based on a good number of observations, R-squared is typically 50–80%. The higher the R-squared in an EGQ regression the more the observed stock prices agree with their DCF estimated share prices (i.e. market-implied EGQ agrees with estimated EGQ).

27.4   RELIABILITY OR CONFIDENCE IN THE QUANTIFIED RELATIONSHIP

27.4.1   Standard error (of beta)

Any estimate of beta is a point estimate; calling into question how much confidence to have in that single number, this is where standard errors help. A small standard error suggests more confidence in the beta estimate. Because of the mathematical properties of a normal distribution, we can use standard error to construct a "confidence interval" around beta. For example, if we calculate beta ± two standard deviations, we can state that we are 95% confident the "true beta" lies within this range. For Microsoft, we can be 95% confident that the true beta lies between 1.19 and 2.37 ($1.19 =$ beta of $1.782 - [2 \times$ std. err. of $0.294]$ and $2.37 = 1.782 + [2 \times 0.294]$). This might seem like a large range, but is quite typical for this type of market model.

Applying EGQ analysis, we view a large deviation from the regression line as an indication that a security is either overvalued or undervalued relative to its peers.

27.4.2 t-Statistic

The t-statistic allows for a more formal quantification of statistical significance. A t-statistic is a standardized measure, so a t-stat of ± 1.96 or greater will always indicate significance at the 95% level or above. In our example, the t-statistic on the beta is 6.063, meaning we can say with an extremely high degree of confidence (well over 99%) that our beta is significantly different from zero.

Alternatively, if the null hypothesis (beta $= 0$) is true, the probability of getting a t-stat of ± 1.96 or higher is 5% or lower. Thus, a p-value of 0.05 or less usually indicates that the coefficients are statistically significant (different from zero).

27.5   REGRESSION OUTLIERS

27.5.1   Influence outliers

These are outliers that result from the y variable being very far from the average of all the other y variables observed.

27.5.2   Leverage outliers

These are outliers that result from the x variable being very far from the average of all the other x variables observed. Because this lone observation is to the far left or right of the others it exerts more influence on the tilt of the line than the other observations. This kind of outlier can be particularly problematic and is usually removed from regressed data sets.

27.6   BEWARE OF OUTLIERS IN EGQ REGRESSIONS

For EGQ regressions it is helpful to ensure that outliers do not overly influence the regression. Outliers often represent bad data and even if the data is correct, influence outliers are typically the result of some company specific issue complicating valuation comparisons with the other companies. Some common causes of influence outliers are (when the issue is specific to that one company): litigation risk, M&A activity, significant size difference, non-cash producing assets, financial distress, pension or health care liability concerns, etc. Adjusting for these issues will improve the quality of this observation in the regression.

A reliable market value line (MVL) is usually well littered with observation points throughout its course. If only one or two observation points exist at either extreme of the x-axis, it is likely best to remove these leveraged outliers and use the more center part of the line supported by more observations. It is generally fine if clusters of several or more companies exist along the line, as these clusters are likely logical subgroups within the larger peer group. If the cluster is of numerous companies it may make for a good regression universe of its own.

Appendix Discussions

28.1   EGQ'S MUTED SENSITIVITY TO ASSUMED WACC

Provided the initial cost of capital assumption is a reasonable estimate (we base it on CAPM), EGQ will very reliably measure a company's value-added growth potential relative to its EBV without distortions caused by an incorrect cost of capital assumption. This allows investors to compare the worth of a company's expected value-added growth potential (relative to the value of its existing earnings) to that of peer companies without distortions from minor inaccuracies in the assumed cost of capital. This allows EGQ regressions to identify the market's assigned cost of capital for a group of peer companies independent of the cost of capital assumptions made in the DCF to calculate company EGQs.

Consider a firm with yearly NOPAT from existing business of $100 and incremental opportunities as shown in Figure 28.1.

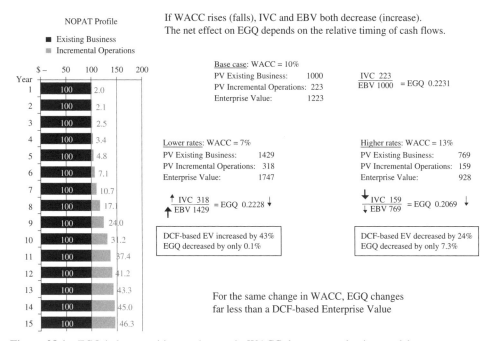

Figure 28.1   EGQ is less sensitive to changes in WACC than most valuation models

Figure 28.1 demonstrates important aspects of EGQ related to the assumed cost of capital.

(1) Given a decrease in WACC, the DCF-based enterprise value will increase, but so will both the present value of existing business (EBV) and the present value of incremental opportunities (IVC).
(2) Accordingly, EGQ is far less sensitive to changes in the cost of capital assumption than a traditional DCF-based share or enterprise value measures.
(3) The direction of change in IVC and EBV does not determine the direction of change in EGQ (as seen above, increases and decreases in IVC and EBV can lead to a decrease in EGQ).

Rather, it is the relative change in IVC and EBV (as influenced by the timing of the incremental economic profits) that determines the direction of change in EGQ. We have highlighted one possible set of cash flows in the chart in Figure 28.1 but consider if incremental opportunities all occurred in the near-term, or if economic profits from existing business were to decline over time.

28.2   EV/IC VS. ROIC/WACC REGRESSIONS

The EV/IC versus ROIC/WACC regression fails to satisfy the condition of X variable independence to the Y variable. NOPAT acts as a circular link between the two axis inputs. NOPAT is in the X variable as the numerator in ROIC and is also in the Y variable as a significant but somewhat-masked component of enterprise value. Market enterprise value is the summation of NOPAT in perpetuity (capitalized at WACC) plus the market estimated present value of growth opportunities (PVGO). It is mostly because of this circular link that EV/IC versus ROIC/WACC regressions produce a high R-squared.

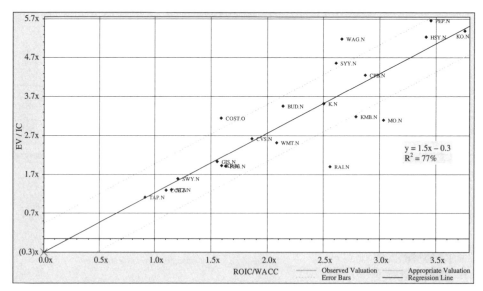

Figure 28.2   EV/IC vs. ROIC/WACC (Source: UBS VCAM)

Upon careful consideration, it should come as no surprise that a high return on a certain amount of invested capital should cause a high market multiple on that same invested capital. High returns are inherent to high NOPAT relative to invested capital, so enterprise value, which is significantly influenced by current NOPAT, should also be high relative to the invested capital base.

The only part of market enterprise value not wholly dependent on current ROIC is the market's assessed present value of growth opportunities (PVGO). However, current ROIC/WACC is not a good indicator of the market's estimated growth prospects for a company (or PVGO). This is precisely why we use VCAM to forecast the future and the EGQ metric in valuation regressions.

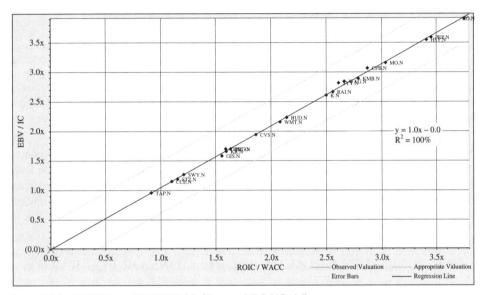

Figure 28.3   EBV/IC vs. ROIC/WACC (Source: UBS VCAM)

Once market enterprise value is stripped of the value determined by today's NOPAT in perpetuity (leaving market implied PVGO) correlation declined to 12%. It appears that current ROIC levels poorly predict the market's expectations for value-added growth and, thus, appropriate valuation.

$$\text{Enterprise value} = \text{NOPAT/WACC} + \text{PVGO}$$

In our view, the ROIC/WACC regression fails to reflect future performance. It does not account for the likely changes to ROIC/WACC in the future or the interaction of future ROIC/WACC, the economic profit margin, with the future invested capital base to derive economic profits. The amount of invested capital is as important as the economic profit margin. In short, ROIC/WACC regressions neglect major valuation determinants.

Relative company positions in ROIC/WACC regressions are the same as would be produced by a relative ordering by PE. Just like PE analysis, ROIC/WACC regressions lack

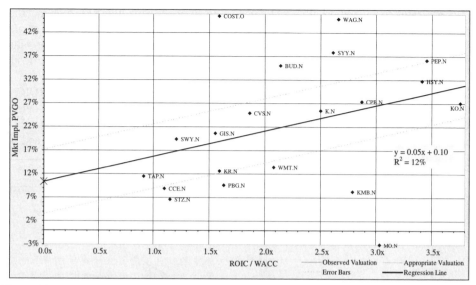

Figure 28.4   MI PVGO vs. ROIC/WACC (Source: UBS VCAM)

consideration for differences in future value-added growth performance among the companies. Unfortunately, we think ROIC regressions provide investors with a false sense that a high ROIC/WACC justifies a high PE or EV multiple. It is future economic profit growth potential that justifies premium multiples, not current high returns on capital or economic profits.

28.3   PE VS. EPS GROWTH REGRESSIONS OR PEG RATIOS

Conceptually, the PE to EPS growth ratio or "PEG" is similar to EGQ regressions. The Y-axis of EGQ regressions is EV/NOPAT, which is an unlevered PE multiple. EGQ, on the X-axis, can be thought of as a cleaned-up version of EPS growth, having made adjustments for the investments required to support that growth and eliminate distortions from financial engineering.

However, EGQ regressions have the important benefit of capturing value-added growth potential vs. appropriate EV/NOPAT multiple in a linear relationship (made possible by the DCF model underlying EGQ). Appropriate PEG ratios do not have a linear relationship between PE and EPS growth.

The bold diagonal line in the matrix in Figure 28.5 shows the appropriate PEG for companies that are at steady state (value-added growth potential is exhausted) and do not pay dividends (if dividend paid add yield to expected EPS growth).

This matrix uses DCF concepts to prove that PEGs less than 1 are not necessarily attractive and PEGs above 1 or even 2 or 3 are not necessarily unattractive. Even for companies at steady state the appropriate PEG can differ significantly owing to varying cost of equity. If two companies were at steady state, but one had a higher cost of equity, it would deserve a lower PEG.

We advise against using PEG ratios to compare companies with differing cost of capital. Tech PEGs are not comparable to health care PEGs, and caution investors to be careful

Appropriate PEG for steady-state companies paying no dividend							
Cost of equity							
12%	1.08	0.99	0.93	0.89	0.87	0.87	**0.88**
11%	1.23	1.14	1.09	1.06	1.05	**1.07**	1.11
10%	1.45	1.36	1.32	1.31	**1.33**	1.40	1.52
9%	1.75	1.68	1.67	**1.71**	1.82	2.02	2.38
8%	2.22	2.20	**2.27**	2.47	2.86	3.64	5.56
7%	3.03	**3.17**	3.57	4.44	6.67	18.18	(16.67)
6%	**4.76**	5.71	8.33	22.22	(20.00)	(6.06)	(3.33)
LT EPS Growth	**6%**	**7%**	**8%**	**9%**	**10%**	**11%**	**12%**

Figure 28.5   No Linear relationship between PE and EPS growth

using PEGs in general, even with companies that have similar systematic risk, as the steep non-linear relationship between appropriate PEGs and cost of equity/growth often makes this valuation measure very misleading.

28.4   RETURN METRICS: ROIC VS. CFROI

Investors often ask us to explain the differences between the varying return on capital and economic profit measures used by other research firms. We tend to shy away from commenting specifically on the numerous branded metrics offered by others, as most are a variation or exactly the same thing as one of the generic metrics used by academics and practitioners. For instance, the well-known EVA® metric by Stern Stewart is the economic profit measure that has existed in concept since Adam Smith, but was first specified in the context of valuation by academics in the Edwards-Bell-Ohlson (EBO) valuation model.[1]

Differences between branded metrics typically exist only in application or in the estimates used within the calculation (such as invested capital) and usually not in the metric conceptually. In our view, the greatest value of any metric to investors is the aspect of the metric that represents a forecast. We believe it is in the quality of the forecasts that branded metrics will have varying degrees of success in predicting stock performance. If the metric is not based on forward-looking analysis then the metric should not be used for stock selection without making other explicit decisions. For instance, one must decide if a company's historical returns are indicative of its future returns on investment.

The two principles underlying the concept of economic profit are return and opportunity cost. The risk adjusted opportunity cost of capital is reflected in the WACC component of economic profit. WACC estimates are generally based on models such as CAPM. We will not address the opportunity cost component of economic profit here, but rather we will focus on the measurement of return.

---

[1] The expression "Edwards-Bell-Ohlson (EBO)" valuation model was first used in Bernard (1994). The EBO model is a residual income model measuring the value of the firm to equity holders in terms of current and forecast accounting numbers. Bernard (1994), pp. 1–3, Edwards and Bell (1961), Ohlson (1995).

28.5   ACCRUAL VS. CASH FLOW RETURN MEASURES

Conceptually there are two types of return on investment measures, accrual and cash flow based. The accrual-based return measures incorporate accrual accounting provisions like depreciation and amortization. These provisions allow for meaningful finite period profit measurements such as annual net income. Accrual-based return measures include return on assets (ROA = NI/assets), return on equity (ROE = NI/equity), return on invested capital (ROIC = NOPAT/Invested capital). ROIC represents unlevered returns.

Cash flow-based return measures do not incorporate accruals (although in practice they often include provisions other than D&A for retiree obligations, warranties, etc.). Instead cash flow return measures are based on multi-year cash flow forecasts. The key word being "flow" as this analysis requires multiple years of cash flow projections in order to calculate meaningful return measures. Single period cash flow measures can be distorted by lumpy capital expenditures, customer payments, working capital changes, deferred taxes, etc. Proper multi-period cash flow-based return measures include internal rate of return (IRR) and cash flow return on investment (CFROI). DCF and NPV analysis are also cash flow based.

28.6   ROIC VS. CFROI

In principle ROIC and CFROI are essentially the same and when used in practice to measure overall corporate returns they generally produce very similar results.[2] However, even when all other aspects of the two return calculations are consistent (such as properly measuring profit or cash flow to financial claimholders after accounting for stock options, pensions, etc. and consistently measuring invested capital) there will still be some minor difference between ROIC and CFROI. This difference is related to time value. Accrual accounting measures generally do not take time value into consideration. For instance, depreciation expense, which is a non-cash provision intended to represent the future cost of replenishing assets, is not time value adjusted. Therefore, depreciation expense and ROIC do not differentiate between expected cash expenditures for maintaining assets one year or 20 years away.

Consider the difference between two investments, as depicted above, both producing $100 of cash revenue annually. Both investments require a $1000 investment upfront for equipment. However, one investment requires $1000 to be invested in a piece of equipment that will never require any expenditure on repairs or maintenance, but in 20 years the equipment must be replaced entirely for another $1000. The second investment also requires $1000 upfront for equipment but this equipment will last forever, as long as it is maintained and certain components replaced yearly at a cost of $50 annually.

The annual depreciation on the assets underlying both of these investments will be $50. Thus, assuming the only expense is depreciation and no taxes, NOPAT will be $50 and the measured ROIC will be 5% on both investments. However, the IRR and true return on the first investment is higher than the second. ROIC assumes that the invested capital base is maintained annually. But if the invested capital base is not maintained annually then ROIC, as measured on the starting invested capital base, will understate the true return of the investment.

---

[2] The CFROI model is discussed by Larsen and Holland in Part III of this book.

Time	0	1	5	10	15	19	20	21 ...
Investment in asset requiring maintenance:								
Cash revenue		100	100	100	100	100	100	100
NOPAT		50	50	50	50	50	50	50
Invested capital	1000	1000	1000	1000	1000	1000	1000	1000
ROIC		**5.0%**	**5.0%**	**5.0%**	**5.0%**	**5.0%**	**5.0%**	**5.0%**
Depreciation		50	50	50	50	50	50	50
Capex	1000	50	50	50	50	50	50	50
Free cash flow	−1000	50	50	50	50	50	50	50
IRR/CFROI	**5.0%**							
Investment in asset requiring replacement:								
Cash revenue		100	100	100	100	100	100	100
NOPAT		50	50	50	50	50	50	50
Invested capital	1000	950	750	500	250	50	1000	950
ROIC		**5.0%**	**6.3%**	**9.1%**	**16.7%**	**50.0%**	**100.0%**	**5.0%**
Depreciation		50	50	50	50	50		50
Capex	1000						1000	
Free cash Flow	−1000	100	100	100	100	100	−900	100
IRR/CFROI	**7.75%**							

Figure 28.6 ROIC vs. CFROI

ROIC as measured on the invested capital base after the first year will suffer from a distortion causing it to overstate the true return of the overall investment because the net capital employed will decline owing to the delayed and sporadic capex. Some call this false signal of high returns as measured by ROIC after the first period when invested capital is temporarily depressed between large but infrequent maintenance capital expenditures a cheap assets trap.

CFROI's more precise consideration of time value makes it better for evaluating individual projects when detailed information on the timing of capital expenditures is known (ROIC's invested capital distortion will not occur at year 1). This is why IRR or NPV is the basis of most corporate budgeting decisions. However, ROIC is an effective measure for an investor assessing a company with numerous projects and depreciation expense that reasonably proxies annual maintenance capital expenditures. If a company has a history of significant stoppages in capex for many years with very large capital expenditures only every several years then CFROI may be better. But while a temporary reduction in net assets may overstate the true return in certain periods, this measure of net assets does not misrepresent the book value of the business at that point in time. Also, high ROIC caused by cheap assets only justifies a higher multiple on the cheap assets. Choosing to measure returns using ROIC or CFROI will not affect DCF valuation or UBS VCAM valuation.

Although ROIC may suffer from temporary distortions, CFROI calculations have implementation drawbacks. CFROI is a cumbersome multi-year IRR calculation based on gross corporate assets (before accumulated D&A) and forecasted gross cash flow (before D&A expense), thus the calculation requires an assumed life for the gross corporate assets. This assumption is typically estimated by dividing gross assets by the accounting depreciation expense. CFROI/WACC determined EV/IC multiples must still be based on net assets.

We note that the example in Figure 28.6 is extreme. If the capex surge described above for the investment without any annual maintenance expenditures until the asset is completely replaced was reduced from 20 years to 5 years, still an uncommonly large surge for a company overall, the difference between ROIC and CFROI in year 1 is less than 50 basis points and there is next to no difference between CFROI and the average ROIC measured over the 5 years.

ROIC and CFROI are not the most important single period performance measures. Economic profit is the most important single period performance measure, whether that be: (CFROI–WACC) * IC or (ROIC–WACC) * IC. Only economic profit accounts for both the return and the size of the investment. The larger a company becomes the more difficult it is to earn a return above the cost of capital. It is incorrect to attempt to standardize economic profitability by looking at only return in excess of the cost of capital.

In our view too much effort has been placed by some on trying to perfect the return on capital and economic profit measures and not enough effort placed on forecasting or assessing a company's potential to generate economic profit growth. It is the ability to generate economic profit growth, regardless of current return and economic profit levels, that justifies placing a higher multiple on company earnings or cash flows. Similarly, it is the ability to generate economic profit growth that justifies a multiple on invested capital greater than that of the company's return to its cost of capital ratio (ROIC/WACC).

28.7   ADJUSTING INVESTED CAPITAL IMPORTANT, BUT NOT FOR EGQ

A good adjusted invested capital base estimate, adjusted for the numerous historical distortions stemming from inflation and accounting issues, is required to understand how much of a company's profits are truly economic profits. It is also important for understanding how much of the company's current total market value is supported by its assets, as opposed to current and future nominal economic profits.

However, an accurate invested capital base estimate is not needed to imply how much of a company's current market value is attributed to the company's incremental economic profits or value-added growth potential. Although both are important, it is useful to distinguish between market expectations for future economic profits and economic profit growth when assessing observed values.

Just as the portion of an observed EV/IC multiple greater than the ROIC/WACC ratio is attributable to expected economic profit growth, so is the portion of an observed EV greater than NOPAT/WACC or the proportion of the EV/NOPAT multiple greater than 1/WACC. Thus, market expectation for economic growth can be revealed without invested capital base estimates. Below are the top 10 most important invested capital base adjustments for historical ROIC and EP Analysis:

(1) Add back all accumulated goodwill amortization, all after-tax asset write-downs/impairments, all after-tax losses on asset sales (net of gains).
(2) Add back all after-tax restructuring and other one-time special charges.
(3) Adjust for historical acquisitions accounted for under the pooling method.
(4) Adjust for the cumulative effect of historical inflation on asset book values.
(5) Capitalize operating leases (affects ROIC but not economic profit).
(6) Capitalize expensed investments, such as portions of R&D and marketing.
(7) Add historical operating losses in order to capitalize as start-up investments.
(8) Adjust pension and other post employment benefit accounts.

(9) Ensure that depreciation expense adequately reflects maintenance capex.

(10) Deduct non-operating income producing assets, like excess cash/corporate assets.

Be sure to adjust NOPAT for any unrecognized employee stock option expense, but no historical invested capital-based adjustment is required for stock options. The UBS Valuation and Accounting team has published numerous detailed reports on the economics and accounting of employee stock options.

The UBS Economic Profitability of Invested Capital (EPIC) model has historical return on capital and economic profit analysis for all S&P 500 companies with the above and other recommend adjustments to company reported financial statements. This model is available to UBS clients upon request. Please contact the UBS Valuation and Accounting team for access to the UBS VCAM or UBS EPIC models.

References

Bell, F.W. (1974), The relation of the structure of common stock prices to historical, expectational and industrial variables, *Journal of Finance*, 29, 187–197.

Bernard, V.L. (1994), Accounting-based valuation methods, determinants of market-to-book ratios, and implications for financial statement analysis, Working Paper, Michigan Business School, January.

Bianco, D., and Burkett, A.H. (2006), UBS value creation analysis model, regression-based valuation, UBS Investment Research, Research Report, 18 August.

Bianco, D., Cooper, S., and Burkett, A.H. (2004), Value creation analysis model VCAM: a new analytical tool, UBS Investment Research, Research Report, 5 March.

Bower, D., and Bower, R. (1970), Test of a stock valuation model, *Journal of Finance*, 25, 483–492.

Edwards, E.O., and Bell, P.W. (1961), *The Theory and Measurement of Business Income*, University of California Press.

Malkiel, B., and Cragg, J. (1970), Expectations and the structure of share prices, *American Economic Review*, 60, 601–617.

Ohlson, J. (1995), Earnings, book values and dividends in security valuation, *Contemporary Accounting Research* 11, 661–687.

Sharpe, W.F., and Alexander, G.J. (1990), *Investments*, Fourth Edition, Prentice Hall.

Whitbeck, V., and Kisor, M. (1963), A new tool in investment decision making, *Financial Analysts Journal*, 19, 55–62.

Part VI
Leverage Buyout (LBO) Models[1]

Jan Viebig[2], Daniel Stillit[3] and Thorsten Poddig[4]

[1] DWS Investment GmbH, © 2008 Jan Viebig. UBS AG & UBS Securities LLC, © 2008 UBS. All rights reserved.
[2] Managing Director, DWS Investment GmbH.
[3] Managing Director, Restructuring/Special Situations Research, Equities, UBS Investment Bank.
[4] Professor of Finance, University of Bremen.

29

Introduction

The coffers of private equity firms are flush with cash. In 2006, private equity funds had raised over USD 215 billion in the United States alone from pension funds, wealthy individuals and other qualified investors.[1] 2007 saw a number of record breaking deals. Fueled by significant amounts of "dry powder", private equity firms such as The Blackstone Group, Kohlberg Kravis Roberts & Co., TPG and The Carlyle Group will likely undertake more and increasingly larger leverage buyout (LBO).

Investors of publicly listed companies can benefit from leveraged buyouts as private equity investors typically pay a control premium when they take a public company private. Many leading investors and investment banks have developed LBO models to screen for potential LBO candidates. Financial sponsors use similar LBO models when analyzing potential leveraged buyouts. In this part of the book, we describe the methodology and the mechanics of LBO models developed by leading investment banks such as Deutsche Bank, Goldman Sachs, Credit Suisse, Morgan Stanley and UBS.[2]

In the previous parts of this book we discussed discounted cash flow models which value companies from the perspective of investors that do not seek to gain control of a company. Unlike DCF models, LBO models value companies from the perspective of a private equity investor who recapitalizes the financial structure of a company and restructures operations to enhance profitability and capital efficiency. Used in combination, DCF models and LBO models might give a more complete view how companies are valued by different groups of potential buyers. LBO models reveal that the value of controlling a company can be substantial from the perspective of a financial investor.

In Chapter 30, we explain the deal mechanics of leveraged buyout transactions. In Chapters 31 and 32, the structure of and the basic assumptions behind LBO models are discussed. Using Continental AG as a practical example, we demonstrate in Chapter 33 how financial analysts at UBS Investment Research assess LBO candidates in practice. Chapter 34 concludes with a word of caution.

---

[1] Lehman Brothers (2007), p. 2.

[2] Deutsche Bank (2007), Goldman Sachs (2007), Credit Suisse (2007a), Credit Suisse (2007b), Morgan Stanley (2003), UBS (2006). Financial analysts value LBO candidates from the perspective of a private equity investor who tries to gain control of a company. The structures of LBO models used by financial analysts and private equity investors are therefore similar, if not identical. However, the knowledge base of a financial analyst not directly involved in an LBO deal is usually less far-reaching than that of the financial sponsor planning a concrete deal. LBO models used by financial sponsors are typically more detailed.

30

Leveraged Buyouts

A leverage buyout (LBO) is an acquisition of a target company which is predominantly financed by debt. The purpose of an LBO is to gain control of a target company without committing a large amount of equity capital. The equity capital is usually provided by private equity funds. The debt capital employed usually consists of a combination of senior debt in the form of bank loans, high yield debt ("junk bonds"), and mezzanine debt. The use of financial leverage allows equity investors to earn higher returns on equity but also makes the transaction more risky. The assets of acquired companies are usually used as collateral and their cash flows repay debt. Private equity investors expect their capital to be committed to the company only for a limited period of time, typically three to five years. Often, they realize high rates of return on their capital when they sell the acquired company to new investors either in one transaction or in stages. Given the leverage, a private equity sponsor will attempt to reduce overall risk by lowering operating risk. UBS estimates that 31% of LBO exits over the period 2003 to August 2006 were by way of initial public offering (IPO), as compared with 26% via a secondary buyout and 44% via a sale to a trade (corporate) buyer.

Figure 30.1 explains the basic principles of an LBO deal. Let us assume that a private equity fund buys company A for an enterprise value, or EV, of EUR 20 billion at the end of 2007. The company generated EUR 2.5 billion in earnings before interest, taxes, depreciation and amortization (EBITDA) and EUR 1 billion in free cash flow in 2007. The deal implies a trailing EV/EBITDA ratio of 8× (EUR 20 billion/EUR 2.5 billion). The multiple is usually referred to as "entry multiple". If the deal is financed with 30% equity and 70% debt, the private equity fund has to provide EUR 6 billion in cash to gain control of the company. For simplicity, we ignore fees paid to bankers and lawyers. We also assume that company A's assets are used as collateral for the debt.

On completion of the acquisition, the private equity investor may install a new management team, and set to work on the implementation of a 100-day plan. Key components of the plan will be expense reduction and cash flow generation. As a result of these and other restructuring efforts, assume that EBITDA increases by 12.5% per annum in each of the next four years. In 2011 the company generates EUR 4.0 billion in EBITDA (EUR 2.5 billion * 1.125^4). After investing in fixed assets and working capital, and meeting its interest obligations, the company produces each year EUR 1 billion in free cash flow which is used completely to pay down debt, i.e. no dividends are paid to the private equity investor in the interim period 2008–2011. At the end of 2011 the debt is reduced to EUR 10 billion (EUR 14 billion initial debt −4* EUR 1 billion free cash flow).

Then comes the exit. Assume that after a lengthy process of pursuing a trade sale and/or IPO (sellers increasingly pursue both via a dual-track process for as long as is commercially feasible), all the shares of company A are sold in an initial public offer to institutional and retail investors at the end of 2011. In the IPO, company A is valued at an enterprise value of EUR 32 billion, again equivalent to an EV/EBITDA multiple of 8× (EUR 4.0 billion *

$8 = $ EUR 32 billion) and a market capitalization of EUR 22 billion after subtracting EUR 10 billion in debt. We assumed that the "entry multiple" and the "exit multiple" are equal. Figure 30.1 illustrates our example.

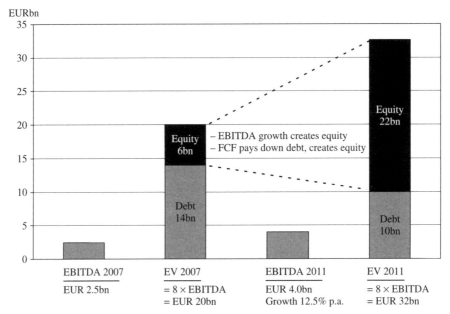

Figure 30.1   LBOs: the basic principle

The equity capital increases from EUR 6 billion in 2007 to EUR 22 billion in 2011 which translates into an internal rate of return of 38.4% (EUR 6 billion $*1.384^4 = $ EUR 22 billion). Some private equity houses also assess their return using a "money multiple" or "return multiple". This is simply the total amount(s) received from the investment divided by the amount(s) invested. No adjustment is made for time value. In our simplified example, the money multiple is $3.7\times$ (EUR 22 billion/EUR 6 billion).

The beneficiaries of a successful LBO deal are primarily the investors of the private equity fund and the private equity firm. Private equity funds are usually organized as limited partnerships which are controlled by a private equity firm. The investors in the fund are limited partners benefiting from the fund's performance. The private equity firm acts as general partner, makes all investment decisions and receives a management fee (typically 1% to 2% of assets under management) and a "carried interest" (typically 20% of all profits above a specified hurdle rate). The beneficiaries of the deal also include the banks providing loans and the investment banks charging fees in M&A transactions. The example illustrates that private equity firms can create value for their investors (and themselves) mainly in three ways:[1]

(1) *Financial restructuring*: Private equity firms usually employ a significant amount of borrowed money and debt to finance an LBO transaction in order to enhance (leverage)

---

[1] The sources of value creation in LBOs are discussed in detail in Loos (2005).

the expected return on equity. The presence of debt lowers the overall cost of capital and can act to condition management to maximize free cash flow generation over its life.

(2) *Operational restructuring*: After an acquisition, private equity firms usually establish new management and restructure operations to enhance operating earnings and cash flows. Higher free cash flows (FCF) can be used to pay down debt or to pay dividends. Paying down debt increases the equity stake of the new owners. Higher EBITDA levels usually translate into higher exit values.

(3) *Multiple expansion*: Ideally, a target company is bought at a low entry multiple and sold at a higher exit multiple. In the example above, we assumed no multiple expansion. One of the risks in an LBO transaction is the uncertainty of the exit price. The exit price depends on the overall conditions of financial markets at the exit date and the ability of the private equity firm to negotiate and execute an exit.

Table 30.1 summarizes the key criteria of an ideal LBO target from the perspective of a private equity firm.

Table 30.1 Criteria of an ideal LBO target (Source: KKR/Morgan Stanley)[2]

Financial criteria	Business criteria
(1) A history of demonstrated profitability and the ability to maintain above average profit margins [. . .]	(1) A strong management team.
(2) Strong, predictable cash flows to service the financing costs related to the acquisitions.	(2) Products with well-known brand names and a strong market position.
(3) Readily separable assets or businesses which could be available for sale, if necessary.	(3) Status as a low cost producer within an industry, thereby creating a competitive advantage.
	(4) Potential for real growth in the future.
	(5) Not subject to prolonged cyclical swings in profitability.
	(6) Products which are not subject to rapid technological change.

For a long time, the acquisition of the food and tobacco giant RJR Nabisco was the biggest leverage buyout by a private equity firm. After a bidding war Kohlberg Kravis Roberts & Co. (KKR) agreed to a record USD 25 billion buyout and took RJR Nabisco private in the late 1980s. The battle for control of RJR Nabisco during October and November 1988 was later immortalized in the bestselling book *Barbarians at the Gate* by two reporters of the *Wall Street Journal*.[3] Since 2006 the record has been broken several times. Bain Capital, KKR and Merrill Lynch paid USD 21 billion and assumed USD 12 billion in debt to gain control of the hospital operator Hospital Corporation of America (HCA) in a club deal in

---

[2] Kohlberg Kravis Roberts & Co. (1989), p. 66.
[3] Burrough and Helyar (2004).

July 2006.[4] Also in 2006, Blackstone Group announced a leveraged buyout of Equity Office Properties for a total value of USD 34 billion including net debt.

Table 30.2 All-time largest LBO deals–global (Source: Bloomberg)[5]

Announce date	Target name	Acquirer name	Announced total value (USD mil.)
2/26/2007	TXU CORP	MULTIPLE ACQUIRERS	43 218
11/20/2006	EQUITY OFFICE PROPERTIES	BLACKSTONE GROUP	34 102
7/24/2006	HCA INC	MULTIPLE ACQUIRERS	32 193
10/19/1988	RJR NABISCO INC	KOHLBERG KRAVIS ROBERTS & CO	30 062
4/2/2007	FIRST DATA CORP	KOHLBERG KRAVIS ROBERTS & CO	27 497

On Monday, February 26, 2007, TXU Corp. confirmed in a press release that an investor group led by KKR and Texas Pacific Group (TPG) agreed to acquire the Dallas-based energy group for a total value (including net debt) of USD 43 billion. The acquisition of TXU Corp. marks a new height in a recent wave of leveraged buyouts. Under the terms of the merger agreement, the financial investors offered existing shareholders USD 69.25 per share which represents a 25% premium to the average closing share price over the 20 days ending February 22, 2007.[6] The acquisition of TXU Corp. would be the largest leveraged buyout in history if completed.

In the next chapter we will explain the structure of LBO models which can help investors to identify future LBO candidates.

---

[4] In a "club deal", several financial investors team up to acquire a target company. The teaming of private equity investors enables them to conduct large takeovers while sharing risk and reward.

[5] Bloomberg defines the "Announced Total Value" as ". . . the total dollar value of the entire offer, which includes all disclosed payment types (cash, stock, net-debt, or a combination). Bloomberg M&A derives Announced Total Values by using 20-day trading average prior to announcement date for target and acquirer as the basis of all calculations. In a cash deal offer is multiplied by the number of shares outstanding to arrive at the total value (the net-debt is also applied to this value). In a stock offer, we take the offer ratio and multiply it by the 20-day average of the acquirer stock to arrive at a cash value of the offer. The cash offer is multiplied by the shares outstanding to arrive at the total value (debt assumption is added as well)" (Bloomberg M&A term definitions). Data obtained from Bloomberg on April 9, 2007.

[6] The Wall Street Journal Online (2007b).

31

IRRs and the Structure of LBO Models

In Part I, we have argued that the fundamental value of each investment is the present value of its expected, future cash flows discounted at an appropriate risk-adjusted rate. Discounted cash flow models are based on the premise that a company will employ its assets to generate cash flows and will continue its operations. The going concern assumption does not hold if a company is bought and restructured by a strategic or financial investor. Financial investors usually pay a "control premium" to gain control of a target company. After the acquisition, they typically establish new management, restructure operations, divest non-core assets and undertake a variety of other measures to increase the efficiency of the acquired company.

LBO models try to capture the effects of a potential recapitalization and a subsequent operational restructuring of a company. Deutsche Bank, UBS, Goldman Sachs, Credit Suisse and Morgan Stanley have made the frameworks of and the assumptions behind their LBO models more or less transparent to investors.[1] The structure of their models is very similar. The purpose of LBO models is to identify potential LBO candidates. In all of these models, the attractiveness of a potential LBO candidate is quantified by its internal rate of return (IRR). Financial analysts at Goldman Sachs, for example, advise their clients explicitly to buy shares of potential LBO candidates: "Equity investors can profit by buying shares of companies likely to receive a buyout offer. The median stock in our 937 company coverage universe has a five-year implied internal rate of return (IRR) of 10.6%. We recommend investors buy 117 companies with 20% + implied IRRs (. . .). For a more focused approach, buy the 40 companies with the highest implied IRRs . . . "[2] UBS' Restructuring/M&A Situations group is similarly focused on identifying stocks with private equity potential and a take-out premium. In Chapter 33, an IRR-based LBO model to measure the attractiveness of a potential LBO developed by UBS Restructuring/M&A Situations Research is discussed in detail.

From a modeling perspective, a leveraged buyout is a very simple transaction: A private equity firm or another financial investor agrees to pay a transaction price in $t = 0$ to gain control of a company. The transaction price is typically predominantly financed by debt and borrowed money D_0. Financial investors usually commit only a small amount of equity E_0 in $t = 0$ to finance the deal. The initial equity investment is a negative cash (out)flow CF_0 from the perspective of the financial investor. After acquiring the company, the financial investor usually sells non-core assets to raise cash and restructures operations to increase operational cash flows. Often the private equity firm forces the acquired company to pay out excess cash and cash equivalents not needed for day-to-day operations. The financial investor receives positive cash flows CF_t if the acquired company pays dividends or undertakes a "dividend recap" (a debt-financed super-dividend) in the interim period. For simplicity, financial analysts usually assume that free cash flows after investing of the releveraged

---

[1] Deutsche Bank (2007), UBS (2006), Goldman Sachs (2007), Credit Suisse (2007a, 2007b), Morgan Stanley (2003).
[2] Goldman Sachs (2007), p. 3.

company are completely used to pay down debt and that no dividends are paid in the interim period $t = 1, \ldots, T$.[3] Proceeds from disposals may be modeled as being used to pay down debt or be distributed in alternative proportions to the debt providers and buy-out sponsors (equity providers).

After T years, financial investors usually exit their investments by selling the acquired company to new investors and hence receive a final cash flow CF_T. To simplify matters, it is usually assumed that the entire business is sold in T. In practice, financial investors often sell their equity stakes in the business in several steps over time. The equity capital which belongs to the financial investor equals the enterprise value EV_T less (net) debt D_T in period T. The debt in period T is simply the difference between the initial debt D_0 and the sum of all free cash flows used to pay down debt in the interim period. The ability of a company to pay down debt depends on its ability to generate free cash flows. In Part I of this book we explained that free cash flows are a function of sales, EBIT margins, tax rates, capital expenditures and change in net working capital. The success of an LBO depends on the ability of management to restructure operations in order to enhance its profitability and capital efficiency. Financial analysts can incorporate expected profitability and efficiency gains into an LBO model, when modeling sales, EBIT margins and investment needs.

Figure 31.1 illustrates the cash flow stream from the perspective of a private equity investor.

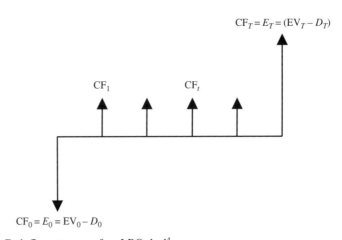

Figure 31.1 Cash flow streams of an LBO deal[4]

We assumed that private equity investors initially pay a cash flow CF_0, receive possible cash flows CF_t in the form of dividends during the interim period and a final cash flow CF_T when they exit their investment. Given these assumptions, they can expect to make an internal rate of return, or IRR, which can be obtained by solving the following net present value (NPV) equation which is set to zero for the internal rate of return:

---

[3] Financial analysts usually implicitly assume that the assets of the acquired company are used as collateral for the debt used to finance the acquisition price and that the cash flows generated by the acquired and releveraged company are used to pay down debt. Financial analysts usually do not assume that the acquired company is merged with another company when they search for potential LBO candidates.

[4] Please note that CF_0 represents a negative number. The initial investment is a cash outflow from the perspective of the private equity investor.

$$\text{NPV} = \text{CF}_0 + \frac{\text{CF}_1}{(1+\text{IRR})} + \frac{\text{CF}_2}{(1+\text{IRR})^2} + \cdots + \frac{\text{CF}_t}{(1+\text{IRR})^t} + \cdots + \frac{\text{CF}_T}{(1+\text{IRR})^T} = 0$$

Excel users can solve for the internal rate of return by using the Excel Solver or the function IRR. In our example above, an initial cash flow of minus EUR 6 billion in 2007, zero cash flows in the years 2008–2010 and a final cash flow of EUR 22 billion in 2011 were used to calculate an IRR of 38.4%. Figure 31.2 illustrates that the IRR is simply the discount rate at which the net present value equals zero.

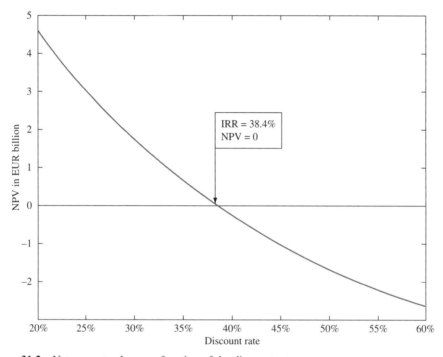

Figure 31.2   Net present value as a function of the discount rate

From a theoretical perspective, the use of IRRs to measure the attractiveness of an LBO has several drawbacks:[5]

Drawback 1: The IRR often materially overestimates the attractiveness of an LBO. When calculating IRRs, financial analysts implicitly assume that interim cash flows can be reinvested at the IRR. In reality, private equity investors can only reinvest interim cash flows at the IRR if equally attractive investment opportunities are available. If the calculated IRR is higher than the true rate at which private investors can reinvest interim cash flows, the IRR overestimates the attractiveness of an LBO. The overestimation can be material (a) if the true reinvestment rate is significantly lower than the IRR and (b) if cash flows are

---

[5] Brealey *et al.* (2006), pp. 91–99.

distributed to private equity investors at the beginning of the interim period (in which case the true reinvestment rate is overestimated for a longer period of time). By definition, the opportunity cost of capital – not the IRR – is the expected rate of return which investors can achieve elsewhere on a comparable investment with the same characteristics. Therefore, the opportunity cost of capital and not the IRR is the correct reinvestment rate from a theoretical perspective.

Drawback 2: Comparing IRRs of different LBOs ignores the fact that buyout companies usually do not bear the same risk. Only very few private equity investors would seriously argue that two LBOs with the same IRR are equally attractive if they are differently risky. Private equity investors usually prefer LBO candidates that have unused debt capacity and generate stable and predictable cash flows. Even if IRRs are identical, the LBO of a utility company with stable, predictable cash flows and the LBO of a highly cyclical technology company with unstable, unpredictable cash flows are not equally attractive, simply, because the risk of the two deals is different. Logically, the IRR of a potential LBO deal should be compared with its opportunity cost of capital (which includes a risk premium) instead of the IRR of other LBO deals which usually do not bear the same risk.

Drawback 3: There can be many solutions when solving the NPV equation for the IRR. The internal rate of return is the rate of discount at which the net present value of a stream of cash flows is zero. Whenever the expected cash flows change sign, many internal rates of return can exist. Financial analysts should be aware of the problem of multiple solutions when calculating IRRs and always ask if possible solutions make economic sense.

Financial analysts usually avoid drawbacks (1) and (3) by assuming that there are only two cash flows at the beginning and the end of the interim period and that no dividends are paid to the new owners during the interim period. There are mainly two reasons why practitioners use LBO models based on IRR calculations instead of DCF models when evaluating potential LBO deals:

(1) *The calculation and interpretation of IRRs is highly intuitive.* Well-constructed LBO models based on IRRs realistically reflect the mechanics of a leveraged buyout transaction.
(2) *LBO models based on IRRs do not require financial analysts to estimate the effect of financial leverage on the equity beta and the cost of equity.* From a modeling perspective, an LBO is first and foremost a recapitalization of a potential acquisition target with unused debt capacity. When constructing DCF models, financial analysts usually apply the CAPM to estimate the cost of equity. In Part I of this book we explained that the equity beta and the cost of equity increase when more debt is used to finance a business. In a DCF framework, the effect of financial leverage on the cost of equity can be estimated in three steps. First, the unleveraged equity beta β_{unl} has to be calculated to remove the effect of the historical debt to equity ratio $(D/E)_{hist}$ on the current equity beta β_{curr}:[6]

$$\beta_{unlev} = \frac{\beta_{curr}}{\left[1 + (1 - \tau)\left(\frac{D}{E}\right)_{hist}\right]}$$

---

[6] Damodaran (2005b), pp. 339–395.

The term τ represents the tax rate. Applying the debt to equity ratio after releveraging the financial structure, or $(D/E)_{rel}$, financial analysts can calculate the releveraged equity beta β_{rel}:

$$\beta_{rel} = \beta_{unlev} \times \left[1 + (1 - \tau) \left(\frac{D}{E} \right)_{rel} \right]$$

Assuming that the CAPM holds, the cost of equity i_E can be estimated by inserting the releveraged beta in the CAPM equation:

$$i_E = r_f + \beta_{rel} \times \pi$$

The terms r_f and π represent the risk-free rate and the market risk premium, respectively. The process of releveraging betas to incorporate the effect of financial leverage into a DCF model has a material drawback: From a theoretical perspective it is more than questionable if releveraged betas are well suited to calculate the risk premium and the opportunity cost of capital required by private equity investors. The CAPM assumes that investors are only rewarded for market risk which cannot be eliminated by diversification. Private equity investors, however, will most likely ask for additional risk premia to compensate for the liquidity risk, the bankruptcy risk and other deal specific risks involved in LBO transactions. LBO models do not require financial analysts to estimate risk premia and costs of equity. Using LBO models based on IRRs avoids the time-consuming process of releveraging equity betas. In an LBO model, the attractiveness of a leveraged buyout is usually measured by a single measure: its internal rate of return. As discussed earlier, some private equity houses will also focus on an additional measure: the money multiple, or the equity value and flows received over the lifetime of the deal divided by the equity capital invested over the lifetime. Note that this metric is unadjusted for time value.

32

Assumptions of LBO Models

Private equity firms and investment banks advising them on a deal use LBO models to analyze the attractiveness of leveraged buyouts. Financial analysts use similar models to screen for potential LBO candidates. Valuation models are well constructed if they are simple and realistic and help investors to gain insights. Like any other model, LBO models are based on simplifying assumptions. To model the attractiveness of a potential LBO transaction several assumptions must be made:

(1) *Transaction value and control premium:* Private equity firms seeking to acquire attractive target companies compete with other financial and strategic investors. Acquiring firms usually have to pay a premium above the current market price to gain control of a target company. Table 32.1 reflects the deal premia paid in the largest global M&A deals in history.

An acquiring firm can offer cash, stock, debt or a combination of financial instruments to acquire a target company from selling shareholders. On Monday, January 10, 2000, America Online (AOL) announced that it was buying Time Warner. At the time, AOL, which was later renamed Time Warner Inc., had a market capitalization of about USD 164 billion, while Time Warner had a market capitalization of just USD 83 billion. AOL offered 1.5 own shares for each share of Time Warner (Historic TW INC) which equated to a "deal premium" of 81.13% according to Bloomberg.[1] More recently the German sports car manufacturer Porsche AG offered EUR 100.92 for each common share and EUR 65.45 for each preferred share of Volkswagen AG. The mandatory offer was triggered when Porsche raised its stake in Volkswagen AG to 30.94%. Porsche's bid was 16% below the market value on March 23, 2007, the day prior to the announcement.[2] The two examples illustrate that the control premium which a potential acquirer offers can vary dramatically. One key area of difference in buyouts versus industrial deals such as the two examples is that the financial buyer's valuation is referenced to operating uplift and the impact of leverage and is unlikely to be able to rely on industrial synergies. Table 32.2 reflects the deal premia of the largest private equity deals announced in the first quarter of 2007.

Based on 61 private equity deals announced in the first quarter of 2007 for which Bloomberg provided the data field "Deal Premium", we calculated an average deal premium of 18.38% with a standard deviation of 13.88%. This is important; the output of LBO models is highly sensitive to assumed transaction prices. Financial analysts usually model the expected transaction value paid in an LBO by adding (net) debt, D_0, to the

---

[1] The acquisition of Time Warner by America Online is vividly narrated in Munk (2004).
[2] Bloomberg (2007a).

Table 32.1 All time largest M&A deals – global (Source: Bloomberg)[3]

	Announce Date	Target Name	Acquirer Name	Announced Total Value (mil.)	Payment Type	Deal Premium in %
1	1/10/00	HISTORIC TW INC	TIME WARNER INC	186 236	Stock	81.13
2	11/14/99	VODAFONE HOLDING GMBH	VODAFONE GROUP PLC	185 066	Stock and Debt	104.63
3	11/4/99	WARNER-LAMBERT CO	PFIZER INC	87 319	Stock	30.18
4	3/26/07	VOLKSWAGEN AG	PORSCHE AG-PFD	85 750	Cash	0.16
5	3/5/06	BELLSOUTH CORP	AT&T INC	83 105	Stock	19.45
6	12/1/98	MOBIL CORP	EXXON MOBIL CORP	80 338	Stock	26.23
7	10/28/04	SHELL TRANSPRT&TRADNG	ROYAL DUTCH SHELL	80 138	Stock	
8	7/9/01	COMCAST CABLE COMM	COMCAST CORP-CL A	76 057	Stock	
9	1/21/06	ENDESA SA	E.ON AG	75 404	Cash	79.26
10	1/26/04	AVENTIS SA	SANOFI-AVENTIS	72 704	Cash and Stock	21.68
11	1/17/00	SMITHKLINE BEECHAM PLC	GLAXOSMITHKLINE PLC	72 445	Stock	−0.61
12	7/28/98	GTE CORP	VERIZON COMMUNICATIONS	71 127	Stock	3.84
13	4/6/98	CITICORP	CITIGROUP INC	69 892	Stock	8.06
14	5/11/98	AMERITECH CORP/DEL	AT&T INC	68 219	Stock	23.05
15	7/15/02	PHARMACIA CORP	PFIZER INC	64 264	Stock	31.51
16	1/31/07	KRAFT FOODS INC-A	SHAREHOLDERS	62 014		
17	4/13/98	BANKAMERICA CORP (OLD)	BANK OF AMERICA CORP	57 466	Stock	−2.61
18	1/5/99	VODAFONE AMERICAS ASIA INC	VODAFONE GROUP PLC	57 355	Cash and Stock	38.97
19	1/28/05	GILLETTE COMPANY	PROCTER & GAMBLE CO	57 279	Stock	20.67
20	4/11/00	NORTEL NETWORKS CORP	SHAREHOLDERS	56 029		
21	8/11/98	AMOCO CORP	BP PLC	55 947	Stock	32.17
22	2/27/06	SUEZ SA	GAZ DE FRANCE	55 754	Stock	−11.49
23	4/22/99	COMCAST MO GROUP INC	AT&T CORP	55 422	Cash, Stock and Debt	24.25
24	1/14/04	BANK ONE CORP	JPMORGAN CHASE & CO	55 066	Stock	8.28
25	7/5/99	ELF AQUITAINE	TOTAL SA	52 297	Stock	29.98

[3] The initial "Deal Premium" is "…calculated based off the 20-day trading average price prior to the announcement date" (Bloomberg M&A term definitions). Data obtained from Bloomberg on March 31, 2007.

Table 32.2 Private Equity Deals in the First Quarter of 2007 – Deal Premium (Source: Bloomberg)[4]

	Announce Date	Target Name	Acquirer Name	Announced Total Value (mil.)	Deal Premium in %
1	2/26/07	TXU CORP	MULTIPLE ACQUIRERS	43 218	23.89
2	3/9/07	ALLIANCE BOOTS PLC	KOHLBERG KRAVIS ROBERTS & CO	21 500	29.37
3	3/20/07	AFFILIATED COMPUTER SVCS	CERBERUS CAPITAL MANAGEMENT	8244	14.07
4	3/12/07	DOLLAR GENERAL CORP	KOHLBERG KRAVIS ROBERTS & CO	7321	28.33
5	3/19/07	SERVICEMASTER COMPANY	CLAYTON DUBILIER & RICE	5071	15.71
6	1/26/07	MOELNLYCKE HEALTH CARE AB	MULTIPLE ACQUIRERS	3680	
7	2/8/07	EDGARS CONSOLIDATED	BAIN CAPITAL LLC	3673	17.38
8	1/29/07	LAUREATE EDUCATION INC	MULTIPLE ACQUIRERS	3402	18.43
9	3/13/07	SPIRIT FINANCE CORP	REDFORD HOLDCO LLC	3312	11.62
10	3/23/07	ISTA	CHARTERHOUSE CAPITAL	3190	
11	3/20/07	CLAIRE'S STORES INC	APOLLO MANAGEMENT LP	2846	2.38
12	3/13/07	WCI COMMUNITIES INC	MULTIPLE ACQUIRERS	2845	2.94
13	2/12/07	PINNACLE FOODS GROUP INC	BLACKSTONE GROUP	2160	
14	3/12/07	VITUS WOHNIMMOBILIEN GMBH	MULTIPLE ACQUIRERS	2110	
15	3/5/07	TUSSAUDS GROUP	BLACKSTONE GROUP	1977	
16	1/25/07	APN NEWS & MEDIA LIMITED	MULTIPLE ACQUIRERS	1937	0.93
17	3/23/07	KRONOS INC	HELLMAN & FRIEDMAN	1726	33.50
18	3/20/07	EGL INC	APOLLO MANAGEMENT LP	1682	14.41
19	2/9/07	GNC PARENT CORP	MULTIPLE ACQUIRERS	1650	
20	2/26/07	HUB INTERNATIONAL LTD	MULTIPLE ACQUIRERS	1643	25.00

[4] Data obtained from Bloomberg on March 31, 2007.

product of the current market capitalization times one plus a historical deal premium, DP, offered or paid for a comparable peer group p of companies which recently received buyout bids. The following equation shows how analysts usually model the expected transaction or enterprise value, EV, of an LBO target j:

$$EV_{j,0} = \left(P_{j,0} \times S_{j,0}\right) \times \left(1 + DP_{p,hist}\right) + D_{j,0}$$

The terms P, S and D represent the current market price, the current number of shares outstanding and the current amount of debt and debt-deemed liabilities of a potential LBO candidate. Financial analysts usually multiply current earnings before interest, taxes, depreciation and amortization, or EBITDA, by a historical EBITDA multiple paid in recent LBO transactions to check if the assumed transaction price is realistic:

$$EV_{0,j} = EBITDA_{0,j} \times \left(\frac{EV}{EBITDA}\right)_{hist,p} = Rev_{0,j} \times \left(\frac{EBITDA}{Rev}\right)_{0,j} \times \left(\frac{EV}{EBITDA}\right)_{hist,p}$$

Typically 12 months' trailing revenues and EBITDA margins are used to calculate EBITDA. A potential LBO candidate and a peer group p of companies are usually only comparable if they operate in the same sector (and country) and have comparable EBITDA margins.

(2) *Financial leverage and cost of debt*: Private equity investors typically use a significant senior debt, 2nd lien debt, mezzanine debt and junk bonds to finance the transaction price. When modeling an LBO transaction, analysts have to make assumptions as to how much initial debt a possible LBO candidate can carry. Private equity firms usually look for companies with unused borrowing capacity and high, predictable and stable cash flows which can be used to pay down debt. The ability to generate stable cash flow and therefore the maximum leverage potential depends on a variety of business risk factors such as:

- Visibility and cyclicality of revenues.
- Degree of product and geographic diversification.
- Amount of operating leverage.
- Flexibility of capital expenditures.
- Market structure, e.g. concentration, barriers of entry.
- Regulatory risk.

Companies that operate in highly cyclical industries, for example, can usually carry less debt than companies that are less sensitive to economic cycles. To simplify matters, financial analysts usually apply financial ratios to determine the leverage potential of an LBO candidate. Analysts at Goldman Sachs, for example, use sector specific debt/EBITDA ratios to determine the initial debt level.[5] Their colleagues at Deutsche

---

[5] Goldman Sachs (GS) analyzed debt/EBITDA multiples of historical LBO deals and assigned for each sector a sector-specific debt/EBITDA multiple. The base case debt/EBITDA multiples for the GS sectors "food" and "steel", for example, are 6.5 and 4.5, respectively. The leverage potential for steel companies is usually lower than for food companies due to the higher sensitivity of the steel industry to economic cycles. In addition, analysts at GS cap debt at two times interest coverage or 80% enterprise value. Goldman Sachs (2007), pp. 21–26.

Bank apply interest coverage ratios to determine the maximum amount of debt a company can carry.[6] Analysts at Morgan Stanley simply assume as base case that private equity firms finance LBO transactions with 30% equity and 70% debt.[7] UBS uses sector specific debt/EBITDA multiples and interest coverage ratios but adjusted to allow for an acceptable long-term debt repayment schedule and deal size.[8] All three metrics are subject to flux and are market determined.

Different companies require different capital structures. There is not a single capital structure that fits for all leveraged buyouts.[9] Modeling an LBO, financial analysts have to formulate assumptions not only on the degree of leverage but also on the cost of debt. As the base case for its standardized LBO model, Goldman Sachs assumes that 60% of debt is bank debt at LIBOR plus 250 basis points, 30% senior debt at LIBOR plus 375 basis points and 10% subordinated debt at LIBOR plus 500 basis points.[10]

(3) *Operational assumptions*: ". . . 'Any fool can buy a company, just pay enough.' The hard and important part of our job was what we did with the company to create shareholder value once we acquired it. . . . " (Henry R. Kravis, co-founder of KKR).[12] After acquiring a target company, private equity investors typically establish new management, reduce wasteful expenditures, restructure operations, and divest non-core assets to enhance free cash flows. The success of a leveraged buyout depends to a large degree on the execution of the restructuring by management. Agency theory states that conflicts arise between the owners and the managers of a company as a consequence of diverting interests.[13] The problem is also known as "principal/agent problem". Financial sponsors usually try to align the interest of management with their own interests by granting equity, stock options and other incentive schemes. In LBO transactions sponsored by KKR, for example, management typically holds 10–20% of the company.[14] In Part I, we explained that free cash flows to the firm are a function of revenue growth, operating margins, tax rates, capital expenditures and change in net working capital. Free cash flows to the firm, or FCFF, can be defined as earnings before interest, taxes, depreciation and amortization, or EBITDA, minus cash taxes T, minus capital expenditures CAPEX and minus change in net working capital ΔNWC:

$$FCFF_t = EBITDA_t - T_t - CAPEX_t - \Delta NWC_t \pm Adj_t$$

$$= Rev_{t-1}(1 + g_t)\left(\frac{EBITDA}{Rev}\right)_t - T_t - CAPEX_t - \Delta NWC_t \pm Adj_t$$

Financial analysts usually formulate assumptions on revenue growth, or g, and EBITDA margins when modeling FCFF of a potential LBO candidate. Free cash flows after investing can be used to pay down debt or to pay dividends. The result of an LBO model is highly sensitive to expected top line growth, operating margins and investment needs.

---

[6] Deutsche Bank (2007), p. 12.
[7] Morgan Stanley (2003), p. 3.
[8] UBS (2006), p. 22.
[9] Kohlberg Kravis Roberts & Co. (1989), p. 65.
[10] Goldman Sachs (2007), pp. 24f.
[11] Credit Suisse (2007b), p. 5, Goldman Sachs (2007), pp. 24f.
[12] Kravis (2007).
[13] Loos (2005), pp. 17–19.
[14] Kohlberg Kravis Roberts & Co. (1989), p. 65.

After an acquisition, management usually tries to create shareholder value by a variety of actions such as:[15]

- Investments in new products and sales force to increase sales.
- Cost reductions, e.g. elimination of inefficiencies, reduction of overstaffed workforce, outsourcing, moving operations to countries with lower labor costs.
- Reduction of tax burden, e.g. moving operations to tax havens.
- Improvement of inventory and accounts receivable and payable management.
- Divestment or redeployment of poorly performing assets.
- Replacement of outdated equipment and labor by more efficient equipment.
- Reassessing capital expenditure plans and associated payoffs.
- Distribution of excess cash to the new owners.
- Generally setting more aggressive stretch-targets across the business through a management and governance structure that differs from that in the public market.

It is also worth mentioning that some of the debt, particularly the more senior debt, with it covenants will have some impact on how the business is managed. This may include cash flow covenants, restrictions on dividends and acquisitions.

When modeling an LBO, financial analysts have to make assumptions as to how profitable and how efficiently a company will be run after the acquisition.

(4) *Use of free cash flows and length of the interim period*: Critiques of leveraged buyouts often argue that private equity companies not only commit little capital and load up companies with massive amounts of debt but also milk them before they finally resell them to new investors. In fact private equity firms often receive dividends, management and transaction fees from their portfolio companies. Some financial sponsors will recapitalise an LBOd company, borrowing additional capital to pay dividends. For simplicity, most financial analysts assume that all free cash flows are used to pay down debt and that no dividends are paid to private equity investors in the interim period. At the exit date the amount of debt D_T equals the initial debt D_0 minus the sum of all cash used for debt repayment, or DR:

$$D_T = D_0 - \sum_{t=1}^{T} \mathrm{DR}_t$$

Paying down debt increases the equity stake of the financial sponsor in the business. Table 32.3 demonstrates how financial analysts usually model debt outstanding. In our simplified example we assumed that total debt consists entirely of senior debt. Of course, in reality buyouts are not completely financed with senior debt, but the amount of senior debt to subordinated debt to finance buyouts has increased considerably in the last few years. Today, an increasing amount of so-called "second lien" loans is used to fund leveraged buyouts which are collateralized in the form of tangible or intangible assets. In case of default, second lien holders are second in line to recover capital from a forced asset sale, behind "first lien" holders but before unsecured bond holders. The template in Table 32.3 clarifies that private equity investors can choose from a variety of different

---

[15] Damodaran (2005a), pp. 10–16.

Table 32.3 Debt outstanding and debt repayment – template

[in EUR million]	Year 0	Year 1	Year 2	Year 3	Year 4	Year 5	Year 6	Year 7	Year 8	Year 9	Year 10
Senior debt A outstanding	14 000	13 000	12 000	11 000	10 000	9000	8000	7000	6000	5000	4000
Senior debt A repayment		–1000	–1000	–1000	–1000	–1000	–1000	–1000	–1000	–1000	–1000
Senior debt B											
Senior debt C											
Total senior debt	**14 000**	**13 000**	**12 000**	**11 000**	**10 000**	**9000**	**8000**	**7000**	**6000**	**5000**	**4000**
Mezzanine											
High yield											
Total debt	**14 000**	**13 000**	**12 000**	**11 000**	**10 000**	**9000**	**8000**	**7000**	**6000**	**5000**	**4000**
PIK											
Total debt plus PIK	**14 000**	**13 000**	**12 000**	**11 000**	**10 000**	**9000**	**8000**	**7000**	**6000**	**5000**	**4000**
Leverage and coverage ratios											
Total senior debt/EBITDA											
Total debt/EBITDA											
EBITDA/interest expense											

debt instruments including unsecured, subordinated mezzanine debt,[16] high yielding junk bonds and pay in kind, or PIK,[17] notes. For illustration purposes, we assumed that the company pays down EUR 1 billion in debt each year. In reality, the ability to pay down debt depends on the amount of free cash flows generated and therefore on the operational assumptions discussed above. Financial analysts usually calculate a variety of leverage and coverage ratios to check if their assumptions are realistic.

The analysis can be modified such that dividends are assumed to be paid to the private equity investor during the interim period. Of course, distributing cash means that debt is reduced at a slower pace.[18] Analysts at Deutsche Bank and UBS[19] assume that excess cash not needed for daily operations is immediately used to pay down debt.[20] For simplicity, it is usually assumed that the entire business is sold in T. In practice, financial investors often sell their equity stakes in the business in several steps over time. The length of the period over which private equity investors hold their investment varies considerably. Some financial sponsors exit after a few months. Others hold companies for several years in their portfolios. When modeling LBOs, analysts typically assume as base case that private equity investors exit after five years and calculate five-year IRRs accordingly.[21] As we show below, UBS works on a basis of three to five years, with four years taken to be the base case.

(5) *Final cash flows and exit multiples*: Private equity investors usually exit their investment by selling the acquired company to new investors or listing it on a stock exchange in an initial public offering after a few years. The final cash flow to the private equity sponsor equals the exit enterprise value less net debt in the exit year T. Most financial analysts use average EV/EBITDA exit multiples of a comparable peer group of companies to determine the ex ante unknown enterprise value EV of a potential buyout candidate j at the exit date T:[22]

$$\text{EV}_{T,j} = \left(\frac{\text{EV}}{\text{EBITDA}} \right)_{T,p} \times \text{EBITDA}_{T,j}$$

Table 32.4 provides an overview of EV/EBITDA multiples of companies that recently received leveraged buyout offers from private equity investors. The choice of the exit multiple is highly subjective. Like other valuation multiples, EV/EBITDA multiples expand and compress over time. Some financial analysts use long-term historic average EV/EBITDA multiples, some apply current multiples to calculate the exit enterprise value. Financial analysts can apply company specific or industry specific exit multiples. To calculate the equity value E_T which belongs to the private equity investor, (net) debt

---

[16] The term "mezzanine debt" typically refers to deeply subordinated, unsecured, high yield debt or preferred stock. Mezzanine debt is usually only senior to shareholder's equity and therefore more expensive than senior, secured debt to compensate for the higher credit risk. Mezzanine debt is often provided by specialized lenders, e.g. mezzanine funds, which are willing to take high credit risk. Mezzanine lenders often generate high rates of returns from upfront arrangement fees, interest payments (and/or payments in kind), and warrants.

[17] Bonds usually pay cash interest in the form of coupon payments. The term "pay in kind", or PIK, is used in finance for payments other than in cash. Payments in kind usually accrue over time and increase the principal which is due at maturity.

[18] Goldman Sachs (2007), p. 24.

[19] UBS (2006), p. 26.

[20] Deutsche Bank (2007), p. 14.

[21] Morgan Stanley (2007), p. 3, Goldman Sachs (2007), p. 24, Deutsche Bank (2007), p. 12.

[22] Goldman Sachs (2007), p. 26, Morgan Stanley (2003), p. 3, Deutsche Bank (2007), p. 13, UBS (2006), p. 22.

Table 32.4 Private equity deals in the first quarter of 2007 – EV/EBITDA multiples (Source: Bloomberg)[23]

	Announce Date	Target Name	Acquirer Name	Announced Total Value (USD mil.)	EBITDA Multiple
1	2/26/07	TXU CORP	MULTIPLE ACQUIRERS	43 218	8.08
2	3/9/07	ALLIANCE BOOTS PLC	KOHLBERG KRAVIS ROBERTS & CO	21 500	28.33
3	3/20/07	AFFILIATED COMPUTER SVCS-A	CERBERUS CAPITAL MANAGEMENT	8244	
4	3/12/07	DOLLAR GENERAL CORP	KOHLBERG KRAVIS ROBERTS & CO	7321	12.30
5	3/19/07	SERVICEMASTER COMPANY	CLAYTON DUBILIER & RICE	5071	
6	1/26/07	MOELNLYCKE HEALTH CARE AB	MULTIPLE ACQUIRERS	3680	
7	2/8/07	EDGARS CONSOLIDATED	BAIN CAPITAL LLC	3673	9.55
8	1/29/07	LAUREATE EDUCATION INC	MULTIPLE ACQUIRERS	3402	16.97
9	3/13/07	SPIRIT FINANCE CORP	REDFORD HOLDCO LLC	3312	19.32
10	3/23/07	ISTA	CHARTERHOUSE CAPITAL PARTNER	3190	
11	3/20/07	CLAIRE'S STORES INC	APOLLO MANAGEMENT LP	2846	9.58
12	3/13/07	WCI COMMUNITIES INC	MULTIPLE ACQUIRERS	2845	37.16
13	2/12/07	PINNACLE FOODS GROUP INC	BLACKSTONE GROUP	2160	
14	3/12/07	VITUS WOHNIMMOBILIEN GMBH	MULTIPLE ACQUIRERS	2110	
15	3/5/07	TUSSAUDS GROUP	BLACKSTONE GROUP	1977	
16	1/25/07	APN NEWS & MEDIA LIMITED	MULTIPLE ACQUIRERS	1937	10.97
17	3/23/07	KRONOS INC	HELLMAN & FRIEDMAN	1726	16.28
18	3/20/07	EGL INC	APOLLO MANAGEMENT LP	1682	13.02
19	2/9/07	GNC PARENT CORP	MULTIPLE ACQUIRERS	1650	
20	2/26/07	HUB INTERNATIONAL LTD	MULTIPLE ACQUIRERS	1643	12.82

[23] Bloomberg calculates EBITDA multiples " . . . by dividing Bloomberg M&A announced total value of the deal by the underlying target fundamental. EBITDA is a trailing 12-month figure" (Bloomberg M&A term definitions). Note that LBO analysis tends to rely on trailing rather than $t + 1$ multiples. Data obtained from Bloomberg on April 1, 2007.

D_T must be subtracted from the enterprise value EV_T at the exit date T:

$$E_{T,j} = EV_{T,j} - D_{T,j}$$

Determining (net) debt requires several subjective assumptions, too. The debt reported on the balance sheet usually does not reflect the true debt burden of a company. Looking from an economic instead of an accounting perspective, most financial investors would arguably consider pension obligations, lease obligations and other off-balance sheet obligations as debt. However, when running LBO screens on a large universe of potential LBO candidates, most analysts usually make only a few adjustments, if any, on reported debt.

   In the next chapter we use Continental AG as an example to demonstrate how financial analysts value potential LBO candidates in practice.

33

Example: Continental AG

Before running through an LBO analysis of Continental AG, it is worth setting some context on the situation that arose around the company starting in late July 2006. After providing some background information, we will discuss the key LBO parameters and run you step-by-step through our LBO analysis of Continental AG.

33.1 BACKGROUND

Continental ("Conti") is today one of the world's leading automotive industry suppliers, with extensive operations in rubber, tire, braking technology, driving dynamics control, electronics, sensor systems and telematics.

On September 19, 2006, Conti announced it had been approached by a private equity investor in connection with a bid for the company, but that the talks had lapsed at an early stage. On the same day, the *Financial Times* reported that a Bain Capital-led consortium had approached the company with regard to the buyout at a generous premium. On September 27 at the Paris auto show, Conti informed the market that an unidentified private equity firm had made a "reasonable" offer for the company. Management had determined that the firm had no plans to break up the company and that its strategic plans were aligned with the management's. However, talks ended after the shares rose ca. 11% in the week of discussions. Given the stock price progression, UBS believed at the time that the talks took place during the second and third week of July. Applying an assumed 20–25% premium to the stock price range of EUR 72–74.5 that prevailed during this period suggested a takeout price range of EUR 86–93 per share. Our task was to establish an LBO valuation and the level at which the stock would become "interesting" to a private equity investor. This floor valuation has been referred to by some as the private equity "put" – a floor that transforms the payoff profile on the stock into an asymmetric one, with no downside combined with upside.

A prospective buyer of the business would have been attracted by Conti's industry-leading operating margins and attractive operating free cash flow (EBITDA minus capex) margins. Some of this derived from its product positioning versus its peers and some due to its scale and efficiency. Conti was also arguably further ahead in restructuring than many of its peers. Conti's operating free cash flow margins were also strong by industry standards, suggesting less operating leverage – something a leveraged buyer would be keen to see. Conti was also arguably grossly underleveraged. Our forecasts envisaged it being debt free by the end of 2007.

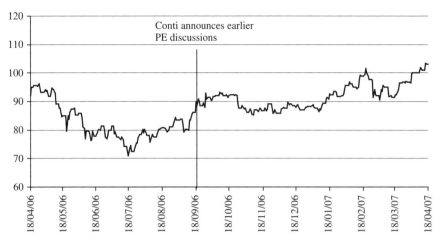

Figure 33.1   Continental AG: share price April 2006–April 2007

33.2   LBO MODELING APPROACH – APPROPRIATE LEVEL OF DETAIL

Key to any LBO analysis is the decision on the level of detail likely to be required. This will depend on the scenarios that are expected to be run – taking into account variations in sales, margins, capex and working capital, tax, alternative financing structures and potential disposals. Also key is the structure of the company being analyzed and the data that is publicly available.[1] Prior to the acquisition of VDO in Q3 2007, Continental was organized around four main business divisions: Automotive Systems, Passenger and Light Truck Tyres, Commercial Vehicle Tyres and ContiTech.

Continental's CEO, Dr. Wennemer, and CFO, Dr. Hippe, stated at the time that the board would likely not block a bid which met certain conditions. Aside from price, two conditions appeared to be that a bidder would not break up the company and second that the company's strategy would remain intact. A stated part of the strategy is a desire to undertake another acquisition in the next year. Accordingly, we elected to model Conti at the group rather than divisional level[2] and not model any disposals.[3]

33.3   KEY LBO PARAMETERS

In this section we will discuss the key parameters of our LBO model. The model we use is a conventional industrial LBO model, which is distinct from an infrastructure buyout model

---

[1] Investment banking advisors and private equity investors that have been granted due diligence rights and access to non-public information will likely develop more detailed financial models. These models will also likely be structured to model proposed alternative LBO financing structures in considerable detail. The example we provide pertains to an actual model relied upon to generate an LBO valuation on the public side of the Chinese wall.

[2] A further round of analysis might have involved modeling separate divisions, including a possible disposal of ContiTech (the least "core" of the divisions in our view) and analyzing a turnaround or disposal of the relatively poorer performing US tire business. This would entail recalibration of the analyst's forecasts to strip out the disposed-of business and a stronger turnaround in the US tire business than in the base case figures.

[3] We were aware that others were modeling an LBO involving a disposal of ContiTech.

that would typically be used to assess a buyout of long cash flow duration infrastructure-type businesses.[4] Below are the key building blocks of the model:

- *Market price of the stock and the takeout premium*: Historic analysis suggests a figure of close to 20% should be used.[5] Financial sponsors assessing an LBO opportunity early in its life will often use a figure in the range of 20–30%. It is not unusual for a stock to jump by more than 10% once it becomes public that a private equity buyer is assessing a company. It is possible to plug in the current market price plus a premium into the model and see, subject to operating and capital structure assumptions, what IRR emerges. However, we were interested to see what price would be implied or be necessary to ensure a financial buyer could expect to achieve a sufficient target IRR.

- *The target or expected IRR from the transaction*: The focus is on the IRRs rather than the "money multiple" described earlier. We use a range of 15% to 20% IRR. Where in this range the IRR should sit will partly be a function of the perceived risk underlying the business on a geared basis. Were Conti a significant restructuring situation, an IRR of at least 20% would likely be demanded. Private equity investors expect their capital to be committed to the company only for a limited period of time, typically three- to five years. Thus we tend to model IRRs over a three- to six-year window.

- *Entry and exit multiples*: Multiples reflect the valuation paid for the business by the financial sponsor and the value achieved on exit. In assessing both of these, LBO practitioners typically use trailing (last 12 months (LTM)) and current year forecast multiples rather than forward multiples. This in part derives from the fact that the banks providing the leverage finance will tend base their lending on an LTM or current year basis. EV/EBITDA is a commonly used multiple, though will be accompanied by others such as EV/sales, price/earnings and free cash flow yield. The relationship between assumed entry and exit multiples is critical. An assumption of exiting at a multiple superior to that of entry is aggressive and tantamount to building in an instantaneous revaluation into the valuation.[6] Terminal exit multiples should also be set within the context of peer valuations and historic trading valuations of the company and its peers. Another reason for applying caution to the exit multiple is that the exit may be by way of an IPO rather than trade sale or secondary buyout and as such may not incorporate the control premium that was implicit in the purchase.

- *Capital structure*: Three complementary metrics usefully define this: the net debt/EBITDA multiple, the percentage of equity in the buyout capital structure and lastly, the fixed charge cover ratio. The latter refers to the ratio of post interest-free cash flow to interest cost. The level of each that private equity sponsors and leveraged acquisition finance providers deem appropriate will vary from industry to industry and transaction to transaction. It is fair to say, however, that the percentage of equity in the capital structure will decline with the size of the transaction. In a buoyant credit environment it would not be unusual to see a EUR 5 billion plus transaction where ca. 20% of the purchase EV comprises equity. For Europe as a whole, the figure for 2007 was 32.5%.[7]

---

[4] The principal differences are that an infrastructure buyout aims to retain ongoing maximal levels of gearing over the long term, with financing structured accordingly. The target IRR in such a transaction is likely to be in the range of 8–12%.

[5] For historical deal premia paid in M&A deals and private equity deals, see Table 32.1 and 32.2, respectively.

[6] This is not to say that multiple enhancement has not been a driver of value creation in LBOs in the past. The buyout of Celanese in Germany and subsequent IPO in the US benefited from such "multiple arbitrage".

[7] Standard & Poor's European LBO review 2007.

- *Debt capital structure and paydown*: Our model broadly mirrors the financing of a typical buyout. That is, it comprises a mix of three tiers of senior debt, A, B and C tranches, a tier of subordinated high yield (junk) debt and higher yielding, more subordinated, mezzanine debt. The A tranche is traditionally amortizing, although it was increasingly common in the year proceeding the credit crisis for A loans to carry bullet repayment schedules. The A, B and C tiers are usually seven, eight and nine years' maturity. Buyouts in the last two years have increasingly utilized a tier of second lien debt, so-called for its subordination to the three tiers of senior debt, which have a first lien on the assets of the credit. We see no loss of analytical power through allocating the finance from this tier to higher levels of senior debt. Similarly, we model the B and C tranches as amortizing, which provides some cushion of comfort as in practice repayment is likely to be a bullet. The maturities involved require cash flow forecasts 10 years out.
- *Mezzanine and high yield debt*: The high yield and mezzanine markets have traditionally offered nowhere near the depth of liquidity as the senior debt market and largely fill some if any funding gaps. Mezzanine debt is considerably more costly than high yield debt (see below), reflecting its subordination to high yield bond holders. Mezzanine debt is often half PIK (pay in kind), half cash-pay.
- *Operating impact of private equity ownership*: We use UBS' Autos research team forecasts as a starting point and collectively make some (generally small) adjustments, in this case to capex and working capital investment, to arrive at a central case operating scenario. While private equity is often successful in bringing about improvements in key performance and cash flow metrics, we endeavor to get confident that the buyout economics do not rest on a very material operating impact.

After discussing the key parameters of our model, we will discuss in the next section how we calculated the IRR of a potential buyout of Conti.

33.4   STEP-BY-STEP WALK THROUGH THE MODEL

In this section we will discuss our LBO analysis of Conti step by step. As mentioned above, the objective is to see what price range would correspond to an acceptable IRR range. The analysis provided us with a sense of what a private equity buyer could afford to pay.

- *Transaction details*: In Table 33.1 we show key assumptions relating to timing, prices and aggregate values. To keep the modeling tractable we assume a transaction date at the nearest future year end (December 31, 2006). A share price of EUR 87, a takeout premium of 20% and 145.5 million shares suggested a takeout equity value of EUR 15.2 billion. Adding net debt, an IFRS pension deficit and an assumed cost of buying out minorities suggests a takeout enterprise value of EUR 17.7 billion. This figure is then lowered by an assumed sale of a small amount of peripheral assets to reach a takeout enterprise value of EUR 17.5 billion.

    Table 33.2 shows the valuation multiples implied by those acquisition values. We show current year multiples (defined as the year of the acquisition) and the one-year prospective multiples. Given the quality of Conti's operations (best in class margins) and where auto parts peers were trading, we felt a prospective buyer[8] would be able to justify these multiples.

---

[8] From the size of a potential transaction it was clear that a consortium of buyers would be involved.

Table 33.1 Transaction details – assumptions

Transaction details	
Transaction date	31-Dec-06
Shares outstanding, m	145.5
Current price, EUR	87.00
Premium	20%
Price, EUR	104.40
EUR, m	
Equity value	15 185
Net debt (cash)	927
Pension provision	1111
Buyout minorities	221
Fees (1.5%)	228
Enterprise value	17 671
Non-core/peripheral assets	−127
Core EV	17 544

Table 33.2 LBO valuation multiples – assumptions

	2006	2007
EV/sales	1.2×	1.1×
EV(core)/EBITDA	7.1×	6.8×
EV(core)/EBITA	10.2×	9.8×
PER	13.3×	12.7×
FCF yield	4.9%	6.7%

Table 33.3 sets out the capital structure assumed for the buyout. It starts by splitting the financing of the EUR 17.7 billion takeout EV between debt and equity. The 58% debt in the overall capital structure – shown in the implied debt burden table – corresponds to 4.1× 2006E net debt/EBITDA. This figure was lower than the average multiple for European LBO financings of ca. 6.0×. Important was that the pro forma fixed charge cover ratio stood at only 1.2× for 2006E; this figure was effectively setting an upper bound to the amount of possible debt burden. As will be apparent below, this was further backed up by the forecast debt repayment profile.

The third table, the Debt Split shows the assumed debt capital structure. We set the A tranche of the senior debt at 1.5× EBITDA, with the B tranche representing an additional turn; that is, an additional 1.0× EBITDA, such that the cumulative leverage through the two tranches was 2.5× (1.5× +1.0×). The third, C, tranche was modeled as an additional tranche. Given our belief that at that point in time the high yield market could support ca. EUR 1 billion of Conti paper, we split the remaining 15% of the debt capital for the buy-out as 10% high yield and 5% mezzanine.

Table 33.4 shows the calculation of the initial interest costs based on market rates. It also shows the overall blended cost of debt at 7.0%.

Table 33.3   Financing structure – assumptions

Financing structure		
Debt %		**58%**
Equity %		42%
Debt		10 249
Equity		7422
Total		17 671
Implied debt burden		58%
Total net debt		10 249
Net debt/EBITDA 2006E		4.1×
Senior debt/EBITDA 2006E		3.5×
EBITDA interest cover 2006E		3.5×
Fixed charge cover 2006E		1.2×
Debt split	Split	EUR m
Bank debt A	36.2%	3714
Bank debt B	24.2%	2476
Bank debt C	24.2%	2476
High yield	10.0%	1025
Mezzanine	5.4%	558
Total	100.0%	10 249

Table 33.4   Interest cost – assumptions

[in EUR million]	Rate	Spread	Cost
Euribor	3.8%		
Bank debt A	6.1%	225bp	225
Bank debt B	6.6%	275bp	162
Bank debt C	7.1%	325bp	175
High yield	8.5%		87
Mezzanine	12.0%		67
Total			716
Average cost of debt	7.0%		

- *Summary financial statements*: Tables 33.5 and 33.6 are a summary profit and loss (P&L) and a pre-LBO summary cash flow statement. We show 2005–2011 and 2015. As discussed earlier, these can be substituted by more detailed statements, with divisional drivers. We chose to proxy these by consolidated business drivers. The P&L shows our assumed slowdown in revenue in 2008 and a further slowdown in 2011. We also modeled some EBIT margin erosion from 2007 after a slight increase forecast for 2006.

In terms of cash flow, we believed that private equity would make a concerted attempt and be successful in stemming net working capital outflow and reduce capital intensity slightly. However, we retained a material amount of annual restructuring cost. We assume

Table 33.5 Pre-LBO sales and profit assumptions

[in EUR million]	2005	2006	2007	2008	2009	2010	2011	2015
Gross sales	13 837	14 709	15 721	16 350	17 004	17 684	18 126	20 008
% change in revenue		6.3%	6.9%	4.0%	4.0%	4.0%	2.5%	2.5%
EBIT margin	11.2%	11.7%	11.4%	11.0%	11.0%	11.0%	11.0%	11.0%
EBIT	1545	1716	1794	1798	1870	1945	1994	2201
Depreciation	742	760	800	899	935	973	997	1000
% of sales	5.4%	5.2%	5.1%	5.5%	5.5%	5.5%	5.5%	5.0%
EBITDA margin	17%	17%	16%	17%	17%	17%	17%	16%
EBITDA	2287	2476	2594	2698	2806	2918	2991	3201
EBIT	1545	1716	1794	1798	1870	1945	1994	2201
Margin	11.2%	11.7%	11.4%	11.0%	11.0%	11.0%	11.0%	11.0%

Table 33.6 Pre-LBO cash flows

[in EUR million]	2005	2006	2007	2008	2009	2010	2011	2015
EBITDA	2287	2476	2594	2698	2806	2918	2991	3201
Capex	−872	−890	−890	−899	−935	−973	−997	−1100
Capex as a % of sales	6.3%	6.1%	5.7%	5.5%	5.5%	5.5%	5.5%	5.5%
ΔNWC	−185	−200	−20	−50	−50	−50	−20	−20
Interest	−104	−86	−80	−28	29	91	159	470
Tax	−432	−489	−514	−531	−570	−611	−646	−801
Restructuring costs	−69	−74	−79	−82	−85	−88	−91	−100
FCF	624	737	1011	1107	1195	1287	1396	1649

no acquisitions are made, however, and believed some room could be made for Conti's acquisition strategy through an additional acquisition facility.

In Table 33.7, we show the cash flow statement pro forma for the LBO financing. The impact can be seen from 2007 (the first year post buyout) in the tax and interest charges. It is here that we calculate the cash available for debt reduction. Our financing structure leaves in the first year some EUR 640 million available to pay down debt, rising to EUR

Table 33.7 Post-LBO free cash flows

[in EUR million]	2005	2006	2007	2008	2009	2010	2011	2015
EBITDA	2287	2476	2594	2698	2806	2918	2991	3201
Capex	−872	−890	−890	−899	−935	−973	−997	−1100
ΔNWC	−185	−200	−20	−50	−50	−50	−20	−20
Tax	−432	−489	−329	−343	−377	−414	−444	−592
Restructuring cost	−69	−74	−79	−82	−85	−88	−91	−100
FCF	728	823	1276	1324	1358	1393	1439	1388
Disposals	0	0	64	0	0	0	0	0
Interest	−104	−86	−696	−656	−614	−566	−513	−226
Cash for debt reduction	624	737	643	668	745	827	926	1162
Tax (%)	30%	30%	30%	30%	30%	30%	30%	30%

830 million by 2010.[9] Two major differences between the pre- and post-LBO cash flows (Tables 33.6 and 33.7) are the interest line and the tax charge. It is not unusual to see a pre-LBO interest line showing net interest receivable, reflecting an undergeared balance sheet. At the same time, the benefits of gearing – tax deductibility of interest costs – will be evident in the post-LBO cash flow statement. In addition, an important part of the LBO analytical process is forecasting and modeling potential operating improvements that arises on account of the transfer of ownership from the public market into the hands of the buy-out group and the concommitant incentivisation of management and an intense focus on profitability and cash flow. Also in the cash flow forecasts are assumed proceeds from disposals reflected, as the buy-out group works to reduce excess capital and generate cash to repay debt.

In Table 33.8 below we show a summarized debt repayment schedule. It should be evident that the 2007 forecast net debt figure of EUR 9.6 billion is lower than the initial debt taken on in the LBO by the amount of the cash available to pay down debt. This cash flow is used to pay down the A tranche until it is fully repaid, at which point the cash flow is directed at the B tranche and later the C tranche. The high yield and mezzanine tranches are modeled as bullet repayments. This schedule is important, as it very much dictates debt capacity and is a market-determined phenomenon. Our analysis was based on the view that the leveraged finance providers to Continental would be keen to finance a transaction involving Conti which might involve some degree of refinancing risk (i.e. no full repayment of senior debt). The analysis below shows that by 2011, 44% of the senior debt could likely be repaid and 95% repaid by 2015.

Table 33.8 Debt paydown

[in EUR million]	2007	2008	2009	2010	2011	2015
Bank debt A	3071	2403	1658	832	0	0
Bank debt B	2476	2476	2476	2476	2381	0
Bank debt C	2476	2476	2476	2476	2476	441
High yield	1025	1025	1025	1025	1025	1025
Mezzanine	558	558	558	558	558	558
Total	9606	8938	8194	7367	6441	2024
% of opening debt repaid	6%	13%	20%	28%	37%	80%
Net debt/EBITDA	3.7×	3.3×	2.9×	2.5×	2.2×	0.6×
% of senior debt repaid	7%	15%	24%	33%	44%	95%

- *Results*: The IRR Table 33.9 is the critical "output" from the analysis. It shows the range of IRRs for three different exit multiples and four potential exit years, 2009–2012. The mid-point of the multiples, 7.1×, corresponds to the current year entry multiple.[10] The highlighted cell is our central reference point; it relates to the central multiple exit assumption and the central assumption holding period of four years. While 16.3% is below the IRR traditionally desired or targeted by private equity, we felt it would be acceptable for a private equity buyer and its lenders, in part due to a combination of

---

[9] We have seen a multitude of LBO runs which we would have expected to be attractive but whose IRRs fell short for want of deleveraging.
[10] The implicit assumption is that the buyer will ultimately recoup the upfront control premium.

Table 33.9 IRR matrix

Exit multiple EV/EBITDA (×)	Exit year			
	2009	2010	2011	2012
6.6×	12.4%	13.1%	12.8%	12.5%
7.1×	17.2%	16.3%	15.2%	14.4%
7.6×	21.6%	19.4%	17.4%	16.1%

increased market pressure to deploy funds, the quality and scarcity value of Conti's business and perhaps even its position as a DAX 30 company.[11] Our uncertainty as to the precise IRRs that different financial buyers would deem acceptable motivates our use of a valuation interval with a central figure.

Table 33.10 shows the computation of the central case 16.3% IRR assuming a four-year exit at 7.1× trailing EBITDA. The equity investment at the inception of the deal is EUR 7.42 billion; this is equivalent to 42% of the enterprise value at the time the LBO takes place. A small amount, EUR 64 million, is assumed to be raised from the disposal of non-core investments. Otherwise the only cash flow is that received on exit of the business.[12] At a trailing exit multiple of 7.1× and thus an EV of EUR 20.86 billion, the residual debt of EUR 7.37 billion implies an exit equity value of EUR 13.49 billion. This generates an IRR of 16.3%.

Table 33.10 Computation of central case 4-year IRR and IRRs for other exit years

	2006	2007	2008	2009	2010
Transaction multiple (×)	7.1				
EV		18 542	19 286	20 057	20 860
Opening debt		10 249	9606	8938	8194
Paydown		−643	−668	−745	−827
Closing debt		9606	8938	8194	7367
Exit equity		8936	10 348	11 864	13 493
Proceeds from disposal		64			
Flows to equity					
2007 exit	(7422)	8999			
2008 exit	(7422)	64	10 348		
2009 exit	(7422)	64	0	11 864	
2010 exit	(7422)	64	0	0	13 493
2011 exit	(7422)	64	0	0	0
2012 exit	(7422)	64	0	0	0
IRRs		21.3%	18.5%	17.2%	16.3%

Recall from Table 33.1 that the IRR of 16.3% maps back to a price of EUR 87 per share. This IRR should be viewed being at the low end of returns typically targeted

---

[11] We perceived a strong interest among the private equity community to complete a DAX 30 LBO.
[12] In practice, the exit may not be a full realization but a partial sale or IPO.

by financial sponsors. The analysis thus suggests that private equity interest could well remain strong and a bid could emerge, if the stock were to trade below EUR 87. It is worth pointing out the complicating factor of the assumed takeout premium. As the share price chart above showed, Conti's share price began to rise materially from its low of EUR 71.57[13] in mid-July 2006 and in the month after the disclosure of the private equity approach the stock traded within a range of EUR 88 and EUR 92. We took the view that a premium of 20% would still be required to achieve a recommendation from Conti's board and be acceptable to shareholders. Thus, including a premium, this suggested a takeout price per share of EUR 104 to EUR 106.

The IRR matrix – shown in Table 33.9 – illustrates the intuition that the IRR is highly sensitive to the assumed exit multiple. What the table cannot illustrate, however, is the "optionality" available to the private equity owner in terms of being able to exit early if market and peer valuations emerge as attractive or to defer exit to some extent should valuations be otherwise.

- *Sensitivity analysis*: Table 33.11 shows implied IRRs based an alternative levels of net debt, or ND, to takeout EV; that is, the amount of leverage in the buyout capital structure. The column begins at the highest amount of leverage we felt could be supported by the business. The other variable is the takeout price or corresponding premium to the current market price. The IRRs assume the central case exit multiple and an exit in 2010 pertain. The IRR of 16.3% (when ND/EV is 58%, with a 20% premium) can be cross-referenced with the preceding table. This matrix was valuable in the light of the uncertainty surrounding the potentially acceptable premium. We were comfortable with the IRRs in the table, as generated by our takeout valuation per share of EUR 87 to EUR 88 plus a 20% premium.

Table 33.11 IRR sensitivity to proportions of debt consideration and premium paid (exit year 2010, exit multiple 7.1×)

	EUR 95.7 10%	EUR 100.05 15.0%	EUR 104.4 20.0%	EUR 108.75 25.0%	EUR 113.1 30.0%
58%	20.7%	18.5%	16.3%	14.2%	12.1%
53%	19.5%	17.5%	15.5%	13.6%	11.7%
48%	17.3%	15.6%	14.0%	12.4%	10.9%

A critical sensitivity analysis to complement the foregoing would be to assess the impact of alternative operating performance scenarios on the IRRs and debt coverage and paydown metrics.

In conclusion, the analysis above – conducted during a very favorable credit environment and keeness amongst private equity sponsors to undertake a large German take-private transaction – represents an alternative approach to modeling and LBO situation simply yet sufficiently realistically. In doing so, it generated a valuation of Conti – mapping a price, premium, takeout price, exit multiple and forecast cash flow through to an IRR. In doing so,

---

[13] Closing price of Continental AG's shares as of July 18, 2006.

it suggested a level for the stock at which there was likely to be strong interest from private equity. As at the time of writing, until the acquisition of Siemens' VDO business, Conti had not traded below EUR 87 – and no private equity bid has emerged. The acquisition of VDO was said by some to have the secondary benefit to Conti of reducing the probability of further buyout approaches.

34

A Word of Caution

LBO models value companies from the perspective of a financial investor who acquires a company, recapitalizes its financial structure and restructures operations to increase profitability and capital efficiency. Used in combination, DCF and LBO models give a more complete picture on how companies are valued in competitive financial markets. From the perspective of a private equity investor, the value of controlling a company can be substantial. Investors of publicly listed companies can benefit from leveraged buyouts as private equity investors usually have to offer a control premium to take a public company private. Studying LBO models helps investment professionals, students and anyone else interested in equity valuation to understand how an increasingly important investor group values equity.

Financial analysts at leading investment banks such as UBS, Deutsche Bank, Morgan Stanley, Goldman Sachs and Credit Suisse use LBO models to identify future LBO candidates. Like any other model, LBO models are based on simplifying assumptions. Before interpreting the results of an LBO model, investors should always carefully review the assumptions made, including those not immediately evident within the published research. Financial sponsors, of course, use similar LBO models when analyzing potential leveraged buyouts and in some cases – especially as a deal becomes live – considerably more detailed models. However, the knowledge base of a financial analyst not directly involved in an LBO deal is usually less far-reaching than that of the financial sponsor planning a concrete deal and who may already be in contact with a prospective management team with a working knowledge of the industry and business. We strongly encourage investors to analyze different scenarios before making investment decisions based on the result of an LBO model.

Above we explained in detail how analysts at UBS Investment Research value potential LBO candidates. We used Continental AG as an example. It is public knowledge that many automotive companies are viewed as attractive targets by private equity firms.[1] While it is entirely possible that private equity investors will acquire and restructure automotive assets, we have no knowledge that Continental AG is currently a target of a private equity investor. The purpose of the example was solely to demonstrate LBO analysis around a historic situation.

For a long time, academics have warned that the use of internal rates of return has material theoretical deficiencies. Most important, the IRR materially overestimates the attractiveness of a potential leveraged buyout if cash flows are paid to the financial sponsor in the interim period and the true reinvestment rate is substantially lower than the IRR. There are mainly two reasons why all LBO models of leading investment banks which we have seen are based on IRR calculations. First, well-constructed LBO models realistically reflect the mechanics

---

[1] Merrill Lynch (2007), p. 4.

of an LBO deal. In addition, they avoid the time-consuming process of releveraging equity betas which is usually applied to incorporate the effect of financial leverage into DCF models.

In our opinion there are additional reasons why investors should interpret the results of LBO models with great caution:

(1) *Low interest rates and announced IPOs*: No doubt, the coffers of private equity investors are flush with cash waiting to be invested. According to Goldman Sachs private equity firms have USD 300 billion of uninvested equity capital which could fund leverage buyouts in the amount of USD 1.3 trillion.[2] The last wave of LBOs was driven by large inflows of capital from investors into LBO funds, low interest rates and aggressive lending practices by financial institutions. The recent wave of LBO activity ended abruptly with the unwillingness of institutional investors to continue to buy large quantities of leveraged loans that formed the bedrock of LBO financing. At the same time, risk aversion made for a significant reduction of leverage levels that could be appiled to potential buy-outs. In February 2007, Fortress Investment Group, an alternative asset manager with USD 17.5 billion of assets under management (AUM) in private equity, USD 9.4 billion AUM in hedge funds and USD 3 billion AUM in other alternative investment vehicles as of September 30, 2006, went public. The IPO priced at the top of the price range at USD 18.50. Due to large demand by investors, shares of Fortress opened at USD 35, reached an intraday high of USD 37 and closed at USD 31 on its first trading day in February 2007. With little over 1 billion in total revenues in the nine months ended September 30, 2006, Fortress's current market capitalization of roughly USD 12 billion is demanding for an asset manager.[3] Attracted by the success of Fortress, other alternative asset managers such as Blackstone have already announced to list their shares in an initial public offering.[4] A string of IPOs is usually an unmistakable sign that a particular sector is hyped. Unfortunately, investors usually realize a bubble only after it has burst.

(2) *Do not solely rely on IRR calculations*: A high IRR on an LBO screen is no guarantee that the current owners of a company will sell it to financial investors. One of the authors recently met with the management of a company that produces auto parts in the south of Germany. The company generates high cash flows and has a lot of unused debt capacity. During a management meeting we asked the CEO incidentally if he has recently received a buyout offer. The CEO smiled and responded that private equity firms have offered to buy the company several times in the past but that it is highly unlikely that a buyout will ever occur. The publicly listed company is majority owned by an extremely wealthy family. Whenever the CEO forwards a new buyout offer to the family owners, they simply neglect it. The ability to control "their" company is more important for them than a high price offered by a private equity investor. The anecdote illustrates that it is not sufficient to screen for high IRRs if majority shareholders will likely block even the most attractive takeover bid. Sometimes dual share classes and other legal structures separate the economic interest in and the control of a company. The probability of a buyout decreases if the main objective of majority or other controlling shareholders is not to maximize returns but to keep the control of a company.

---

[2] Goldman Sachs (2007), p. 1.
[3] Fortress Investment Group (2007).
[4] Bloomberg (2007b).

As a response to the wave of hostile takeovers in the 1980s, corporate lawyers have developed a variety of defense tactics to avoid takeovers. The most common form of a "poison pill" is the issuance of shareholder rights which can be converted into shares if a third party tries to gain control of the company. Another defense tactic is to grant employees stock options that can be cashed in immediately when a third party acquires the company. These and other defense tactics make hostile takeovers more expensive and sometimes economically infeasible. Good analysts do not solely rely on their IRR calculations but also screen for blocking shareholders and legal impediments to a takeover before advising their clients to buy a potential buyout candidate.

References

Bloomberg (2007a), Porsche's low-ball bid values VW at EU35.8 billion (Update 6), March 28, 2007, 17:44.

Bloomberg (2007b), Fortress investment group's 2006 net income doubles (Update 6), April 17, 2007.

Brealey, R.A., Myers, S.C., and Allen, F. (2006), *Corporate Finance*, Eighth International Edition.

Burrough, B., and Helyar, J. (2004), *Barbarians at the Gate*, First Published in Great Britain in 1990.

Credit Suisse (2007a), Reed Elsevier, Mispricing LBO risks, Research Report by Robert Lambert *et al.*, January 10.

Credit Suisse (2007b), Pearson, LBO approaches, Research Report by Giasone Salati *et al.*, January 19.

Damodaran, A. (2005a), The value of control: implications for control premia, minority discounts and voting share differentials, Working Paper, Stern School of Business, June.

Damodaran, A. (2005b), *Applied Corporate Finance*, Second Edition, John Wiley & Sons.

Deutsche Bank (2007), Retail LBO screen revisited, another look at LBO candidates, Research Report by Vin Chao *et al.*, February 13.

Financial Times (2007), KKR buys first data as private equity booms, April 3, 2007, p. 18.

Fortress Investment Group (2007), Prospectus Dated February 2.

Goldman Sachs (2007), Private equity and the GS LBO model, Research Report by David J. Kostin *et al.*, March 22, 2007.

Kohlberg Kravis Roberts & Co. (1989), Leveraged buy-outs, *Journal of Applied Corporate Finance*, Spring, Volume 2.1, 64–70.

Kravis, H.R. (2007), Industry speeches, SuperReturn 2006, European Private Equity & Venture Capital Summit, February 21, 2006, www.kkr.com/news/speeches/02-21-06.html.

Lehman Brothers (2007), European strategy weekly, Research Report by Jane Pearce, January 29.

Loos, N. (2005), Value creation in leveraged buyouts, Dissertation No. 3052, University of St. Gallen, 2005.

Merrill Lynch (2007), Suppliers of value, Research Report by Thomas Besson *et al.*, April 5.

Morgan Stanley (2003), Barbarians can wait: LBO as a valuation tool, Research Report by Adam M. Jonas *et al.*, July 22, 2003.

Munk, N. (2004), *Fools Rush In: Steve Case, Jerry Levin, and the Unmaking of AOL Time Warner*, Harper-Collins, New York.

The Wall Street Journal Europe (2007), KKR agrees to buy first data for $29 billion, April 3, p. 6.

The Wall Street Journal Online (2007a), Buyout firms seek utility TXU for $32 billion, February 24.

The Wall Street Journal Online (2007b), Full text of TXU press release on firm being taken private, February 26.

UBS (2006), How big is the private equity factor?, Research Report by Daniel Stillit, July 7.

UBS (2007), Barbarians at the gate again, UBS Global Strategy, February.

Part VII

Valuation 101: Approaches and Alternatives

Aswath Damodaran[1]

---

[1] Professor of Finance at New York University's Leonard N. Stern School of Business.

35

Introduction

In recent years, managers, under pressure from stockholders and activist investors, have turned their attention increasingly to ways in which they can increase firm value. A number of competing measures, each with claims to being the "best" approach to value creation, have been developed and marketed by investment banking firms and consulting firms. In this part, we look at four basic approaches to valuation and how value enhancement is framed in each one. First, we look at discounted cash flow models and their variants – certainty equivalents, excess return models and adjusted present value models – and note that to increase value in these models, we have to generate a tangible impact on either cash flows or discount rates. Second, we examine accounting valuation models – book value and liquidation value – and why value enhancement in these models is often cosmetic, tailored to accounting conventions and considerations rather than what is best for the firm in the long term. Third, we evaluate relative valuation models, where assets are priced based upon how the market is pricing similar assets, and look at how value enhancement can be adapted to meet market considerations. Finally, we consider real options models, where value can be derived from increasing flexibility and potential opportunities in the future, and the interaction between corporate strategy and finance in value enhancement.

Financial theorists have long argued that the objective in decision making should be to maximize firm value. Managers and practitioners have often criticized them for being too single minded about value maximization and for not considering the broader aspects of corporate strategy or the interests of other stakeholders. In the last decade, however, managers seem to have come around to the view that value maximization should be, if not the only, at least the primary objective for their firms. This turnaround can be partly attributed to the frustration that many managers have felt with strategic consulting and its failures, partly to an increase in their ownership of equity in the firms that they manage but mostly to pressure that they have felt from activist investors to increase stock price. Whatever the reason, the shift of focus to value maximization has created an opening for investment bankers and consultants to offer their advice on the best ways to create value.

To exploit this opening and differentiate their offerings, consultants and investment bankers have come up with measures that they claim offer new insights into value enhancement. In some cases, these measures have been promoted as needing less information than traditional approaches, and in other cases, the claim is made that value is better estimated using these new measures. In this part, we return to basics. We begin by laying out the different approaches to valuation and then introduce a generic model of value, where we relate value to expected cash flows in the future and consider all of the potential routes that are available for a firm to create value. In the process, we hope to show that all value enhancement measures are variations on common themes in valuation.

36
Overview of Valuation

Analysts use a wide spectrum of models, ranging from the simple to the sophisticated. These models often make very different assumptions about the fundamentals that determine value, but they do share some common characteristics and can be classified in broader terms. There are several advantages to such a classification – it makes it is easier to understand where individual models fit into the big picture, why they provide different results and when they have fundamental errors in logic.

In general terms, there are four approaches to valuation. The first, *discounted cash flow valuation*, relates the value of an asset to the present value of expected future cash flows on that asset. The second, *liquidation and accounting valuation*, is built around valuing the existing assets of a firm, with accounting estimates of value or book value often used as a starting point. The third, *relative valuation*, estimates the value of an asset by looking at the pricing of "comparable" assets relative to a common variable like earnings, cash flows, book value or sales. The final approach, *contingent claim valuation*, uses option pricing models to measure the value of assets that share option characteristics. This is what generally falls under the rubric of real options.

Within each of these approaches lie a myriad of sub-approaches, sharing common themes while varying on the details. Discounted cash flow valuation models can take three forms – *cash flow models*, where aggregate cash flows are discounted back at a risk-adjusted rate to arrive at a current value, *excess return models*, where excess returns are separated from normal returns and valued, and *adjusted present value* (APV) models, where the cash flows from debt are valued independently of the cash flows from operations. Accounting valuation models begin with accounting book value but diverge on how best to adjust this book value to arrive at an estimate of market or liquidation value. Relative valuation models can be structured around different multiples (earnings, book value and revenues) and an asset can be valued relative to very similar companies, the sector or even against the entire market. Real option models can be built around options to delay making investments (useful for valuing patents, licenses and undeveloped natural resource reserves), options to expand (for companies in growing markets, where unexpected opportunities may present themselves) and options to abandon.

37

Discounted Cash Flow Valuation

In discounted cash flow valuation, the value of an asset is the present value of the expected cash flows on the asset, discounted back at a rate that reflects the riskiness of these cash flows. This approach gets the most play in academia and comes with the best theoretical credentials. In this chapter, we will look at the foundations of the approach and some of the preliminary details on how we estimate its inputs.

37.1   ESSENCE OF DISCOUNTED CASHFLOW VALUATION

We buy most assets because we expect them to generate cash flows for us in the future. In discounted cash flow valuation, we begin with a simple proposition. The value of an asset is not what someone perceives it to be worth but it is a function of the expected cash flows on that asset. Put simply, assets with high and predictable cash flows should have higher values than assets with low and volatile cash flows.

Using discounted cash flow models is in some sense an act of faith. We believe that every asset has an intrinsic value and we try to estimate that intrinsic value by looking at an asset's fundamentals. What is intrinsic value? Consider it the value that would be attached to an asset by an all-knowing analyst with access to all information available right now and a perfect valuation model. No such analyst exists, of course, but we all aspire to be as close as we can to this perfect analyst. The problem lies in the fact that none of us ever gets to see what the true intrinsic value of an asset is and we therefore have no way of knowing whether our discounted cash flow valuations are close to the mark or not.

There are four variants of discounted cash flow models in practice, and theorists have long argued about the advantages and disadvantages of each. In the first, we discount expected cash flows on an asset (or a business) at a *risk-adjusted discount rate* to arrive at the value of the asset. In the second, we adjust the expected cash flows for risk to arrive at what are termed risk-adjusted or *certainty equivalent cash flows* which we discount at the risk-free rate to estimate the value of a risky asset. In the third, we value a business first, without the effects of debt, and then consider the marginal effects on value, positive and negative, of borrowing money. This approach is termed the *adjusted present value approach*. Finally, we can value a business as a function of the *excess returns* we expect it to generate on its investments. As we will show in the following section, there are common assumptions that bind these approaches together, but there are variants in assumptions in practice that result in different values.

37.2   DISCOUNT RATE ADJUSTMENT MODELS

Of the approaches for adjusting for risk in discounted cash flow valuation, the most common one is the risk-adjusted discount rate approach, where we use higher discount rates to discount expected cash flows when valuing riskier assets, and lower discount rates when valuing safer assets. There are two ways in which we can approach discounted cash flow valuation. The first is to value the entire business, with both assets-in-place and growth assets; this is often termed firm or enterprise valuation (Figure 37.1).

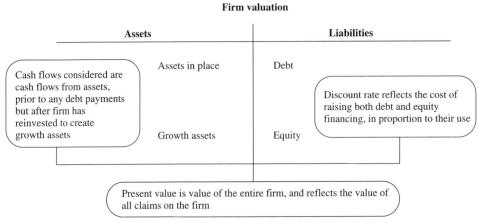

Figure 37.1   Firm or enterprise valuation

The cash flows before debt payments and after reinvestment needs are termed *free cash flows to the firm*, and the discount rate that reflects the composite cost of financing from all sources of capital is the *cost of capital*.

The second way is to just value the equity stake in the business, and this is called equity valuation (Figure 37.2).

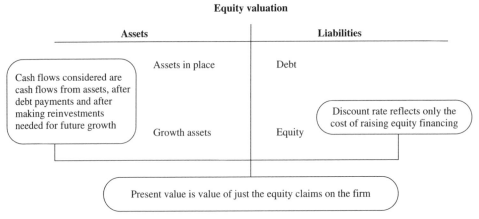

Figure 37.2   Equity valuation

The cash flows after debt payments and reinvestment needs are called free cash flows to equity, and the discount rate that reflects just the cost of equity financing is the cost of equity.

Note also that we can always get from the former (firm value) to the latter (equity value) by netting out the value of all non-equity claims from firm value. Done right, the value of equity should be the same whether it is valued directly (by discounting cash flows to equity at the cost of equity) or indirectly (by valuing the firm and subtracting out the value of all non-equity claims).

37.2.1 Equity DCF models

In equity valuation models, we focus our attention of the equity investors in a business and value their stake by discounting the expected cash flows to these investors at a rate of return that is appropriate for the equity risk in the company. The first set of models examined take a strict view of equity cash flows and consider only dividends to be cash flows to equity. These dividend discount models represent the oldest variant of discounted cash flow models. We then consider broader definitions of cash flows to equity, first by including stock buybacks in cash flows to equity and then by expanding out analysis to cover potential dividends or free cash flows to equity.

The oldest discounted cash flow models in practice tend to be dividend discount models. When investors buy stock in publicly traded companies, they generally expect to get two types of cash flows – dividends during the holding period and an expected price at the end of the holding period. Since this expected price is itself determined by future dividends, the value of a stock is the present value of dividends through infinity.

$$\text{Value per share of stock} = \sum_{t=1}^{t=\infty} \frac{E(\text{DPS}_t)}{(1+k_e)^t}$$

Where: $E(\text{DPS}_t) = $ expected dividends per share in period t
$\quad\quad k_e = $ cost of equity

The rationale for the model lies in the present value rule – the value of any asset is the present value of expected future cash flows discounted at a rate appropriate to the riskiness of the cash flows. There are two basic inputs to the model – expected dividends and the cost on equity. To obtain the expected dividends, we make assumptions about expected future growth rates in earnings and payout ratios. The required rate of return on a stock is determined by its riskiness, measured differently in different models – the market beta in the CAPM, and the factor betas in the arbitrage and multi-factor models. The model is flexible enough to allow for time-varying discount rates, where the time variation is caused by expected changes in interest rates or risk across time.

The free cash flow to equity model does not represent a radical departure from the traditional dividend discount model. In fact, one way to describe a free cash flow to equity model is that it represents a model where we discount potential dividends rather than actual dividends.

$$\text{Value per share of stock} = \sum_{t=1}^{t=\infty} \frac{\text{FCFE}_t}{(1+k_e)^t}$$

Damodaran (1994) provides a measure of free cash flow to equity that captures the cash flow left over all reinvestment needs and debt payments:

$$FCFE = \text{Net income} + \text{Depreciation} - \text{Capital expenditures} - \text{Change in non-cash}$$
$$\text{working capital} - (\text{New debt issued} - \text{Debt repayments})$$

When we replace the dividends with FCFE to value equity, we are doing more than substituting one cash flow for another. We are implicitly assuming that the FCFE will be paid out to stockholders. There are two consequences:

- There will be no future cash build-up in the firm, since the cash that is available after debt payments and reinvestment needs is paid out to stockholders each period.
- The expected growth in FCFE will include growth in income from operating assets and not growth in income from increases in marketable securities. This follows directly from the last point.

The FCFE model treats the stockholder in a publicly traded firm as the equivalent of the owner in a private business. The latter can lay claim on all cash flows left over in the business after taxes, debt payments and reinvestment needs have been met. Since the free cash flow to equity measures the same for a publicly traded firm, we are assuming that stockholders are entitled to these cash flows, even if managers do not choose to pay them out. In essence, the FCFE model, when used in a publicly traded firm, implicitly assumes that there is a strong corporate governance system in place. Even if stockholders cannot force managers to return free cash flows to equity as dividends, they can put pressure on managers to ensure that the cash that does not get paid out is not wasted.

37.2.2 Firm DCF models

The alternative to equity valuation is to value the entire business. The value of the firm is obtained by discounting the free cash flow to the firm at the weighted average cost of capital. Netting out the market value of the non-equity claims from this estimate yields the value of equity in the firm. Implicit in the cost of capital approach is the assumption that the cost of capital captures both the tax benefits of borrowing and the expected bankruptcy costs. The cash flows discounted are the cash flows to the firm, computed as if the firm had no debt and no tax benefits from interest expenses. While there are varying definitions of the expected after-tax operating cash flow in use, the most common one is the free cash flow to the firm, defined as follows:

$$\text{Free cash flow to firm} = \text{After-tax operating income} - (\text{Capital expenditures}$$
$$- \text{Depreciation}) - \text{Change in non-cash working capital}$$

In essence, this is a cash flow after taxes and reinvestment needs but before any debt payments, thus providing a contrast to free cash flows to equity that are after interest payments and debt cash flows.

There are two things to note about this model. The first is that it is general enough to survive the relaxing of the assuming of financing irrelevance; in other words, the value of the firm is still the present value of the after-tax operating cash flows in a world where the cost of capital changes as the debt ratio changes. Second, while it is a widely held preconception that the cost of capital approach requires the assumption of a constant debt ratio, the approach is flexible enough to allow for debt ratios that change over time. In fact, one of the biggest strengths of the model is the ease with which changes in the financing mix can be built into the valuation through the discount rate rather than through the cash flows. The most revolutionary and counterintuitive idea behind firm valuation is the notion that equity investors and lenders to a firm are ultimately partners who supply capital to the firm and share in its success. The primary difference between equity and debt holders in firm valuation models lies in the nature of their cash flow claims – lenders get prior claims to fixed cash flows and equity investors get residual claims to remaining cash flows.

37.3   CERTAINTY EQUIVALENT MODELS

While most analysts adjust the discount rate for risk in DCF valuation, there are some who prefer to adjust the expected cash flows for risk. In the process, they are replacing the uncertain expected cash flows with the certainty equivalent cash flows, using a risk adjustment process akin to the one used to adjust discount rates and then discounting these adjusted cash flows at the risk-free rate. The practical question that we will address in this section is how best to convert uncertain expected cash flows into guaranteed certainty equivalents.

- The first (and oldest) approach to computing certainty equivalents is rooted in the utility functions for individuals. For instance, an individual with a log utility function would demand a certainty equivalent of $93.30 for a risky gamble with a 90% chance of winning $100 and a 10% chance of making nothing.

$$\text{Utility from gamble} = .90\ln(100) + .10\ln(50) = 4.5359$$

$$\text{Certainty equivalent} = \exp^{4.5359} = \$93.30$$

- A more practical approach to converting uncertain cash flows into certainty equivalents is offered by risk and return models. In fact, we would use the same approach to estimating risk premiums that we employ while computing risk-adjusted discount rates but we would use the premiums to estimate certainty equivalents instead.

$$\text{Certainty equivalent cash flow} = \text{Expected cash flow}/(1 + \text{Risk premium in risk-adjusted discount rate})$$

- A far more common approach to adjusting cash flows for uncertainty is to "haircut" the uncertain cash flows subjectively. Thus, an analyst, faced with uncertainty, will replace uncertain cash flows with conservative or lowball estimates. This is a weapon commonly employed by analysts, who are forced to use the same discount rate for projects of different risk levels, and want to even the playing field. They will haircut the cash flows of riskier projects to make them lower, thus hoping to compensate for the failure to adjust the discount rate for the additional risk.

Adjusting the discount rate for risk or replacing uncertain expected cash flows with certainty equivalents are alternative approaches to adjusting for risk, but do they yield different values, and, if so, which one is more precise? The answer lies in how we compute certainty equivalents. If we use the risk premiums from risk and return models to compute certainty equivalents, the values obtained from the two approaches will be the same. After all, adjusting the cash flow, using the certainty equivalent, and then discounting the cash flow at the risk-free rate is equivalent to discounting the cash flow at a risk-adjusted discount rate.

37.4   EXCESS RETURN MODELS

In the excess return valuation approach, we separate the cash flows into excess return cash flows and normal return cash flows. Earning the risk-adjusted required return (cost of capital or equity) is considered a normal return cash flow but any cash flows above or below this number are categorized as excess returns; excess returns can therefore be either positive or negative. With the *excess return valuation* framework, the value of a business can be written as the sum of two components:

$$\text{Value of business} = \text{Capital invested in firm today} + \text{Present value of excess}$$
$$\text{return cash flows from both existing and future projects}$$

If we make the assumption that the accounting measure of capital invested (book value of capital) is a good measure of capital invested in assets today, this approach implies that firms that earn positive excess return cash flows will trade at market values higher than their book values and that the reverse will be true for firms that earn negative excess return cash flows.

Excess return models have their roots in capital budgeting and the net present value rule. In effect, an investment adds value to a business only if it has positive net present value, no matter how profitable it may seem on the surface. This would also imply that earnings and cash flow growth have value only when it is accompanied by excess returns, i.e returns on equity (capital) that exceed the cost of equity (capital). Excess return models take this conclusion to the logical next step and compute the value of a firm as a function of expected excess returns.

It is relatively simple to show that the discounted cash flow value of a firm should match the value that you obtain from an excess return model, if you are consistent in your assumptions about growth and reinvestment. In particular, excess return models are built around a link between reinvestment and growth; in other words, a firm can generate higher earnings in the future only by reinvesting in new assets or using existing assets more efficiently. Discounted cash flow models often do not make this linkage explicit, even though you can argue that they should. Thus, analysts will often estimate growth rates and reinvestment as separate inputs and not make explicit links between the two.

37.5   ADJUSTED PRESENT VALUE MODELS

In the *adjusted present value (APV) approach*, we separate the effects on value of debt financing from the value of the assets of a business. In contrast to the conventional approach, where the effects of debt financing are captured in the discount rate, the APV approach attempts to estimate the expected dollar value of debt benefits and costs separately from the value of the operating assets.

In the APV approach, we begin with the value of the firm without debt. As we add debt to the firm, we consider the net effect on value by considering both the benefits and the costs of borrowing. In general, using debt to fund a firm's operations creates tax benefits (because interest expenses are tax deductible) on the plus side and increases bankruptcy risk (and expected bankruptcy costs) on the minus side. The value of a firm can be written as follows:

$$\text{Value of business} = \text{Value of business with 100\% equity financing} + \text{Present}$$
$$\text{value of expected tax benefits of debt} - \text{Expected bankruptcy costs}$$

The first attempt to isolate the effect of tax benefits from borrowing was in Miller and Modigliani (1963), where they valued the present value of the tax savings in debt as a perpetuity using the cost of debt as the discount rate. The adjusted present value approach, in its current form, was first presented in Myers (1974) in the context of examining the interrelationship between investment and financing decisions.

Implicitly, the adjusted present value approach is built on the presumption that it is easier and more precise to compute the valuation impact of debt in absolute terms rather than in proportional terms. Firms, it is argued, do not state target debt as a ratio of market value (as implied by the cost of capital approach) but in dollar value terms. There are numerous variants of the adjusted present value model, with the variations primarily revolving around the discount rate used to compute the present value of tax benefits from debt. The original version of the model used the pre-tax cost of debt but subsequent versions developed by Ruback and Kaplan (1995) use the unlevered cost of equity; the latter are called compressed adjusted present value models and yield the same values as conventional cost of capital models. The former, however, generate slightly higher values.

37.6   VALUE ENHANCEMENT IN THE DCF WORLD

While we could look at any of the variations on discounted cash flow models, listed above, it is easiest to consider value enhancement in the cost of capital model. In this section, we will first quickly review the determinants of value in a discounted cash flow model and follow up by looking at how value enhancement fits into the model.

37.6.1   Determinants of value

In the fullest version of firm value models, the value of a firm is the present value of cash flows generated both by existing assets and by future investments. Thus, there are five key inputs that determine value:

- *Cash flows from existing assets*: The cash flow from existing assets is the cash flow left over after taxes and reinvestment to maintain these assets, but before debt payments.

$$\text{Free cash flow to the firm} = \text{EBIT}(1 - t)(1 - \text{Reinvestment rate})$$

This cash flow will reflect how efficiently the firm manages these assets.

- *Expected growth rate during extraordinary growth period*: The value of a firm should be a function is the expected growth rate in operating income. The fundamentals that drive growth are simple and growth itself has two parts to it. The first component is growth from new investments, which is the product of a firm's reinvestment rate, i.e. the proportion of the after-tax operating income that is invested in net capital expenditures and changes in non-cash working capital, and the quality of these reinvestments, measured by the return on the capital (ROC) invested.

$$\text{Expected growth}_{New\ investments} = \text{Reinvestment rate}^* \text{Return on capital}$$

The second component is the growth from managing existing investments more efficiently. This is the additional growth from generating a higher return on capital from existing investments and can be written as follows:

$$\text{Growth}_{efficiency} = (\text{ROC}_{t,\ Existing\ investments} - \text{ROC}_{t-1,\ Existing\ investments})/ \\ \text{ROC}_{t-1,\ Existing\ investments}$$

If the improvement in return on capital on existing investments occurs over multiple years, this growth rate has to be spread over the period.[1] The key difference between the two components of growth lies in their sustainability. Growth from new investments can continue in the long term, as long as the company continues to reinvest at the specified return on capital. Growth from existing assets can occur only in the short term, since there is a limit to how efficiently you can utilize existing assets.

- *Length of the extraordinary growth period*: Given that we cannot estimate cash flows forever, we generally impose closure in valuation models by assuming that cash flows, beyond the terminal year, will grow at a constant rate forever, which allows us to estimate the terminal value. Thus, in every discounted cash flow valuation, there are two critical assumptions we need to make on stable growth. The first relates to when the firm that we are valuing will become a stable growth firm, if it is not one already. The answer to this question will depend in large part on the magnitude and sustainability of the competitive advantages possessed by the firm. The second relates to what the characteristics of the firm will be in stable growth, in terms of return on capital and cost of capital. Stable growth firms generally have small or negligible excess returns and are of average risk.
- *Cost of capital*: The expected cash flows need to be discounted back at a rate that reflects the cost of financing these assets. Recapping the discussion in section 37.2, the cost of capital is a composite cost of financing that reflects the costs of both debt and equity, and their relative weights in the financing structure. The cost of equity represents the rate of return required by equity investors in the firm, and the cost of debt measures the current cost of borrowing, adjusted for the tax benefits of borrowing. A firm's cost of capital will be determined by the mix of debt and equity it chooses to use, and whether the debt reflects the assets of the firm; long-term assets should be funded with long-term debt and short term assets by short term debt. Using a sub-optimal mix of debt and equity to fund

---

[1] If the doubling in return on capital occurs over 5 years, for instance, the growth rate each year can be estimated as follows:

$$\text{Annual growth rate} = \{1 + (\text{ROC}_t - \text{ROC}_{t-1})/\text{ROC}_{t-1}\}^{1/n} - 1 = (1 + (.10 - .05)/.05)^{1/5} - 1 = .1487$$

The compounded annual growth rate will be 14.87%.

its investments or mismatching debt to assets can result in a higher cost of capital and a lower firm value.

• *Cash, cross holdings and other non-operating assets*: Once the operating assets have been valued, we generally add on the value of cash, cross holdings and other assets owned by the firm. While the conventional view is that cash holdings are neutral, the evidence suggests that cash, at least in the hands of some companies, is viewed as value destructive. The same can be said about cross holdings in other companies.

In summary, then, to value any firm, we begin by estimating how long high growth will last, how high the growth rate will be during that period and the cash flows during the period. We end by estimating a terminal value and discounting all of the cash flows, including the terminal value, back to the present to estimate the value of the operating assets of the firm. Adding back the value of cash, cross holdings and non-operating assets yields the firm's value. Figure 37.3 summarizes the process and the determinants of a firm's value.

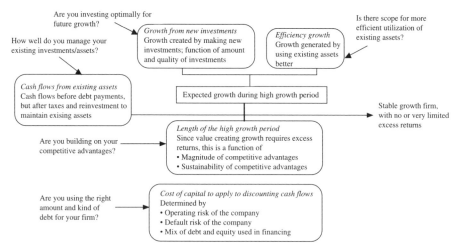

Figure 37.3   Determinants of firm value

37.6.2   Ways of increasing value

A firm can increase its value by increasing cash flows from current operations, increasing expected growth and the period of high growth and by reducing its composite cost of financing.[2] In reality, however, none of these is easily accomplished and whether these changes can be made is a function of all of the qualitative factors that we are often accused of ignoring in valuation – the quality of management, the strength of brand name, strategic decisions and good marketing.

Increase cash flows from assets in place

The first place to look for value is in the assets in place of the firm. These assets reflect investments that have already been made by the firm that generate the current operating

---

[2] In practical terms, this firm will have to raise external financing, either from debt or equity or both, to cover the excess reinvestment.

income for the firm. To the extent that these investments earn less than the cost of capital, or are earning less than they could, if optimally managed, there is potential for value creation. In general, actions taken to increase cash flows from assets in place can be categorized into the following groups:

- *Asset redeployment*: To the extent that the assets of a business are poorly invested, you can increase the cash flows and value of the firm by divesting poorly performing assets[3] or by moving assets from their existing uses to ones that generate higher value. One example would be a retail firm that owns its stores and decides that the store spaces would be worth more developed as commercial real estate instead of being used in retailing.
- *Improved operating efficiency*: When a firm's operations are riddled with inefficiencies, reducing or eliminating these inefficiencies will translate into an increase in operating cash flows and value. Thus, a telecommunications firm that is overstaffed should be able to generate value by reducing the size of its workforce. A steel company that is losing money because of outdated equipment in its plants may be able to increase its value by replacing them with newer, more efficient equipment. In recent years, manufacturing companies in developed markets like the United States and Western Europe have been able to generate substantial savings in costs by moving their operations to emerging markets where labor costs are lower.
- *Reduce tax burden*: It is every firm's obligation to pay its rightful due in taxes but not to pay more than its fair share. If a firm can legally reduce its tax burden, it should do so. A multinational firm may be able to reduce its taxes by moving more of its operations (and the ensuing earnings) to lower tax locales. Risk management can also play a role in reducing taxes by smoothing out earnings over periods; spikes in income can subject a firm to higher taxes.
- *Reduce capital maintenance and working capital investments*: A significant portion of after-tax operating income is often reinvested in the firm not to generate future growth but to maintain existing operations. This reinvestment includes capital maintenance (which is capital expenditure designed to maintain and replace existing assets) and investments in inventory or accounts receivable. Much of this reinvestment may be unavoidable, because assets age and firms need working capital to generate sales. In some firms, though, there may be potential for savings, especially in working capital. A retail firm that maintains inventory at 10% of sales, when the average for the sector is only 5%, can increase cash flows substantially if it can bring its inventory levels down to industry standards.

Increase expected growth

A firm with low current cash flows can still have high value if it is able to grow quickly during the high growth period. As noted earlier, higher growth can come either from new investments or from more efficiently utilizing existing assets.

- With new investments, higher growth has to come from either a *higher reinvestment rate or a higher return on capital on new investments or both*. Higher growth does not always translate into higher value, since the growth effect can be offset by changes elsewhere in

---

[3] At first sight, divesting businesses that are earning poor returns or losing money may seem like the ticket to value creation. However, the real test is whether the divestiture value exceeds the value of continuing in the business; if it is, divestiture makes sense. After all, when a business is earning poor returns, it is unlikely that a potential buyer will pay a premium price for it.

the valuation. Thus, higher reinvestment rates usually result in higher expected growth but at the expense of lower cash flows, since more reinvestment reduces free cash flows at least in the near term.[4] To the extent that the return on capital on the new investments is higher (lower) than the cost of capital, the value of the business will increase (decrease) as the reinvestment rate rises. Similarly, higher returns on capital also cause expected growth to increase, but value can still go down if the new investments are in riskier businesses and there is a more than proportionate increase in the cost of capital.

• With existing assets, the effect is more unambiguous, with higher returns on capital translating into higher growth and higher value. A firm that is able to increase its return on capital on existing assets from 2 to 8% over the next 5 years will report healthy growth and higher value.

Which of these two avenues offers the most promise for value creation? The answer will depend upon the firm in question. For mature firms with low returns on capital (especially when less than the cost of capital), extracting more growth from existing assets is likely to yield quicker results, at least in the short term. For smaller firms with relatively few assets in place, generating reasonable returns, growth has to come from new investments that generate healthy returns.

Lengthen the period of high growth

As noted above, every firm, at some point in the future, will become a stable growth firm, growing at a rate equal to or less than the economy in which it operates. In addition, growth creates value only if the return on investments exceeds the cost of capital. Clearly, the longer high growth and excess returns last, other things remaining equal, the greater the value of the firm. Note, however, that no firm should be able to earn excess returns for any length of period in a competitive product market, since competitors will be attracted by the excess returns into the business. Thus, implicit in the assumption that there will be high growth, in conjunction with excess returns, is also the assumption that there exist some barriers to entry that prevent firms from earning excess returns for extended time periods.

Given this relationship between how long firms can grow at above-average rates and the existence of barriers to entry, one way firms can increase value is by increasing existing barriers to entry and coming up with new barriers to entry. Another way of saying the same thing is to note that companies that earn excess returns have significant competitive advantages. Nurturing these advantages can increase value.

Reduce the cost of financing

The cost of capital for a firm was defined earlier to be a composite cost of debt and equity financing. The cash flows generated over time are discounted back to today at the cost of capital. Holding the cash flows constant, reducing the cost of capital, will increase the value of the firm. There are four ways in which a firm can bring its cost of capital down, or more generally, increase its firm value by changing both financing mix and type:

---

[4] Acquisitions have to be considered as part of capital expenditures for reinvestment. Thus, it is relatively easy for firms to increase their reinvestment rates but very difficult for these firms to maintain high returns on capital as they do so.

- *Make products/services less discretionary*: The operating risk of a firm is a direct function of the products or services it provides and the degree to which these products/services are discretionary to its customers. The more discretionary they are, the greater the operating risk faced by the firm. Consequently, firms can reduce their operating risk by making their products and services less discretionary to their customers. Advertising clearly plays a role, but coming up with new uses for a product/service may be another.
- *Reduce operating leverage*: The operating leverage of a firm measures the proportion of its costs that are fixed. Other things remaining equal, the greater the proportion of the costs of a firm that are fixed, the more volatile its earnings will be, and the higher its cost of equity/capital will be. Reducing the proportion of the costs that are fixed will make a firm less risky and reduce its cost of capital.[5]
- *Changing financing mix*: Debt is always cheaper than equity, partly because lenders bear less risk than equity investors and partly because of the tax advantage associated with debt. Offsetting this advantage is the fact that borrowing money increases the risk and the cost of both debt (by increasing the probability of bankruptcy) and equity (by making earnings to equity investors more volatile). The net effect will determine whether the cost of capital will increase or decrease if the firm takes on more debt. One way of defining the optimal financing mix is to define it as the mix at which the cost of capital is minimized.
- *Match financing to assets*: The fundamental principle in designing the financing of a firm is to ensure that the cash flows on the debt match as closely as possible the cash flows on the asset. Firms that mismatch cash flows on debt and cash flows on assets (by using short-term debt to finance long-term assets, debt in one currency to finance assets in a different currency or floating rate debt to finance assets whose cash flows tend to be adversely impacted by higher inflation) will end up with higher default risk, higher costs of capital and lower firm values. To the extent that firms can use derivatives and swaps to reduce these mismatches, firm value can be increased.

Manage non-operating assets

In the first four components of value creation, we have focused on ways in which a firm can increase its value from operating assets. A significant chunk of a firm's value can derive from its non-operating assets – cash and marketable securities, holdings in other companies and pension fund assets (and obligations). To the extent that these assets are sometimes mismanaged, there is potential for value enhancement here.

Cash and marketable securities   In conventional valuation, we assume that the cash and marketable securities that are held by a firm are added on to the value of operating assets to arrive at the value of the firm. Implicitly, we assume that cash and marketable securities are neutral investments (zero NPV investments), earning a fair rate of return, given the risk of the investments. Thus, a cash balance of $2 billion invested in Treasury bills and commercial paper may earn a low rate of return but that return is what you would expect to earn on these investments.

There are, however, two scenarios where a large cash balance may not be value neutral and thus provide opportunities for value enhancement. The first is when cash is invested

---

[5] Outsourcing and more flexible wage contracts, both phenomena that have been widely reported on over the last decade, can be viewed as attempts by firms to reduce their fixed costs.

at below market rates. A firm with $2 billion in a cash balance held in a non-interest bearing checking account is clearly hurting its stockholders. The second is when investors are concerned that the cash will be misused by management to make poor investments (or acquisitions). In this case, there will be a discount applied to cash to reflect the likelihood that management will misuse the cash and the consequences of such misuse. Reverting back to the example of the company with $2 billion in cash, assume that investors believe that there is a 25% chance that this cash will be used to fund an acquisition and that the firm will over pay by $500 million on this acquisition. The value of cash at this company can be estimated as follows:

Value of cash = Stated cash balance − Probability of poor investment ∗
          Cost of poor investment = $2 billion − 0.25 ∗ 0.5 billion = $1.875 billion

In either of these scenarios, returning some or all of this cash to stockholders in the form of dividends or stock buybacks will make stockholders better off.

Holdings in other companies   When firms acquire stakes in other firms, the value of these holdings will be added on to the value of operating assets to arrive at the value of the equity of the firm. In conventional valuation, again these holdings have a neutral effect on value. As with cash, there are potential problems with these cross holdings that can cause them to be discounted (relative to their true value) by markets. Cross holdings are difficult to value, especially when they are in subsidiary firms with different risk and growth profiles than the parent company. It is not surprising that firms with substantial cross holdings in diverse businesses often find these holdings being undervalued by the market. In some cases, this undervaluation can be blamed on information gaps, caused by the failure to convey important details on growth, risk and cash flows on cross holdings to the markets. In other cases, the undervaluation may reflect market skepticism about the parent company's capacity to manage its cross holding portfolio; consider this a conglomerate discount.[6] If such a discount applies, the prescription for increased value is simple. Spinning off or divesting the cross holdings and thus exposing their true value should make stockholders in the parent company better off.

Pension fund obligations (and liabilities)   Most firms have large pension obligations and matching pension assets. To the extent that both the obligations and assets grow over time, they offer both threats and opportunities. A firm that mismanages its pension fund assets may find itself with an unfunded pension obligation, which reduces the value of its equity. On the other hand, a firm that generates returns that are higher than expected on its pension fund assets could end up with an overfunded pension plan and higher equity value.

There are ways of creating value from pension fund investments, though some are more questionable from an ethical perspective than others. The first is to invest pension fund assets better, generating higher risk-adjusted returns and higher value for stockholders. The second (and more questionable approach) is to reduce pension fund obligations, either by renegotiating with employees or by passing the obligation on to other entities (such as the government) while holding on to pension fund assets.

---

[6] Studies looking at conglomerates conclude that they trade at a discount of between 5 and 10% on the value of the pieces that they are composed of.

38

Liquidation and Accounting Valuation

The value of an asset in the discounted cash flow framework is the present value of the expected cash flows on that asset. Extending this proposition to valuing a business, it can be argued that the value of a business is the sum of the values of the individual assets owned by the business. While this may be technically right, there is a key difference between valuing a collection of assets and a business. A business or a company is an ongoing entity with assets that it already owns and assets it expects to invest in the future. This can be best seen when we look at the financial balance sheet (as opposed to an accounting balance sheet) for an ongoing company in Figure 38.1:

Assets			Liabilities	
Assets in place Existing investments generate cash flows today	Investments already made	Debt	Borrowed money
Growth assets Expected value that will be created by future investments	Investments yet to be made	Equity	Owner's funds

Figure 38.1 A simple view of a firm

Note that investments that have already been made are categorized as assets in place, but investments that we expect the business to make in the future are growth assets.

A financial balance sheet provides a good framework to draw out the differences between valuing a business as a going concern and valuing it as a collection of assets. In a going concern valuation, we have to make our best judgments not only on existing investments but also on expected future investments and their profitability. While this may seem to be foolhardy, a large proportion of the market value of growth companies comes from their growth assets. In an asset-based valuation, we focus primarily on the assets in place and estimate the value of each asset separately. Adding the asset values together yields the value of the business. For companies with lucrative growth opportunities, asset-based valuations will yield lower values than going concern valuations.

38.1   BOOK VALUE-BASED VALUATION

There are some who contend that the accounting estimate of the value of a business, as embodied by the book value of the assets and equity on a balance sheet, represents a more reliable estimate of value than valuation models based on shaky assumptions about the future. In this section, we examine book value as a measure of the value of going concern and then extend the analysis to look at book value-based valuation models that also use forecasted earnings to estimate value. We end the section with a short discussion of fair value accounting, a movement that has acquired momentum in recent years.

38.1.1 Book value

The original ideals for accounting statements were that the income statements would provide a measure of the true earnings potential of a firm and that the balance sheet would yield a reliable estimate of the value of the assets and equity in the firm. Daniels (1934), for instance, lays out these ideals thus:

> In short the lay reader of financial statements usually believes that the total asset figure of the balance sheet is indicative, and is intended to be so, of the value of the company. He probably is understanding this "value" as what the business could be sold for, market value – the classic meeting of the minds between a willing buyer and seller.[1]

In the years since, accountants have wrestled with how to put this ideal into practice. In the process, they have had to weigh how much importance should be given to the historical cost of an asset relative to its estimated value today and have settled on different rules. For fixed assets, they have largely concluded that the book value should be reflective of the original cost of the asset and subsequent depletion in and additions to that asset. For current assets, they have been much more willing to consider the alternative of market value. Finally, they have discovered new categories for assets such as brand name where neither the original cost nor the current value is easily accessible.

While there are few accountants who would still contend that the book value of a company is a good measure of its market value, this has not stopped some investors from implicitly making that assumption. In fact, the notion that a stock is undervalued if is market price falls below its book value is deeply entrenched in investing. It is one of the screens that Ben Graham (1949) proposed for finding undervalued stocks and it remains a rough proxy for what is loosely called value investing.[2] Academics have fed into this belief by presenting evidence that low price to book value stocks do earn higher returns than the rest of the market (Fama and French, 1992).

Is it possible for book value to be a reasonable proxy for the true value of a business? For mature firms with predominantly fixed assets, little or no growth opportunities and no potential for excess returns, the book value of the assets may yield a reasonable measure of the true value of these firms. For firms with significant growth opportunities in businesses where they can generate excess returns, book values will be very different from true value.

38.1.2 Book value plus earnings

In the context of equity valuation models, we consider earnings-based models that have been developed in recent years, primarily in the accounting community. Most of these models

---

[1] Daniels (1934), p. 114.
[2] Morningstar categorizes mutual funds into growth and value, based upon the types of stocks that they invest in. Funds that invest in low price to book stocks are categorized as value funds.

are built on a combination of book values and expected future earnings and trace their antecedents to Ohlson (1995) and Feltham and Ohlson (1995). Ohlson's basic model states the true value of equity as a function of its book value of equity and the excess equity returns that the firm can generate in the future. As a consequence, it is termed a residual income model and can be derived from a simple dividend discount model:

$$\text{Value of equity} = \sum_{t=1}^{t=\infty} \frac{E(\text{Dividends}_t)}{(1 + \text{Cost of Equity})^t}$$

Now substitute in the full equation for book value (BV) of equity as a function of the starting book equity and earnings and dividends during a period (clean surplus relationship):

$$\text{Book value of equity}_t = \text{BV of equity}_{t-1} + \text{Net income}_t - \text{Dividends}_t$$

Substituting back into the dividend discount model, we get

$$\text{Value of equity} = \sum_{t=1}^{\infty} \frac{(\text{Net income}_t - \text{Cost of equity}_t \times \text{BV of equity}_{t-1})}{(1 + \text{Cost of equity}_t)^t}$$

Thus the value of equity in a firm is the sum of the current book value of equity and the present value of the expected excess returns to equity investors in perpetuity. In effect, this is an excess return model framed in terms of equity, rather than the firm.

38.1.3   Fair value accounting

In the last decade, there has been a strong push from both accounting rule makers and regulators towards "fair value accounting". Presumably, the impetus for this push has been a return to the original ideal that the book value of the assets on a balance sheet and the resulting net worth for companies are good measures of the fair value of these assets and equity.

The move towards fair value accounting has not been universally welcomed even within the accounting community. On the one hand, there are some who believe that this is a positive development increasing the connection of accounting statements to value and providing useful information to financial markets (Barth et al., 2001). There are others who believe that fair value accounting increases the potential for accounting manipulation, and that financial statements will become less informative as a result (Holthausen and Watts, 2001). In fact, it used to be commonplace for firms in the United States to revalue their assets at fair market value until 1934, but the SEC discouraged this practice after 1934 to prevent the widespread manipulation that was prevalent (Fabricant, 1938). While this debate rages on, the accounting standards boards have adopted a number of rules that favor fair value accounting, from the elimination of purchase accounting in acquisitions to the requirement that more assets be marked to market on the balance sheet.

The question then becomes an empirical one. Do fair value judgments made by accountants provide information to financial markets or do they just muddy up the waters? We believe that fair value accounting, at best, will provide a delayed reflection of what happens in the market. In other words, goodwill will be impaired (as it was in many technology companies in 2000 and 2001) after the market value has dropped and fair value adjustments will convey little, if any, information to financial markets. If in the process of marking to market, some of the raw data that is now provided to investors is replaced or held back, we will end up with accounting statements that reflect neither market value nor invested capital.

38.2   LIQUIDATION VALUATION

One special case of asset-based valuation is liquidation valuation, where we value assets based upon the presumption that they have to be sold now. In theory, this should be equal to the value obtained from discounted cash flow valuations of individual assets but the urgency associated with liquidating assets quickly may result in a discount on the value. The magnitude of the discount will depend upon the number of potential buyers for the assets, the asset characteristics and the state of the economy.

The research on liquidation value can be categorized into two groups. The first group of studies examines the relationship between liquidation value and the book value of assets, whereas the second takes apart the deviations of liquidation value from discounted cash flow value and addresses directly the question of how much of a cost you bear when you have to liquidate assets rather than sell a going concern.

While it may seem naïve to assume that liquidation value is equal or close to book value, a number of liquidation rules of thumb are structured around book value. For instance, it is not uncommon to see analysts assume that liquidation value will be a specified percentage of book value. The relationship between liquidation and discounted cash flow value is more difficult to discern. It stands to reason that liquidation value should be significantly lower than discounted cash flow value, partly because the latter reflects the value of expected growth potential and the former usually does not. In addition, the urgency associated with the liquidation can have an impact on the proceeds, since the discount on value can be considerable for those sellers who are eager to divest their assets.

In summary, liquidation valuation is likely to yield more realistic estimates of value for firms that are distressed, where the going concern assumption underlying conventional discounted cash flow valuation is clearly violated. For healthy firms with significant growth opportunities, it will provide estimates of value that are far too conservative.

38.3   VALUE ENHANCEMENT IN THE ACCOUNTING WORLD

If we accept the notion that value is determined by accounting measures of value or liquidation value, our perspectives on value enhancement change accordingly. In general, what we do to create value will be tailored to accounting rules and conventions rather than cash flows and fundamentals. As an extreme example, consider a world where the book value of assets is considered the best measure of a firm's value. Everything firms do will then be directed towards increasing the book value of assets, even if doing so makes no economic sense. Conversely, if value is driven by accounting returns – return on equity and return on invested capital are two widely used measures – actions that increase these returns will be considered to be value enhancing. In the 1990s, for instance, the focus on return on invested capital resulted in massive stock buybacks even at firms that could not afford to do these buybacks, motivated by the desire to bring the book value of capital down (and return on capital up).

While the notion of catering to accounting convention sounds misconceived, a great deal of what passes for value enhancement is really built around it. Note that most value enhancement measures are structured around a key accounting measure or dependent on accounting numbers – return on invested capital and capital invested for Economic Value Added (EVA) and gross investment in fixed assets (for CFROI). Concurrently, firms are often willing to spend considerable sums of money to qualify for accounting treatment that either increases the reported earnings or reduces the book value of capital.

39

Relative Valuation

In relative valuation, we value an asset based upon how similar assets are priced in the market. A prospective house buyer decides how much to pay for a house by looking at the prices paid for similar houses in the neighborhood. A baseball card collector makes a judgment on how much to pay for a Mickey Mantle rookie card by checking transactions prices on other Mickey Mantle rookie cards. In the same vein, a potential investor in a stock tries to estimate its value by looking at the market pricing of "similar" stocks.

39.1 STEPS IN RELATIVE VALUATION

Embedded in this description are the three essential steps in relative valuation. The first step is *finding comparable assets that are priced by the market*, a task that is easier to accomplish with real assets like baseball cards and houses than it is with stocks. All too often, analysts use other companies in the same sector as comparable, comparing a software firm to other software firms or a utility to other utilities, but we will question whether this practice really yields similar companies later in this part. The second step is *scaling the market prices to a common variable* to generate standardized prices that are comparable. While this may not be necessary when comparing identical assets (Mickey Mantle rookie cards), it is necessary when comparing assets that vary in size or units. Other things remaining equal, a smaller house or apartment should trade at a lower price than a larger residence. In the context of stocks, this equalization usually requires converting the market value of equity or the firm into multiples of earnings, book value or revenues. The third and last step in the process is *adjusting for differences across assets* when comparing their standardized values. Again, using the example of a house, a newer house with more updated amenities should be priced higher than a similar sized older house that needs renovation. With stocks, differences in pricing across stocks can be attributed to all of the fundamentals that we talked about in discounted cash flow valuation. Higher growth companies, for instance, should trade at higher multiples than lower growth companies in the same sector. Many analysts adjust for these differences qualitatively, making every relative valuation a story telling experience; analysts with better and more believable stories are given credit for better valuations.

39.2 BASIS FOR APPROACH

There is a significant philosophical difference between discounted cash flow and relative valuation. In discounted cash flow valuation, we are attempting to estimate the intrinsic value of an asset based upon its capacity to generate cash flows in the future. In relative valuation, we are making a judgment on how much an asset is worth by looking at what the market is paying for similar assets. If the market is correct, on average, in the way it prices assets, discounted cash flow and relative valuations may converge. If, however, the market is systematically overpricing or underpricing a group of assets or an entire sector, discounted cash flow valuations can deviate from relative valuations.

Harking back to our earlier discussion of discounted cash flow valuation, we argued that discounted cash flow valuation was a search (albeit unfulfilled) for intrinsic value. In relative valuation, we have given up on estimating intrinsic value and essentially put our trust in markets getting it right, at least on average. It can be argued that most valuations are relative valuations. Damodaran (2002) notes that almost 90% of equity research valuations and 50% of acquisition valuations use some combination of multiples and comparable companies and are thus relative valuations.

39.3 STANDARDIZED VALUES AND MULTIPLES

When comparing identical assets, we can compare the prices of these assets. Thus, the price of a Tiffany lamp or a Mickey Mantle rookie card can be compared to the price at which an identical item was bought or sold in the market. However, comparing assets that are not exactly similar can be a challenge. After all, the price per share of a stock is a function both of the value of the equity in a company and the number of shares outstanding in the firm. Thus, a stock split that doubles the number of units will approximately halve the stock price. To compare the values of "similar" firms in the market, we need to standardize the values in some way by scaling them to a common variable. In general, values can be standardized relative to the earnings firms generate, to the book values or replacement values of the firms themselves, to the revenues that firms generate or to measures that are specific to firms in a sector.

- One of the more intuitive ways to think of the value of any asset is as a *multiple of the earnings that asset generates*. When buying a stock, it is common to look at the price paid as a multiple of the earnings per share generated by the company. This price/earnings ratio (P/E) can be estimated using current earnings per share, yielding a current PE, earnings over the last four quarters, resulting in a trailing PE, or an expected earnings per share in the next year, providing a forward PE. When buying a business, as opposed to just the equity in the business, it is common to examine the value of the firm as a multiple of the operating income or the earnings before interest, taxes, depreciation and amortization (EBITDA). While, as a buyer of the equity or the firm, a lower multiple is better than a higher one, these multiples will be affected by the growth potential and risk of the business being acquired.
- While financial markets provide one estimate of the value of a business, *accountants often provide a very different estimate of value* for the same business. As we noted earlier, investors often look at the relationship between the price they pay for a stock and the book value of equity (or net worth) as a measure of how over- or undervalued a stock is; the price/book value ratio that emerges can vary widely across industries, depending again upon the growth potential and the quality of the investments in each. When valuing businesses, we estimate this ratio using the value of the firm and the book value of all assets or capital (rather than just the equity). For those who believe that book value is not a good measure of the true value of the assets, an alternative is to use the replacement cost of the assets; the ratio of the value of the firm to replacement cost is called Tobin's Q.
- Both earnings and book value are accounting measures and are determined by accounting rules and principles. An alternative approach, which is far less affected by accounting

choices, is to use the *ratio of the value of a business to the revenues it generates*. For equity investors, this ratio is the price/sales ratio (PS), where the market value of equity is divided by the revenues generated by the firm. For firm value, this ratio can be modified as the enterprise value/sales ratio (VS), where the numerator becomes the market value of the operating assets of the firm. This ratio, again, varies widely across sectors, largely as a function of the profit margins in each. The advantage of using revenue multiples, however, is that it becomes far easier to compare firms in different markets, with different accounting systems at work, than it is to compare earnings or book value multiples.

- While earnings, book value and revenue multiples are multiples that can be computed for firms in any sector and across the entire market, there are some *multiples that are specific to a sector*. For instance, when internet firms first appeared on the market in the later 1990s, they had negative earnings and negligible revenues and book value. Analysts looking for a multiple to value these firms divided the market value of each of these firms by the number of hits generated by that firm's website. Firms with lower market value per customer hit were viewed as undervalued. More recently, cable companies have been judged by the market value per cable subscriber, regardless of the longevity and the profitably of having these subscribers. While there are conditions under which sector-specific multiples can be justified, they are dangerous for two reasons. First, since they cannot be computed for other sectors or for the entire market, sector-specific multiples can result in persistent over- or undervaluations of sectors relative to the rest of the market. Thus, investors who would never consider paying 80 times revenues for a firm might not have the same qualms about paying $2000 for every page hit (on the website), largely because they have no sense of what high, low or average is on this measure. Second, it is far more difficult to relate sector-specific multiples to fundamentals, which is an essential ingredient to using multiples well. For instance, does a visitor to a company's website translate into higher revenues and profits? The answer will not only vary from company to company, but will also be difficult to estimate looking forward.

39.4   DETERMINANTS OF MULTIPLES

In the introduction to discounted cash flow valuation, we observed that the value of a firm is a function of three variables – its capacity to generate cash flows, the expected growth in these cash flows and the uncertainty associated with these cash flows. Every multiple, whether it is of earnings, revenues or book value, is a function of the same three variables – risk, growth and cash flow generating potential. Intuitively, then, firms with higher growth rates, less risk and greater cash flow generating potential should trade at higher multiples than firms with lower growth, higher risk and less cash flow potential.

The specific measures of growth, risk and cash flow generating potential that are used will vary from multiple to multiple. To look under the hood, so to speak, of equity and firm value multiples, we can go back to fairly simple discounted cash flow models for equity and firm value and use them to derive the multiples. In the simplest discounted cash flow model for equity, which is a stable growth dividend discount model, the value of equity is:

$$\text{Value of equity} = P_0 = \frac{\text{DPS}_1}{k_e - g_n}$$

where DPS_1 is the expected dividend in the next year, k_e is the cost of equity and g_n is the expected stable growth rate. Dividing both sides by the earnings, we obtain the discounted cash flow equation specifying the PE ratio for a stable growth firm:

$$\frac{P_0}{EPS_0} = PE = \frac{\text{Payout ratio}^*(1+g_n)}{k_e - g_n}$$

The key determinants of the PE ratio are the expected growth rate in earnings per share, the cost of equity and the payout ratio. Other things remaining equal, we would expect higher growth, lower risk and higher payout ratio firms to trade at higher multiples of earnings than firms without these characteristics.

Dividing both sides of the stable growth dividend discount model by the book value of equity, we can estimate the price/book value ratio for a stable growth firm:

$$\frac{P_0}{BV_0} = PBV = \frac{ROE^*\text{Payout ratio}^*(1+g_n)}{k_e - g_n}$$

where ROE is the return on equity and is the only variable in addition to the three that determine PE ratios (growth rate, cost of equity and payout) that affects price to book equity.

Finally, dividing both sides of the dividend discount model by revenues per share, the price/sales ratio for a stable growth firm can be estimated as a function of its profit margin, payout ratio, risk and expected growth:

$$\frac{P_0}{Sales_0} = PS = \frac{\text{Profit margin}^*\text{Payout ratio}^*(1+g_n)}{k_e - g_n}$$

The net margin is the new variable that is added to the process. While all of these computations are based upon a stable growth dividend discount model, we will show that the conclusions hold even when we look at companies with high growth potential and with other equity valuation models.

We can do a similar analysis to derive the firm value multiples. The value of a firm in stable growth can be written as:

$$\text{Value of firm} = V_0 = \frac{FCFF_1}{k_c - g_n}$$

Dividing both sides by the expected free cash flow to the firm yields the value/FCFF multiple for a stable growth firm:

$$\frac{V_0}{FCFF_1} = \frac{1}{k_c - g_n}$$

The multiple of FCFF that a firm commands will depend upon two variables – its cost of capital and its expected stable growth rate. Since the free cash flow the firm is the after-tax operating income netted against the net capital expenditures and working capital needs of the firm, the multiples of EBIT, after-tax EBIT and EBITDA can also be estimated similarly.

In short, multiples are determined by the same variables and assumptions that underlie discounted cash flow valuation. The difference is that while the assumptions are explicit in the latter, they are often implicit in the use of the former.

39.5   COMPARABLE FIRMS

When multiples are used, they tend to be used in conjunction with comparable firms to determine the value of a firm or its equity. But what is a comparable firm? A comparable firm is one with cash flows, growth potential, and risk similar to the firm being valued. It would be ideal if we could value a firm by looking at how an exactly identical firm – in terms of risk, growth and cash flows – is priced. Nowhere in this definition is there a component that relates to the industry or sector to which a firm belongs. Thus, a telecommunications firm can be compared to a software firm, if the two are identical in terms of cash flows, growth and risk. In most analyses, however, analysts define comparable firms to be other firms in the firm's business or businesses. If there are enough firms in the industry to allow for it, this list is pruned further using other criteria; for instance, only firms of similar size may be considered. The implicit assumption being made here is that firms in the same sector have similar risk, growth, and cash flow profiles and therefore can be compared with much more legitimacy. This approach becomes more difficult to apply when there are relatively few firms in a sector. In most markets outside the United States, the number of publicly traded firms in a particular sector, especially if it is defined narrowly, is small. It is also difficult to define firms in the same sector as comparable firms if differences in risk, growth and cash flow profiles across firms within a sector are large. The tradeoff is therefore a simple one. Defining an industry more broadly increases the number of comparable firms, but it also results in a more diverse group of companies.

39.6   CONTROLLING FOR DIFFERENCES ACROSS FIRMS

No matter how carefully we construct our list of comparable firms, we will end up with firms that are different from the firm we are valuing. The differences may be small on some variables and large on others and we will have to control for these differences in a relative valuation. There are three ways of controlling for these differences:

- *Subjective judgments*: Relative valuation begins with two choices – the multiple used in the analysis and the group of firms that comprises the comparable firms. In many relative valuations, the multiple is calculated for each of the comparable firms and the average is computed. One issue that does come up with subjective adjustments to industry average multiples is how best to compute that average. To evaluate an individual firm, the analyst then compares the multiple it trades at to the average computed; if it is significantly different, the analyst can make a subjective judgment about whether the firm's individual characteristics (growth, risk or cash flows) may explain the difference. If, in the judgment of the analyst, the difference on the multiple cannot be explained by the fundamentals, the firm will be viewed as overvalued (if its multiple is higher than the average) or undervalued (if its multiple is lower than the average). The weakness in this approach is not that analysts are called upon to make subjective judgments, but that the judgments are often based upon little more than guesswork. All too often, these judgments confirm their biases about companies.
- *Modified multiples*: In this approach, we modify the multiple to take into account the most important variable determining it – the companion variable. To provide an illustration, analysts who compare PE ratios across companies with very different growth rates often divide the PE ratio by the expected growth rate in EPS to determine a growth-adjusted PE

ratio or the PEG ratio. This ratio is then compared across companies with different growth rates to find under- and overvalued companies. There are two implicit assumptions that we make when using these modified multiples. The first is that these firms are comparable on all the other measures of value, other than the one being controlled for. In other words, when comparing PEG ratios across companies, we are assuming that they are all of equivalent risk. If some firms are riskier than others, you would expect them to trade at lower PEG ratios. The other assumption generally made is that the relationship between the multiples and fundamentals is linear. Again, using PEG ratios to illustrate the point, we are assuming that as growth doubles, the PE ratio will double; if this assumption does not hold up and PE ratios do not increase proportional to growth, companies with high growth rates will look cheap on a PEG ratio basis

- *Statistical techniques*: Subjective adjustments and modified multiples are difficult to use when the relationship between multiples and the fundamental variables that determine them becomes complex. There are statistical techniques that offer promise when this happens. In a regression, we attempt to explain a dependent variable by using independent variables that we believe influence the dependent variable. This mirrors what we are attempting to do in relative valuation, where we try to explain differences across firms on a multiple (PE ratio, EV/EBITDA) using fundamental variables (such as risk, growth and cash flows). Regressions offer three advantages over the subjective approach:

(a) The output from the regression gives us a measure of how strong the relationship is between the multiple and the variable being used. Thus, if we are contending that higher growth companies have higher PE ratios, the regression should yield clues to both how growth and PE ratios are related (through the coefficient on growth as an independent variable) and how strong the relationship is (through the t-statistics and R-squared).

(b) If the relationship between a multiple and the fundamental we are using to explain it is non-linear, the regression can be modified to allow for the relationship.

(c) Unlike the modified multiple approach, where we were able to control for differences on only one variable, a regression can be extended to allow for more than one variable and even for cross effects across these variables.

In general, regressions seem particularly suited to our task in relative valuation, which is to make sense of voluminous and sometimes contradictory data.

39.7   VALUE ENHANCEMENT IN THE RELATIVE VALUATION WORLD

If we begin with the presumption that the value of a company is based upon how the market values similar companies, value enhancement has to be directed towards what the market values and what it does not. In particular, if the market seems to be attaching a high value for growth and not charging much for risk, growth strategies, even if risky, will create value for firms. This was the case during the technology boom in the 1990s and companies responded accordingly by shifting to high risk, high growth strategies. One of the useful by-products of the sector regressions described in the last section is that we can quantify the effects of those variables that the market is weighing into value. Thus, regressing the price to book ratios for banks against growth rates and bad loan provisions may allow us to judge how much the market rewards earnings growth and punishes high risk loans at commercial banks. The output can then provide a template for deciding the best value enhancement strategy for a small bank. A similar regression of price earnings ratios for drug companies against profit margins and the depth of the product pipeline (measuring new drugs that are in various stages of development) may let us decipher how much the market values current profits and future growth at these companies. This can be used to determine how much to invest in R&D at a pharmaceutical company.

Will the actions taken to enhance value on a relative basis coincide with those taken to increase value on a discounted cash flow basis? The answer depends upon how well we set up the discounted cash flow model and how efficient the market is in pricing the fundamentals that go into those models. In one scenario (albeit an unlikely one), where markets are efficient and discounted cash flow models reflect fundamentals, actions taken to maximize value will be identical in both approaches. In a second scenario, where discounted cash flow models are deeply flawed and incomplete but markets are reasonably efficient, actions taken to increase relative value will have a much bigger and more long-term impact than actions taken to increase discounted cash flow value. In the third scenario, where market prices deviate from intrinsic value in the short term but converge in the long term, it is entirely possible that actions taken to increase relative value may be good for stock prices in the short term but hurt the firm in the long term.

40
Real Option Valuation

Perhaps the most significant and revolutionary development in valuation is the acceptance, at least in some cases, that the value of an asset may not be greater than the present value of expected cash flows if the cash flows are contingent on the occurrence or non-occurrence of an event. This acceptance has largely come about because of the development of option pricing models. While these models were initially used to value traded options, there has been an attempt, in recent years, to extend the reach of these models into more traditional valuation. There are many who argue that assets such as patents or undeveloped reserves are really options and should be valued as such, rather than with traditional discounted cash flow models.

40.1 BASIS FOR APPROACH

A contingent claim or option pays off only under certain contingencies – if the value of the underlying asset exceeds a pre-specified value for a call option, or is less than a pre-specified value for a put option. Much work has been done in the last 20 years in developing models that value options, and these option pricing models can be used to value any assets that have option-like features.

Figure 40.1 illustrates the payoffs on call and put options as a function of the value of the underlying asset.

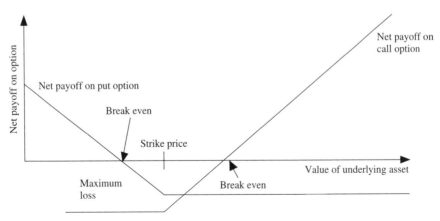

Figure 40.1 Payoff diagram on call and put options

An option can be valued as a function of the following variables – the current value, the variance in value of the underlying asset, the strike price, the time to expiration of the option and the riskless interest rate. This was first established by Black and Scholes (1973) and has been extended and refined subsequently in numerous variants. While the Black-Scholes option pricing model ignored dividends and assumed that options would not be exercised early, it can be modified to allow for both. A discrete-time variant, the binomial option pricing model, has also been developed to price options.

An asset can be valued as an option if the payoffs are a function of the value of an underlying asset. It can be valued as a call option if the payoff is contingent on the value of the asset exceeding a pre-specified level. It can be valued as a put option if the payoff increases as the value of the underlying asset drops below a pre-specified level.

40.2 THE ESSENCE OF REAL OPTIONS

To understand the basis of the real options argument and the reasons for its allure, it is easiest to use a different risk assessment tool – decision trees. Consider a very simple example of a decision tree in Figure 40.2.

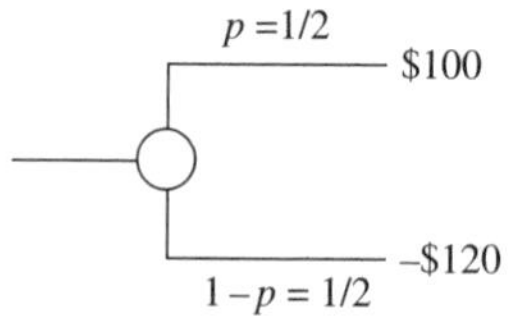

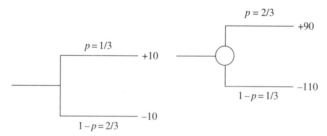

Figure 40.2 Simple decision tree

Given the equal probabilities of up and down movements, and the larger potential loss, the expected value for this investment is negative:

$$\text{Expected value} = 0.50(100) + 0.5(-120) = -\$10$$

Now contrast this with the slightly more complicated two-phase decision tree in Figure 40.3.

Figure 40.3 Two-phase decision tree

Note that the total potential profits and losses over the two phases in the tree are identical to the profit and loss of the simple tree in Figure 40.2; your total gain is $100 and your total loss is $120. Note also that the cumulative probabilities of success and failure remain at the 50% that we used in the simple tree. When we compute the expected value of this tree, though, the outcome changes:

$$\text{Expected value} = (2/3)(-10) + 1/3[10 + (2/3)(90) + (1/3)(-110)] = \$4.44$$

What is it about the second decision tree that makes a potentially bad investment (in the first tree) into a good investment (in the second)? We would attribute the change to two factors. First, by allowing for an initial phase where you get to observe the cash flows on a first and relatively small try at the investment, we allow for *learning*. Thus, getting a bad outcome in the first phase (-10 instead of $+10$) is an indicator that the overall investment is more likely to be money losing than money making. Second, you act on the learning by abandoning the investment, if the outcome from the first phase is negative; we will call this *adaptive behavior*.

In essence, the value of real options stems from the fact that when investing in risky assets, we can learn from observing what happens in the real world and adapting our behavior to increase our potential upside from the investment and to decrease the possible downside. In the real options framework, we use updated knowledge or information to expand opportunities while reducing danger. In the context of a risky investment, there are three potential actions that can be taken based upon this updated knowledge. The first is that you build on good fortune to increase your possible profits; this is the *option to expand*. For instance, a market test that suggests that consumers are far more receptive to a new product than you expected them to be could be used as a basis for expanding the scale of the project and speeding its delivery to the market. The second is to scale down or even abandon an investment when the information you receive contains bad news; this is the *option to abandon* and can allow you to cut your losses. The third is to hold off on making further investments, if the information you receive suggests ambivalence about future prospects; this is the *option to delay or wait*. You are, in a sense, buying time for the investment, hoping that product and market developments will make it attractive in the future.

We would add one final piece to the mix that is often forgotten but is just as important as the learning and adaptive behavior components in terms of contributing to the real options arguments. The value of learning is greatest when you and only you have access to that learning and can act on it. After all, the expected value of knowledge that is public, where anyone can act on that knowledge, will be close to zero. We will term this fourth condition *exclusivity* and use it to scrutinize when real options have the most value.

40.3   EXAMPLES OF REAL OPTIONS

There are many assets that generally are not viewed as options but still share several option characteristics. We can categorize these assets using the three types of options that we described in the last section:

(1) *The option to delay*: Investments are typically analyzed based upon their expected cash flows and discount rates at the time of the analysis; the net present value computed on that basis is a measure of its value and acceptability at that time. The rule that emerges is a simple one: negative net present value investments destroy value and should not be accepted. Expected cash flows and discount rates change over time, however, and so does the net present value. Thus, a project that has a negative net present value now may

have a positive net present value in the future. In a competitive environment, in which individual firms have no special advantages over their competitors in taking projects, this may not seem significant. In an environment in which a project can be taken by only one firm (because of legal restrictions or other barriers to entry to competitors), however, the changes in the project's value over time give it the characteristics of a call option. There are at least three possible areas in valuation where this can be relevant. The first is with *patents* on products or services, where the company has the option to develop the patent (but not the obligation). The argument goes that some patents may not have much value from a discounted cash flow perspective (negative net present values) but they can still create option value for their owners. The second and related point is that the *exclusive rights to a technology*, even if it is not viable, can be valuable from an option perspective. Finally, *undeveloped reserves* of oil, gold or any natural resource may give its owners an option; even if the reserves are not viable today, the volatility in the prices of natural resources will give them value as options.

(2) *The option to expand*: In some cases, a firm will take an investment because doing so allows it either to make other investments or to enter other markets in the future. In such cases, it can be argued that the initial investment provides the firm with an option to expand, and the firm should therefore be willing to pay a price for such an option. Consequently, a firm may be willing to lose money on the first investment because it perceives the option to expand as having a large enough value to compensate for the initial loss. The extensions of this option into valuation can be significant. Firms investing in large, emerging markets such as China and India may derive significantly more value from these investments than suggested by conventional discounted cash flow valuation. Exclusive or proprietary licenses to manufacture or sell goods may be worth more than discounting the cash flows would suggest, because they allow firms to expand in these markets. At the limit, this argument has been used to justify paying premiums over discounted cash flow values for high growth and technology firms; the reasoning is that these firms may be able to seize on unanticipated good fortune or opportunities to add value.

(3) *The option to abandon*: Firms that preserve the flexibility to back out of risky investments, if these investments do not pay off, should have the option to abandon built into their value.

40.4   VALUE ENHANCEMENT IN THE REAL OPTIONS WORLD

The actions taken to increase firm value in a real options world will seldom find their place in finance text books or accounting measures, because their focus is either on increasing flexibility in responding to crises or in keeping open the possibility of exploiting future opportunities. In fact, it is entirely possible for an action to be value destructive in the discounted cash flow model and value enhancing in a real options framework. At the risk of oversimplifying, the following are some of the ways in which a firm's real options value can be enhanced.

• *Play the upside*: Options models stand apart from other valuation models because risk is treated as an ally rather than an adversary; options increase in value as variance increases. In keeping with this link, value enhancement in a real options framework is much more attuned to taking advantage of risk rather than avoiding it. Thus, a drug company will increase its value by redirecting research to those areas where the least is known rather than the areas where more is known; the value of patents derived in the former will be worth more than patents in the latter.

- *Increase flexibility*: If there is a key word in the real options framework, it is flexibility. Actions that maintain or augment financial and operating flexibility will generate value for firms, by preserving the options that these firms have to expand or abandon investments in the future. Following this proposition, firms should try to make big investments in stages (allowing for stopping and reassessing at each stage) and not enter into long-term commitments unless they have significant economic benefits.
- *Value strategic considerations*: In finance, strategic considerations have been viewed with suspicion since the term is almost always used to override financial analyses. As a consequence, firms take negative net present value investments and pay premiums over estimated value in acquisitions for strategic considerations. While skepticism is still warranted, there are at least some scenarios where these strategic considerations refer to real options that a firm may acquire as a result of the negative net present value investment or acquisition.
- *Go for exclusivity*: Real options derive their value from the exclusive access (or as close to it) of opportunities. Anything that firms can do to increase this exclusivity will pay off as higher value. While some of this exclusivity can be garnered from legal sources (patents, trademarks, etc.) much of it has its source in competitive advantages acquired by the firm over time.

Value enhancement in the real options framework requires us to bring in strategic and financial considerations into play. As a consequence, it can be hard to quantify and measure but the potential payoff can be large.

41

Closing Thoughts on Value Enhancement

Value enhancement can take varied forms, depending in large part on how we approach valuation. With discounted cash flow valuation, the emphasis is on the fundamentals that drive value – cash flows, growth and risk. For an action to create value, it has to affect one or more of these levers of value. Accounting-based valuation models are focused on accounting earnings and book value. Not surprisingly, value enhancement is tailored to changing one or both of these measures, with tenuous connections to intrinsic value. With relative valuation, the focus shifts to multiples and how the market is pricing the peer group or sector. Consequently, value enhancement is much more tailored to market moods and perceptions, even if such perceptions may be unrelated to fundamentals. Real option valuations are not alternatives but supplements to conventional valuation models and consider the value added by increased flexibility and access to opportunities. Value enhancement in this framework has a heavy strategic component with the benefits often unlikely to show up in conventional valuation models.

So which value enhancement approach should you pick? The answer depends upon a number of factors. If you believe that markets are efficient, your choices become easier since relative and discounted cash flow approaches converge. If markets are not efficient, you have a fundamental decision to make on whether you want to emphasize price enhancement or value enhancement. If the focus is on increasing prices, your odds are better with relative valuation measures, since you will cater to what the market wants and values right now – higher earnings per share or higher growth, or instance. If you intend to increase value, you should consider discounted cash flow measures, since they take into account the fundamentals that determine long-term value, and hope that markets adjust at least over the long term. Focusing on accounting-based measures is almost never a sensible strategy since it will neither keep markets happy nor deliver higher value. Finally, option-based value enhancement measures can be used as a supplement to discounted cash flow models but only for firms that have exclusivity when it comes to taking advantage of opportunities.

Value enhancement is clearly on the minds of many managers today. As they look at various approaches to value enhancement, they should consider a few facts. The first is that no value enhancement mechanism will work at generating value unless there is a commitment on the part of managers to making value maximization their primary objective. If managers put other goals first, then no value enhancement mechanism will work. Conversely, if managers truly care about value maximization, they can make almost any mechanism work in their favor. The second is that while it is sensible to connect whatever value enhancement measure you have chosen to compensation, there is a down side. Managers, over time, will tend to focus their attention on making themselves look better on that measure even if that can be accomplished only by reducing firm value. Finally, there are no magic bullets that create value. Value creation is hard work in competitive markets and almost involves a tradeoff between costs and benefits. Everyone has a role in value creation, and it certainly is not the sole domain of financial analysts. In fact, the value created by financial engineers is smaller and less significant than the value created by good strategic, marketing, production or personnel divisions.

References

Barth, M., Beaver, W., and Landsman, W. (2001), The relevance of the value-relevance literature for financial accounting standard setting: another view, *Journal of Accounting and Economics*, 31, 77–104.

Black, F., and Scholes, M. (1973), The pricing of options and corporate liabilities, *Journal of Political Economy*, 86, 637–654.

Damodaran, A. (1994), *Damodaran on Valuation*, John Wiley & Sons.

Damodaran, A. (2002), *Investment Valuation*, 2nd Edition, John Wiley & Sons Ltd, New York.

Daniels, M.B. (1934), Principles of asset valuation, *The Accounting Review*, 9, 114–121.

Fabricant, S. (1938), *Capital Consumption and Adjustment*, National Bureau of Economic Research.

Fama, E.F., and French, K.R. (1992), The cross-section of expected returns, *Journal of Finance*, 47, 427–466.

Feltham, G., and Ohlson, J. (1995), Valuation and clean surplus accounting for operating and financial activities, *Contemporary Accounting Research*, 11, 689–731.

Graham, B. (1949), *The Intelligent Investor*, HarperCollins.

Holthausen, R., and Watts, R. (2001), The relevance of the value-relevance literature for financial accounting standard setting, *Journal of Accounting and Economics*, 31, 3–75.

Kaplan, S.N., and Ruback, R.S. (1995), The valuation of cash flow forecasts, *Journal of Finance*, 50, 1059–1093.

Modigliani, F., and Miller, M. (1963), Corporate income taxes and the cost of capital: a correction, *American Economic Review*, 53, 433–443.

Myers, S. (1974), Interactions in corporate financing and investment decisions – implications for capital budgeting, *Journal of Finance*, 29, 1–25.

Ohlson, J. (1995), Earnings, book values and dividends in security valuation, *Contemporary Accounting Research*, 11, 661–687.

Part VIII

Final Thoughts on Valuation[1]

Armin Varmaz[2], Thorsten Poddig[3] and Jan Viebig[4]

---

[1] DWS Investment GmbH, © 2008 Jan Viebig.
[2] Research Fellow, Chair of Finance, University of Bremen.
[3] Professor of Finance, University of Bremen.
[4] Managing Director, DWS Investment GmbH.

42
Introduction

The goal of this book is to explain to our readers how portfolio managers and financial analysts at leading investment banks analyze companies. The models presented in this book are all rooted in the present value framework for equity valuation pioneered by Merton Miller and Franco Modigliani in the early 1960's.[1]

In this final Part we discuss the underlying theory of valuation models from a theoretical perspective. Models are based on simplifying assumptions. In our opinion, a good understanding of the underlying assumptions of a valuation model can help investors avoid costly mistakes when interpreting its results. A good valuation model is simple and helps investors to make informed decisions in a complex and uncertain world. Simplicity, applicability and costs are important criteria for practitioners constructing and applying valuation models. A valuation model should be simple (but not too simple) so that the user can easily understand it, estimate its input parameters, as well as interpret and communicate its results. The benefits of a model must be weighed against the costs related to it. Anyone applying valuation models in practice should be aware of possible theoretical shortcomings and should be familiar with alternatives. It is then up to the user to decide whether to accept a valuation model or to reject it in favor of a more sophisticated approach – at the disadvantage of losing its simplicity, applicability and of higher costs.

The value of a firm depends on the ability of its managers to grow sales, reduce costs, control capital and ultimately to generate cash flows in excess of the claims against them. Portfolio managers and financial analysts apply discounted cash flow (DCF) models to translate cash flows into intrinsic or fair values. In Chapter 43, we discuss three alternatives to incorporate risk in the DCF framework. Most, but not all, professional investors apply the capital asset pricing model (CAPM) to estimate risk-adjusted discount rates. In the literature, certainty equivalents (CEQ) and risk neutral probabilities (RNP) are proposed as alternatives for considering uncertainty. While these models are rarely applied by investment professionals today, they have implications for pedagogy, practice and further research.

Reviewing the literature, we have to admit that valuation and asset allocation are not well integrated. They often appear to be isolated from each other and it is not always obvious how to integrate stock selection and asset allocation. In Chapter 44, we introduce the reader to multi-asset valuation and show how asset allocation and DCF valuation can be linked in practice. At the end of this Part, the reader will be familiar with important valuation concepts in academic literature.

---

[1] Miller and Modigliani (1961).

Valuation in Theory:
The Valuation of a Single Asset

43.1 CERTAIN CASH FLOWS

The starting point of the analysis is the premise that the value of a security can be derived from the cash flows which an investor obtains from owning it. Let us assume that an investor holds a stock for one period which pays a dividend D_1 at the end of the period. The cash flows to the stock holder in period 1 are the dividend payments D_1 and the proceeds P_1 from selling the stock at the end of period 1.[1] In the case of certainty, the fair value P_0 of the security today $(t=0)$ equals the sum of the cash flows CF_t to the stockholder discounted at the risk-free interest rate i_f.

$$P_0 = \frac{D_1}{(1+i_f)^1} + \frac{P_1}{(1+i_f)^1} = \frac{CF_1}{(1+i_f)^1}$$

As the present value PV of the stock price P_1 at the end of period 1 equals the discounted dividend paid in year 2, D_2, and the discounted value of the price in period 2, P_2, we can write:[2]

$$PV(P_1) = \frac{D_2}{(1+i_f)^2} + \frac{P_2}{(1+i_f)^2}$$

and thus

$$P_0 = \frac{D_1}{(1+i_f)^1} + \frac{D_2}{(1+i_f)^2} + \frac{P_2}{(1+i_f)^2}$$

Using the same technique for $t = 1, \ldots, \infty$ we can derive a general DCF formula under certainty. As the present value of the stock price approaches zero in infinity $(T \to \infty)$, we can stop discounting future prices at a period T in the distant future:[3]

$$P_0 \approx \frac{D_1}{\left(1+i_f\right)^1} + \frac{D_2}{\left(1+i_f\right)^2} + \frac{D_3}{\left(1+i_f\right)^3} + \cdots + \frac{D_T}{\left(1+i_f\right)^T}$$

The general DCF formula under certainty states that the value of any security is the present value of future net cash flows discounted at the risk-free rate.

---

[1] Elton *et al.* (2003), pp. 445–447.
[2] Levy (2002), pp. 254–257.
[3] Elton *et al.* (2003), p. 446, Levy (2002), p. 255.

The present value approach assumes complete competition and arbitrage-free pricing. According to the law of one price, in competitive markets financial instruments with *identical* cash flows must have the same price. If two identical assets do not trade at the same price, arbitrageurs can generate risk-free profits by buying the less expensive asset and short selling the more expensive but otherwise identical asset. A market is said to be in equilibrium, if no arbitrage opportunities exist (arbitrage-free pricing). In perfect financial markets, investors can make investment decisions based on objective criteria, e.g. the net present value rule, without regard to subjective preferences (Fisher separation principle). The net present value rule does not hold if investors cannot borrow and lend at the same risk-free rate i_f.[4]

From the general DCF formula above, we can deduce a large number of different variants of DCF models if we make appropriate assumptions. For example, if we assume that dividends D grow at a constant rate g in periods $t = 1, \dots, \infty$, the fair value P_0 equals:

$$P_0 = \sum_{t=1}^{\infty} \frac{D_0 (1+g)^t}{(1+i_f)^t} = D_0 \sum_{t=1}^{\infty} \frac{(1+g)^t}{(1+i_f)^t}$$

For $i_f > g$, we can derive the well known dividend growth model (DGM) discussed in Part I using a property of geometric series:

$$P_0 = D_0 \frac{1+g}{i_f - g} = \frac{D_1}{i_f - g} \qquad \left| note: \quad \sum_{t=1}^{\infty} \frac{(1+g)^t}{(1+i_f)^t} = \frac{1+g}{i_f - g} \right.$$

While other variants of DCF models can be derived from the general DCF formula if appropriate assumptions are made, for the purpose of this Part, the general DCF formula is sufficient.

43.2   UNCERTAIN CASH FLOWS

In this chapter we will show that the general DCF formula under certainty is not applicable in an uncertain world. In addition, we will discuss different approaches which allow investors to incorporate uncertainty into valuation models. Uncertainty means that more than one outcome or realization of a future cash flow at any point in time is possible. In literature, several concepts are discussed to incorporate uncertainty into valuation models.[5] The most prominent approach uses expected values which are well known in mathematics and statistics. The expected value approach requires that investors are able to determine all possible outcomes (cash flows) at time t and their probabilities ex ante.[6] The aim of this Part is not to discuss how to estimate future cash flows but to discuss alternative concepts to incorporate uncertainty (risk) in the stock valuation framework. For simplicity, we assume that investors are able to determine future outcomes and probabilities, i.e. expected cash flows.

---

[4] Copeland *et al.* (2005), pp. 3–14.
[5] In the following paragraphs, we discuss three methods which allow investors to incorporate risk into the valuation framework. The estimation of cash flows is not affected by the choice of the risk-adjustment method.
[6] Judge *et al.* (1988), pp. 11–36.

Let $cf(t, s)$ be the (uncertain) cash flow at time t in state s and $\pi(t, s)$ the probability of state s at time t. The most tempting way to value a stock under uncertainty is to apply the DCF formula under certainty and simply replace certain cash flows CF_t by expected cash flows $E(cf(t, s))$:

$$P_0 = \sum_{t=1}^{T} \frac{E(cf(t, s))}{(1+i_f)^t} \qquad \text{where: } E(cf(t, s)) = \sum_s \pi(t, s) \cdot cf(t, s)$$

The following example illustrates that simply replacing certain cash flows by expected cash flows does not work if investors are risk-averse. Let us assume that a stock is currently priced at EUR 82, no dividends are paid and two possible stock price realizations, $cf(t,1) = \text{EUR}$ 80 and $cf(t,2) = \text{EUR } 100$, might occur with a probability $\pi(t,1) = \pi(t,2) = 0.5$ at the end of a one-period valuation horizon. The expected cash flow of the stock is EUR 90 ($= \text{EUR}$ 80 * 0.5 + EUR 100 * 0.5). If the risk-free rate is 6%, the present value of the expected, future cash flows is EUR 84.905:

$$P_0 = \frac{90}{(1+0.06)} = 84.905$$

Is this an indication that the stock is undervalued at a current market price of EUR 82? Not at all! Risk-averse investors are willing to invest in risky assets only if they expect to be compensated for bearing risk. The price of a risky asset must therefore be lower than the price of a risk-free but otherwise identical asset. But what is the appropriate price of risk? Risk can be incorporated into the general DCF formula by either adjusting the denominator or the enumerator.[7]

Risk-adjust the denominator (discount rate): Investors usually incorporate risk into the valuation framework by discounting expected cash flows by the sum of one plus the risk-free rate i_f plus a risk premium rp. The following equation shows that the fair value P_0 decreases when the risk premium increases and vice versa:

$$P_0 = \sum_{t=1}^{T} \frac{E(cf(t, s))}{(1+i_f+rp)^t}$$

Risk-adjust the enumerator (cash flows): The enumerator can be adjusted by either applying a utility-based valuation approach or a risk neutral probability (RNP) valuation approach.

Utility-based valuation approach: A utility function f representing investor-specific preferences is applied to transform expected cash flows into investor-specific utility adjusted values of expected cash flows. Investor-specific utility adjusted values are then discounted at the risk-free rate to derive the investor-specific, fair value P_0.

$$P_0 = \sum_{t=1}^{T} \frac{f(cf(t, s))}{(1+i_f)^t}$$

---

[7] Kruschwitz and Löffler (2006), pp. 20–30.

Risk neutral probabilities (RNP) approach: Instead of using probabilities of future outcomes as weighting factors, so-called risk neutral probabilities (RNP), or π^*, are applied to calculate expected values.

$$P_0 = \sum_{t=1}^{T} \frac{\sum_{s=1}^{S} \pi^*(t, s) \cdot cf(t, s)}{(1+i_f)^t} = \sum_{t=1}^{T} \frac{E^*(cf(t, s))}{(1+i_f)^t}$$

Risk neutral expected values, $E^*(cf(t,s))$, are not investor specific.

In the following chapters, we will discuss the three approaches, their assumptions and drawbacks in more detail. Please note these approaches modify the DCF formula in order to incorporate risk into the valuation.

43.3   RISK PREMIA

Virtually every sophisticated valuation model used in practice today is a discounted cash flow model. The most common way is to discount expected cash flows at risk-adjusted discount rates. The risk-adjusted discount rate is composed of the risk-free rate and a risk premium which adequately reflects the risk of the investment.[8] As risk-averse investors are willing to invest in risky assets only if they are compensated for bearing risk in the form of a positive risk premium, the risk-adjusted rate always exceeds the risk-free rate. The following example shows how to derive market implied risk premia. Let us assume again that a stock currently trades at EUR 82, the expected cash flow for the next period is EUR 90, and the risk free interest rate is 6% (see the example presented above). If we solve the present value formula for the risk premium, *rp,* we obtain a market implied risk premium of 3.756%:

$$82 = \frac{0.5 \cdot 80 + 0.5 \cdot 100}{1 + 0.06 + rp} \Leftrightarrow rp = 0.03756$$

But how can we estimate the risk premium in real world applications? Future cost of equity and equity risk premia are not readily observable in financial markets. Financial economists have therefore formulated a wide range of models which can be used to estimate cost of equity.[9]

Because of its simplicity, most investors apply the Capital Asset Pricing Model (CAPM) to estimate cost of equity. In Part I, Viebig and Poddig showed that the CAPM can be logically derived from a few assumptions.[10] According to the CAPM, the expected return r_i of an asset is a linear function of the risk-free rate i_f and the excess return of the market portfolio M above the risk-free rate:

$$r_i = i_f + \beta_i(r_M - i_f)$$

where r_i, r_M and β_i represent the risk-adjusted, required return of stock i, the expected return of the market portfolio M, and the sensitivity of returns on stock i to the returns on the

---

[8] Viebig and Poddig, Part I, Chapter 2, of this book.
[9] In the literature, the most prominent alternatives to the CAPM are Ross' arbitrage theory of capital asset pricing and the Fama-French model. Ross (1976b), Fama and French (1992, 1995).
[10] Viebig and Poddig, Part I, section 3.3.3 in this book.

market portfolio M, respectively. The term $\beta_i(r_M - i_f)$ is the risk premium. According to the CAPM, investors are compensated only for bearing systematic market risk.

At first glance, it seems smart to apply the CAPM in a DCF framework to estimate the cost of equity. The following formula shows that we can derive a single-period, risk-adjusted DCF valuation model directly from the CAPM:

$$E\left(\frac{cf(t)_i - P_0}{P_0}\right) = i_f + \beta_i(r_M - i_f) \Leftrightarrow$$

$$P_0 = \frac{E\left(cf(t)_i\right)}{1 + i_f + \beta_i(r_M - i_f)} \Leftrightarrow$$

$$P_0 = \frac{E\left(cf(t)_i\right)}{1 + r_i}$$

where $E(cf(t)_i)$ is the expected stock value at time 1. Both the standard CAPM equation and DCF/CAPM approach yield the same results if consistent inputs are used. However, the CAPM is a single-period model. A multi-period valuation DCF model can be derived directly from the CAPM only if a number of restrictive assumptions are made. These assumptions include, among others, that betas, risk premia and risk-free rates are constant over time, that expected returns are not auto-correlated and that investors' preferences are not state-dependent[11].[12]

A vast amount of empirical studies suggests that betas and risk premia are not constant over time.[13] Ang and Liu (2004) find that time-varying betas, equity risk premia and risk-free rates have a substantial impact on the outcome of a valuation model.[14] Despite strong evidence, practitioners often ignore time variation in betas, equity risk premia and risk-free rates. Scenario analysis and the simulation of stochastic variables can be used to build more realistic valuation models. In Part II of this book, Viebig and Poddig discuss Monte Carlo simulation which can be used to more realistically model stochastic, economic variables.

The assumption that investors evaluate portfolios by looking at expected returns and standard deviations over a single-period horizon is not the only assumption behind the CAPM.[15] The capital market in the CAPM framework is assumed to be competitive and always in equilibrium. The CAPM further assumes that investors have homogeneous expectations and can borrow and lend at the same risk-free rate. In the CAPM world taxes and transaction costs are irrelevant. The CAPM suggests that the required return is a linear function of the risk-free rate and the equity risk premium (security market line). Financial economists have shown that this linear relationship generally does not hold if the restrictive assumptions of the CAPM are relaxed. Ross (1976a), for example, analyzes the implication of disallowing risk-less lending and borrowing and short sales and shows that it is impossible to derive a simple, general equilibrium if these assumptions are relaxed simultaneously. Practitioners should keep in mind that the CAPM is an equilibrium model when applying it to estimate cost of equity.

---

[11] A process is called "not state dependent" if its outcomes do not depend on one specific future state among other possible future states.

[12] Brennan (1973), Bogue and Roll (1974), Fama (1977), Myers and Turnbull (1983), Brennan (1997), Ang and Liu (2004), among others.

[13] Ferson and Harvey (1991), pp. 50–54, Evans (1994), pp. 660–675, DeSantis and Gérard (1997), pp. 1892–1909.

[14] Ang and Liu (2004), p. 2775.

[15] Elton et al. (2003), pp. 309–328.

For a practitioner it is more important whether a model yields accurate predictions rather than whether its assumptions are realistic.[16] Unfortunately, Roll (1977) shows that it is practically impossible to test the CAPM without knowledge of the complete market portfolio as the linear return/beta relationship and the assumption that the market portfolio is efficient are mathematically equivalent.[17] In his famous critique of the CAPM, Richard Roll quotes Pirsig (1974): "If the horn honks and the mechanic concludes that the whole electrical system is working, he is in deep trouble …".[18] Tests of the CAPM are heavily influenced by the choice of the "true" market portfolio. Practitioners usually use market indices such as the S&P 500 index as proxies for the market portfolio. The choice of the index and the time period over which betas are estimated can have a substantial impact on beta estimates. Empirical evidence suggests that not only equity risk premia, but also other economic variables such as size (market capitalization) and book-to-market equity ratios, explain some of the variation in average equity returns.[19]

In the literature, several other approaches are proposed to estimate risk-adjusted, required returns r_i. An alternative is to use the DCF model itself to estimate r_i. The result is an implied risk-adjusted market return on a stock. A further method is to calculate the historical average return on a stock.[20] In Part IV of this book, Harris et al. argue that attempts to estimate precise cost of capital are futile and recommend using a required return on equity of 3% to 4% above government bond yields as a starting point. Sophisticated financial analysts carefully analyze the sensitivity of their price targets to changes in cost of equity

43.4   CERTAINTY EQUIVALENTS AND UTILITY-BASED VALUATION

The certainty equivalent (CEQ) concept is closely related to the expected utility theory and the utility-based valuation framework. The basic idea was initially proposed by Bernoulli (reprinted 1954). Based on Bernoulli (reprinted 1954) and on a set of axioms, von Neumann and Morgenstern (1944) developed the expected utility theory. The expected utility theory became important in economics and is deemed to be a key concept of (neoclassical) economics.

A utility function transforms outcomes of different states, e.g. cash flows $cf(t, s)$, to investor-specific utility values of these outcomes $U(cf(t,s))$. The expected utility, $E(U)$, equals the sum of the utility values weighted with the probability of the outcomes $\pi(t, s)$:

$$E(U) = \sum_s^S \pi(t, s) \, U\,(cf(t, s)).$$

The CEQ approach suggests that investors make decisions not on the basis of expected values but on the expected utilities. Utility-based valuation requires that a set of axioms of

---

[16] Sharpe and Alexendar (1990), p. 195.
[17] Roll (1977).
[18] Roll (1977), p. 129.
[19] Fama and French (1992, 1995).
[20] See Levy (2002), pp. 286–288.

utility are defined. There are 5 central axioms of utility: *Comparability, Transitivity, Strong independence, Measurability* and *Ranking*.[21]

In neoclassical economic theory, it is assumed that investors always make rational decisions based on these axioms. If the utility axioms hold and investors prefer more utility to less utility, it is said that investors maximize expected utility. The maxim of expected utility maximization is logically deducible if we accept the five axioms above. The concept of expected utility maximization is a key concept of neoclassical economics; almost all important theories in (neoclassical) economics assume utility maximizing individuals.

Utility theory requires that investors specify their relevant type of utility function which transforms different outcomes in measurable utility and expresses their degree of risk aversion. The utility function must posses at least two properties: i) it must be order preserving (i.e. if $x \succ y$ then the transformation of outcomes to utility preserve the order $U(x) \succ U(y)$) and ii) the expected utility $E(U)$ can be used to rank risky alternatives.[22] In the context of utility theory, risk aversion is usually described in form of a risk premium which is the difference of expected value of future cash flows and the CEQ (which we will explain in more detail below). Please do not confuse the risk premium in the utility theory and the risk premium according to the CAPM.

A positive risk premium indicates risk aversion (and a strictly concave form of utility function), a negative risk premium a risk-seeking investor (and a strictly convex form of the utility function), and a zero risk premium a risk-neutral investor (linear utility function).

In the literature, a multitude of different utility functions and approaches to estimate risk aversion are discussed.[23] Utility theory is a normative theory. It describes how investors *should* rationally decide and not how investors really decide. The evidence from empirical research in the field of behavioral finance indicates that investors are not always rational. The seminal empirical analysis of DeBondt and Thaler (1985), for example, shows that most investors tend to "overreact" to unexpected and dramatic news events. This is in contrast to the assumptions of utility theory. The findings from behavioral finance should not be misinterpreted. They do not offset the rationality behind the expected utility maximization principle. Any investor who wants to decide rationally should do so. However, if investors behave irrationally, it is difficult to specify investor-specific utility functions.

If utility-based valuation is applied, all values are investor-specific. Consider the following utility function:

$$U\left(cf(t, s)\right) = \exp\left(\frac{cf(t, s)}{\lambda}\right)$$

and

$$E(U) = E\left(U\left(cf(t, s)\right)\right)$$

[21] See von Neumann and Morgenstern (2004), pp. 24–29 and 73–78. A more intuitive approach is presented in Markowitz (1998), pp. 228–256. *Comparability* means that for a set of uncertain alternatives, an investor can state whether outcome x is preferred to outcome y ($x \succ y$) or y is preferred to x ($y \succ x$) or that they are indifferent ($x \sim y$). *Transitivity* states that if an investor prefers x to y and y to z, then x is preferred to z (if $x \succ y$ and $y \succ z$ then $x \succ z$). *Strong independence* assumes that if the probability of receiving an outcome x in a gamble G is α and the probability of receiving an outcome y equals 1-α, we can write $G(x, y: \alpha)$. Strong independence implies that if an investor is indifferent to x and z, then she will also be indifferent to $G(x, y:\alpha)$ and $G(z, y:\alpha)$. *Measurability* means that if $x \succ y \succ z$, an unique probability α, exists such that $y \sim G(x, z : \alpha)$. To explain *Ranking* assume that alternatives z and u both rank between x and y. Assume further that an investor is indifferent between i) z and a gamble between x with a probability α and y and ii) between u and a gamble between x with a probability β and y. Then z is preferred to u if α is greater than β.
[22] For a proof of these properties of any utility function see Copeland *et al.* (2005), p. 48.
[23] Copeland *et al.* (2005), pp. 52–56.

Then we can write:

$$CEQ = U^{-1}(E(U))$$

where CEQ is the certainty equivalent, and λ is a weighting factor which expresses the investor-specific risk aversion (risk aversion parameter). Let us assume that a stock currently trades at EUR 82. One period later, the value of the stock is expected to be either $cf(t,1) =$ EUR 100 or $cf(t,2) =$ EUR 80. Both outcomes are assumed to have a probability of 0.5. Thus, the expected value of the cash flows equals EUR 90. The risk free interest rate is 6%. The weighting factor λ is assumed to be 1.141. According to the utility function above, the certainty equivalent is 86.9199.

$$U(100) = \exp\left(\frac{100}{1.141}\right)$$

$$U(80) = \exp\left(\frac{80}{1.141}\right)$$

$$E(U) = \sum_{s=1}^{S} p_s \cdot U_s = 0.5 \cdot U(100) + 0.5 \cdot U(80) = 5.608 \cdot 10^{37}$$

$$CEQ = U^{-1}(E(U)) = \ln(E(U)) = 86.9199$$

The value of the stock for this special investor with a risk aversion parameter λ of 1.141 is:

$$P_0 = \frac{CEQ}{1 + i_f} = \frac{86.9199}{1.06} = 82$$

As mentioned above, the valuation process is investor-specific. For another investor with a different risk aversion parameter, the result will differ. From a theoretical perspective, it is worth noting that we do not assume equilibrium conditions.

A popular approach for determining risk aversion in portfolio optimization is discussed in Grinold and Kahn (2000). Sharpe *et al.* (1995) describe a more general way to estimate risk aversion parameter.[24]

At first glance, it seems that the discussion of the theory of choice under uncertainty offers little or no value for practitioners. Utility-based valuation is subjective and arbitrary in nature, often criticized as useless for "real world" valuation purposes, and not widely used in practice. Everybody who ever dealt with real clients knows how difficult it is to measure their "risk aversion". However, the CEQ framework discussed above stresses two important points. First, standard DCF models do not adjust for the individual risk aversion of investors. Whether an investment is suitable for a specific client depends on her risk aversion. Secondly, risk aversion is an important factor which drives the demand for stocks. Shifts in investor risk aversion can cause substantial rallies and corrections in financial markets.

---

[24] Grinold and Kahn (2000), pp. 96–98, and Sharpe and Alexander (1995), pp. 883–887.

Investors who mechanically discount corporate earnings without carefully analyzing the risk aversion of investors ("investor sentiment") might miss an important factor influencing stock prices.

43.5 RISK NEUTRAL PROBABILITIES

A third alternative for incorporating uncertainty into the valuation framework is the use of risk neutral probabilities (RNP). The valuation approach with RNP is closely related to the time state preference model and to option pricing theory.[25] In the RNP approach, the risk adjusted expectation E^* is defined as:

$$E^*(cf(t)) = \sum_{s=1}^{S} \pi^*(t, s) \cdot cf(t, s)$$

where $\pi^*(t, s)$ are risk neutral probabilities. Risk neutral probabilities range between 0 and 1 and sum up to one. The name "risk neutral probabilities" is misleading. Risk neutral probabilities are not real probabilities. Risk neutral probabilities are weighting factors for risky cash flows. The RNP framework assumes arbitrage-free markets.

Arbitrage is the practice of taking advantage of price differentials between identical assets which are priced differently in financial markets. An arbitrage portfolio in a perfect capital market has no sensitivity to any risk factor and has a positive expected return. The arbitrage portfolio provides cash inflows in some future states but does not require any net cash outflows. Arbitrageurs seek out arbitrage opportunities to generate risk-free profits.

An example might clarify these points. Assume two different assets. An investor expects future cash flows $cf(s,1)$ at different states s in one period from now:

Table 43.1 A capital market with arbitrage opportunities

Asset	$cf(1,1)$	$cf(2,1)$	P_0
A	80	100	82
B	40	50	43

The "market" represented in Table 43.1 is not arbitrage-free. A clever investor can implement an arbitrage strategy to generate a risk-free profit. According to the law of one price, two goods with identical future cash flows must have the same price.

$$1 \cdot A = 2 \cdot B \Leftrightarrow$$
$$1 \cdot A - 2 \cdot B = 0$$

However, in our example the law of one price does not hold:

$$1 \cdot A + (-2) \cdot B = 82 - 86 = -4$$

An investor can sell short two stocks of B and buy one stock of A. The arbitrage portfolio does not require any investment, has no risk and has a positive expected return. The proceeds

---

[25] See Cox and Ross (1976).

from short selling two stocks of B is EUR 86. From these proceeds, an investor can buy one stock of A for EUR 82. The arbitrage transaction generates a profit of EUR 4 and is risk-free. If state 1 occurs, the net cash flow is zero (2 * EUR 40 − EUR 80 = 0). If state 2 occurs, the net cash flow of the arbitrage portfolio is also zero (2 * EUR 50 − EUR 100 = 0). Our arbitrage portfolio is perfectly hedged.

Now assume that investors recognize this arbitrage opportunity, buy stock A and sell short stock B. As a result of these transactions, stock A increases and stock B decreases in value. The arbitrage process lasts until equilibrium is reached (2 stocks of B equal 1 stock of A).

An important principle to value securities is known as risk-neutral valuation. In a risk-neutral world, investors are by definition indifferent to risk and require no compensation for risk; the expected return on all assets is the risk-free interest rate.[26] In a risk neutral-world, the value of an asset is the sum of its future cash flows discounted at the risk-free interest rate. Risk neutral probabilities $\pi^*(t, s)$ can be used to risk-adjust cash flows. The adjusting factor $\pi^*(t, s)$ transforms risky cash flows into 'risk-free' cash flow streams.

From the definition of risk-adjusted expected cash flows, $E^*(cf(t,s))$, we can derive the following valuation formula:[27]

$$P_0 = \sum_{t=1}^{T} \frac{E^*(cf(t))}{(1+i_f)^t}$$

The formula can be used to value multi-period cash flow streams. For practical and empirical applications of the RNP approach, it is necessary to determine risk-neutral probabilities $\pi^*(t, s)$. RNP can be derived directly from market prices if the current prices are arbitrage-free. In order to illustrate the RNP approach, let us use the above-mentioned example of two stocks in an arbitrage-free market and a risk-free interest rate of 6%. In our example, the risk-neutral probabilities (weighting factors) π^* for stock A can be derived from the following equation:

$$84 = \frac{\pi^*(1, 1) \cdot 80 + \pi^*(2, 1) \cdot 100}{1 + 0.06} = \frac{\pi^*(1, 1) \cdot 80 + (1 - \pi^*(1, 1)) \cdot 100}{1 + 0.06}$$

We can rearrange the equation and solve for $\pi^*(1,1)$:

$$84 \cdot 1.06 = \pi^*(1, 1) \cdot 80 + 100 - \pi^*(1, 1) \cdot 100 \Leftrightarrow$$

$$\pi^*(1, 1) = \frac{84 \cdot 1.06 - 100}{80 - 100} = 0.548$$

Solving the equation for $\pi^*(1,1)$, we obtain a RNP of 0.548 for state 1. The risk-adjusted expectation $E^*(cf(t))$ equals EUR 89.04. Discounting the risk-adjusted expectation at the risk-free interest rate yields a fair value of EUR 84. In our example, the fair value and the assumed market price are equal. RNP can be interpreted as adjusting factors. As we assumed

---

[26] Hull (2003), pp. 200–205. A valuation using RNP is not in contrast to the widely accepted assumption of risk-averse investors. RNP translate "real" world valuation and "physical" probabilities into a risk-neutral world considering risk-averse investors. Real world risk aversion is reflected in RNP as long as markets are arbitrage-free. In analogy to mathematics, one can think of an "isomorphism" between "real" and risk-neutral world.

[27] Grinold and Kahn (2000), p. 205.

only arbitrage-free pricing, RNP are neither investor-specific nor stock-specific. RNP can be estimated directly from market data.

In our example, we assumed two future states, 1 and 2. Please note that we did not assume that investors know state-specific probabilities ex ante. Instead of estimating future states, a return-generating process, e.g. a random walk, or option prices can be applied to estimate RNP.[28] The basic idea of the estimation procedure of RNP remains the same if return-generating processes or option prices are used to estimate RNP. However, the estimation procedure becomes much more complicated and requires the use of sophisticated parametric and non-parametric models. The practical application of these models is challenging. However, economists have formulated sophisticated models to estimate RNP.[29] The discussion of these models is beyond the scope of this article.[30]

---

[28] Financial analysts usually discount future cash flows over multi-year periods. Unfortunately, for most stocks there are no liquid options with long-dated maturities available which could be used to estimate RNP over multi-year periods.

[29] Ross (1976a) shows that in a complete capital market, risk neutral distributions can be derived from a set of European call option prices. Huynh et al. (2002) and Härdle and Zheng (2002), among others, apply non-parametric regressions to estimate risk neutral probabilities, while Clement et al. (2000) apply a parametric approach. In addition, Bakshi and Chen (2005) develop and implement stock valuation models using the RNP approach. Schwartz and Moon (2000) applied this approach to value an internet start-up (Amazon.com) at the end of 1999.

[30] Risk-neutral valuation is an important principle in option pricing.

44

Outlook: The Multi-asset Valuation and Allocation Case

DCF models are based on the maxim that investors should maximize the present value of future cash flow. DCF models might help skilled investors to identify attractive securities. However, the use of DCF models does not ensure that portfolios have the risk and return characteristics which investors desire. Markowitz (1952) states:

"[...] The hypothesis (or maxim) that the investor does (or should) maximize discounted return must be rejected. If we ignore market imperfections the foregoing rule never implies that there is a diversified portfolio which is preferable to all non-diversified portfolios. Diversification is both observed and sensible; a rule of behavior which does not imply the superiority of diversification must be rejected both as a hypothesis and as a maxim."[1]

According to Markowitz (1998) investors evaluate portfolios by looking at the expected returns and variances (or standard deviations) of the portfolios and seek to maximize their utility. A widely-used utility function states:

$$E(r_p) - \lambda \cdot Var(r_p) \to \max$$

where $E(r_p)$ and $Var(r_p)$ are the expected return and future variance of a portfolio p, respectively. The term λ represents the risk aversion parameter of an investor.[2] According to Markowitz (1952), the portfolio selection approach can be formulated as an optimization problem. If $\mathbf{w}$ is the vector of these asset weights, the investor-specific utility function can be written as objective function:

$$\mathbf{w}^T \mathbf{r} - \lambda \cdot \mathbf{w}^T \mathbf{V} \mathbf{w} \to \max$$

$$s.t.$$

$$\mathbf{e}^T \mathbf{w} = 1$$

$$\mathbf{w} \geq 0$$

where $\mathbf{w}^T$ denotes the transposed vector of the asset weights, λ is the risk aversion, and $\mathbf{r}$ and $\mathbf{V}$ indicate the vector of expected returns and future covariance matrix, respectively. The term $\mathbf{e}$ represents a vector of ones. In the example above, the optimization problem is subject to the budget restriction $\mathbf{e}^T \mathbf{w} = 1$, and to the restriction that short sales are disallowed ($\mathbf{w} \geq 0$).

---

[1] Markowitz (1952), pp. 77–78.
[2] Approaches to estimate the risk aversion parameter are described in Grinold and Kahn (2000), pp. 96–98, and Sharpe and Alexander (1995), pp. 883–887.

Return-based analysis can be applied to estimate expected returns:[3]

$$r_i = \alpha_i + \sum_{j=1}^{N} \beta_{ij} F_j + \varepsilon_i$$

where r_i is the return of stock i, α_i is a constant term, called autonomous asset return, F_j is the value of risk factor j, β_{ij} is the sensitivity of stock return i to factor j, ε_i is a random error term and N the number of factors. The term $(\alpha_i + \varepsilon_i = \hat{r}_i)$ is usually referred to as firm-specific residual return. We will use the residual return later for benchmark-oriented portfolio optimization. The return-based factor model can be used for estimation in cross-section as well as in time series regression analysis. The valuation approach represents a multi-factor asset pricing model.

The model assumes that the return on a security is sensitive to the movements of one or more systematic risk factors. Return-based analysis examines past returns and attributes those returns either to firm-specific variables or to macroeconomic risk factors. Often, different types of risk factors, such as macroeconomic indicators, firm-specific data or synthetic factors are used as return-based variables. In the simplest case, the single index model, only one risk factor affects the returns on an asset i. The single index model is similar to the structure of the CAPM.[4]

We can use the results of the return-based approach to estimate the input parameters, i.e. expected returns r_i, variances σ_i and co-variances σ_{ik}, of the Markowitz portfolio optimization model:[5]

$$r_i = \alpha_i + \sum_{j=1}^{N} \beta_{ij} E(F_j)$$

$$\sigma_i^2 = \sum_{j=1}^{N} \beta_{ij} Var(F_j) + Var(\varepsilon_i)$$

$$\sigma_{ik} = \sum_{j=1}^{N} \beta_{ij} \beta_{kj} Var(F_j)$$

Unfortunately, asset pricing theory does not clearly define which economic factors F_j ($j = 1, \ldots, N$) affect asset returns. Even the number of explaining factors remains unclear. Multi-factor models can be used to explain historical stock returns and to predict future returns.[6] Empirical studies suggest that probably more than one pervasive factor affects historical returns.[7] A widely used return-based valuation model is developed by the consulting company BARRA.[8]

The standard Markowitz portfolio optimization model is based on estimations of absolute returns. "Absolute" portfolio optimization procedures are not widely used in practice since the estimated optimal portfolio weights $\mathbf{w}$ are very sensitive to changes in expected returns.

---

[3] Elton et al. (2003), pp. 130–174, Sharpe and Alexander (1995), pp. 293–315, Grinold and Kahn (2000), pp. 248–254.
[4] Sharpe and Alexander (1995), pp. 314–315.
[5] Elton et al. (2003), pp. 176–177.
[6] Sharpe (1995), pp. 298–3003.
[7] Chen et al. (1986), Aprem (1989), Fama and French (1992), Ferson and Harvey (1997), Ferson and Harvey (1999).
[8] http://www.barra.com for more details. BARRA is now part of MSCI-BARRA.

The lack of robustness of the Markowitz portfolio optimization leads to frequent rebalancing of the optimal portfolio and therefore to high transaction costs. The Markowitz portfolio optimization approach tends to generate an unbalanced portfolio structure with high ("extreme") portfolio weights on few investments. The problem of extreme portfolio weights is not due to the Markowitz portfolio optimization but to imprecise forecasting of asset returns.[9]

Investors can try to generate exceptional (active) returns by deviating from the benchmark portfolio. The active return describes the difference between portfolio return and return on the benchmark portfolio. Assuming a linear return generating process, the objective function of a relative portfolio optimization procedure is:

$$\alpha_P - \lambda \omega_P^2 \to \max$$

where α_P represents the expected active return and ω_P^2 is the active risk of portfolio P. To find an optimal portfolio we have to solve the following optimization problem:[10]

$$\mathbf{w}_P^T \boldsymbol{\alpha} - \lambda(\mathbf{w}_A^T \mathbf{V} \mathbf{w}_A) \to \max$$

$s.t.$

$$\mathbf{e}^T \mathbf{w}_P = 1$$

$$\mathbf{w}_P^T \geq 0$$

$$\mathbf{w}_P^T \boldsymbol{\beta} = 1$$

where $\boldsymbol{\alpha}$ is a vector of asset alphas, $\mathbf{w}_P$ is the vector of portfolio weights, $\mathbf{w}_A$ is the vector of active portfolio weights with $\mathbf{w}_A = \mathbf{w}_P - \mathbf{w}_{B.} \mathbf{w}_B$ represents the vector of weights of the benchmark portfolio, and $\mathbf{V}$ is the future covariance matrix of asset returns. The challenge for an investor is to estimate ex-ante asset alphas, $\boldsymbol{\alpha}$, and the future covariance matrix $\mathbf{V}$. To estimate $\mathbf{V}$, we can apply the multi-factor model mentioned above. For the estimation of $\boldsymbol{\alpha}$ at least two solutions exist. Firstly, multi-factor models can be used. Secondly, the alpha refinement method proposed by Grinold (1994) and Grinold and Kahn (2000) can be applied. We can use the results of the DCF models, described in section 43, to calculate future alphas. According to Grinold (1994) alphas can be estimated as follows:

$$\alpha_i = IC_i \cdot Vola_i \cdot Score(i)$$

where IC_i is the information coefficient, $Vola_i$ is defined as $Var(\hat{r}_i)^{1/2}$, $\hat{r}_i$ is the residual return, and $Score(i)$ is a standardized measure expressing the relative desirability of asset i. IC_i is defined as:

$$IC_i = \frac{Cov\left(\hat{r}_i^{forecast}, \hat{r}_i^{realized}\right)}{std\left(\hat{r}_i^{forecast}\right) \cdot std\left(\hat{r}_i^{realized}\right)}$$

---

[9] Scherer (2002), pp. 98–99.
[10] The restriction in the optimization problem that the portfolio beta (with respect to the benchmark) equals one (beta-neutral, no benchmark-timing) is not necessary, but often required in practical applications.

and represents the correlation coefficient between the forecast residual return $\hat{r}_i^{forecast}$ and the realized residual return $\hat{r}_i^{realized}$ of asset i. IC measures the forecasting skills of an asset manager. As a correlation coefficient, IC can take values between -1 and 1. An IC value of 1 indicates a perfect forecasting ability, while negative values indicate that the forecasts are systematically wrong.[11]

Grinold and Kahn (2000) state that a simple scoring scheme can be used to determine $Score(i)$, which assigns assets to five ordinal categories: 'strong buy' (2), 'buy' (1), 'hold' (0), 'sell' (–1), 'strong sell' (–2). In practice, DCF models can be used to generate stock scores. The scoring process links DCF valuation and asset allocation.

The theoretical framework of modern asset allocation is based on the Markowitz portfolio selection theory. The input parameters needed for the Markowitz portfolio optimization can be estimated by applying multi-factor models. However, due to different practical challenges, investors usually prefer relative portfolio optimization. Applying relative portfolio optimization, an investor has to estimate alpha parameters. DCF models can be used to determine asset-specific scores. Applying a simple scoring scheme, practitioners can elegantly link security selection and asset allocation.

---

[11] Grinold (1994) also provides an illustrative example how to generate and use the refined alphas.

45

Summary

The aim of this Part is to give a brief overview of some general valuation concepts and principles from a theoretical point of view. We showed that three alternatives exist to incorporate uncertainty into the DCF valuation framework. First, risk-adjusted cost of equity can be used to discount expected cash flows. Practitioners usually apply the CAPM to estimate cost of equity. Above we argued that the CAPM is based on a number of restrictive assumptions. The wide acceptance of the CAPM in practice is probably based on the simplicity of the underlying economic model.

Secondly, risk can be incorporated into the valuation framework by applying utility-based valuation. Utility-based valuation requires only a few assumptions of the decision behavior of investors and no assumptions about capital markets. The utility-based valuation framework requires that investor-specific utility functions can be estimated. Most practitioners reject this approach as, in practice, it is almost impossible to adequately determine and aggregate individual utility functions and estimate risk aversion parameters. Thirdly, risk neutral probabilities can be applied to incorporate uncertainty into the valuation framework. The estimation of RNP requires the use of sophisticated econometric models.

Despite these difficulties, a lot of academic research is done on RNP valuation. In addition, financial economists have formulated more sophisticated factor models which better explain average historical returns on stocks than the CAPM.[1] The future will show whether practitioners will use these methods to incorporate risk into the valuation framework.

A serious disadvantage of DCF models is the inherent decision rule which states that investors should invest in securities with the highest net present value. This decision rule is in contrast to the findings of modern financial theory. Unfortunately, stock selection and asset allocation are often viewed in isolation. We showed how investors can use scoring schemes to incorporate the results of DCF models into the asset allocation process. We hope that the bibliography is useful for readers who are interested to learn more about valuation theory.

---

[1] Fama and French (1992, 1995).

References

Ang, A., and Liu, J. (2004), How to discount cashflows with time-varying expected returns, *Journal of Finance*, 59, 2745–2783.

Bakshi, G., and Chen, Z. (2005), Stock valuation in dynamic economics, *Journal of Financial Markets*, 8, 111–151.

Bernoulli, D. (1954), Specimen theoriae novae de mensura sortis', *Commentarii Academiae Scientiarum Imperialis Petropolitanae*, reprinted as: Exposition of a new theory on the measurement of risk, *Econometrica*, 22, 23–36.

Bogue, M., and Roll, R. (1974), Capital budgeting of risky projects with 'imperfect' markets for physical capital, *Journal of Finance*, 29, 601–613.

Brennan, M. (1973), An approach to the valuation of uncertain income streams, *Journal of Finance*, 28, 661–674.

Brennan, M. (1997), The term structure of discount rates, *Financial Management*, 26, 81–90.

Chen, N., Roll, R., and Ross, S. (1986), Economic forces and the stock market, *Journal of Business*, 59, 383–403.

Clement, E., and Gourieroux, C., and Monfort, A. (2000), Econometric specification of the risk neutral valuation model, *Journal of Econometrics*, 94, 117–143.

Copeland, T., Weston, J., and Shastri, K. (2005), *Financial Theory and Corporate Policy*, Pearson/Addison-Wesley.

Cox, J., and Ross, S. (1976), A survey of some new results in financial option pricing theory, *Journal of Finance*, 31, 383–402.

DeBondt, W., and Thaler R. (1985), Does the stock market overreact?, *Journal of Finance*, 40, 793–805.

DeSantis, G., and Gérard, B. (1997), International asset pricing and portfolio diversification with time-varying risk, *Journal of Finance*, 52, 1881–1912.

Elton, E., Gruber, M., Brown, S., and Goetzmann, W. (2003), *Modern Portfolio Theory and Investment Analysis*, John Wiley & Sons.

Evans, M. (1994), Expected returns, time-varying risk, and risk premia, *Journal of Finance*, 49, 655–680.

Fama, E. (1977), Risk-adjusted discount rates and capital budgeting under uncertainty, *Journal of Financial Economics*, 5, 3–24.

Fama, E., and French, K. (1992), The cross-section of expected stock returns, *Journal of Finance*, 47, 427–465.

Fama, E., and French, K. (1995), Size and book-to-market factors in earnings and returns, *Journal of Finance*, 50, 131–155.

Ferson, W., and Harvey, C. (1991), Sources of predictability in portfolio returns, *Financial Analysts Journal*, 47, 49–56.

Ferson, W., and Harvey, C. (1997), Fundamental determinants of national equity market returns: A perspective on conditional asset pricing, *Journal of Banking and Finance*, 21, 1625–1666.

Ferson, W., and Harvey, C. (1999), Conditioning variables and the cross section of stock returns, *Journal of Finance*, 54, 1325–1360.

Grinold, R. (1994), Alpha is volatility times IC times score, *Journal of Portfolio Management*, 20, 9–16.

Grinold, R., and Kahn, R. (2000), *Active Portfolio Management*, McGraw-Hill.

Härdle, W., and Zheng, J. (2002), How precise are price distributions predicted by implied binomial trees?' in: Härdle, W., Kleinow, T., and Stahl, G. (eds.) *Applied Quantitative Finance*, Springer.

Hull, J. (2003), *Options, Futures and Other Derivatives*, Prentice-Hall.

Huynh, K., Kervella, P., and Zheng, J. (2002), Estimating state-price densities with nonparametric regression, in: Härdle, W., Kleinow, T., and Stahl, G. (eds) *Applied Quantitative Finance*, Springer.

Judge, G., Hill, R., Griffiths, W., Lütkepohl, H., and Lee, T. (1988), *Introduction to the Theory and Practice of Econometrics*, John Wiley & Sons.

Kruschwitz, L., and Löffler, A. (2006), *Discounted cash flow: a theory of the valuation of firms*, John Wiley & Sons.

Levy, H. (2002), *Fundamentals of Investments*, Financial Times Prentice Hall.

Markowitz, H. (1952), Portfolio selection, *Journal of Finance*, 7, 77–91.

Markowitz, H. (1998), *Portfolio selection,* Blackwell.

Miller, M.H., and Modigliani, F. (1961), Dividend policy, growth, and the valuation of shares, *Journal of Business*, October, 411–433.

Myers, S., and Turnbull, S. (1983), Capital budgeting and the capital asset pricing model: good news and bad news, *Journal of Finance*, 32, 321–333.

Roll, R. (1977), A critique of the asset pricing theory's tests, *Journal of Financial Economics*, 4, 129–176.

Ross, S.A. (1976a), Options and efficiency, *Quarterly Journal of Economics*, 90, 75–89.

Ross, S.A. (1976b), The arbitrage theory of capital asset pricing, *Journal of Economic Theory*, 13, 341–360.

Scherer, B. (2002), Portfolio resampling: review and critique, *Financial Analysts Journal*, 58, 98–109.

Sharpe, W., and Alexander, G.J. (1990, 1995), *Investments*, Prentice Hall.

Schwartz, E., and Moon, M. (2000), Rational Pricing of Internet Companies, *Financial Analysts Journal*, 62–75.

von Neumann, J., and Morgenstern, O. (1944, 2004), *Theory of Games and Economic Behavior*, Princeton Univ. Press.

Index